REGIONAL ECONOMICS AND REGIONAL PLANNING

REGIONAL ECONOMICS AND REGIONAL PLANNING

O.S. Shrivastava

ANMOL PUBLICATIONS PVT. LTD.
NEW DELHI - 110 002 (INDIA)

ANMOL PUBLICATIONS PVT. LTD.
H.O.: 4374/4B, Ansari Road, Daryaganj,
New Delhi-110 002 (India)
Ph.: 23278000, 23261597
B.O.: No. 1015, Ist Main Road, BSK IIIrd Stage
IIIrd Phase, IIIrd Block,
Bangalore - 560 085 (India)
Visit us at: www.anmolpublications.com

Regional Economics and Regional Planning

First Edition, 2009
ISBN 978 81-261-4044-2

PRINTED IN INDIA

Printed at Balaji Offset Press, Delhi.

Countries."

28 M.P. Todaio : "Development Planning: Models and Methods." "Planning for Economic Development."

29 U.N.O. : "Planning Techniques," seminar, Moscow, 1960," planning and plan implementation," 1971. "Techniques of Annual Planning, "1970. "Long-Term planning, "1971. "Integration of Economic and Physical Planning," 1975.

30 F.A. von hayck : "Road to Serfdom."

31 Albery Waterston : "Development Planning: Issued and Experiences."

32 L.J. Zimrnerman : "Economic Planning."

33 Mydral : "Op. cit."

34 Edward Hemiann : "Types and Potentialities of Economic Planning."

35 P. Dasgupta, A. Sen, & S. Marglin : "Guidelines for project Evaluation."

36 E.J. Mishan : "Cost-Benefit Analysis."

37 A.C. Harberger : "Project Evaluation."

38 Little and Scoit : "Using shadow Prices."

CONTENTS

PART-III: REGIONAL FLOWS

PART-IV: PRICE THEORY, APPLIED TO REGION

PART-V: DYNAMIC MODELS OF REGIONAL GROWTH

PART-VI: SPECIAL THEORIES OF REGIONAL GROWTH

PART-VII: REGIONAL PLANNING

Perface

This book is divided into seven parts:

1. Regions : types : delineation: regional activities.
2. Economics of location: Theories.
3. Regional flows: of capital and labour.
4. Price Theories applied to regions/space.
5. Dynamic Models of Regional Growth.
6. Special Theories of Regional Growth.
7. Multi-level planning; regional planning and project planning.

The grand goal of any nation is to have development with social justice or acceptable redistribution. This is now called "inclusive growth". Though all the objectives are national objectives, there are spatial/regional components of the same as also components for the targeted groups. This is the disaggregation. The regional growth process is unbalanced because of agglomeration economies, indivisibilities in investment, differences in natural and manpower resourcs, and the uneven spatial distribution of growth advantages and shortcomings. Regional economics promotes inequalities and at the same time aims at bringing equalities through creation of such imbalances that undo the past imbalances!

Growth should not be enclave growth. It is unacceptable that a developed region should be surrounded by many backward or under-developed regions. Regional differences will remain but there should be a movement from divergence to convergence. *We need planning for that. Planning is based upon certain. policies, Policies are based upon pure theories. No policy can succeed if it contravenes fundamental truths spelled out in theories.*

This book is on theories. Policy propositions are implicitly present in them. There is the section on regional planning. *[A sister book studies " Economic Development of India in Inter-regional] (Inter state) perspective"].* Regional economics that is discussed in this book is not of parochial nature but integrated *for* a balanced view.

The concept of regional balance is too subjective and nebulous yet complementarities are to be promoted. Before a nation can be efficient, the regions have got to be efficient. Sectoral efficiency has got to be diffused. Growth should not bypass some categories of people.

This book was the first on the pure theory of regional economics written by an Indian. The book has its pedagogic aspects as well as pragmatic aspects. The book explores and explains. It has its positive and normative aspects. This time we have added chapters on micro-level and regional planning.

A sister book examines the State-wise development of economic sectors in India. The author thanks the publishers for bringing out the second edition of this book. I am also indebted in the production manager, Dr. S.S. Tiwary.

—O.S. Shrivastva
Ph.D.

Retired Professor and Head of Economics, Department of Regional Planning and Economic Growth,
Ex-Dean Faculty of Social Sciences,
Ex-State Bank of India Chair Professor for Rural Economy,
Ex-Director Designate of MBA Institute of the University,
Bhopal University (now known as Barkatullah Uni),
BHOPAL (MADHYA PRADESH).

88 Sector A, Kasturbanagar, BHOPAL-24
Phones: 0755 2588549
9981831318

PART-I

Regional Economics, Regions, Regional Activities

1

Regional Economics, Scope and Discipline

APPOGGIATURA

(A short note of summary at the outset before a long one)

Every thing happens in space and the persons/activities over the space are not the same/uniform. *Regional economics studies all regional economic differentiations and reduces / promotes wherever necessary.* Regional economics cannot make all the regions same but can aim at helping in the generation of same levels of income. Regional economics aims at furthering regional specialisation yet at the same time reducing regional dichotomies and inequalities. Inequalities are to be made tolerable. People in all regions, *and in their rural areas in particular,* should have acceptable decent levels of living. No region should be in abject penury while there are highly developed/industrialised regions elsewhere *in the country.* Regional growth theory is for a country. Regional disparities are to be reduced, if not abolished all together. There should be less and less divergence of income. All sub-disciplines of economics (e.g., monetary or agricultural or demography-------) have regional dimensions.

Regional economics is not parochial. A region is not a nation within a nation. Regional development subserves national development. However national growth has to be "inclusive" i.e. should not bypass poor persons, backward regions and laggard activities.

Regional economics is for balanced growth. There can be deliberate unbalancing of growth in regions to undo the past unbalancing for ultimate balancing! Material outputs value-adding, provision of infrastructure, employment generation and income propagation should be for/in all the regions of the country.

Some regions, or rather the people of some regions do not accept development! They stick to their culture which may not be materialistic. Here the challenges of regional development are daunting. Regional economics is pro-poor regions, sectors and ethnic groups.

There has not to be regional inventory of physical and human resources and growth strategies to ensure regional growth. Regional economics should reduce and end regional distress. Regional are not isolated. Regional economics studies the linkages, interface and inter-relationships between differentiated regions. Specialisations, mobilities, net migration rates, flows of goods and services (and counterflows of money) unilateral transfers, factors incomes etc. are all discussed. *Regional, economics is tailor made economics and not readymade economics.*

Regional growth should be equity-oriented also. Economics of regional locations and transportations are important in regional economics. Regional economics studies regional pattern of agricultural, industrial and infrastructural development. *The rich region / person come in the way of developing poor regions / persons.* Regional economics devisers ways and means to combat this. Regional economics seeks to increase regional economics efficiency. Complementarities are to be promoted in increase regional competitiveness. Economic nodes are to be developed even in physical homogeneous space. There are non-economic aspects also in regional studies like regional politics or regional culture.

Regional economics developed as regional disparities required better solutions. Economists never neglected space but paid less attention to it because regional disparities themselves were less. All economic theories had their own changing spatial dimensions.

"International economics is but a special case of inter-regional economics." Ohlin. (Ohlin to be pronounced as OLEEN).

Price theory has important component of transport costs and transport is space-related and distance related. Rural-urban economics is the most important part of regional economics.

REGIONAL ECONOMICS — SCOPE AND DISCIPLINE*

Prolegomenon

Regional study from the angle of the geographer related to settlements in space. Regional studies mostly related to just three topics: (i) location, (ii) transportation, and (iii) migration. Economists and geographers contributed in this study.

Regional economics, as a sub-discipline of Economics, concentrated on the inter-slate, intra-state and inter-district differences with reference to various economic variables e.g., cropping pattern, savings, investment pattern in various lines of manufacture, employment and income generation, exports and imports etc. Regional economic studies are

---

* When one examines the 'scope' of a subject one's concern is not to exclude what should be included, and when one discusses the 'discipline' of the subject his concern is not to include what should be excluded.

related to inter-sectoral linkages between urban and rural areas and also between various economic regions.

Regional 'science' is a broad-based subject while Regional Economics is a part of it. Problems of economic change, social development, demographic transition, etc. can be studied in regional perspective as well as in the national perspective. It is the inter-regional difference that is of main concern to the regional economists. A nation may be doing well but certain regions may be stagnating of even may be decelerating. However, regional economics will give greater emphasis to the *people and sectors in different regions* rather than to merely space as such.

In the Words of Hallet, Randall and West

"Regional Economics now attempts also to incorporate other parts such as macro-economics, welfare economics, public finance, labour economics, and input-output analysis. In addition, its own hybrids have now appeared — the agglomeration economics, the growth-point economics, the polarisation economics, or the industrial complex, analysis. However, regional economics still suffers *from* inadequate assimilation of some of the older and more established branches of formal economics."

We can say: "'Regional Economics is what economists interested in regional economic problems do".

Regional economics is both a theoretical (pedagogic) science, concentrating on theory as also a behaviouralistic or normative science, concentrating on inducing inequalities. Regional *science* is multi-disciplinary but regional economics has to remain a sub-discipline of general economics. Regional planning and national planning require cooperation of persons of all and sundry vocations and disciplines, but 'planning' will always remain more associated with Economics.

Regional economics emphasises that as the national income increases and various sectors and regions contribute unequally to the gross domestic product, we should find out why some regions have not been contributing their due share. Agriculture, industry and tertiary sector services are unequally concentrated in different regions; due to reasons other than geographical. These aspects are to be studied and correctives are to be introduced.

Regional economics is biased in favour of the depressed regions because in depressed regions live persons who are much more deprived. Urban-rural chasm is not only an important part of rural economics (rural persons are over-represented in poverty), and of urban economics but also of regional economics. Regional economics will disaggregate the man-made and natural causes of non-uniform development of sectors in different regions.

Regional economics, however, cannot provide policy prescriptions or tools which, will end all inequalities and differences but can only help in keeping them under control. Regional differences were not due to investment on the principle of comparative advantage principle but due to a host of other reasons. *'Economics of poverty' is not due to 'poverty of Economics'*, but because good economics is not put into practice by bad politics.

There can be no such solutions that regions can progress while the nation decays. Infact when the nation develops, all the regions should develop, subject to the natural constraints. All regional solutions have to be compatible with the national interests and interest of other regions. *A nation is not in inferior position to a region; a region is not a nation within a nation and those who try to study problems of region without the knowledge of general economics, are apt to be less than perfect.*

Perloff took the view that *regional science* is indivisible whole which will include regional economics, regional demography, study of the regional resource inventory, regional geo-physical conditions, and even regional socio-cultural aspects. He was for integration as against disaggregation. He was against categorisation and acknowledged that mix of various disciplines was necessary to form a new discipline.

Isard wanted to discuss *only regional economic problems in regional economics,* though many economic problems have non-economic aspects also.

Lafeber, regarded regional economics as the economics of spatial separation. Location, agglomeration, migration, settlements, transport networks would constitute the subject matter of regional economics.

Lafeber would prefer a narrower approach compared with even to Isard. If, for the sake of arguments, all regions are more or less same in various economic and non-economic aspects, regional economics will have no relevance.

Meyer defines regional economics in still narrower sense as "economics of resource immobility". Immobilities between regions simply do not exist and if this is the sole criterion, then regional economics becomes still-born.

In the opinion of the present author economics of the development of sectors and people, if studied in the inter-regional and intra-regional perspective, becomes regional economics in which we move from disaggregated levels to the aggregation, Regional economics studies the linkages, interface and inter-relationships between differentiated regions. It studies how locational economies overcome locational diseconomies; how immobilities lead to specialisation and trade and how restrictions lead to mobilities of factors between regions. We study how different degrees of scarcities of resources/facilities in different regions give rise to different sets of prices and how these prices *perform* the allocative functions or *require* the allocative functions. Regional economics tackles the regional inequalities, while the national economic planning tackles the problems of low national income. Regional economics would concentrate on undoing; the imbalances perpetuated by market mechanism, though it is not to say that market mechanism is discarded here. Regional economics is the child and father of 'planning from below'.

Regional economics is *tailor-made economics* rather than the ready-made economics. Regional economic development is not left to *happenstance economics* but there is conscious planning to reduce economic inequalities between regions in the shortest possible period. If planning is for the development of the sectors, regions and socio-economically handicapped people, it will not ignore the social consequences of economic transformation and will be truly welfare economics. *Regional economics is regional economic grievance redressal economics.*

Regional economics cannot end relative and absolute inequalities but can bring them within the socio-economically tolerable limits. *Poverty and under-development, if they are location specific, require regional economic tools.* Regional economics comes into its own if the regional inequalities are not self-correcting. Regional economic policies cannot be implemented without the State intervention.

Renowned monetary economist Milton Friedman has argued:

> "Regional Policy Issues become important in industrial and post-industrial period"

In the pre-industrial transitional phase of development, it is the growth aspect rather than the equity aspect which should be more important. Even infrastructure development serves more the 'development' purpose than 'social service' purpose. It is during the industrialisation period that locational optimisation can be linked to ending the distortions of the previous development and to ensure that distortions do not get accentuated over a wide area to develop all the regions as tied industries (tied to the source of raw material which was low value in high bulk and requires load-shedding activities at the point of obtaining the raw materials; cannot be distributed according to the will of the planners. Over industrialisation and over-specialisation of certain regions would create diseconomies of the same regions as also keep other regions depressed. Economics of industrialisation, rural or urban development are *now* part of not only sectors-development economics but also of regional economies.

Regional Economics will study in details the regional pattern of industrialisation {economies and diseconomies of scale, of firms concentrated in a region), and the rural-urban growth differential in a return. A policy of optimum utilisation of material and human resources for regional self-sufficiency in basic goods (as far as possible), should precede policy measures for strengthening the export base. Some regions may specialise in one or two commodities and then they will have to strengthen their export base in such a manner that the region can import the basic necessities. It a region has achieved self-sufficiency in basic necessities and has also strengthened its export-base, then the take-off stage can be said to be around.

One important task of regional planning will be planned location of new industries to reduce the regional imbalances. If necessary, some industries may have to be shifted to new locations, a task which is exceedingly difficult even for the most congested regions. *The moot question is whether the developed regions will accept the stop' signal, while the backward regions are given 'go' signal. Still more important question is whether the developed regions, sectors and groups themselves will finance the development of the backward counterparts. For this the central planning has to be very effective.* The fall of socialist by 1991 has made this even more difficult. Hence strong packages of incentives and disincentives have to be devised which will not negate the market mechanism altogether. One big problem with the non-planned poor countries is that vested interest groups make phantom piles of money for themselves by siphoning off funds meant for the development of backward regions and depressed classes.

A region is considered 'developed' when it has high "value-adding" as also can ensure better 'physical quality of life'. Adequacy of food, good housing conditions, high literacy rates, better medical facilities, absence of crime, low growth rate of population, low pollution, high savings, high capital formation and investment are indicators of a region being well placed.

Regional Problems and Relevance of Regional Economics

The basic regional problem is how to increase the complementary relations between regions and inside a region.

This task is as onerous as *trying to please God without offending the Devil!*

The main task of regional policy is to solve regional problems. *Under-development and over-development* (development of urban areas accompanied by solving the problems of congestion and pollution) both are to be tackled. However, it will not be regional economics or 'general economics' alone which can solve all economic problems: this will depend upon the efficiency of the economic *system.* Exogenous support can overcome many endogenous disadvantages of a region and secure the least-cost position.

One of the problems of national and regional development, is how to reconcile the incompatibilities of narrow individual objectives. A regional policy is necessary for the application of development tools in a spatial framework for the optimum utilisation of the physical, material and human resources of the regions while trying to balance the 'balance of payment disequilibria ' between regions. *Perloff* went on to remark that complementary characteristics of the problems distinguish one region from the other and complementarities are to be promoted.

Regional economics will primarily take into account the (a) homogeneity, (b) nodality and (c) programming or planning.

(A) *Homogeneity:* There can be economic homogeneity, socio-cultural homogeneity or physical homogeneity that is to be taken care of. Inter-regional and intra-regional differences require being lessened as far as possible.*

(B) *While homogeneity emphasizes the uniformity, nodality emphasizes the heterogeneous nature of the areas and hence the inter-dependence.* Some nodes of economic activities emerge in space and these nodal regions are composed of heterogeneous units, but closely connected with each other functionally. Towards the centres of agglomeration of economic activities (the dominant centres) money, men and materials gravitate. There can be found in a nucleus or nuclei where most of the business and industrial activities (with high 'density' or intensity) take place. Each node will have a concentric zone of influence around it and all types of flows will be very thick near the region; but, they will thin out with the distance. Two concentric circles of two nodal points may have some overlapping area and within that area, the two nodal points (centres) will have an "indifferent" clientele. The outer limits of a nodal centre are set by a certain radius and the cost of covering the distance set the limits of the

* More follows on this topic and theme elsewhere in this book.

critical radius. There are two-way flows from the nodes to the periphery and from the periphery to the nodes, though the nature and extent of the flows will differ. The heaviest flows tend to polarize towards and from the dominant node or nodes, usually large cities. *KA Fox* argued that these flows vary directly with the size or attraction of the node and inversely with the distance from it. These flows form the basis of the study of the *Gravity Models,* which provide important operational technique for polarization analysis.

Thus the economics of nodal regions is the study of the upstream and downstream linkages between the centres of higher and lower economic order and thus inter-regional framework is hierarchal; some regions dominating the others-the disadvantaged ones. The hierarchy can be observed thus:

(a) if the thickest flows are to a smaller centre from the node, then the node is 'independent'; and
(b) if the flows are towards a larger centre, then the node is subordinate.

From this we can deduce the *transitivity* i.e., the hierarchy. If nodal point 'A' is subordinate to 'B', and 'B' is subordinated to 'C, then 'A' is subordinate to 'C' also. Production and service flows (they become polarization flows if they are very large), determine the nodal hierarchy. Thus, one important part of regional economics is the study of concentration/ agglomeration versus dispersal.

(C) *Planning:* Geo-physical conditions may set the parameters of development, but economic planning can reduce the 'deterministic' element in the development process. With real and financial transfers/ investments/ subsidies, backward regions can be developed to appreciable extent In relation to the national planning, the regional planning/ programming is 'open' and hence more dynamic and difficult. Regional economics thus becomes a part of the dynamics of economic development. From the sixties of the last decade, attention is being paid to (or recommended to be paid to) *the planning of things, population and people,* thus regional planning will give more emphasis to backward areas, usually rural areas.

Regional economics should include the economics of the depressed ethnic groups. Very poor persons, living below the mythical poverty line, belong to certain categories (SC & ST persons in India, for example). Women are over-represented in the poverty number. Starving persons can be found living in rich urban areas or rich regions. Regional economics" has theories for these issues.

All centralized planning gives back-seat to the market mechanism. However, as the events since 1989 in the erstwhile socialist USSR showed, "mutual consistency through centralized planning" remained a myth because no computer could handle the 'mutual consistency between 25 million goods and services. Hence market mechanism cannot be done away with and effective planning would infact accept the signals from market mechanism. Regional 'planners' have traditionally been antagonistic to market mechanism but will have to make good use of it now in future.

Regional problems give rise to complementarities as also competitiveness. Demand for separate 'States' like Telangana or Vidharbha comes because people believe that this is the only way development disparities could be ended. The reorganisation of States in India on linguistic lines was done to enable people to develop the State economies while maintaining the socio-cultural identities.

However, developing a region for effective flood control, or for arresting the onward movement of desert, or for developing a power grid, or developing forests, mining or river valley project area are examples of the needed complementarities as administrative regions may be transgressed.

Filial Background

Regional economics, in the words of *Brown,* started as an *ad hoc* study with a piece-meal approach. Regional economics is the filial descendent of the oldest branch of economics — the international economics. It originated with special analysis of the problems of depressed areas. We now have regional *science:* and, not only economists but geographers, sociologists, anthropologists, environmentalists, agronomists, public men and even scientists have contributed to the development of the subject.

A False Charge

Isard, an important name in regional science, made an observation about the *classical* economists that they used to wander in the wonderland of no space'. In the first instance this remark is not well founded and in the second place it was directed towards the *classical* economists only. However, some writers quote Isard for *all economists!*

Refutation: This remark of Isard is unfortunate, to say the least but the slavish quoting of the same by many regional analysts is a misfortune. No economist ever thought that economic activity takes place in a vacuum. The classical economists were not the dwellers in the ethereal regions. In the rudimentary economies there was 'equality in poverty' and economic problem was: "how to increase the national income of the country' through sectoral development." Wide disparities did not exist between various sub-sectors and sub-regions. As capitalism gained strength, inter-personal differences became glaring. Since spatial differentiation was not a grave problem not much was written on it. The classical economists are to be judged with reference to the time and conditions when they wrote.

(1) *Even Adam Smith, the founder of Economics, took space into consideration*

The father of economics started his book *The Wealth of Nations* with a chapter on division of labour, which included discussion on territorial division of labour — a space related subject. The economics of the classical writers was economics of *truck, barter and exchange* — activities which are always related to space. Smith even discussed the economics of the developed and depressed regions. India's Bengal was cited by him as the prospective depressed region where stationary state' will be reached! Smith discussed in details the problems of the colonising countries and the colonies.

Much earlier than him Sir William Petty (1682) recognized the existence of location rent. Richard Cantillon (1730) propounded a market theory of towns: about the transient markets and the permanent markets.

(2) *Immediate- disciples also gave adequate attention to space: as much as was necessary*

Malthus and Ricardo were quite worried about the decreasing returns in agriculture and exponential rate of demographic explosion and that there should be control on population wherever the man-land ratio crossed the optimum sustainable limit at that time. Infact Alexander Gray, an important name amongst the writers on history of economic thought, wrote that "Ricardo was not a dweller in ethereal region but very much in the thick of life". Ricardo discussed the economics of virgin territories and old territories separately. Malthus wanted control on population growth for higher capital formation.

The rent theory of Ricardo provided locational inferences. *JS Mill* extended the classical theory of rent to urban land. *Theory of international trade developed by the classical economists had locational implications because comparative advantage in costs and prices depended upon the location.* The rules of trade in the classical theory were simple: (a) immobilities lead to specialisation and trade and (b) trade leads to changes in income and prices and to mobilities. Neither the mobilities are absent nor they are perfect. *Marshall* wrote about location rent also, though it is a fact that he wrote more with reference to time than with reference to space. Yet discussion about space was not absent, as much as was necessary at the time the classical economists wrote.

(3) *Surprising it may seem, but it is true that J.B. Say's s famous ' Law of the Market' — "Supply creates its own demand and hence demand creates own supply through price signals — had a regional dimension.*

In his system:

Over production is a condition where all the producers, in sum, produce *too little.*

In J.B. Say's system there is no general over-production: it is sub-sectoral and regional. If there is overproduction *somewhere,* it is necessary that something else should be produced, *somewhere else,* based on the territorial or functional division of labour. If cloth remains unsold, it means that the potential buyers of cloth do not have the necessary purchasing power to acquire which they should produce something else so that they can have purchasing power by selling their product/service. In this type of discussion of sub-sectoral activities, the territorial division of labour was also included.

(4) *Thunen, the pioneer of location economics of agricultural activities, was an immediate disciple of the classical Trinity of Smith, Malthus and Ricardo.*

While the British economists were 'liberal and cosmopolitan' in their outlook, the German economists were 'nationalistic' first. While the British economists largely concentrated on the laws of universal applications, there were some amongst them who examined the local problems and thus protectionism emerged. It was not a sin to have examined the laws of universal applications because such laws are not historico-relative nor space related. The downfall of socialism in 1989-90 in European countries was the victory of these very universal laws!.

*von Thunen's theory of rent was developed with reference to a central point and concentric circles of different uses of land.

So far as studies about rural and urban areas are concerned, some writers used mathematical tools and geographers cartographic illustrations to study the settlements. It is their forte and no one can improve upon them. The civil engineers and architects studied the problems of physical planning of the settlements and their public health engineering. Environmentalists are bothered about the pollution problems. The administrators and policemen write about crime control. Economists were concerned with the occupational and income patterns. Writers of different discipline study different socio-cultural, technological or other problems. In such a situation it cannot be accepted that 'general economists' were/are not *ipso facto* regional economists.

Thus, even in the theory of location it was the *contribution of economists which was more significant.* Geographers and sociologists contributed in the analysis of urban-regional *cartographic* relations, in the words of Richardson.

(5) *Price theory did not neglect space*

The theory of price determination under perfect

* von to be pronounced as "fon" and v is to be small and not a capital letter.

competition was developed under several qualifying assumptions for homogenous commodities. It was, however, recognized that competition can be 'perfect' only in concentric circles. It was in the two-commodity and two-country model that transport costs were *assumed* to be equal and hence were not included. Assumptions are assumptions only and they are relaxed also. This is the process with which we study the laws of motion by first studying the laws of stand-still. Infact while writers of other disciplines might have taken the 'distance costs of transport' into account, economists also took into considerations the 'opportunity cost of moving over the distance' — in terms of time wasted, or other opportunities lost. Transport costs were ignored by regional analysts also over the uniform space, which seldom is the real situation.

Where transport costs mattered, they were incorporated in the product differentiations or market imperfections. *It should be remembered that industrial revolution had just begun in the time of Smith and products were not differentiated for the sake of differentiations,* as today.

When the concept of representative firm of Marshall was questioned and when it was acknowledged that differing costs of production of different firms producing under increasing returns at different rates were incompatible with the perfect competition the foundations of the theory of imperfect competition became solid. *Even Adam Smith had taken space into account in the discussion of monopoly pricing.* His monopolies were rather local and natural because multi-nationals or transnational companies had not emerged. Infact it can be said that the neo-classical theory of imperfect competition was the starting point of

* "The area now defined as regional economics has been woven out of several separate strands. Some of these strands have been developed out of a direct interest of *economists in spatial problems as Location theory.*" * *"Regional Economics Reader" p. 14.*

regional economics also: of the present day regional economics, that is. In 1933, EH Chamberlain showed that:

Location was merely one aspect of product differentiation.

(6) Roots of present-day *regional economics have to be traced from the classical international economics.*

> The old international trade theory was based on location economics and in turn developed the location economics: *it was regional economics itself.* Ohlin wrote ('to be pronounced as Oleen):
>
> "To demonstrate that the theory of international trade is only a part of a general localisation theory, wherein the space aspects of pricing are taken into full account."
>
> (Quoted from Richardson's *Reader,* p. 9)

Ohlin clearly differentiated between a spatial and non-spatial theory of pricing. His price theory was extended to several markets and these were obtained by assuming that there were geographical immobilities of factors of production. After taking into account the transport and factor-mobility constraint, he developed his spatial price equilibrium. Commodity prices for separate markets differ by transport costs mainly. Thus, the basis was laid of the analysis of spatial price equilibrium in multiple market:, in the 1950s by S. Enke (1951)., Paul Samuleson (1952) M.J. Beckmann (1952 and 1953)-, and K.A Fox (1953).

Price theory incorporated both factor mobility as well as immobility and different solutions were worked out. Ohlin had pointed out that whereas inter-regional trade results from differences in regional specialisation following from variations in relative factor endowment, differences in factor prices may also induce locational adaptation associated with inter-regional factor movements. However, because normally there are constraints on the movement of productive factors, commodity trade frequently compensates for the relative immobility of factors, and hence promotes a tendency to both commodity and factor price equalisation.

Trade and location were studied by economists in an integrated manner: infact the separation is inconceivable because goods to be traded start from a location. In the words of Richardson:

> "With the growth of interest in regional economics as distinct from the much narrower economics of location, the development of regional income theory was a logical next step, even though it meant a temporary loss of interest in distance factors and transport costs. Regional income analysis stems from the integration of Keynesian economics with international trade theory."
>
> (Reader, p. 10)

(7) Economists discussed the problems of migration not as movement of the automations, but of human beings, taking all ramifications of migration in consideration.

Infact economists discussed the problems of migration and mobility in juxtaposition. As is well known, there can be mobility without migration and migration without horizontal and vertical mobility. If Thunen and Weber were pioneers of location theory, Reilly (1929), S.A. Stouffer (1940), G.K. Zipf (1941 & 1949, J.Q. Stewart (1947 & 1948), Walter Isard and G. Freutel (1954), W. Warntz and Ronald Artle (1959) made important contributions about the gravity models'. Economists and sociologists have studied the problems of migration in terms of economic and social distances. Isard and others discussed how trading centres attract people or how better employment and income earning opportunities exercise the 'gravitational pulls'.

W. Launhardt (1882 and 1885) also wrote about the location but his work remained less popular than Weber's because the work of Weber was translated in English! Both opined that location follows the least cost principle. T. Polander. FA Fetter, Hysons, Hoover, Greennut and I sard extended the works on location. Waber's theory was theory of *capitalist location* and it was a general theory.

The urban hierarchy with its rank-size rule was analysed by Christaller and Losch. The rank size rule was popularized by Zipf. The roots of the CFT are traced back to Auerback (1931).

Economists discussed in details the barriers of mobility and migration and also their spurs. It is part of elementary economics that

(a) transport economies overcome the locational diseconomies; and (see foot note on last page of this chapter.)
(b) if the transport diseconomies cannot be overcome, then the locational indivisibilities have to be overcome i.e., locational economies have to be ensured.

Metzler, Machlup, Vining, Kahn, R.M. Goodwill and J.S. Chipman—the well known names in economics of growth and economics of international trade wrote about regional business cycles and regional multipliers also. The *economic base theory* was also developed by the German nationalist economists who argued that rather than emphasizing the importance of exports, development of domestic market is even more important for national growth.

G. Hildebrand — a great name in international economics — brought about the integration of economic base theory and Keynesian general theory. Vining developed the regional business cycle theories after this integration was accomplished and regional income models were developed. The fifties of the 20th century witnessed these developments.

Economists studied the regional income theory, which made them study every sector or policy in regional perspective regional differences in cropping pattern and productivity, regional industrial structure, regional fiscal differentiations, regional grants and subsidies, regional wage differentiations etc. were studied by the economists in the inter-State and inter-district systems. Administrative regions rather than the geo-physical regions were considered by the economists for such analysis.

Economists who wrote about multi-level planning — a subject which is inter-disciplinary but always associated with economics. (For example, district level planning and even block level planning were suggested right from the Second Five Year Plan of India.) An economist, however, does not treat *a region as a nation within a nation.*

(8) *Sectoral development is still more important than spatial development, though it will be necessary that sectoral development should take care of spatial development and the development of the people.*

Unless plentiful supplies of real goods necessary for the people are produced locational aspects are of no consequence. Similarly in India there are many *ad hoc* programmes for the development of the depressed ethnic groups' under the *clientele approach to development,* adopted by the Government of India. However, they too are proving palliatives because they have not been properly integrated with the development programmes of sectors. Infact because of the high cost-benefit ratio or low benefit-cost ratio and corruption leakages programmes become inflationary as investment costs go up.

In Conclusion we can say that it will be wrong to say

that economists neglected space or that the geographers were unconcerned with the sectors. Every writer wrote with reference to his time and circumstances. As it was found that certain areas were neglected and spatial dualism became unacceptable, economists drew attention to this. As it became apparent that growth was not percolating to all, and certain groups were experiencing real and relative immiserisation during the growth process, economists started having clientele approach i.e. targetting the disadvantaged poor.

It is to be re-emphasized that development of the sectors is most important. The space development programmes and the clientele development programmes should be integrated with the development programmes of the sectors. It is the generation of real wealth through the development of the sectors which can provide real resources for consumption, savings, capital formation and investment.

* In the mountaneous Himachal Pradesh it will be better that factories for processing apples and preparing apple juice, jams, marmalada etc. be established there. Locational economics will overcome transport diseconomies. [Low value apples will be taken out at high costs.]

If there are locational diseconomies (infrastructure not being there) Then raw materials, can be taken to a good place.

2

Regions and Their Types

APPOGGIATURA

Geographers define a region according to geophysical features; economic planners usually take a planning (administrative) region. They then go down to a district or even a taluka or a block as the bottom of the hierarchy of regions. Planners also take into account (i) forest regions (ii) desert region, (iii) mining region, (iv) river vally/irrigation region, (v) agro-climatic region and the like.

Everyone defines a region as it suit him/her objective of the study. Geographers unfortunately criticise economists for neglecting space, which is not correct. They themselves do not go beyond natural features. In their scheme they seem to plan regional development without incorporating monetary and fiscal factor and commodity/good prices, productivities (capital- output ratios) and investment coefficients etc.

The chapter arrangement given hereafter is self-explanatory.

REGIONS AND THEIR TYPES

Chapter Arrangement

A region is a sub-system within a system (the country itself) and if sub-systems develop greater inter-connectivity, the greater will be the efficiency of the system. All regions are 'problem regions' in one way or the other, level of development notwithstanding. A structural set of different types of regions has its own 'dualism' everywhere. The essential task of planning is to bind various regions into a system in which only those inequalities remain which simply cannot be obliterated.

(A) Regional Economics accords highest importance to these regions
1. Homogeneous Regions of various hues. Formal regions.
2. Nodal, Polarized, Heterogeneous, or functional regions.
3. Planning and Programming Regions.

(B) *In Multi-level Planning, these regions receive attention*
1. Macro region.
2. State region.
3. Meso region.
4. Micro region.
5. Micro Minor region.

(C) *In the 'stages-of-development' analysis, we distinguish between the*
1. Developed Region.
2. Backward and Depressed Region. (Vestigial regions also)
3. Neutral and Intermediate Regions.

(D) *In the activity status analysis, following types are mentioned*
1. Mineral regions.
2. Manufacturing regions.
3. Urban and or Congested regions.

Regions have been delimited on several criteria: economic, administrative, physical or activity regions. Geographers, economists and administrators invariably delimit the regions in different manner. Harry W. Richardson wrote

> "Defining regions precisely is such a nightmare that most regional economists prefer to shy away from the task, and are relieved when they work with administrative regions on the grounds that policy considerations require it or that data are not available for any other spatial units."

Too small sub-regions arc less significant for comprehensive planning. In the words of *Carter:*

> "Countries differ enormously both in size and in the variety of localised economic communities that they contain, but in most of them there is some sort of awareness of a small number usually from two to a dozen — spatially distinguishable division, different in economic respects that bear upon national policy. Beyond them there lie an indefinite number of smaller divisions, sometimes with very clear differences of welfare and interest separate towns and rural districts, working-class and middle-class suburbs, manufacturing— which we exclude from the discussion for a variety of reasons."

> "There has been a great deal of discussion of the regional concept, but this has not led to any firm agreement. Probably the most prevalent view is that there is no unambiguous method of defining an ideal region, and that wherever possible spatial analysts should work with the more neutral concept of space. It is clear that a region is a supra-urban on the one hand, and a sub-area of the nation on the other. A common procedure is to delimit the region by reference to physical criteria, administrative boundaries or data availability. Certainly, most researchers accept that it is easier to define the core of a region [usually a central city] than to map its outer boundary."*

Ohlin defined a region in terms of factor mobility, and

* See: Richardson: Regional Economics Reader: pp. 12 & 13.

labour catchment or general supply areas as an alternative to market area analysis and polarisation [nodal] studies of the urban hierarchy.

North opined that a region should be defined in terms of its export base.

Many writers belonging to disciplines other than economics were more inclined to define region as a homogeneous geographical region.

(A) Regions Popular with Regional Economists

A.1. Homogeneous Regions

They are formal regions and if the basis of homogeneity is topography, rainfall, climate or other geo-physical characteristic, they are geographer's darling.

Economic homogeneity is more relevant for planning. The structure of employment, the occupational pattern, the net migration, the density of population, the resource and industrial structure, if similar in a space, the regions become homogeneous in economic sense. The greater the economic similarities, the greater the interest the economists will have in homogeneous regions. Internal differences in a region are unimportant. Sometimes, however, a clearcut homogeneous region nay have as many differences in sub-regions as to make them quite different yet a region may remain 'homogeneous'. Scotland or Uttar Pradesh are clear-cut homogeneous regions but in topography the hilly districts of Uttar Pradesh have nothing in common with the districts of the plains. Eastern and Western districts are also different but Uttar Pradesh remains a homogeneous region in administrative terms. Thus, a homogeneous economic region can have differing physical characteristics. A homogeneous region on economic or political criterion may have a lot of heterogeneity from several other standpoints.

Regional macro-economic growth models treat a region

as homogeneous and they are spaceless for intra- regional differences. This should be kept in mind by those who always criticise economists of "neglecting space"

The methodology of formulating macro-economic regional growth models for homogeneous regions is the same as that of the national models e.g., assumptions of perfect competition, perfect mobility and the same capital -output ratio. There is no difference between national and regional growth models for homogeneous regions, in that both ignore differences in space. A region being a collectivity of people is a sociological phenomenon and thus a region goes parallel to the concept of community also. A homogeneous region is therefore a homogeneous problem-bound entity.

A.2. Polarized or Nodal Regions

Polarized or nodal region looks to a centre — a large town usually — for services. Its influence extends beyond the area of the city. The villages are dependent upon it for services and marketing. There is little concern for uniformity when a polarized or nodal region is taken. Cohesiveness is due to internal flows, contacts and interdependencies. The city region need not correspond to the administrative region because hinterland of several clear-cut regions may be served by a city. (For example even the persons of Gwalior may visit Delhi for buying some consumer durables of high value. A capital city may attract customers from several districts around the capital city).

A nodal region will have heterogeneous economy around it. Regional economists are more concerned with what happens within a nodal region and spatial dimension of the nodal region assumes importance Population and industries agglomerate and there are *core* regions with higher per capita income generation through higher production of goods and services. Within regions there are dominant cities or nodes to which flows of inputs, goods, people and traffic gravitate. Within the cities there are nuclei that form business and social centres and which are discernible at a glance from an intra-metropolitan traffic-flow density map. (Richardson). If the 'size of the mass' of the nodes is large then there will be great pull effects of the centre. However, as the distance increases, the costs of 'overcoming frictions' will rise and the people of distant areas will look for a different nodal point. Each region will have one or more dominant nodes and it will be interesting to find and record as to which interior areas form the areas of influence of one or the other •node. A binary graph can reduce the complex flows into a network of points and lines, giving indications of the inflows and outflows and their strength.

A node is independent if its largest flow is to a smaller centre, but subordinate if flow is to a big centre. There is also hierarchy of subordination e.g., if region 'A' is subordinate to 'B' and 'B' is subordinate to 'C, then 'A' is subordinate to 'C' also this is *transitivity principle.* Different internal and external flows have greater or smaller intensity for various categories of services, commodities and persons.

Nodal regions provide an understanding of the functional relationship between settlements which fill up the space. Big, medium, small and tiny settlements dot the space and because of their intra-regional differentiations, flows emanate. These heterogeneous units in rural and urban areas are functionally related because each settlement cannot have all the functions and facilities.

All functions require a particular threshold population and other facilities (each settlement cannot have a college; or, unless there is electricity there cannot be cinema hall; or a bank branch will require not only a critical minimum population but also a critical minimum deposit-credit ratio). The size of the settlements and the hierarchy of functions are mutually determining. Lower and higher order functions can naturally be found in the same order hierarchy of the settlements. Thus between hamlets and metropolitan cities there are lower and higher order functions in all types of services (from one-man post office to head post office; from primary school to Institutes of higher learning and so on). Since not all settlements can afford to sustain all types of functions, they depend upon other settlements/areas for meeting their needs of services and goods and thus functional linkages develop. Markets of various orders exist. Nothing can be bought unless something is sold and thus all exchanges are ultimately barter, unless supported by grants, donations and subsidies. Functional linkages are revealed by the flows of men, materials, and money, such linkages result in the emergence of the dominant nodes — focal points which attract and provide all types of flows. In a hierarchy of settlements we find several nodal points which receive and provide flows and functions. Each node has some settlements to support and receive sustenance e.g., a city receives its food items from the villages; while the villages receive goods of the secondary sector from the urban nodes. (Nodal points are always urban centres). *Thus a nodal region is composed of heterogeneous units which are closely inter-related with each other functionally.* Functional linkages give unity to nodal region and a certain amount of functional coherence/utility/ interdependence is always present.

Nodes attract labour while the hinterland becomes the labour catchment area if the hinterland cannot provide jobs to the people. In *some respects the boundary of a nodal region may extend far and beyond for some facility e.g., Bombay attracts persons from distant places in Uttar Pradesh and Bihar because these persons can find employment in Bombay. Similarly even the rural areas of Punjab attract labour from Chhattisgarh from Eastern Uttar Pradesh or Bihar because highly paying (comparatively speaking) employment can be found in Punjab in agricultural operations.*

All functional linkages keep on changing in nature and volume. While economic activities are scattered in a homogeneous region, they are concentrated in or around specific foci of activities. Inter-dependence is a rule in *heterogeneous region and thus nodal region is heterogeneous region.* The demand and supply conditions at different points/settlements in the heterogeneous region differ and that is the reason for inter-dependence. Around a node (a focal point in space) revolve not only economic but political and cultural activities also. Yet, it can be said that all activities become weak with the distance and ultimately terminate also. The forces of distance weaken the linkages of all types, unless it is the linkage of all areas of the country with the capital of the nation. The size of a nodal region shall depend upon the efficiency of means of communications and transportation and all those facilities which give rise to localisation of industries/activities at a certain place. An improvement in transportation, communications, finance, accommodation and other facilities will widen the radius of influence and the hinterland will get enlarged and the node will get further strength.

In a sense there is an element of homogeneity in a nodal region! *A nodal region is homogeneous in that it combines areas dependent in some trade or functional sense on a specific centre.* (Meyers). There are a number of possible sets of nodal regions depending on the level of activity one is specifying. (Smaller node for vegetables: bigger node for (automobiles).

All nodes have their own periphery but different nodes have interdependence with other nodes outside their region.

Formal Regions: or Functional Regions

A formal region is homogeneous with reference to some geo-physical characteristic such as topography, climate or vegetation. This is *physical* formal region.

Lateron there was a shift from this narrow approach to a broader approach and economic, social and political criteria were also applied. An industrial or agricultural or plantation region is a formal economic region; or a State is a formal political region.

As against this, the *functional region* is concerned with inter-dependence. There is a geographical area in which there is economic interdependence. The nodal regions are functional regions between which there are flows of men, material and money.

In practice, the formal and functional regions very rarely overlap neatly, and often vary markedly. We have to "carve out" a planning region after compromising the two approaches. That region becomes the planning region (formal or functional) which is administratively viable. All regions are geographical regions because they exist on space and all regions are economic regions because people cannot remain alive without there being economic activity. Functional regions have important nodal points in them and intra-regional and inter-regional spatial differentiations are emphasized.

Functional Regions and Flow Analysis

This is relevant for nodal regions with considerable degree of inter-dependence. The actual flows of men, money and materials can be studied (flow analysis) and/or simulation may be made as to how they would flow (gravity model). Functional regions can be delineated on the basis of the direction and intensity of flows between the dominant centre and surrounding satellites. Each flow will show (a) decreasing intensity as it becomes more distant from the main centre and (b) increasing intensity as it approaches another centre. If a small town "A" is 100 km. from Delhi but just 10 km. from another city, then flows to Delhi will be weaker, unless those flows can be exclusively to and from Delhi. Thus the boundary of the sphere of influence of the dominant centre will be where the flow intensity tapers of or becomes minimum.

Export and import of goods, transfers of money, migration of persons in search of jobs etc. are all 'flows'. Students going to colleges in big cities or to specialized hospitals, or girls going to the place of their husbands are "social flows". People going to pilgrimage are cultural flows, also involving economic flows as the people spend money on the way. Information flows (newspapers) also involve monetary transactions. Nystuen, Dacey, and Boudeville plotted these flows on graphs. The intensity becomes an indication as to which flows emanate from where or end up to a particular place. The dominant centre can be identified and the regions covered by flows from and to a dominant flow can also be demarcated.

A.3 Planning Regions

Planning regions depend upon the *type of multi-level planning* in the country. A very small country will naturally have one level planning. Markedly different geo-physical or agro-climatic areas may be chosen as planning region for special cases e.g., developing a mining or plantation or power grid region. A planning region in a multi-level setup requires a regional plan, which is a spatial plan for the systematic location of functions and facilities in relation to human settlements so that people may use them to their maximum advantage. Infact more important than reducing the regional disparities, is the task of ensuring that backward regions and rural areas have basic minimum needs. Planning region for different activities can be different and a regional plan will be locational in character for that activity/function. For *comprehensive* planning, there has to be a national plan and then a State plan and finally district/block plans. Since a planning region is a sub-national area demarcated for the purpose of translating national objectives into regional programmes and policies, and since plan formulation and implementation need administrative machinery, administrative regions are generally accepted as planning regions. This may be not wholly correct as administrative boundaries may be inconsistent with regional boundaries, derived from economic criteria. However, in some cases a planning region can be small, say a city but a village cannot be (and, probably not even a custer of villages) a planning region unless the objective is too limited.

The hierarchy of planning region would be (i) national level (ii) macro level (iii) State level, (iv) Meso level, (v) and micro level.

A planning region is (or should be) large enough to enable substantial changes in the distribution of population and employment to take place within its boundaries, yet small enough for its planning problems to be tackled effectively. It should have a viable resource base, a manpower base, and internal homogeneity/cohesiveness. It should be such that satisfactory levels *of mutually satisfying* levels of production, exchange, and consumption levels obtained.

Boudeville defines a planning region in the following words:

> "It is an area displaying some coherence or unit of economic decisions."

Klassen defines it as:

> A planning region must be large enough to take investment decisions of an economic size, must be able to apply its own industry with the necessary labour, should have a homogeneous economic structure, contain atleast one growth point and have a common approach to and awareness of its problems. In short, a region should be defined according to the purpose of one's analysis.

Planning ensures that under the direction of those

> who know how to plan, the scarce human and natural resources are used and utilised for the satisfaction of maximum number of wants within a specified time period. A planned economy can supercede the market mechanism but it will come to grieve soon and, though a planned economy is a regulated economy, it *should not* be over-regulated.

Ideally a planning region should have adequate resources to establish a satisfactory pattern of savings, capital formation, investment, production, employment, income generation and consumption pattern. It means that the area should be economically viable. This usually is not the case. The States of East India are rich in natural resources and poor in logistics/infrastructure support. Unless the aid comes from the Centre, these States cannot be viable as planning regions. As the things stand at present, these States are not capable of being self-sufficient at higher levels of economic activity and are not able even to develop at a reasonable growth rate of income, comparable to some of the developed States of the country. Thus planning regions are spatial units of different sizes, (city, block, district or State) depending upon the objectives in view and the problems to be tackled. In rare cases only, a planning region extends beyond a State.

B.I. & B.2: Macro-Major Region

We coin this term to define a "cluster of adjoining States" which may form a 'zone of planning' of certain sub-sectors or functions. There are in India zonal councils of States. The Chief Ministers (along with others involved in planning) meet to decide about certain things like "agro-climatic zonal planning of agricultural activities" "planning of a power grid"; or "planning mining activities in a region"; "forestry planning"; or "planning all complementarities of a river valley project". Zone of 'seven sister States of the East' or 'zone of Southern States' is an example of macro-major region. Planning in or for a macro-major region does not exclude the importance of the strong centre. For some specific purposes, an "Authority" may be created e.g., Narmada Valley Region Authority which will have its jurisdiction in all the States involved e.g., Madhya Pradesh, Gujarat, Maharashtra and Rajasthan.

The Zonal councils can plan the sharing the water of the rivers and irrigation projects or power amongst them. Zonal 'aggregation' is only for sharing the common resources. For all practical purposes the States remain the second level planning regions. However, unless the zonal councils (usually consisting of the Chief Ministers of the States) agree, certain schemes, projects, or programmes cannot be included in the plans of the States, and hence of the country. There is no zonal administration for execution the administrative machinery of Zonal States have to cooperate. Zonal cooperation is very necessary for the development of infrastructure and industries in complementary manner.

Macro Region

Macro region is naturally bigger than the micro region and comprises of a few micro regions, having industrial nucleus rooted in a strong power and infrastructure base, when will serve as apex centre for the entire macro region. Emergence of a central place of a high order in a macro region is of importance. A metropolitan centre with its area of influence, if it is quite wide, is also a macro region. Metropolitan areas with not only strong industrial base but services base (education and training facilities, medical facilities, legal aid, to innovations, demonstration effect and cultural entertainment) will serve as foci of development. Considerable degree of self-sufficiency can be achieved in such regions, though not complete autarky. All macro regions do not have the same type of sectoral development. *Macro region can be a State or even a group of States,* if the States of a country are not big enough. Macro regions are second in hierarchy, next to the national level. It is also possible that a *physical* macro region may comprise parts of different States of a country for *project* planning purposes (e.g., big river valley projects. An electric grid, or a big industrial unit (steel plant) may require resources of the *parts* of different States, and, for the purpose of that particular activity (facility) planning, the macro region will be parts of different States. State boundaries are not respected in the sense that the macro region may transcend or cut-across administrative boundaries of the States of a country. *A macro region may not be uniform or homogeneous in all respects. It may have homogeneity in one respect (physical complementcrity of an industrial facility or a project) and may have heterogeneity in other respect (administrative boundaries).* A macro region should have a common resource base and specialisation in that resource base so that production activities can develop on the principle of comparative advantage based on territorial division of labour. (India has been divided into 11 to 20 macro regions — agro-climate or resource based by different authors/ agencies e.g., Dr. Chen-Hen, The Census of India, Dr. Danial Throner, or Regional Survey Unit of the Indian State Institute). The Planning Commission of India would have just 5 Zonal councils — Eastern, Northern, Central, Western, and Southern comprising of certain Stales but beyond this there is no systematic *macro-regionalisction* in India.

These so-called macro regions of India have to have inter-State cooperation in the matter of utilisation of river water and electricity grids etc. For all practical purposes, after the national level, there are the State level planning units.

B.3 Meso Region

Meso region can be identified with a 'division' of a State. Bundelkhand region, Baghelkhand region, Mahakoshal region, or Malwa region are meso region of

Madhya Pradesh. Meso region is usually a sub-division of a State, comprising of several districts. There should be some identifiable affinity in the area which may even facilitate planning. It can be a cultural or administrative region, and it will be even better if it is a homogeneous physical region (resource) region. *A meso region can also become a nodal region* provided the combined micro regions or parts thereof can be developed in a complementary manner. (NSS of India has identified 58 meso regions of India but they are not shown on maps as planning regions).

B.4 Micro Regions

In multi-level planning a district is the micro region. It becomes the lowest territorial unit of planning in the hierarchy of planning regions, The most important reason why a district is the most viable micro region for planning, is the existence of data base and compact administration. This is the area which is viable for plan formulation with administration for plan implementation and monitoring.

A metropolitan area can be one micro region and the area of influence can be another micro region. A nodal point is also a micro region, though in many cases micro regions are basically rural areas which may have a number of minor nodes without any organisational hierarchy influencing the entire area. The basic characteristic of a micro region is its smallness. There can be some specific micro regions such as belts of extraction of minerals or a reclaimed area, or a not-so-big command area of an irrigation project.

B.5 Micro-minor Region

This is the region which is associated with, what is called, the grass-root planning. A micro-minor region can be a block for which also data exists now and for which there may be a plan. (So far as the quality of data is concerned, there is hardly any activity, or sector, or region or field for which data is not cooked by the vested interest groups: but, that is another story).

This block level plan is integrated with the national plan, through the district and State level plans. A block level plan is not surgically cut portion of the district plan but a plan which has its own logic and linkage.

At block level, most of the officers will be more concerned with the implementation of the plans than formulating the plans. At block level, the main exercise will be to take account of the physical and human resource inventories and to find out the prime moving activities which will enable the block people to make best use of the development potential of the block for providing the basic needs of the people

Minimum needs can be satisfied with the production of basic goods with the help of low entropy local resources. Yet it cannot be said that 'external help' will not be necessary. Infrastructure support has to come from the developed regions. Infact, planning of the development of the transport, communications, banking, education, medical and many service facilities has got to be done at the national level.

At the panchayat level, basic goods and services can be arranged through the efforts of the local people. *Many activities can be so planned being the part of the national plan.* Several activities can be undertaken with the cooperation of the local people, with minimum of financial and real resource support from outside e.g., development of dairying, animal husbandry, pisciculture, poultry etc. Soil conservation measures, optimisation of the cropping pattern, production of inputs locally, improving the storage and transport facilities can be done at the micro-minor level. Many agro-based industries and tiny sector guild-type activities can be developed at the micro-minor level. *A good planning can secure 'realisation of the industries'* *instead of 'industrialisation of rural areas' . This will involve production of goods 'by the masses, for the masses and near the masses'.**

The most important test of micro-minor planning is that the people need not look towards the centre for it. Now a days a lot of importance is given to 'water harvesting'. Water is proxy for the use of modern inputs in agriculture. Much of the run-off water goes waste and the infiltration rate is also low. If this water can be harvested, not only the run-off water can be stored, but sub-soil water reserves can also become rich. Micro-minor water-shed development programme probably will be the most important programme for a country like India. The optimum land use planning can start from the micro-minor area only.

Regions, Delimitation on the Basis of Stages of Economic Development

Developed/ Development Regions

Developed regions are naturally those which are having a high rate of accretion in goods and services i.e., their share in the GDP of the country is relatively higher. This may be with or without rich natural resources but most certainly because of the use of upgraded technology by highly skilled and motivated persons. The locus of infrastructure facilities in abundance will put a region in the state of "nothing succeeds like success" and the region may continue to forge ahead of the backward regions at a higher rate.

A developed region may become 'overdeveloped' in certain respects e.g., it may suffer from the diseconomies

* See "District Level Planning in Multi-Level Planning" elsewhere in the volumes. Other volumes on

"Regional Economics and Planning Policy Issues"

"Regional dimensions of the Sectoral Development in India" "Glossary of Regional Economics and Some Measurement Techniques."

of congestion and the Perroux's 'growth pole' becomes over-critical here.* Infrastructure costs become very high and people can go into the jitters due to pollutions and stresses of various types.

A developed region is the counterpart of the backward region; the 'positive' side is emphasized in case of the developed region while 'negative' aspects are emphasized in case of the backward region. A developed region is one which has exploited its potentialities fully, which has removed the bottlenecks and speed breakers of development. Developed regions emerge on their own because of the comparative advantage or may emerge as a result of the diversion of funds by the government. In any case imbalances emerge between developed and backward regions and these imbalances can be the creation of planners also. Many a times disproportionately high amounts of investments are made in the constituencies of the influential politicians and some regions become far more developed than the neighbouring regions. In a resource short economy such a development may be at the cost of denying legitimate share of investment to some other regions. Those regions where quick maximisation is possible i.e., high outputs are obtained with relatively lower levels of inputs, get further attention and become even more developed.

C.2 Backward Regions

There can be 'backward or depressed' regions in the developing as well as the developed economies. Backward regions in a backward economy are thoroughly depressed regions.

Regions in which the economy is largely a subsistence one, have in the most co-existed with the modern sector regions since long. There is development even in these regions but these regions have not come out of the low

*See Chapter on "Growth Pole."

level equilibrium trap. There can be region which may not be at subsistence level but may be relatively backward. Lack of infrastructure facilities, adverse geo-climatic conditions, low investment rate, high rate of growth of population, and low levels of urbanisation and industrialisation are causes and consequences of backwardness. In less developed countries, even the most ancient occupation (agriculture) is backward and unless it is made progressive with massive real and financial inputs support, the region cannot come out of backwardness. It will be imperative/that for overall development of the backward regions, those industries should be developed on priority basis which supply vital inputs to agriculture as also those industries which take outputs of agriculture as their inputs. *Thus, depressed regions can be very poor under-developed regions which failed to modernise.*

Some *vestigial regions* (as the regions inhabited by the Red Indians in USA) can remain backward and may even remain near the subsistence level. The inhabitants may have ancient traditions and may be smug in their surroundings, but the per capita income may be much lower than in the neighbouring regions. A region can be backward because of the high population density or even without it. If we take some selected indicators of development (e.g., road length per sq. km., literacy rate, beds per thousand population, percentages of villages electrified, percentage of cultivated land under irrigation (under multiple-sequential cropping), longevity, and incidence of low, intermediate and high order functions and facilities), and points or weights are assigned to various levels of these facilities, a low total will suggest backwardness"

Depressed regions have rudimentary type of industrial activity; major centres of industrial and economic activity are not in the region and/or are at a distance from the region. Compared to the developed regions, wide chasms exist in most of the economic activities leading to wide differentials in the per capita income and intensity of productive and well paying employment.

C.3 Neutral Regions: Intermediate Regions

New towns and satellite belts are designated as 'neutral' regions and they promise good prospects of further development because here further employment generation and income propagation are possible without congestion. Such regions can be demarcated around *urban* centres.

Intermediate regions are those regions which are 'islands of development around a sea of stagnation'. Some metropolitan regions are surrounded by areas of utter penury. It should be the task of the planners to develop linkage activities that the hinterland of such intermediate regions also develops.

D.1 Mineral Regions

Many mineral regions promise high growth rates for the region as well as for the prosperity of the country, unless the region suffers from 'Bihar syndrome.'* If mineral based industries can be developed in the region itself, then industrial development will be less costly because much of the load-shedding will be done in the region at low cost. The iron ore deposits of Bailadeela (Bastar District of Madhya Pradesh) are exported abroad; if, however, a plant could be established near the ore deposits, if would have brought tremendous development for the region. Some trade-off is always involved in protecting the forest wealth and extracting minerals in mineral regions.

As the mines continue to yield sufficient minerals and the costs are also not prohibitive, not only the mineral producing region develops but this helps other regions

* It is the richest State of India in terms of mineral deposits, usually at the bottom of the inter-State table in terms of man) economic indicators, thanks to the murky politics feudal and exploitative socio-economic set-up.

also to develop. After the minerals exhaust, the region will bear degraded look; people will move away to other areas and the erstwhile area will bear a deserted look. Germany took great pains to rehabilitate such areas and vast pits and trenches were suitable reclaimed for various purposes like water storage, ecology forestry and even cultivation after enriching the soil. If new deposits of minerals cannot be discovered, there can be several ways of reclaiming wastelands and developing non-mineral based activities. Regional planning will require a long term plan for developing such regions after extraction is no longer a profitable activity. The middle east countries have made adequate planning to diversify their economies so that after the oil wealth exhausts their economies do not relapse to backwardness.

D.2&3 Manufacturing Regions / then Congested Regions

Some regions become big manufacturing regions not because they have rich natural resources but because of the infrastructure development, momentum of an early start, continued government support etc. Autonomous, imitative, supplementary, complementary, induced and speculative investments keep on giving strength to the manufacturing regions. It would be prudent not to develop narrow manufacturing base, otherwise territorial specialisation can become a problem if the crop supplying the raw materials fails or if the minerals which are base for the industries, exhaust. In such regions the internal and external economies are available in ever greater measure and such regions keep on developing. When all the thresholds are crossed, such regions become too congested and the diseconomies overwhelm the economies of production. High density, increasing pollution, reduction in the quality of life result.

Cultural Regions

A cultural region can also be quite well demarcated.

French Canada and English Canada arc such regions. In India various States are primarily demarcated on the basis of language and culture. There are affinities of cultural origin in such region. A rich cultured region should be rich in economic terms also.

Regionalisation

Regionalisation is the process of delineating regions, but each time depending upon the purpose for which the region is to be delineated and a new norm may be taken. If the intention is to develop an arid region, the 'region' will be differently defined, including only arid areas. If the congestion is to be removed then the most congested and polluted areas will be included in the 'congested region'. If the intention is substantially reduce poverty and unemployment, then a 'depressed region' is to be delineated. The homogeneity of a region will differ with the purpose for which delineation is being made.

According to *Groenman* "Regionalisation deals with the differentiation of political measures in space". If the physical region, having homogeneity, is an administrative region also, then all tasks of regional and national planning can be facilitated.

Geographers were always interested in the process of regionalisation and were very fond of pictorial characterisation rather than scientific explanation. (Pokshishevskly, V.V. 1975) Geographers believed that there is some sort of determinism in economic development. We even coin the word *fortunatov* for a region well endowed with resources.

They probably meant that what is physically impossible, money cannot make it possible. However, 'deterministic' situations are not too many and the man and his brain-child — technology — can bring a lot of changes. The *neo-determinism* underlies the fact that as the techno-economic conditions change, the 'degree of determinism' also undergoes a change, to be near the reality, we need adjustments by stages. Infact both 'determinism' and 'possibilism' are facts of life.

REFERENCES

Richardson, H.W. *Regional and Economics,* Pitman, 1978, p. 17.

Brown, A.J. and E.W. Burrows, *Regional Economic Problems,* George alien and Unwin. Carter quoted from this.

Perloff, H.S., E.W. Dunn & E.E. Lanpard and R.F. Muth, *Regions, Resources and Economic Growth.* Baltimore, 1960.

Hansen Niles (Ed) *Public Policy and Region Economic Development,* Cambridge Mass, 1974.

3

Economic Behaviour Related to Space

Prolegomenon

Regional economics should enlighten us now to rationalise regional allocations/investments to optimise so that the region is self-sufficient (in income terms at least) in basic needs. A region cannot practise autarky and hence has to "import from" and "export to" ether regions. It is well known that exports bring imports. Hence there should be such arrangements that "economies of location overcome transport diseconomies" and "economics of transportation overcome locational diseconomies".

A region should have a "strong ordering" system of listing the most important to least important activities. Both market mechanism and planning can ensure regional development. Resource base and unilateral transfers are two leading factors that determine regional activities/incomes. Each region should have optimum combinations of CGS (commodities, goods and services—commodities come from the primary sector; goods from the secondary sector and services from the tertiary sector). *Punctiform* markets should be developed. State intervention can resolve the consumer conflicts i.e., reduce the disparities of income-consumption combinations of different groups of people.

Regional problems and regional solutions differ from region to region. Each region will have to have conditions of "minimum threshold" for getting the fast development started. Each region will have its upper thresholds of income. Earlier the governments used to supply necessary inputs of development at subsidised prices. The "rightist" economists used to talk about using shadow/market prices to know the real benefits-costs of development of a region. Now the disfunctional subsidies are going. The difference between the shadow prices and the planning prices is almost next to nothing now.

Vickerman, in his "Spatial Economic Behaviour" has written about public investment and regional development, but had emphasised that the massive public intervention at prices lower than the market prices may not be "economically optimum". *(* See pp. 1-10).

Regional economic activities give rise to divergence and then efforts are to be made that the divergence created by regional planning moves towards convergence with investments that lead to divergence! In simple words unbalanced investment should be such that it should undo the imbalances of past unbalanced investment! The task is tough.

Public investment in developing backward regions can overcome the disadvantages of poor resource base of the region. Richness in resources and high investment (whether public or private) make the task of regional development easier. It should be planning of the sectors as well as planning for the people in the region. Sectoral planning can take care of the people if the aspect of the market-induced development is high. District level and block level planning are essential features of the multi-level planning for the spatial development. Now that rigorous centralised planning is not there, the upstream (backward) and downstream (forward) spread-effects (developmental) can be expected from market mechanism. Government will have to step in where market mechanism is weak in taking care of the regional development.

> One can list hundreds of reasons for poor development in the countries and regions, but five of them standout as the most important. They are (i) massive corruption leakages in the planning, (ii) lop-sided capitalist development, (iii) population explosion of the indigents, (iv) poor efforts of the communities for self-development and (v) greed of the rich.

Differential rates of growth in different sectors, activities, functions and regions are *both the- causes and consequences* of differential size, composition and structure of regional economic activities.

Lack of infrastructure facilities had been a great cause of regional backwardness. India suffers from the shortage of power and water. There are bad roads in greater part of India. Roads are not bad because the countries and regions are backward. The countries and regions remain backward because the roads are bad. Infrastructure facilities are improving for the classes (upper) and deteriorating for the masses. Production has not been near the masses, by the masses and for the masses. That could have provided full employment as well as basic CGS for all.

Regional growth remains enclave growth in most countries. Project planning has now become more important that planning for the development of the entire space. Tolerable inequalities only should remain after optimum regional development .

Dichotomies in development are everywhere. A five star culture of economic vultures exists simultaneously even as we can find families without a single rupee in the kitty or crores of destitutes who are living in the mean streets, shanties and pigsties like abodes. *Resource inventory and manpower resource inventories should be prepared for spatial development.* Work force should act upon natural resources for regional specialisation first and then for multifarious economic activities. Regional development should ensure socio-cultural development also so that the persons like the tribals do not live in "green deserts" Sectoral and spatial development should totally eradicate *destitution* first and then poverty. Now in details in ten catch points.

ECONOMIC BEHAVIOUR RELATED TO SPACE

[Factors Covering the Size, Composition, and Structure of Regional Activities/Income]

1. Regional differences and the use of natural endowments and resource allocations.
2. Regional differentials in factor prices; prices of commodities and goods.
3. Regional production pattern; location aspects.
4. Monetary transfers and capital formation according to regional differentials.
5. "Production-mix", "price-mix", "place-mix or distribution-mix" and "promotion-mix"——regional dimensions.
6. DPA (directly productive activities) and SOC interface (Socio-economic overhead capital i.e., infrastructure) in the space.
7. Agglutination of the spatial development strategies with the strategies of "clientele development" .
8. Interface of development of economic sectors and stages of development with regional development.
9. Interface between migration and mobility on one hand and spatial development on the other.
10. Fiscal transfers and spatial development: intervention theory; interface between national and regional development.

1. Regional Differences and the Use of Natural Endowments and Resource Allocations

Nations have assortment of natural resources. Small nations may be rich in one or two resources only. Endowment of resources is uneven over the regions. Even the deserts have many natural resources like oil, gas, atomic minerals etc. Other things remaining the same, the richer the country in natural resources the higher *should be* its economic development. This is not so. Africa is very rich in natural resources but not very developed. Japan and Korea import iron, coal and even sand from outside but are global leaders in exports. Agro-climatic zonal planning of crops depends upon natural endowments. Land is inelastic in supply but has use-elasticity. Urban lands lying with sick mills are sought to be used for real estate development. Technological developments and transfer of capital can change the production pattern, a little away from the natural resources. Region specific resources give rise to tied activities and industries. Richer the resources higher the income propagation.

2. Regional Differentiations in Factor Prices; Prices of Commodities and Goods

Rent, wages, interest and profits are factor prices. Wages are high where two employers run after one worker. They are low where two workers run after one job. The relative abundance and scarcity of various types of labourers are space related. Bihar and Chhatisgarh have such super-abundance of the poor workers that they migrate to other States. Punjab in India invites labourers from other States.

Land has no transferability but has use-elastcity i.e., the use pattern can be changed. Urban areas eat away the fringes and their fringes expand. Agricultural land is converted into residential land or even industrial land they higher prices/rents are commanded.

Interest rates are high in rural areas and they remain unaffected by the rates charged by the banks because there is informal market *for* the poor who lack viability of the person and viability of the purpose in borrowing money. *Rates of interest-in-rural-areas- are usually. 3 p.c., 4. p.c . or even 5 p.c . per month. That comes to 36 p.c. 48 p.c. and 60 p.c. per annum. There can be cases of 100 p.c. rate of interest p.a. If a person in rural areas borrows Rs. 10000, Rs. 6000 interest is deducted in advance. If Rs . 10000 in cash are required, the transaction may settle for a loan of Rs. 20000+ (plus).* Capital is very mobile between regions and the rates of interest should not vary so much but the dichotomy is between the formal and informal markets. Loans without securities and collaterals (in addition to security) command high rates of interest.

Regional differences do not play much part in differences in profits. Sometimes there are regional differentiations in prices other than warranted by distance. Hotels in busy season command higher booking prices. In cases of seasonal demand the slack period costs should be deducted.

Commodities originate from the primary sector e.g., wheat or iron are or wood. *Goods* come from the manufacturing sector. Their prices differ due to a host of reasons. (*See chapter on-regional differentiation of- prices- in this book*). Market economy is affected by spatial economics also. In some villages where productivity is high and connectivity is poor, vegetables are taken by those who own all-purpose vehicles at 10 kg. per rupee and the same are sold in the cities at Rs. 10 a kg.! Transport factor can cause such regional differences.

Persons of many hilly regions cannot come to plains and vice versa. They cannot cope with the differences in the climatic conditions and hence differences in incomes remain. *Regions rich in minerals usually have poor persons residing there e.g. tribals living in forests which are rich in minerals.* Here trade-off between maintaining forests and exploiting minerals is there. *People live in green deserts in such case.* Narrow resource base leads to specialisation the production of the commodities and goods and factor use depends upon that.

3. Regional Production Pattern: Location Aspects

Economics of location has been studied earlier in great details. Here a few important points may be mentioned .

It has been seen that location of industrial or any economic activity in the space has got to be such that least costs are ensured. *This does not apply to the public sector activities when welfare of the people is the prime concern.*

Locational economies overcome transport diseconomies, as has been seen. If carrying apples from certain areas of Himachal Pradesh is costly and cumbersome, then a plant that will use apples for jams, pickles, marmalade, juice or wine (or whatever other use) can be located there to cover a lot of hinterland. It will be cheaper to transport finished products of higher value-added.

There- is a- fundamental point of locational economics . It is that the strong order, choices of consumers are translated in the first preference allocations for location of economic activities by the producers.

Regional production pattern should ensure, if possible, self-sufficiency in basic needs. If that is not possible then the specialised lines of production should yield so much "Economic surplus (incomes) that the basic commodities goods and services can be "imported" from other regions. Simulated solutions are necessary to understand the trade-off of locational aspects. There is a game strategy.

Producers play a game to beat each other in cornering greater portion of demand i.e., to have a higher share in production. They play the game of beating ethers in minimising the costs and maximising the revenue.

Buyers and buyers play the game of having best quality things at the cheapest prices, particularly when there is queueing system i.e., when goods are scarce.

The great game is between the buyers and sellers. There is higgling and bargaining for a settled price in informal markets. The buyers would like to pay the low prices while the producers would like to have high prices. There is settlement somewhere in between depending upon the tension of the elasticities of demand and supply. *(See chapter on regional price theory).*

Producers would like to have monopolistic or oligopolistic position in a limited way in the region. Higher than competitive prices can be charged. Strategy of goods produced by the masses for the masses and near the masses is a good strategy for regional production.

4. Monetary Transfers and Capital Formation According in the Regional Differentiations

As in the nation or between the nations, the regions get their monetary inflows if they export commodities, goods and services CGS. The regional monetary outflows of money are due to their imports of CGS. However, there are unilateral transfers also. They are non-reciprocal. They usually come in the form of Government expenditure on planning and development.

Economics studies how different degrees of scarcities give rise to different prices and how different prices help us in allocation of resources to minimise the costs and maximise the returns. When such prices do not exist or do not help, the prices are controlled or manipulated. This used to happen in rigorous planning.

Capital, which is produced means of production, is

now the second engine of growth; the first being technology. Capital is formed with savings—real and monetary and is used for further production. Income-consumption are equal to saving. That what is not consumed becomes savings and leads to capital formation. Capital formation and investments are treated as proxies in the development models, including in the regional models. It is assumed that savings are invested and the rate of interest equates them over the space and time. In rigorous planning investments used to be on the basis of the orders of the government.

> If there is unemployment of resources and/or people that is a sign and consequence of the shortage of capital. Capital investments can be directly productive (as in a manufacturing factory/firm or farm) or can be indirectly production as in the roads or in educational/training institutions.

Backward regions will always depend upon the government or the developed regions for transfer of capital. Developed regions can find their own capital. In the development paradigm of LPG (liberalisation, privatisation and globalisation), developed countries bring capital to developing economies. Regional dimensions have now become wider indeed.

Capital investment must follow the simple logic— first thing first. Agricultural activities should be developed first and the secondary sector should be so developed that it subserves this need. So should be the development of the tertiary sector. However, all have to develop in unison to larger scale and for a bigger widthband. Ultimately there has to be industrialisation and urbanisation. There should be urbanity (rational behaviour) and not merely urbanism of mad-mad consumption. The growth impulses should trigger off from the industrial/urban centres to the periphery and the hinterland.

5. "Production Mix", "Price Mix", "Place or Distribution Mix" "Promotion Mix" Regional Dimensions

"Production- mix" relates to the issues of, (i) what to produce, (ii) where to produce, (iii) how to produce, (iv) how much to produce, and (v) of what quality to procure.

Regional, consumption depends upon regional ethos. People wear attire according to socio-cultural ethos of different regions, including the rural-urban ethos. There are regional differences in food habits and in the construction of the habitats (according to the agro-climatic conditions and availability of construction materials). There are "modern" and "traditional" segments in each country and continents. Africa is very different from Asia but the most modern segments look alike.

> The mix of capital goods (K goods, as they are called), wage goods (w goods), luxury goods (U goods), heavy industrial goods (H goods), White goods (W goods that are used in the modern households), are to be produced *as dictated by the regional economic and socio-cultural differences.*

Product cycle theory-has regional-dimensions also. Product cycle theory tells us that (i) new goods are innovated and/or (ii) old goods are replaced by technically superior goods, (iii) new goods find market slowly or sometimes at a very fast rate, (iv) they oust thc old goods, (v) reach the peak sales level, (vi) their sales find a plateau and (vii) they lose ground to the new goods.

> *TATA NANO* car show-cased in January 2008 will change the car production and sales scenario. There will be mad rush for the same from the lower middle classes and even upper middle classes. Other car manufacturers will bring competitive models. As Indian roads get clogged, the big longish cars may not be demanded much. The market of secondhand

cars will experience a, sort of, crash. Rural and *urban* (partly rural and partly urban areas i.e., small towns too will have fair share of the new cars and more particularly of the second hand cars.

Sun-rise and sun-set industries have spatial implications also. If substitute to jute invented which makes almost total non-use of jute possible, the region producing jute will experience economic depression, till new crops are grown. The region producing synthetic substitutes will experience a boom, *Depth of production (higher, scale) and the width of production (producing a variety of similar/ associated, things)* have different spatial ramifications. There are region -specific projects. One will have a hydro-electricity generating plant at a place where massive waterfall is there. Tied projects are region specific. Differences in the purchasing power has effects on production and sales in different regions in a different way.

"Price mix" (See separate chapters in this book)

Price-mix has got to be cost+ (cost plus i.e., inclusive of profits). Profits are surplus. [Surplus is a kangaroo word —it is "plus" included in it]. Profits are "carrots" or incentives for development. They become the source of investment.

However/ sometimes backward regions may be provided capital at subsidised rates of interest. Various concessions may be offered which may be at variance with the market prices.

Prices are not equal to the values in market economies. Many things have high values (eatables) but prices do not squeeze all the purchasing power of the people. There are some patently economic "bads" which are not goods e.g., cigarettes or atomic weapons. Yet they command higher prices than the values. *Skimming prices* (high) are charged from the rich and in the rich space (urban areas). Backward regions get those things late. Prices can differ in different countries/regions according to the principle of "what the traffic can bear or what the people can pay". Governments conniving with the multinational corporations can mulct the poor persons and poor regions. In India the prices of most medicines have become three to four times during the short span of four years upto 2008, notwithstanding the claims of the government that prices of essential medicines have been brought down.

"Distribution-mix" is transport effect. The lower the transport costs to the production costs, the wider the market. Multi-modal model of transport exists in the space and that completes the work of distribution.

Middlemen of all sorts (financiers, wholesalers, transporters, insurers, handlers, retailers....) help in fanning out development over the entire space. Market thickens and widens.

"Promotion-mix" ultimately covers the backward space. Technovators are bringing new things on daily basis and certain things (e.g., the cars that would fly or float over water) are of far reaching importance. "Promotion-mix" is what is responsible for manufacturing things for persons with low purchasing power (like Nano car of the Tatas). Advertisement, publicity and propaganda increase the size of the potential market; and potential production.

Supportive infrastructure develops. If many cars are to be sold, the business houses will show interest in improving roads" b.o.t. (build, own and transfer) Credit will he provided both to the producers and prospective buyers. Promotion is another name of development.

6. DPA and SOC Should Balance in the Space

Directly productive activities (DPA) can develop only as socio-economic infrastructure facilities facilitate them. Rural areas are generally depressed due to poor water harvesting in most countries. People are lethargic about the same as the governments are guilty of criminal neglect towards the water running off. *Water is to be made to crawl rather-than run- off.* Irrigation development is the most important infrastructural development in rural space. Water is a proxy for the modern inputs in agriculture. Only then the high yielding variety seeds, fertilisers, pesticides, herbicides, modern machinery and other inputs can be used. Expiation costs of the neglect of agriculture are deaths from starvation.

> If SOC (social overhead capital or infrastructure facilities) is there DPA will follow. If DPA do not follow, there will be inflation. This is rather rare. If SOC is lacking, DPA shall remain depressed, more so in neglected regions.

If the scale of regional activities is to be upgraded, all sorts of SOC will be needed. They include facilities and functions relating to (i) finance and credit, (ii) multi-modal model of transport, (iii) health, sanitation and medical facilities, (iv) education and training facilities, (v) communications, and (vi) power, including solar power in rural areas.

7. Agglutination the Spatial Development Strategies with the Strategies of Clientele Development

Clientele development is the current lingo for the anti-poverty programme. The clients are the poor. The poor live in the backward regions, developed regions and vestigial regions (regions with rich natural resources yet inhabitated by the poor)., They are omni-present, thanks to the development process bypassing them. There are certain social groups (as the tribals in most of the countries) who are over-represented in poverty. *Space development projects if agglutinated with the clientele development projects will leave enduring effect on the development of the space.* Poverty is scourge. It is oppressive. Urban poverty is the spill-over of the/rural poverty. This is the spatial dimension.

Poor are also cause of their own poverty as they multiply fast but their social backwardness is due to the apathy of the rich. *Ad. hoc* programmes prove palliatives. The programmes and plans should develop the space on enduring basis.

External assistance (exogenous factors) should come first and then the growth in backward regions may take off due to endogenous factors.

8. Interface of Development of Economic Sections and Stages of Development with Regional Development

Stages-cum-sectors- theory tells us that over a period of time the following should happen related to the regional development.

(A) The absolute share of production, output, productivity and value-productivities of all primary sector activities should go up. However, the *percentage share should decline.* In the USA, the percentage share is just 3 p.c . In India it is about 23 p.c. *For a country like. India, the share may settle at 15 p.c.*

(B) The absolute and percentage contributions of the secondary sector (manufacturing + construction) should go up. This is also a *real sector* (of physical outputs) like the primary sector and its percentage contribution should settle around 35 p.c. in a country like India.

This will ensure that the real goods sectors contribute atleast half of the national income.

There is nothing hard and fast about these percentage figures in the regional economics.)

(C) The percentage contribution of the service sector

should go up both in the absolute terms and in relative terms.

The development of the tertiary sector (socio-economic overheads) should and would help in the development of the primary and secondary sector first. *Sectoral development- theory- of space- emphasises that the relationships are mutual and circular. Transport development needs vehicles that come from the secondary sector. The primary sector supplies the ores and sources of- power. The primary sector provides- food- for all. The transport activity brings inputs of development to agriculture- and.- takes the surplus outputs to the market.* Telecommunications development require raw materials appratus and machineries from the primary secondary sector. Instances can be multiplied.

(4) *Quarternary Sector* is the Most Advanced State of the tertiary sector. (National Institute of Physics is in the quarternary sector while physics taught in school would belong to the tertiary sector. Seven star hotels, wherefrom a helicopter service is available right from the hotel, belongs to the quarternary sector and general transport facilities to the tertiary sector. Super-speciality hospitals which look like "health-hotels" belong to the quarternary sector while a primary health centre in a rural area would belong to the tertiary sector) .

Quarternary sector, in a country like India these two sectors should contribute about 45 and 5 p.c. of the GDP. Interface between migration and mobility on one hand and spatial development on the other.

9. Interface between Migration and Mobility on One hand and Spatial Development on the Other

Mobility can include migration but upward mobility can be there even without migration. People become richer and richer but usually in urban areas. There are no "crorepati" income earners in rural areas. People do migrate to urban areas for upward mobility.

(See a separate chapter on migration in this book).

Push factors work to make people migrate from the rural/depressed areas to urban/developed areas to escape the "idiocy of the country life" (Karl Marx). Limited opportunities for social and economic mobilities upwards push the people to urban areas. Many people do become "faceless" in urban areas. The discriminated persons can hide their identities in urban areas. Absence of good facilities for education, health/ training and high levels of living push people to urban areas.

[We leave aside here the migration of about 50 p.c. population after marriage—i .e., of the brides].

Pull factors are dreams for higher level of living. Urban areas offer more and better employment. In due course of time they inculcate *urbanism* of demonstration effect consumption. Inculcating *urbanity* (rational outlook) may take time. Persons in developed regions lead hectic life and become markedly industrious, innovative, mobile and even workoholics. Persons in the backward regions lead lives which are placid and may be steeped in superstitions.

Migration is not a short soujourn, yet there are sometimes reverse migrations. People of developing economies migrate back from very rich countries. Many people do go back to the small towns, if not to villages. Persons with frustrated ambition who fail in their pursuits in urban areas or developed regions migrate back.

10. Fiscal Transfers and Spatial Development: Invention Theory

This is or should be the sure bet. Fiscal transferences (grants and subsidies and public investment die change the face of the backward regions in the past. There is no *quid pro quo* in such unrequited transfers. They do not depend upon the backward regions exporting CGS (commodities, goods and services). *Fiscal transfers resolve-" consumer conflicts"* i.e., put more money in the hands of those *who* have less purchasing power. Fiscal transfer increase productive capacities and capabilities. They generate employment and propagate income. Divergences are reduced; and convergences are promoted. Enclave growth is dispersed. Such transfers should be problem solving e.g., flood relief works should provide insurance against droughts. Overall welfare should be promoted. But, welfare cannot be prompted in pauper states. The regional incomes should be increased before efforts are directed for the reduction of inequalities. There should be no corruption leakages.

11. Interface between National and Regional Development

If nations develop, regions also develop but not equally and much less equitably. When regions develop, the nation develops for sure.

There can be following combinations of development in the nation and in the regions:

Nation	*Regions*
Developing	Developing
Developing	Stagnating
Developing	Decelerating
Stagnating	Developing
Stagnating	Stagnating
Stagnating	Decelerating
Decelerating	Developing
Decelerating	Stagnating
Decelerating	Decelerating.

As was seen elsewhere also, laggard regions can develop best when (i) individual mode of development, (ii) community mode of development and (iii) intervention (public investment) mode of development combine best.

> Complete regional equality will ensure rural —urban continuum. That is possible in a small nation. Disparities shall remain.

> As far as the individuals are concerned the rules are or should be *(i) there- should- be no equality- between unequals? and (ii) there should be no inequality between the equals.* Skill development should precede drive towards equality.

Top-down and bottom-up strategies should be at work at the same time. Multi-level planning should get juxtaposed with market mechanism. Dichotomies are to be substantially reduced.

Even unbearable regional spatial and inter-personal disparities could not be ended in the developing economies either through socialism or through market mechanism. Equality over the space or between the, people is impossible. Regions differ in resources and work-climate and culture. Persons differ in capabilities and capacities. Even the USA has lakhs of persons who go to sleep without food! Even many white poor take food in the *langars* of Gurudwaras. When the USSR collapsed they had to acknowledge that 40 p.c. of their population was below the poverty line. How could that happen when employment was guaranteed? Work was a matter of right/ duty/ award and honour. China still has destitutes in rural areas despite most rigorous communist planning

> Corruption emerged from 1960s as the most important cause of regional and inter personal inequalities. As the generation that brought freedom to the developing economies died the traditions of honest service of the people were not maintained by the successors.

India ranks amongst the top 10 corrupt nations in the world. Planning is dead in India, Long live five, year plans.*

See this piece that appeared in a foreign newspaper about India.

India and Indian States make provisions in the budgets / plans to the tune of trillions of rupees on ad hoc programmes for "removal" of poverty. The official set-up does not work it self-out. There is a truth to be faced . The officials officers bureaucrats, politicians. Ministers (including the vigilante groups in police or audit), misappropriate in most cases 70 to 100 p.c. of allocations. Not a grain of sand may be used yet thousands and

There is *only one grand goal of development* and that is how to secure a high growth rate with social justice. We want growth that is (as it is called now) that is "inclusive". Earlier we used to call it growth that eliminates or substantially reduces poverty. Destitution is to be ended

* So appeared a caption in EPW. Times of India devoted 1/40'th of a page for the 11th Five Year Plan. It devotes 4 pages daily for commercial news and about 8 pages on budget. What is good for the for spatial and people's development is of little concern to the politicians and the bureaucrats in India.

"One Indian Minister went to a rich country and was invited by his counterpart to a home high-tea. The Indian Minister was surprised to see high level of living of the Minister of that country. On making an inquiry how was that possible, the Minister of the rich country told the Indian Minister, "You see that flyover there: I got 10 p.c. commission." After some time the Indian Minister invited that Minister of the rich country to his place for returning the hospitality. The Minister of the rich country was astounded to see the level of living of the Indian Minister. He made similar inquiry upon which the India Minister said: "Did you see 10 flyovers of the city? ". On being told by the Minister of the rich country that he did not see any, the Indian Minister replied, "well, 100 p.c. commission".

in all cases. Growth should have trickledown effect -its spread effects should percolate to the poor.

Unfortunately *no system could combine the advantages of private initiative (capitalism) in securing higher production with the social justice of 'theoretical' socialism. The middle path proved to be muddled path.* In the middle path many countries could combine the disadvantages of both the systems!

> Democratic path of development is at best the least bad. All political systems have now proved to be bad. Democracy, if it is truly free and fair, can ensure the economic development of the country, regions and all groups of people. *Unfortunately now we have -rabid commercialisation and criminalisation. There is crony capitalism whereby the kith and kins of high powered persons usurp most of the gains. Then there is casino capitalism whereby the freedom for stock marketing and swindling is the criterion of the economy being free. There-is turbo capitalism where the pace of development is sought to be so fast that all cannot keep pace with it, particularly the rural people. Criminalisation has "graduated" to mafia system. Terrorism is another face of criminalisation of the economy and the polity.*
>
> Economics of development and economics of regional development cannot be implemented in such a vicious atmosphere.

of kilometres of roads may be shown as having been constructed/repaired. India is making claims of providing drinking water to all villages within two to three years in each plan. Water harvesting schemes did not last even one monsoon showers and no heads ever rolled. (Nehru, the first Prime Minister of India, had promised to hang the corrupt at the nearest lamp-post!).

> A retired judge of the Karnataka High Court (Dec. 2007) openly said on a TV Channel that when he asked the Bangalore city authorities about what

they did of Rs. 30000 crore collected in tax for improving the city transport system, the reply that was filed claimed that all the money was spent in research!

Not capital but character, building is the first pre-requisite of nation building and for removing/reducing regional/ spatial and inter-personal economic disparities.

PART-II

Economics of Location

4

Economic Factor Analysis of Location of Economic Activities in Space: Economics of Agglomeration in Space

Stefan Valavanis called the study of economics of location and consequent agglomeration as *"fortunate economics"*.

[in "Losch on Location in HW Richardson's Regional Economics: A Reader].

The economic structure/internal structure of the regions depends upon the pattern of locations of economic activities and functions-, and, a change in the existing pattern (planned intervention) can be made by changing the location decisions.

> There are three umbrella approaches of study of the economics at location viz., (i) the least cost approach, (ii) the market area analysis and the (iii) profit maximisation approach. *A recent behavioural approach* emphasises that location is the result of the interaction with the techno-economic environment i.e., the behaviour of the government and the behaviour of the rival firms.

The above three or four approaches are infact only four of the several determinants of the location of economic

---

Location factors are not easy to quantify as they vary from firm to firm and regions to regions. *The factors discussed in this chapter do not conform to the -rank order. It is difficult to put them in strict order of importance. Perhaps the most and the least important can be listed. Rest of them will fit anywhere in the total order.*

activities. We study location economics of not only industries or industrial units or projects but also of agricultural activities (crop selection, mix, substitution) and of infrastructural activities also.

We put the factors that determine location of economic activities in ten catch points.

1. Entrepreneurial decisions.
2. Availability of plentiful raw materials of quality.
3. Availability of adequate and constant flow of power.
4. Availability of efficient labour at comparative advantage in wages.
5. Availability of wide transport connectivity.
6. Availability of adequate and timely finance and banking facilities.
7. Nearness to the market or the market area approach.
8. Decisions of the competitive and complementary firms.
9. Favourable tax structure.
10. Package of incentives and concessions from the governments: Subsides and grants
11. Systems related locations.

While the point number 10 will come under behavioural pattern (as perhaps point number one also), the rest of the points, except related to the market, will come under the principle of "least cost approach". All points can come under the point maximum profit approach.

1. Entrepreneurial Decisions

Wherever free enterprise system exists, the locational decisions depend upon the entrepreneurs. This is true of making decisions of land use pattern in agriculture (location of crops, can we say?), as also of industries and various service centres.

> *Entrepreneurs, follow the principle of "filling the vacuum or gap.'* They enter those fields where none is present or the presence of other entrepreneurs is not upto the requirements of the market. Location has a logic. *It is said about the Indian villages that the villages in past got located where three things could be had at the same time (i) a well, (ii) a moneylender and (iii) a mandir.*

Momentum of an early start means the new entrepreneurs follow what the old entrepreneurs did for the location of any specific economic activity. There is nothing in Ferozabad of India that the glass bangles industry is largely located there. It must have been an accidental and chance decision of a pioneer. Others simply followed. Needless to emphasise that entrepreneurs find everything that they want at the places they choose.

2. Availability of Plentiful Natural Resources of Quality

While location of mining activity cannot be elsewhere than where the minerals are found, industries based upon them can be located elsewhere Infact they can be located very far off! This was d by the imperial powers in the past. They took minerals from Africa and Asia to their countries so the manufactured/finished products of high value-added could be exported from there. Such decisions resulted in the backwash effects in the mineral regions and spread in the non-mineral regions!

Other things being equal, the bulkier the raw material the nearer will be the location of the plant (*See chapter on Weber's location theory in this book ahead*). The load shedding of the waste material is done nearby.

> If sugarcane grows in a region, the sugar factory will be in the centre of the region. If the farmers of the region start cultivating soyabean, many options arise.

(A) The factory land may be used for oil extracting unit and the sugar manufacturing unit may be dismantled.

(B) If the area with the factory is much, then part of the area may be used for oil extraction and the sugar factory can be kept functioning by "importing" sugarcane juice from other regions. Then there will be locational coupling of the two regions.

(C) The sugar factory may be relocated in the new region of sugarcane cultivation.

The higher the *"gross raw material index"* i.e., the ratio of waste to the pure ore, the nearer will be the location of the production unit to the source of raw materials. Transport diseconomies are in direct proportion to the gross weight index. Industrious based on *ubiquitous* raw material found everywhere are "footloose" i.e., can be located anywhere, preferably near the market.

Nations have prospered on the raw materials of other nations which they import as in the case of Japan and South Korea. In such cases, the advantage of having modern technology based on new innovations and the presence of the "technovators" will be necessary.

Perishable raw materials will have their processing units nearby provided the surpluses are of such quantities that a threshold size industrial unit can be established.

3. Availability of the Adequate and Constant Flow of Power

This item is a big issue in developing economies where power generation is not adequate enough to meet the current demand for productive and 'consumption' purposes. In India not only the power generation is inadequate but nearly 60 p.c. of it is pilfered. One can say that most of this is with the connivance of the employees of the State Electricity Boards. In normal cases only 10 p.c. transmission losses are justified. *In India* the pilferage of power is high (even by many industrialists). Voltage fluctuations are erratic and severe and not all regions get adequate power. Load shedding is common in rural areas. Many villages in many States get power for two to three hours in two to three days! (As in Madhya Pradesh).

Private power houses can be solutions in such situations. However, in India these get the *status, of the captive power plants.* Captive power plants mean that the government can pre-empt the power generated by the private power houses for the "public good". *Grid systems become important for orderly supply of motive power, provided the entire system functions with efficiency.*

India has coal reserves that will last minimum 500 years longer than the coal reserves of the rest of the world. Yet the thermal power generation system is messed up in India.

> Entrepreneurs will require cheap and adequate power all the year round without fluctuations in voltage.
>
> [A polypropelene unit requires electricity without least fluctuations otherwise the big balloon of it bursts asunder. Steady current is supplied only when the palms of the officials are greased. *Power supply by the public sector units in India has now become the big bug bear of the locational decisions. Regional differentiations cannot be corrected if power supply is erratic, inadequate and dear.*]

4. Availability of Labour of Comparative Advantage

Location of industries does not depend now on the availability of the cheap unskilled labour but on the skilled and cheap labour. This cheapness is on comparative terms. Japan and Korea have located their automobile plants in India and they intend to take the production in India to higher levels than even in their parent companies because India's labour is *relatively* cheaper. Indians are paid well according to Indian standards and the employees may be quite happy. The companies are happy in such cases because translated in dollar rates and with reference to the cost of living, the wages in the country where outsourcing has been done are comparatively cheaper. Location of industries is promoted where bullying trade unions are not there.

5. Availability of Wide Transport Connectivity

Transport costs promote or protect an industry!

For new industries easy connectivity means that locational weights (total weights of inputs brought in total weight of the outputs taken out) can be transported at lower costs. This will enlarge the market. Market is very enlarged as both production and distributive costs become low.

> High transport costs/ on the contrary, protect the old regional industrial units which must have been located earlier.

Locations are related to the *gross weights to be transported.* For example to manufacture one tonne of steel, nearly five tonnes of coal, limestones, manganese, dolomite, quartizite etc. are required. Hence a steel producing unit becomes "*specific (tied-)*" and has got to be located where the costs of transport of all things prove low.

> Transport system has got to be quick, safe and cheap. *When the Bhilai Steel Plant was constructed in Madhya Pradesh (now that area is in Chhatisgarh), the then USSR government which financed that project had ensured the timely delivery of al1 inputs. In fact a goods train carrying inputs to Bhilai used to be given the right to move through even if the Bombay Calcutta Mail -(via Nagpur) had to wait at a wayside small station. (Now Mumbai-Howrah Mail)*

Pure raw materials and outputs (of high value in low bulk) can bear the burden of transport costs easily.

> If the sources of raw materials and the markets are widely dispersed, the size of the plant would be smaller. A big plant will increase the costs of transport. Small plants have got to be located near the *"dotted"* markets.

If the governments want to locate some plants at particular places they may have to provide transport subsidies. This can be done easily if the transport system is owned by the government. Economists consider government subsidies as "higher real costs" based on "shadow prices. Shadow prices are those imaginary price, which if established, will equate the demand with supply. If the market rate is Rs . 5 per kilometre and the rate charged is Rs. 2 per kilometre/ then the (as the economists say) the shadow rate will be Rs. 5.

6. Availability of Adequate Finance and Banking Facilities

Finance was a big problem in the early 1950s when most of the developing economies of the world started their growth process. International liquidity was also very low. Getting even $ 1 billion a year from the IMF or the World Bank used to be a big deal.

Post-1970s the world saw LPG model (liberalisation, privatisation and globalisation) emerging. The collapse of the Soviet Union and its economic system "saw sudden flush of private finance in the world. *Banks in different countries are flushed with funds. It used to take months of negotiations, for getting funds from the World Bank. Now millions and billions of dollars can be raised in a jiffy.* Even Indian banks are flushed with funds.

> New enterprises trying to find a foothold somewhere can have that anywhere and the financiers are after the entrepreneurs to finance. National savings/income ratios have gone up from nearabout 5 p.c. to 25 p.c. during the period 1950 and 1980 in most developing

> economies, including India. If savings of the "black economy" in any country are taken into account the position is that the supply of loanable funds is greater than even the demand.

Commercial rates of interest for investment in the black economy are almost the same as the "caps" or the peak rates of lending in the formal sector. Once finance used to be arranged by the government finance corporations of various sorts and there used to the subsidy component in the interest rate charged.

Capital is now a days quite mobile thanks to e'banking. Transferences of moneys are easy and quick. The capital stock adjustments are easy now. Finance is available even for the long gestation periods. The cyclical ups and downs have evened out.

> Inflow of financial capital is actually inflow of the real capital. Inflow of real capital is actually inflow of modern technology. The investment patterns diffuse innovations over the space embodied as they are in the goods of high technology. Risk averse entrepreneurs can also locate their units to their liking.
>
> There are both centripetal and centrifugal tendencies in capital movements, investments and consequent location decisions. *Centripetal tendencies bring agglomerations and concentrations. Centrifugal tendencies lead to dispersal of industries. Agglomerations develop to take-advantage of economies; and, when-diseconomies overwhelm the economies new locations are not at the points of agglomerations. Infact some old units may be taken away from the agglomeration points.*

7. Nearness to the Market or the Market Area Approach

Markets are not far off in a country like India. They are everywhere. In sparsely populated countries this assumes importance. Sometimes the producing country may be one and the consuming country may be another. Petrol is used everywhere but location of petrol producing units is near the production reserves. It was the "market area approach" that made Japan and Korea locate their automobile plants in India. Honda (in collaboration with "Hero" Company) became Hero-Honda in India and now the production in India is more than in the parent company. *It is in the buyers market that the location is near the market. The pull effect-of the market is greater than the pull effect of the natural resources in such cases.* Locations move to those markets first where the purchasing power is high and where the demand is very much in favour of the product in question. The locations will be guided by the hierarchy of the markets.

8. Decisions of the Complementary and Competitive Firms

Entrepreneurs may be independent but their economic fortunes are not; they are inter-twined. Entrepreneurs take decisions keeping an eye on the decisions taken by the rival competing firms. However/ this need not always mean that the production units have got to be near each other.

> Tamil Nadu has many automobile producing units in India though it takes a lot of transport cost to deliver the vehicles in north, east and west India. In its comparison production unit located at Gurgaon (a USA city-like city near New Delhi) is better located.
>
> The competing firms take decisions of locations at far off places, if they have in mind the sharing of the markets. Locations will depend upon many circumstances.

In case of the complementary firms, it is easy. There will be clustering of such firms, Momentum of an early start of an important firm/unit of production will decide.

> Complementarities and competitiveness act in different ways. There is nothing *a priori* that will decide that there should be dispersal of locations or clustering of the same. Other factors will decide.

9. Favourable Tax Structure

Locations are also influenced by the tax structure existing at the time of location. Some States may have high "caps" or maximum fixed rates of taxes. Entrepreneurs will not take their units in these States, unless other advantages are overwhelming. Normally the States of a country will impose high taxes only when they want to dispel the further location of economic activities in a region.

Tax concessions like (i) tax holiday for a certain number of year (ii) tax refunds according to certain formulae and (iii) lower rates of taxes for a number of years, attract new units.

If the economic activities get located and the tax structure goes against lateron, probably little can be done. Then the entrepreneurs will adjust their price-cost relations in many other ways.

10. Package of Incentives and Concessions from the Governments

> Subsidies are negative taxes. They are according to a formula as being a certain percentage of something. Grants are outright. There can be conditional or non-conditional grants. Lower rates of taxes are incentives "just as subsidies and grants are.

Various States of India used to grant packages of concessions to the new industrial units. In due course of time the packages of concessions became more or less equal in various States. Thereafter, the entrepreneurs started locating their industrial units on the principle of comparative advantage in costs i.e., on the principle of least costs. The packages of concession became neutral.

The entrepreneurs availed them because they were there. In most cases many entrepreneurs availed land and erected some production machinery. Thereafter declared their units sick and siphoned off capital, land or whatever.

11. System Related Locations

* In socialism—where they were ordered to be located.
* In Singapore or Hong Kong—where there was space.
* In capitalist economies—on the principle of comparative advantage in loast costs.
* In India—in the constituencies of the important politicians.

That was in the initial years of: planning in India. Locations decisions now under the LPG model follow the rules of the game and these rules were listed above.

Factor Analysis

In order to do away with the 'subjectivity' in the delineation of the regions, factor analysis is done so that the delineation is on 'objective' basis.

Agglomeration regions are separate regions and typical agglomeration is also a basis of delineation of a region. Agglomeration economies vary among industries and according to size of the firms. Agglomeration economies are more important for the small firms because they become sort of 'external economies' to them. Large firms 'internalise' the agglomeration economies. Agglomeration economies determine the mobility of capital and labour. In a region/ city, several industries/firms/ activities/functions get localized but it will be easier to examine a few selected cases as to why and how those firms got located in that agglomeration cluster. There are several firms in that agglomeration cluster. There are several reasons for agglomeration economies gaining strength reasons for agglomeration economies gaining strength like (i) efficient labour market, (ii) possibilities of selling more (high purchasing power), (iii) facilities for ancillarisation (beneficial to the main industries as well as to ancillaries), and (iv) tax efficiency (concession package).

To know the nature of the relative development and backwardness and to identify the type of region, *composite index* method can be used. Some indicators are selected and it can be found which regions ranks at which place with respect to various indicators. The number of selected indicators may be large or small, depending upon the nature of inquiry. Regions are to be ranked according to the level of development. Naturally different regions may have different ranks with reference to difference indicators. Kerala may be first with reference to female literacy and Punjab may be first with reference to agricultural productivity.

A simple index can be constructed by adding up the ranks, a composite index can be prepared. For example, if Bihar is at No. 16 with reference to 10 indicators and Punjab at No. 1 with reference to all these 10 indicators, than the total of Punjab is 10 while that of Bihar is 160 and thus the state having the minimum total rank-score (total) will be the most developed and the State with the highest rank score will be least developed or most backward. Composite index becomes necessary because *with reference to each indicator, the ranking order of various States is not the same and hence a composite index is to be constructed.* The above was the simplest method of constructing this composite index.

In the simple composite index, equal weightage is given to each indicator, which is not correct. It can be safely asserted that for the development of agriculture water/irrigation is that most important factor for higher productivity, most certainly more important than a road. The *factor analysis or the principal component analysis* treats different variables differently and assigns weights. Factor analysis *which measures inter-regional disparity, also helps us in delineating regions on the basis of these differences.*

One simple method of assigning weights is *to use the regression results. For example if 55 per cent rise in agricultural productivity is due to irrigation, then water will be given a weight of 55 in those indicators which increase agriculture productivity. However, if we are examining the overall role of various factors in increasing the GDP of the region, then pro rata role of agriculture, and then of irrigation can be calculated. Correlation figures can be used for assigning weights.*

Though the weights are assigned in accordance with their importance, it is common that various researchers assign different weights to the same indicators. The guiding principle is inter-correlation amongst different indicators. Higher weightage is assigned to those which show higher correlation and vice versa. Through multiple regression and/or correlation method we can find the increase in agricultural production due to the application of irrigation, HYV seeds, use of machines, pesticides, or even with non-material inputs e.g., finance. The stronger the association between an indicator to the final output, the greater the weight that can be assigned. If agriculture contributes 1/4 to the GDP of a region and irrigation contributes 1/4 to the agricultural productivity, then 1/4.1/4k or 1/16 or 6.25 per cent can be the weight amongst all the indicators for irrigation.

The set of coefficients (r values) are known as factor-loading (or relative weights). These factor loadings are infact weights, reflecting the relative importance of individual indicators of development.

Sectorial composite indices are combined to prepare a composite index of development. If this is for a region, weights are known as the R values. If CI is for the nation, sectoral weights can be called *n* values. *Giving/assigning weights is known as factor loading.*

Factor analysis ignores qualitative differences in life between two centers/ regions if their indices are the same. The *causes* of backwardness and the *causative factors* of development are different but CI can be the same. The CI cannot throw light on various tendencies is sub-sectoral development. Development potentials are also not taken into account. *Backwardness or development is just not a game of co-effecients.* Understanding the qualitative differences and spelling out the strategy are more important.

A correlation matrix of CIs can be prepared to measure. The association between (say) employment in various sub-sectors. Negative and the degrees of positive relations can be found out. The CI,

Agglomeration and Locations Economics and Economies Concentration Vs, Dispersal

Agglomeration of industries due to concentration of industries, functions and facilities generate external economies of scale. They reduce costs and therefore prices. Agglomeration pulls other industries. Further economies one generated.

Too many industries cause congestion. Diseconomies enter and emerge. All things have upper thresholds. For example transport economies become diseconomies if too many trucks remain stalled on the congested roads. Concentrations are due to centripetal forces. Dispersals are due to centrifugal forces.

We study under the "economies of agglomeration" why and where some industries cluster. We also study why do they not at some other places. We study how the process of agglomeration, once started, becomes self-sustaining, which is known as the snowballing process.

There are strong techno-economic reason for the clustering getting momentum. Some examples of agglomeration be listed thus:

* Vegetable oil, vegetable oil-cakes, hydrogenated vegetable oil, soaps.
* Ginning factories, cotton yarn units, textile mills, textile machinery manufacturing units, ready-made clothes manufacturing units, stuffed dolls etc.,
* drugs and pharmaceutical units, chemical plants, chemical machinery and equipment units.
* telephone equipment industry; storage battery industrial units.
* glass industries, glassware industries, electric goods industries,
* Iron and steel units, metal products, electric motors units.
* Wagons, passenger coaches, locomotives.

Firms which can internalize the external economies will grow in size and can compete out other firms which are not reaping the economies on large scale. The differences in the degree of interalisation of external economies determine the advantages which firms can have over the rival firms. Agglomcration overcomes the indivisibilities and in the agglomeration clusters, external economies become the cause and consequence of the clustering.

As a result of localisation and agglomeration commodities are produced at costs lower than what they would otherwise have been; commodities produced have a ready market because of the goodwill the place earns for itself as production centre; inputs and factors remain available in adequate quantities; markets become wide; imitative, complementary, supplementary and auxiliary industries come up; units that can make good use of the by-products are established and the overall efficiency of the manufacturing sector improves.

In due course of time the boundary between (a) internal economies of large scale production and (b) economies external to the firm but internal to the industry, becomes blurred. Factors which promote agglomeration gain strength and promote further agglomeration. These centres becomes "growth centres" and industries therein act as "growth poles." Quarternary facilities too develop and despite rising prices and costs of land and factors, industrialisation and urbanisation continue for quite a long time.

Myrdal argues that in less developed countries there will be tendencies towards agglomeration/concentration of industries and economic functions and this will result in the divergence of per capita income over the space.

A high 'coefficient of manufacture' efficiency will encourage agglomeration and vice versa.

> This coefficient is related to *index of manufacture* which is the ratio of manufacturing costs to the final weight of the product. *Locational weight* is the total weight to be transported during the process of production. Higher weight handled at low cost increase the manufacturing efficiency.

On the basis of the above, Weber formulated his *Law of Agglolocation.* Industries with high coefficient of manufacture efficiency show a strong tendency to agglomerate and vice versa. As the diseconomies of agglomeration overwhelm the economies of agglomeration, the tendency to agglomerate gets weakened and dispersal becomes beneficial.

"Economies of agglomeration" are efficiency of public services; marketing economies; availability of business consultancy services, advertising agencies, minimisation of computation trips, availability of cultural and recreational facilities; better medical, health and training facilities; better connectivity on surface and through communications considering their efficiency and productivity. Since procuring the inputs, production of output and marketing become efficient, economies of localisation and urbanisation are reaped together. Some units may move in to the cluster from the possible position of least transport cost or least labour costs, since the total cost will be minimised.

Agglomeration ofcourse promotes dualism in the economy and economic development becomes polarized. Though agglomeration makes some factors 'ubiquitious' (as concessional finance or cheap land for all), in the long run external diseconomies may be generated. Many of the differences in regional incomes can be traced to difference in agglomeration.

Darwent holds the view that the economies of agglomeration are virtually immeasurable, while *Marcus* think that they can be measured industry-by-industry. If urban growth rate in a given industry is higher than the national growth rate of the same industry, weighted by the relative growth of population in the area, the extra growth can be attributed to the agglomeration economies:

$A = G_u - G_n [N_u / N_n]$

A = agglomeration economies

G = growth rate of output of an industry

N = Growth rate of Population

U = urban areas

n = nation

Growth rate of the industry in the urban area *minus* growth rate of the nation *weighted* by relative growth of population in the urban area is the measurement of agglomeration economies for a particular industry.

Since the growth of industry is not the function of the agglomeration economies only, but is also a function of the internal economies, this measure is not comprehensive more so because all types of the economies have not been measured.

There cannot be industrialisation without urbanisation, though there can be urbanisation without much industrialisation. Agglomerated industrialisation leads to urbanisation and urbanisation to 'modernisation'. Old values, which come in the way of development, are discarded to a great extent and the quality of the public utilities improves. Not only industry but *business* firms also reap the economies of agglomeration: they make brisk sales as the income elasticity of demand for many products is high in the pockets of high development." In the regions of agglomerated industrilisation "economies" of *household agglomeration* emerge. Families in the city improve their standard of living and enrich the lives of others through interaction. Socio-cultural practices become scientific in out look. Urban households transmit 'growth influences' as also absorb them from others. A city household may be better in most, if not all, respects than a boorish village family. However, economies of 'household agglomeration' are sometimes immeasureable also.

Baumol considers that the population density in a urban centre is a proxy of agglomeration economies. *Lave* measures agglomeration economies in terms of the economies of transport costs which are *not* incurred. *Hansen* would like to measure them in terms of the total facilities available at the point of agglomeration. Not only ail types of services are available but related and non-related industries all develop at the centre (sugar and alcohol/rectified spirits are related but steel goods complexes and chemical complexes are not. *Social, household and business agglomeration economies* further reinforce each other and most of these economies remain intangible but of great consequences and hence a precise measurement becomes difficult. The *agglomeration economies are net balance of external economies and diseconomies and both have immeasureable elements.* Congestion will make some of the external economies negative. Some regional economists have measures the benefits of the agglomeration as each person provides benefits/costs to others.

Richardson is of the opinion that external economies rise upto a particular city size and then diseconomies overwhelm. No one knows when.

Where diseconomies of agglomeration exceed the economies of agglomeration, urban decline follows and symptoms of senescence become visible. Economies of agglomeration help in converting the 'monocentric' city into the 'multicentric' metropolitan region. Development of urban centres accompanies agglomeration.

Economies of agglomeration in a region are assumed to be a function of the size distribution and the spatial distribution of urban population centres. Thus, (a) the larger the number of cities, (b) the greater the relative size of the leading cities and (c) the smaller is average inter-urban distance, the greater are the economies of regional agglomeration.

Richardson is of the opinion that there are several problems in measuring the economies of agglomeration. We are not sure which exponent determines which dependent variable in the economics of measuring the economies of agglomeration or diseconomies of the same. To judge the advantage of one agglomeration centre over the other agglomeration centre, comparisons can be made taking some crucial variables/indicators. We can compare the costs of availing certain services; we can compare the traffic density and holdup; we can compare the profitability of retail business firms. We can even compare the waiting position with regard to getting a telephone connection.

One method can be to take two cities of the same population one with industrial agglomeration and another without it. We can compare the location of functions and facilities in the two. If the agglomerated industrialised centre has a net advantage, the difference can be taken as the 'economies of agglomeration'.

However, the problems will arise as to whether these differences in facilities and functions are due to (i) urbanisation (ii) agglomerated industrialisation, or (iii) the centre being an important administrative centre.

Diseconomies: Decentralisation

There are obvious diseconomies of agglomeration. If agglomeration is due to localisation .of industries of one line of manufacture, then in the even of a crisis on the raw materials front or due to any other reason, the production will get drastically curtailed then the employment of the people of the region and their incomes drop down sharply. If localisation is "territorial division of labour" with the concentration of one type of industry, then in the event of something going wrong with that line of manufacture, not only the complementarities for other sectors/industries/activities are jeopardized, even the national security may be in danger. The skill base of the labour becomes narrow.

In due course of time urban rents become high and urban land prices go up. Poor persons lose the residential places/land as they are 'priced out'. Environmental degradation takes places and the worst sufferers naturally become the dwellers of the mean streets and slums. Soil, air, noise, water and psychic pollution overwhelm the poor persons in particular and the rich in general. All public utilities get strained and people remain in jitters due to strain of commuting.

Decentralisation or dispersal obviously becomes the answer to these problems and those factors which help the localisation of industries at a point are to be made available at other chosen points. This obviously is possible only through the State intervention which alone can make certain localised advantages 'neutral over the space' i.e., regulation of wages everywhere, credit at the same rate of interest every where, or subsidies in various rates and charges. The recent policy of the government to give grants, concessions, tax holidays, tax concessions etc. for industrial units at dispersed industrial estates are steps to counteract the diseconomies of agglomeration and promote external economies for agglomerations at certain chosen points so that techno-economic dualism also ends. Industrial "licensing policy may also be used to promote dispersal and the public sector units may be established in backward regions. The best method is to develop infrastructure facilities in the backward regions.

Some regional analysts have placed too much emphasis on the transport costs as determining agglomeration versus decentralisation. In their over-simplistic analysis improvement in the transport is taken as a proxy for technological development. If localisation of industries reduces transport costs, agglomeration takes place. To say the least, it is a misplaced over-emphasis.

A whole set of economic and non-economic factors determines concentration and decentralisation In the words of Richardson:

> *"The forces behind decentralisation and sub-urbanisation in modern cities are complex. However, it would seem reasonable to express this phenomenon as the outcome of four main factors:*
>
> (a) urbanisation itself as measured by the rate of urban population growth;
>
> (b) rising incomes;
>
> (c) changes in urban transport costs, and
>
> (d) changes in spaces preferences.

The latter may be treated as primarily a function of income. However, it is not easy to devise and suitable measure for decentralisation itself."

Locational preferences and decentralisation have important relationship. Inter-regional migration cannot be explained by inter-regional wage differences and mobility of capital cannot be explained by differences in the rate of interest. Profit-maximisation models 'of industrial location and income-maximisation models of regional choice for household do not explain everything about migration and localisation. Thus even subsidies may not do the trick in sending the new entrepreneurs to backward regions. People have locational preferences: some prefer to live in the centres of agglomeration, whatever the problems; others would rather run away from there and live in serene atmosphere somewhere else. Locational preferences for living an for locating economic units depend upon both economic and non-economic factors, People would take away business/industry from the areas where law and order situation is bad. *Richardson says that the theory of regional growth / location must contain a locational preference function.*

There are both objective (economic and measureable) and subjective (non-economic) factors with determine the locational preferences. *Thus, locational preferences are a function of the potential net income gain. It is the difference between the (i) discounted stream of additional income, and (ii) costs of mobility.*

* Regional Growth Theory: p. 146.

Government arc profoundly interested now a days to decentralise development. However, sometimes their own policies come in the way decentralisation. For example, the owner of the old textile mills in Bombay, Delhi, Ahmedabad or Surat suggested that the mill owners he permitted to use their urban factory land for the development of multi-storeyed complexes. They had promised that from the profits that they make they can apply modern technology in their units without retrenching the workers. They promised to take their units to interior areas long with their workers, who were promised residential accommodation. These proposals were turned down by the 'socialists politicians' who wanted the right to allot the urban land to be vacated by the industrialists to themselves.

There can be savings in transport costs in moving to the centre; and, if this is the case then concentration is promoted. If alternatively, there is saving in transport costs in moving to the sub-centres, dispersal is promoted, If the decentralised sub-centres enjoy a fair amount of self sufficiency, they will be less dependent upon a centre and people will not see advantage in agglomeraton.

Now a days there are three very pronounced tendencies towards decentralisation.

First, the planners and the environmentalists are offering substantial packages, of concession for establishing industries in the backward districts. Defence establishments are kept dispersed. Following industries may be dispersed.

5

Thunen's Theory of Location of Agricultural Activities

von Thunen* made an important contribution to the theory of location of agricultural activities in space in 1826 and his work was based upon the empirical studies which he undertook on his farm *Tallow,* which was located in an interior area. In his book *Der Isolarte Staat (The Isolated State),* he draws a picture of a town surrounded by a belt of land, and shows how cultivation will be distributed in concentric zones around that centre, and how the kind of cultivation adopted will be a function of distance. Thunen was an agriculturist and found that the distance from an urban centre determined the land use pattern of the land surrounding that urban centre. He gave us a deterministic theory of land use and rent. The land use is guided by minimisation of costs and maximisation of profits. Concentric rings alter due to transport efficiency and population pressure and hence relative market prices.

In the words of J. Brian McLoughlin

"Perhaps the most important features of von Thunen's theory are *its uncompromisingly classical structure** and the fact that it is an equilibrium theory. In other words it describes a static climax towards which the system will tend if no disturbances are applied, whilst it admits the possibility of change, such change is simple and discontinuous." p. 60.

---

* to be pronounced as fon

Thunen's theory was basically location theory for agricultural activities. In his model, the transport costs play an important role in determining the agricultural location. Though land use pattern depends upon a host of factors, von Thunen presumes most of the determining factors as being given. There were a few qualifying assumptions.

1. The region is isolated; the area is not hilly and the fertility is the same over the entire region.
2. That there is an urban central place which is surrounded by agricultural and grazing land.
3. The urban area supplies manufactured goods and services, while the rural hinterland supplies the foodgrains and raw materials of agricultural origion.
4. That the centre can be approached from all the parts of the surrounding area or, in other words, there are no transport bottlenecks.
5. That the agriculturalists are rational and are 'economic men' (they want to minimise costs, maximise profits or want to optimise) and are prepared to be mobile.
6. That in this "isolated region" the workers are of uniform efficiency.
7. That in this entire area of one centre and layers of the zones of hinterland, only transport costs differ and not the quality of transport.

Thunen was the second generation classical economist and his views on rent were almost the same as that of Ricardo, but he added a few more points of his own. The basic formulations were as under:

1. Rent is a differential surplus i.e., the excess production of *super-marginal* land over the marginal land, the marginal land being the one on which

only costs of production are recovered, and hence, there is no rent on the marginal land.

2. As the population pressure on land increases, the price of corn rises because its supply becomes relatively scarce. This enables the cultivation on the cultivators to take up cultivation on the hither-to sub-marginal land, which now becomes marginal. The hither-to marginal land becomes super-marginal as the order of the cultivation gets elongated. Rent on all pieces of land which were super-marginal, increases: it accrues for the first time on the hitherto marginal land, which now becomes super-marginal land of the lowest order. Once again there will be no rent on the present marginal land.
3. Rent is the creation of value and not of wealth.

   Rent rises because of the elongation of the order of cultivation made possible by a rise in price (creation of value), and not because of the increase in production (creation of wealth). Rent thus is the product of the scarcity condition.
4. According to the Ricardian theory (implicitly accepted by Thunen), *rent does not enter into the price, and thus:*
   (a) rent rises when the prices rise;
   (b) *but price* does not rise when the rent rises.

   This is because price is equal to the cost of production on the marginal land on which there is no rent. Hence rent is not a constituent of the cost of production and consequently of prices because both are equal. In the Ricardian and Thunen's theories, rent is determined *ex post facto,* though can be anticipated/negotiated *ex ante* (in which case it will be contract rent). Contract rent is real while the economic rent is a theoretical concept and the economists would consider it ideal if both the types of rents conform.

5. Rent is unearned income which accrues to the landlord *for his past labour or labour of his forefathers.* Thunen's rent theory assumes private ownership of land.

Space: Distance: Transport Costs and Rent

It is a common knowledge that rent of land near the centre will be high and of land distant from the centre will be less because (i) with the distance transport costs and hence the total costs rise, and (ii) economic surplus goes down with the rise in costs.

Suppose there are three plots of land: A, B & C. Physical outputs on them are 120,110 and 100 quintals and these three plots of land are cultivated. Then the rents on A & B plots will be 20 (120 -100), and 10 (110-100) quintals respectively. If the cost of cultivation on each plot is Rs. 10000 then the price will be Rs. 100 per quintal (equal to the cost of production of the marginal land which is 10000 divided by 100). Rent multiplied by the price will bc 20 x 100 on A plot and 10 x 100 on B plot i.e., Rs. 2000 & Rs. 1000 respectively.

According to the formulations of Thunen, if the cost of production are not to include the transport costs and are to be shown separately, then the formula can be presented as under;

$$R = E\ (p - a)\ \Sigma fk$$

Here:

R stands for rent per unit of land.

E stands for output per unit of land.

P stands for price per unit of output.

a stands for the cost of production per unit.

f stands for transport cost per unit of distance per unit of commodity; and

k stands for distance from the market; *and this is the only variable in the model of Thunen.*

Efk is thus total transport cost.

If suppose,

E is 10 quintals;

P is Rs. 150

a is Rs. 100

f is Re. 1/- per quintal per kilometre.

k is 5 km.

Then,

R 10 (Σes with the distance;

Σ(p-a) will not vary.

In the model of Thunen, distance increases the transport costs while productivity, price, inputs per unit of cultivation remain the same. A plot of land in the central place earns maximum rent because there are no transport costs. Plots far removed from the distance will have higher total costs because of the transport costs.

It is clear that the farther a place from the centre, the greater are the chances of it being relegated to the cultivation of those crops which simply cannot be transported to the centre. Zonation of production assumes the form of concentric circles or rings. The most desirable by such crops which yield the highest rent or returns. Land distant from the central market town will be relegated to such uses that cannot compete for the prime location. Land which are far distant from the centre can be left for grazing or wilderness. More valuable the product is nearer the cultivation of the same to the centre.

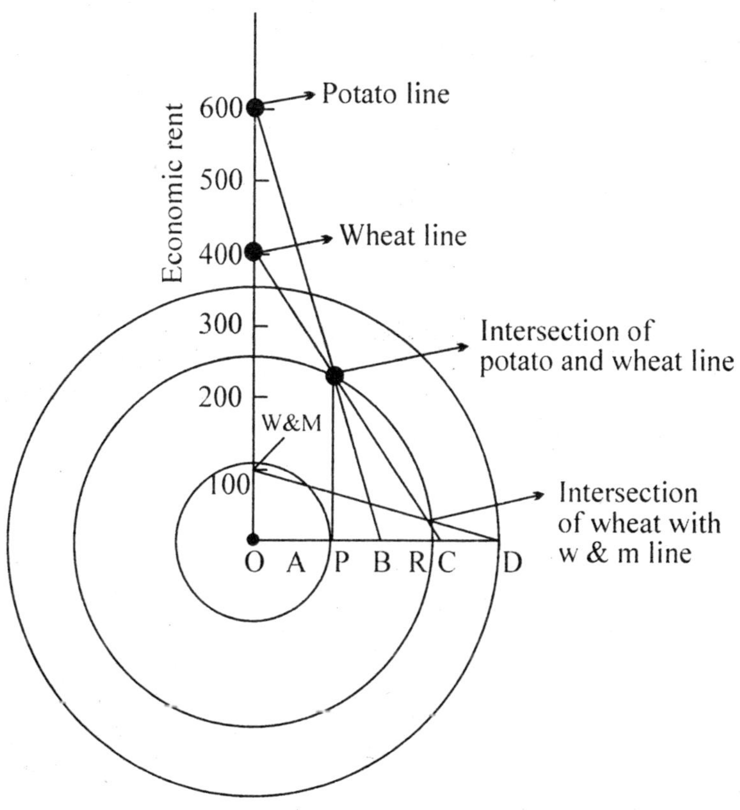

Fig. 1

The above diagram shows the rent and land use association in multi-crop model.

O Urban market

A,B,C,D Different locations

Wool and Mutton

Wheat

Potatoes

O to P Zone of Potatoes

P to R Zone of wheat
R to D Zone of wool and Mutton.

Distance from the Market

(A) Radius of the circle of potato equal to the point of inter-section of potato and wheat OP

(B) Radius of the circle of wheat where the line of wheat intersects the line of wool and mutton OR and wheat circle is PR space.

(C) RD space is for W V M. OD is the radius for wool and mutton.

In the diagram, it has been shown that:

(A) Potatoes command the highest price, have a high yield per acre and get the highest rent—Rs. 600 in this example. The steep decline in the rent curve shows that it will be expensive to transport it over the long distances.

(B) Wheat has a lower yield in terms of money (effect of physical output and price) and yields an economic rent of Rs. 400. Yet compared to potatoes its transport costs per unit prove to be lower. Wheat cannot be grown in the first concentric circle around the central town because of lower economic rent but its rent curve is flatter compared to the rent curve of potatoes.

It is very profitable to produce wheat at P, corresponding to the point of inter-section of rent curves of potatoes and wheat, even though potatoes can yield net return upto point B. The cultivator will, therefore, grow potatoes upto point P and not beyond that i.e., not upto the point R. Here potatoes' zone is delineated.

(C) The third commodity-combination is wool and mutton. If produced at the market, wool and mutton will provide an economic rent of Rs. 100 per acre only.

However, wool is relatively light in weight and the sheep can walk to the market The rent curve is lower than that of wheat but its slope is still flatter.

Wheat can be grown upto point C but earlier to this point, wool becomes profitable to grow. Its economic rent curve intersects the economic rent curve of wheat and corresponding to the point there is point R at which wool becomes profitable to grow because of higher economic rent. Hence another concentric circle of wheat will emerge beyond point R upto point O, there will be grazing grounds where sheep can be reared for producing mutton and wool.

Thunen *not only calculated the economic rent, which he made a function of distance and not merely differences infertility of the land, but also gave a theory of land use pattern in rural areas.* A series of concentric circles were obtained by him around a central city for different land uses. If his first ring was for an important crop, his second ring around the city was for 'forestry' which included horticulture and dairying also. This was relevant for his time when forests used to be the most important source of fire-wood.

As the distance changes from the central point (A) wages which are higher at the central point, go down with the distance; (B) inputs vary in price-outlay in relation to the distance from the city and (C) soil fertility differs.

The price which a product gets and the cost of transport that is incurred in procuring inputs and selling the output determine the production of the output at appropriate place.

The circles of various crops shown around a centre are *the sum of individual decisions made regarding the type of production.* Crops that are grown near the centre are those which require greater tending by the people and that which grow in the outermost circle are those which can grow on their own e.g., grass/fodder.

The determination of rent can be shown in a different way also. Rent on the distant land declines in *Thunen s model not because of the lower fertility alone but because of the distance and costs. Land at the nearby places is higher because of the (i) better fertility and also (ii) lower transport costs, which raises the economic productivity of the land.* Thus not the physical productivity alone but economic productivity determines the rent.

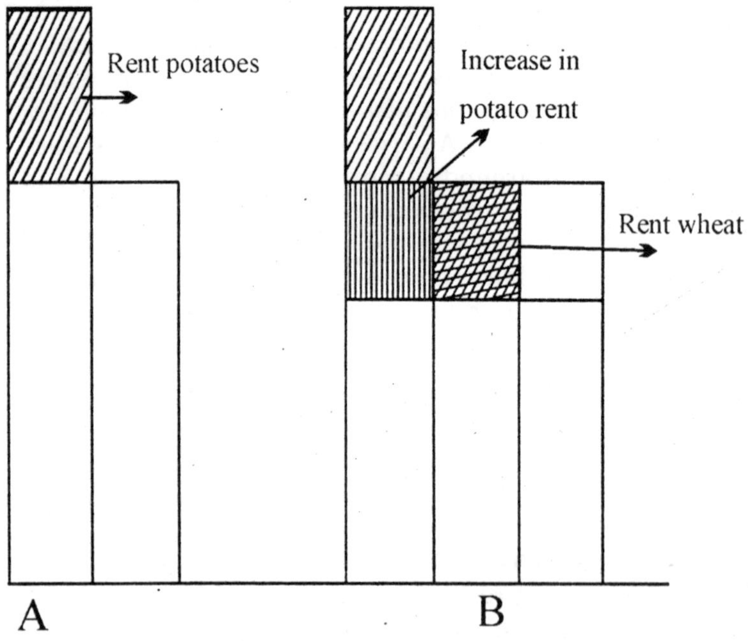

Fig. 2

The are two diagrams above. In the first the economic rent emerging due to differences in fertility is shown. X diagram shown rent when A &B plots are cultivated and B

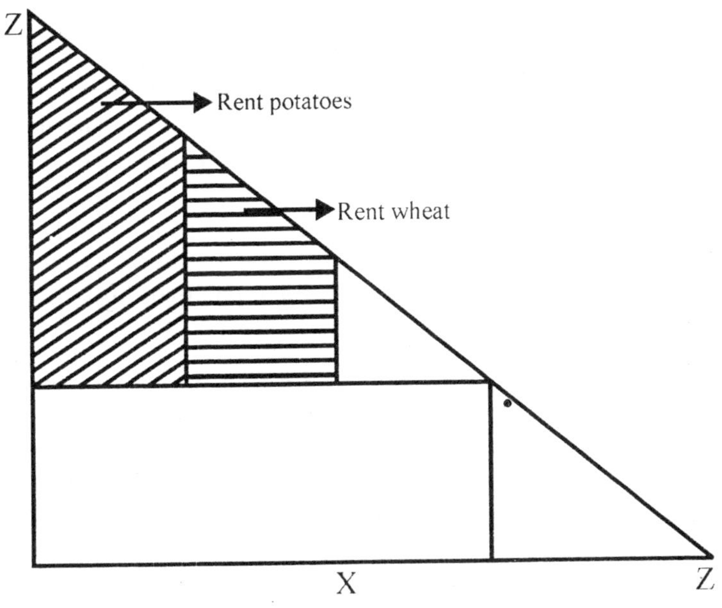

Fig. 3

diagram shows the determination of economic rent when A, B & C plots of land are cultivated.

In the X diagrams above, we show determination of economic rent when distance increases from O. As the distance increases and the cost of transport rises, the margin of advantage declines, shown by ZZ sloping line. Where diagram Y shows economic rent of potatoes and wheat which is diagram Y' when land use is upto C.

Distance and cost of transport alone cannot provide a good explanation of crop selection. If a commodity is intensely demanded and the product has inelastic demand, then the cultivation can be extended to long distances despite increasing cost of transport, if the cost of transport can be included in the price and recovered from the buyers. If transport cost were to be the only element then bulky and less valuable commodities should be grown near the centre, which is not the correct explanation.

Land use pattern depends upon natural characteristics of land as also the demand for the same or for the crop it can grow. The nature of the commodity, the price it can command, the economic rent etc. determine the land use pattern. Transport cost is also one element taken into account in determining the land use pattern but by far not the only factor.

Thunen points out that in a different setting, the size of the circles and rent may differ but the principle will be the same i.e., heavy and bulky commodities which involve huge transport costs and of which economic rent curve falls more steeply will be grown near the city. Perishable goods also follow the same pattern. The first ring will be of such commodities.

The subsequent rings will be of those commodities of which rent curves fall lesser and lesser steeply. Thus Thunen's model assumed the form of concentric zones of rural land use around the urban market.

Critical Estimate

Critics criticise Thunen for assuming same type of natural factors like water availability, soil and fertility. He ignored economies of scale in transport business. As the traffic density increases, the per unit cost of transport declines and his assumption of constant costs per unit over a distance becomes wrong.

Now a days we do not find *one* strong centre but several centres and the concentric circles so much overlap that any pattern of cultivation can emerge. Agricultural development can be in any direction than in concentric circles. Multi-cropping, rather than monocropping, is now common.

6

Weber's Theory of Industrial Location

Weber's theory of industrial location, which was micro-economic in nature, was based on the 'least cost principle', and was a further elaboration of the ideas of a fellow German thinker — Launhardt, The theory took the cost of transport as the most important factor, though other factors also find place in the theory. Weber's theory was a transplantation of Thunen's theory. While Thunen wrote with reference to the agricultural location, Weber developed his ideas with reference to industrial location. Weber's theory was more general than 'specific', the area - specific, market - specific or consumer - specific problems were not discussed in this theory. Lower costs of real inputs and service were considered favourable factors which promote agglomeration while the diseconomies of concentration were considered responsible for dispersal of industrial locations,.

As against the *market approach,* which emphasises that industries will be so located as to maximise the revenue, the *least cost principle* of Weber emphasises that industries will be so located as to keep the costs to the minimum. The first approach emphasises the importance of the nearness to the market, the second theory emphasises nearness of the factors/inputs of production to the place of location. Obviously the first emphasises the demand aspect while the second emphasises the supply aspect.

---

* The Author of the present volume had the privilege with the editing/revising the translation of the Weber's book in Hindi—a work commissioned by Madhya Pradesh Hindi Granth Rachana Academy.

(A recent approach 'behavioural approach' emphasises that location is the result of the interface of the techno - economic environment and the behaviour of the entrepreneurs, who compete amongst themselves).

Weber's theory of industrial location was published in German language in 1909 and was translated in English in 1929, and the title of the book was the same as that of the theory.

Weber's theory comes under the category of 'pure theory', which is not space - related or system - related, and it was very popular not only in Germany but in USA also. This theory accords with the principle of "comparative advantage in trade" developed by Ricardo. Weber's efforts were directed in developing a theory of industrial location which will enable the producer to achieve 'comparative advantage in cost/ price' through least cost location.

Weber gave two important concepts viz.,

(a) locational weights; and
(b) 'critical isodapanes'.

The locational weight is the total weight of all the goods (products, materials, fuel, etc.) that have to be transported to and from the production site, per unit of output. It consists of the weight, of a unit of the finished product plus the weight of localised materials, (that is the materials which are *not* available at *all the* sites), required per unit of output. A very important point that has got to be noted is that the total costs of transporting goods into the space or outside the place should involve minimum of burden. Goods found at the place are to be transported out; while the goods not found at the place are to be transported in.

An Isodapane is the curve of equal transport costs from a point. As the costs go on increasing from a central point, the curve of isodapanes - deviations will become wider.

It is clear that economies of all types should exceed the diseconomies from all sources, Then agglomeration can take place at a place where the transport costs *alone* need not be minimum.

It, is generally held that the agglomeration will take place near the big plants, but this will depend upon the net balance of total economies and diseconomies.

If there are two products from the big and small plants, then it will pay the smaller plane to move adjacent to the larger one if the resulting gains from agglomeration are larger than the increase in transport costs, involved in deviating from its minimum transport cost site. Thus the combined advantages of agglomeration of both the outputs should exceed the advantages of agglomeration of the larger output.

If the two products are *Q* and *q* respectively, then the additional costs of transport are incurred in shifting the production from the smaller unit *(q's)* original site to that next to *Q* and they are equal to:

Q = *Ldqt*

L = 100 tonnes

dq or qd = 100 kms.

t = Rs. 10,000 p.t.p.k.

= Rs. 10 crore.

where,

L is the locational weight,

d is the distance of *q* from Q.

t is the transport cost.

Additional, advantages are to be more than the additional costs.

If the value recovered is higher, then the agglomeration is beneficial, It *can be said that the radius (area of advantage), within which the agglomeration force of a production of output Q is effective, is directly proportional to the value of the agglomeration function.*

If the total costs are greater, then the radius will be smaller. *It (radius) is inversely proportional to the locational weight and transport rate.*

If the total costs of agglomeration exceed the total advantages, then dispersal is promoted, The distance over which the agglomerating force of a large production centre extends is important.

The following diagram gives an idea about the place where the agglomeration should take place.

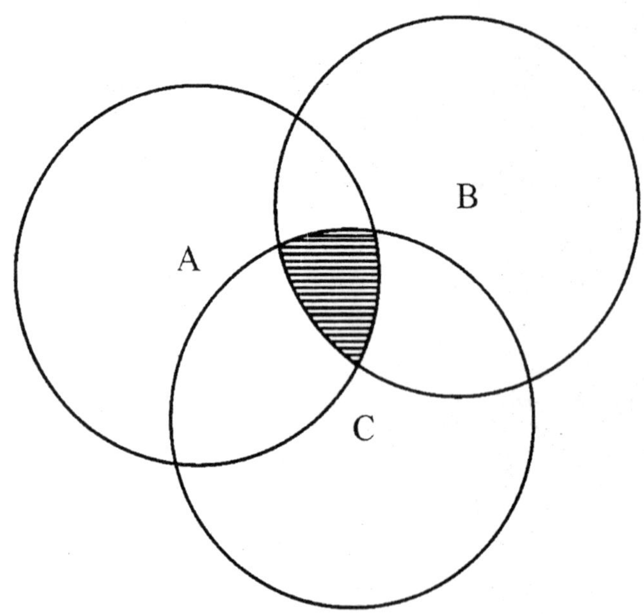

Fig. 1

It is clear that for the industries located at the centres, the minimum transport costs are obtained within the isodapanes, shaded.

However, all the three centres can obtain 'Minimum Transport costs' (MTC) in the shaded portion. Thus agglomeration should take place at a site within the common shaded segment, provided that the combined level of output can be produced at such a site. Every point within the common segment is a *possible* agglomeration' site, since production at any of these points is cheaper than at the three scattered MTC locations.

Thus, according to Weber:

(a) the optimal site will be that which offers the lowest transport cost for the total combined output;
(b) If some big units find a site most suitable, the smaller units will also get attracted there; and;
(c) in all such cases, the total deviations from the MTC will be minimum.

Thus, according to Weber, if location of raw materials is taken as given, spatial distribution of consumption is taken as unchanged and there is just one uniform system of transport, then location of an individual industry will depend on the consideration of transport cost minimisation.

Weber reduced the costs of raw materials into the transport costs by taking 'costlier materials' as being those goods which "originate from distance places." For each locality wages were taken as being fixed. Thus there are two regional factors that determine locations e.g., labour costs and transport costs. If labour costs are taken as given for a region, then transport costs become the *primary causes* that determine the locations.

Secondary causes of location are those which relate to

agglomeration and deagglomeration. Agglomeration refers to the advantages which arise as a result of external economies and deagglomeration refers to the conditions when concentration brings diseconomies which overwhelm the external economies e.g., high cost of land, pollution control, etc. External economies naturally are instrumental in promoting localisation of industries in a region,

Weber relates location to "ubiquitous" and "localised or sporadic" raw materials,

Ubiquities mean those raw materials which can be found everywhere e.g., water, soil, Such raw materials do not influence the location. Water in very arid areas is no longer ubiquitous and hence its shortage discourages location, *Sporadic* raw materials make many industries tied to certain locations e.g., location of iron *and* steel industry.

However, all these three factors (cost of labour, raw materials and transport) were taken *only* to emphasize that the transport costs matter most. He assumed transport costs to be directly proportional to distance and weight carried. Thus the point of least transport costs is that at which the total weight movement of assembling inputs and distributing output is at a minimum.

He gave a locational triangle, where optimum location *T is a balance between the force? exerted by the material sources (*M_1 *and* M_2 *and the consumption point C.* Weber devised a *Material Index* (MI) to indicate whether the optimum location was closer to the source of materials or to the market:

$$\text{MI} = \frac{\text{Weight of local material inputs}}{\text{weight of the final products}}$$

If this index is greater than one (1), the firm is material oriented; if the index is less than then 1, it is market oriented.

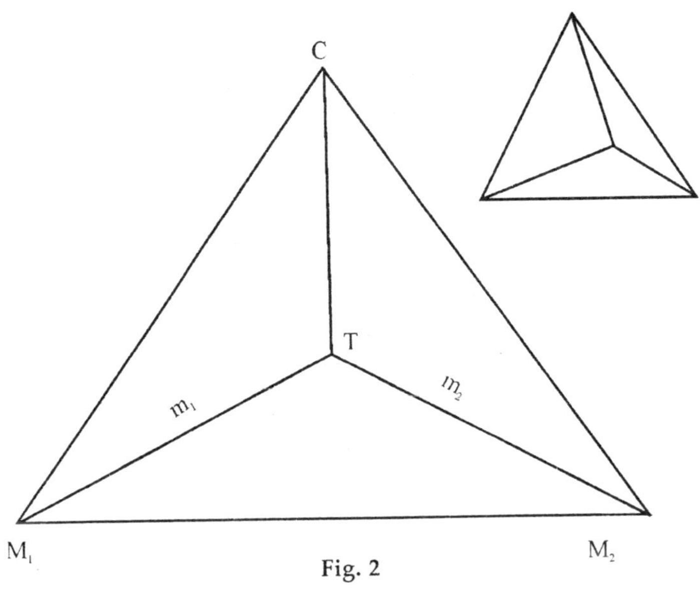

Fig. 2

Sugarcane has more weight than sugarcane — juice, hence sugar industry will be nearer sugarcane growing area. Radios have more weight than any component or raw material in it; hence radios are manufactured near the markets.

The above *kangaroo triangle, which has three triangles inside it, explains the theory that transport cost splay an important part in location and that they are directly proportional to the distance covered and weight carried.*

Here M_1 and M_2 are the sources wherefrom the raw materials are obtained; *C* is the consumption point. If the industry is located at *T*, then M_1 and M, are the distances to be covered.

The finished product is to move to the point C of consumption, and its weight will determine the location. The weights represent the force with the corners of the locational figures draw the location towards themselves.

The ratio between (a) the weight of localized material and (b) the weight of the product, will decide the point of location. This is the material index.

If the index is less than 1, the location is oriented towards the consumption centre while if the index is greater than one, the location is material - oriented, otherwise the transport costs of the bulk will raise the cost. If the costs of the bulk will raise the cost. If the two materials at M_1 & M_2 are 3/4 and 1/4 tonne respectively, they make *1* tonne of the finished product. The optimum location, will be nearer to the first point of material.

Labour Costs

If for any reason, the industry cannot be located at the place of MTC, then some other compensatory factor should be there, e.g., low labour costs. The following diagrammatic representation can be used to show the Weberian point.

If *'A'* is the point of MTC, but *'B'* is the point where the loss in transport cost is Rs. 100 but the gain in the labour cost is Rs. 200, but if the most economical place is 'C', for labour cost, but the transport costs exceed gain in labour cost, then the location will be at A itself. The isodapanes drawn from 'A' for transport costs (in the lump of Rs. 100 show that the *'B'* isodapane can be critical isodapane where the saving in labour cost exactly balances. All this is on the assumption that there are only two costs to be compared i.e., the transport costs and the labour costs. Naturally, *if* only two costs are to be compared, then the location will get attracted towards the point where the total costs are minimum. As simple as that!

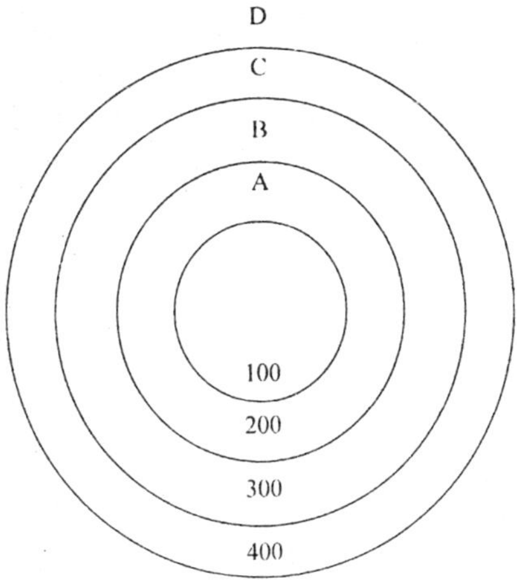

Fig. 3

Weber was in search of the general factors of location rather than specific factors, so that his theory could apply in a more broad - based manner. He considered the regional factors of location e.g., transport costs of raw materials and of the finished products, which depended upon the weight and the distance. He also included in the regional factors, the local factors of agglomeration e.g., savings, capital, marketing facilities, banking facilities, strength of the distribution network and facilities for advertisement.

Weber's theory was based upon several qualifying assumptions. Only railways were considered as mode of transport. Only one point of consumption was taken into account. Raw materials were dispersed. No labour constraint was taken into account and wages were considered to be different at different places but same at one place. Location of an industrial unit was taken as the function of MTC, MLC and agglomeration economies.

Whether the material index is more than one or less than one, entrepreneurs try to have MTC. In this connection the *labour coefficient* has also to be taken into account.

The labour coefficient is the ratio of labour cost to the locational weight. The labour cost index is the ratio of labour cost to the weight of the product, while the locational weight implies the weight to be transported during the whole process of production. (The total weight of all goods of inputs and outputs plus waste — material, fuel and the product — that has to be transported to and from the production site).

The higher the labour productivity coefficient, the greater is the susceptibility of the industry to deviate from the least transport cost location in order to take advantage of cheap labour. Where every conceivable facility for industrial location is available, then agglomerations would emerge and the MTC and MLC principles can be ignored without *net* loss.

In this case the *coefficient of manufacture* efficiency should have to be high, i.e. manufacturing costs should be lowest for the total weights to be transporated.

"It is the ratio of manufacturing costs to the locational weight."

This advantage should be substantial, then there can be deviations from the least transport and/or labour costs principle.

Industries with high coefficients of manufacture efficiency show strong tendency to agglomerate and industries with low coefficient of manufacture efficiency show weak tendency to agglomerate.

Weber observed that there can be cases of *split locations* also which would imply possibilities of location of different stages in production in any industry at different places. Bulk - shedding of the raw materials is done in stages; for example in cement industry, the clinker units can be located at a place near the deposits of lime stone, but grinding unit may be located near the market (The Cement Corporation of India set up a clinker unit at Nayagaon in Mandsaur district of Madhya Pradesh and one near Neemuch in the same district, but the grinding units are located in Hissar in Haryana and Bhatinda in Punjab). At one stage the 'gross raw materials' may be made 'pure' and then at other place it may be converted into the finished product.

There can be cases of *locational couplings* when the by - products of one industry can be used as raw material for another industry and both units are located at the same place. Paper or cloth rag - strings can be used for stuffing in the dolls; molasses of the sugar industry can be used by distilleries or units manufacturing rectified spirits or denatured spirits. The wastes of coal used in iron and steel units can be used as raw material for cement unit. Petroleum crude generates so many by - products that several chemical industries can be located near the petroleum complex.

Critical Evaluation: Weber's theory is based upon uniform gradient of transport space, same rates of fares and charges, and same type of transport and its efficiency. All this was too simplistic. *It is the value of the goods which decides the ratio of transport costs rather than mere weight.* There are multiple points of the sources of raw materials, multiple points wherefrom the demand emanates, and multiple type of transports, which were all ignored by Weber. Weber carried his deductions too far.

The shaded portion in the diagram of Weber is ideal for the industries which are getting started a new but subsequently areas around the shaded portion will be preferred or will have to be preferred as all thresholds are crossed in the shaded portion and diseconomies start appearing. Areas around the shaded portion but within the respective isodapanes would be even more suitable. A time will come when no space may be left; or when environmental considerations forbid location of a unit at the point of least transport cost.

Besides the agglomeration economies and diseconomies are notoriously difficult to measure *unit - wise.* Weber was not aware of the packages of incentives and disincentives which the modern government provide/ inflict on the new units in the backward areas/developed areas, as the economic development is becoming 'sponsored' rather than merely spontaneous.

Location decisions are also a function of the actions of the rivals. For example, if a producer wants to establish a oligopoly type unit then he will locate his plant away from the plant of the rival which may be located at the minimum transport cost point. Then semi - monopolistic position can be obtained in another locality or territory. Weber ignores all non economic factors.

7

Christaller's Central Place Theory in a Hierarchy of Settlements

I. Central Place Theory: Essential Features
II. Assumptions
III. Corner Stones of the Theory
  (A) Settlements: Hierarchy: Centres: Centre of the Centres.
  (B) Functions and Central Functions: Ordering.
  (C) Threshold Population: Market Range: Interaction.
IV. Concentric circles of the market versus Hexagons. The "k" values.. Related Diagrams,
V. Evaluation

The Central Place Theory: Essential Features

Many writers are mentioned for developing the Central Place Theory (CPT). Jefferson (1931), Christaller (1933), August Loch (1939 & 1954), Berry and Garisson (1958), Christaller (again in 1966), Dacey (1966), and Berry/ (again 1967) are important names to be remembered. The most important names are of Christaller and Losch.

While Christaller constructed his system from the "top to the bottom", Losch built his system starting from "bottom to the top". While Christaller takes the commodities with the largest market area first, Losch first selected commodities with the smallest market area and then went on taking commodities with successively large market areas.

These writers attempted to derive in exact a spatial differentiation of economic activity on a homogeneous plain on the basis of economic factors. These *German writers developed hexagonal market areas based on the transport costs and different sizes of the urban settlements.* Like Thunen and Weber of Germany, they were more concerned with the spatial aspects.

In the CPT of Christaller, centrality means importance. It is manifested by the quantity and quality of different services and functions provided by the settlement. It is defined as the functional importance of the settlement as a central place. Functions determine the centrality of a centre and not the location. Central places of different hierarchy provide services and functions of different hierarchy.

In the words of J. Brian McLoughlin

> "... Christaller ... showed the relationship between the 'rarity' of a service and the population needed to support it, the size of the 'field' or 'hinterland' within which such a population v/as contained and the size of the central place itself. In an elegant and rigorous statement, Christaller demonstrated how, under specified conditions, a nested hierarchy of central places would result, distributed in a hexagonal pattern of 'service areas".

Jeremy Alden and Robert Morgan wrote:

> "CPT focuses basically on the relationship between settlement nodes and the areas these nodes serve. . . .The dominating regions of different size vary in importance and are arranged in a hierarchy of several size types in such a way that the total distance moved by residents within a given space for goods

* McLoughlin: "*Urban and Regional Planning*" *A Systems Approach: Faber,* 1969, p. 62 Alden & Morgon: "*Regional Planning —A Comprehensive View*" Leonard Hill Books, 1974, p. 67.

and services of varying cost and frequency of need were minimized."

Christaller's CPT is purely deductive and general theory.

Since all goods and services cannot be produced in any one region, regions import and export to other regions. Movement of factors, transportation of goods and migration of people take place between regions and a network of movement develops. There are some nodal points of advantage in this network, though nodes differ in sizes and importance. There is thus a hierarchy of nodes and there are their zones of influence (also known as hinterland surfaces).

CPT is not based upon the actual pattern of settlements, but it a geographer's dream about the ideal hierarchy as they would like to see and present it on a map.

The Central Place Theory assumes certain situations related to settlements — hamlets, villages, homesteads towns, cities. These assumptions are:

1. The landscape is even with an even distribution of natural resources and an even spread of population — invariably assumed to be fanners. People do the marketing in a circular area.
2. The radius of the circle of the marketing i.e., 'the extent of the market' is the function of transport cost. The circles so overlap that the common areas of overlap provide hexagonal shapes, and *all* consumers and areas are served by various centres.
3. Population is evenly distributed in all the directions and the movement of people in all the directions is unimpeded and involves equal unit transport cost.
4. All people are rational: they want to minimise costs

* More follows on this topic and theme elsewhere in this book.

(transport costs and the time - cost of travelling in particular) and maximise gains.

5. All the consumers have the same purchasing power all the directions and have identical demand schedule!!*
6. Lower order functions are available at lower order places and higher order functions at higher order places, though higher order settlements have many lower order functions also. People so settle in the area that they are not farmer from a centre/function than they are willing to travel to avail the facilities.
7. The relationship between settlement nodes is orderly and not disorderly. There is a hierarchy of functions related to the hierarchy of settlements. In a small village there will be a rural post box and a delivery postman while in a big city most developed modem electronic communication facilities are available. In every field there are facilities ranging from the lowest to the highest order. (Primary school to institutes of specialized learning and research; village dispensary to specialized institutes of surgery/medical treatment; one counter bank to big banks using computers and exchanging all currencies of the world). Big cities and centres are known for *quaternary* facilities and we have this fourth sector now.
8. Each lower or higher order service requires threshold population. A cinema hall will require a minimum film viewing public of (say) 500 persons per show. A

* Economist attach more importance to disposable income than to population. They would attach more importance to the marginal propensities to consume of various sections of the people and to the average propensity to consume rather than to the sheer number of persons. Thousands of persons, devoid of purchasing power, are of little consequence.

Similarly it is not merely the economy in the transport cost which matters in all discussions of regional economies but other costs also. The *ratio* of transport costs to other costs and to the price of the commodity should matter more.

threshold population and efficiency of the transport system (low transport cost) will sustain a facility.

Corner Stones of the Theory

(A) Settlements: Hierarchy: Centres: Centre of the Centres.

The space is dotted with settlements which have a hierarchy. There are farmstead, hamlet, small villages, bigger villages, small - intermediate big towns, cities and metropolises (some of them *miseropolises).* They form the rural and urban areas.

Thus settlements differ in sizes and distribution of population/ functions and in each region there is a centre of central place. These central places are themselves in a hierarchical order. Around a nucleus (town) there is *crystallisation of mass* (mass includes population, function and activities).

As there is ordering of the functions — lower and higher order function — so there is ordering of the centers. There is a centre of the centre. A central place provides goods and services to an area larger than itself and it is related to region. But more importantly it is related to settlements. Not the population of the central place but the functions of the central place are important.

The central places of the lower to higher orders are linked together and constitute the entire system. At each centre, there are certain 'central goods, services and professions' which are produced and offered. The essential point is that the central places of different order are organized into a hierarchy and do not exist in a haphazard manner.

Functions, Central Functions and Ordering

Facilities and functions are the goods and services

available at a place. Primary sector provides agricultural goods, raw materials and food articles. There are manufactured goods made available by the 'secondary' sector and services which make up the 'tertiary sector;. Schools, hospitals, bank branches, wholesale establishments, retail shops, barber's shop, post office are all services. There are lower and higher order services e.g., a small retail shop to higher order services e.g., a Departmental Store in a big city (where one can buy anything from pin to aeroplane!) The quality of service determines the order e.g., primary school to internationally famous Institutes of Higher Learning and Research. Instances can be multiplied in respect of all types of services.

Normally lower order centres will provide lower order functions and facilities and higher order centers will provide higher order facilities. It can be said with fair amount of certainty that higher order functions will provide many, if not all, lower order functions and facilities also. Sometimes we can find higher order facility in a lower order centre (a mission hospital with good medical facilities in a remote small town). Central places provide central functions. These are those goods and services which are produced at a few locations in order to be used by many settlements scattered over the space. Hence the central functions are *un - ubiquitous* in nature and the degree of the importance of a function is supposed to vary inversely with the frequency of its occurrence. If one particular commodity is sold everywhere, there is no central place for the same.

The more developed a country/region, the higher the percentage of the contribution of the secondary and tertiary sectors to the national income. The same is true of the developed central places. Central places develop because of the central functions and central functions are provided by the central places. The central services overcome the disadvantages of the 'friction of distance'. (high cost of transport).

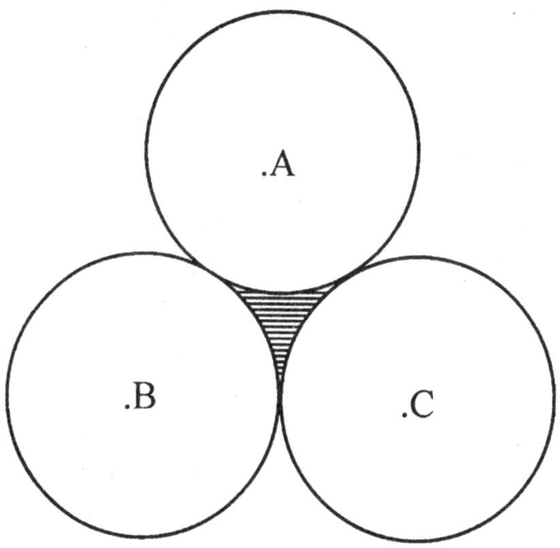

Diagram - 1: Showing areas served from a centre

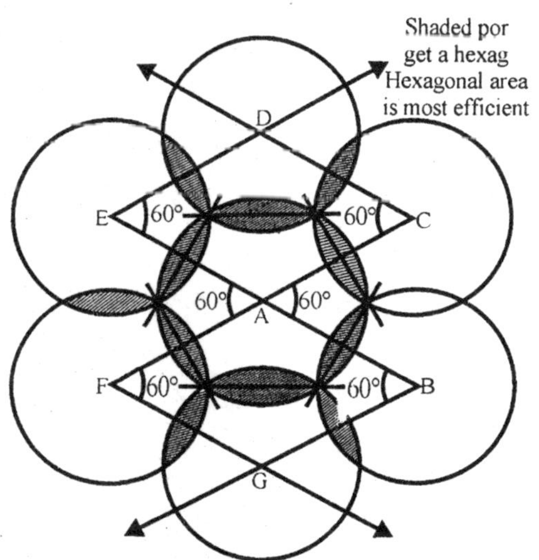

Diagram - 2

Threshold Population: Market Range: Interaction

Various types of the services can be ranked into higher and lower orders, depending on the demand threshold i.e., the minimum viable level of population and income required to support services.

Then there is the range of the service area. There are outer limits of the markets area for each service. These outer limits depend upon the (a) cost of transport and (b) distribution of the centres.

These two factors (threshold and range) determine the number and size of the central places supplying each service, and hence a central place hierarchy develops. Small central places and their complementary regions will be included within the market areas of larger centres.

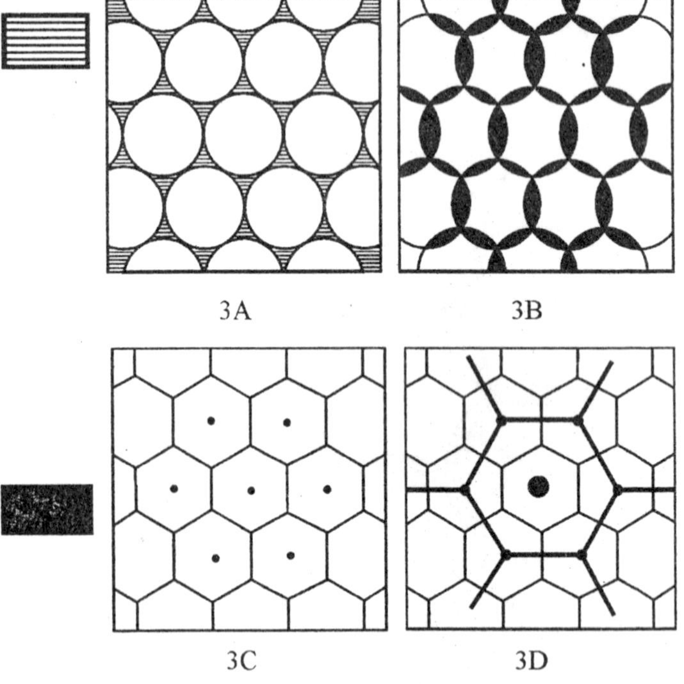

Fig. 3A, 3B, 3C and 3D

In the long run equilibrium, when the whole are of the system is covered, the services areas will be hexagonal in shape. Then the entire space will be covered by several honeycomb lattices with hexagons of different size, superimposed upon each other.

It is right to say that a central point of location can serve an area demarcated by a concentric circle. A, B and C have their own areas but in this arrangement, the shaded area is not served by any centre. Such a situation cannot simply exist. Hence not the circles which are tangent type but overlapping circles are realistic.

The space is shared by circles forming hexagons.

In the diagram 2. A, B, C, D, E, F, G are equi - distant from the nearest points. The circles overlap in some areas (with angles of 60° shown at B,C,E,F and A on both the sides, equi - distant points can be located and with the radius of the circles more than half the distance between the two points, the overlap can be shown). The shaded areas arc shown by two centres. If the shaded area is divided by a line, then the shaded circa can be shared by the two centres on their side of the dividing line in the shaded portion. We get a hexagonal area. Hexagonal arrangement is the most efficient.

Fig. 3A. Shows how the situation of uncovered space is untenable.

Fig. 3B. Shows that if circles overlap, all space is covered by the hexagons that are formed.

Fig. 3C. Shows the neat resultant hexagons that get formed.

Fig. 3D. Shows the overlap of hexagons, dividing hexagons in three part, which themselves result in new hexagons.

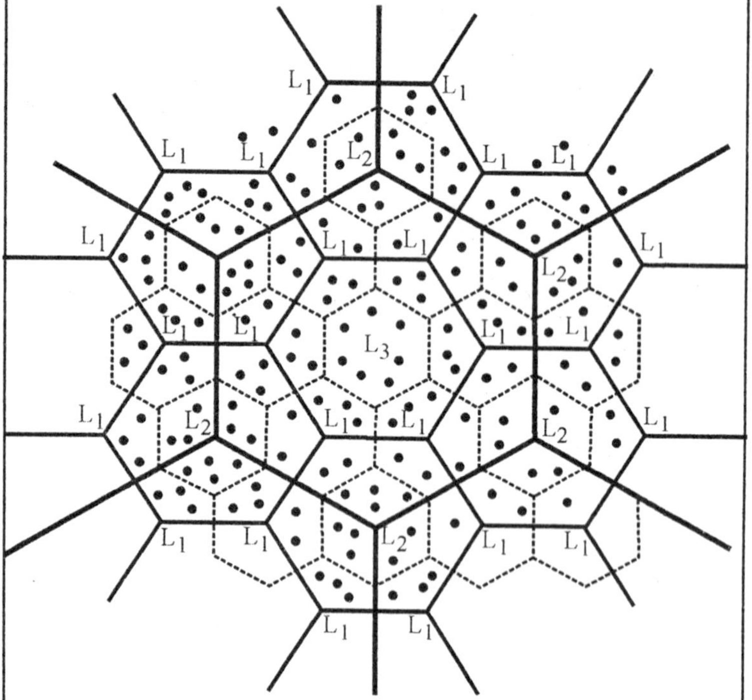

Diagram-3

Hexagonal Development

This diagram shows how each hexagone is divided into three parts and a hierarchy develops.

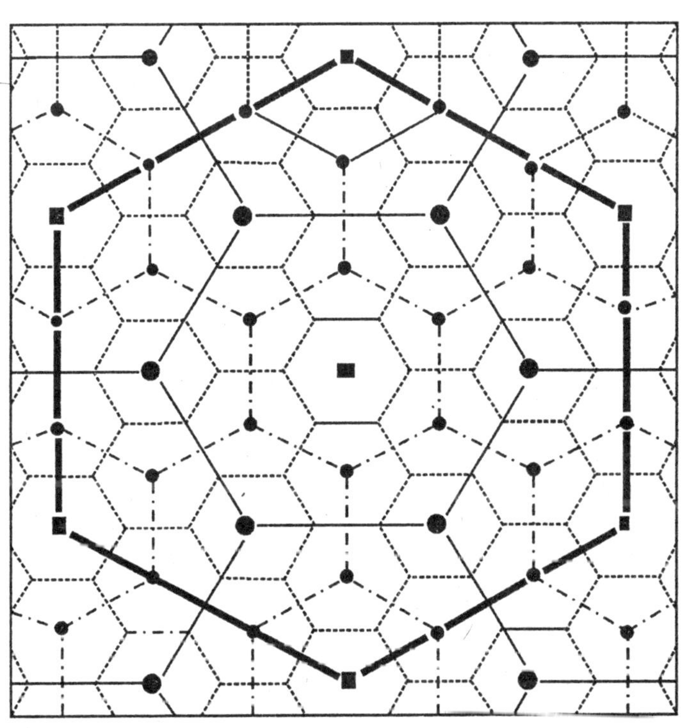

Diagram - 4

Colour Presentation

Honeycomb lattices with hexa - gons of different size, superimposed upon each other.

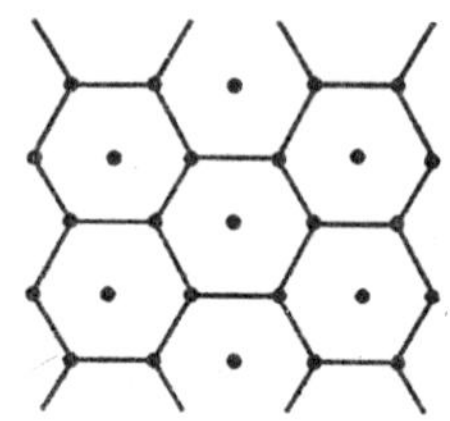

Marketing principla
K= 3

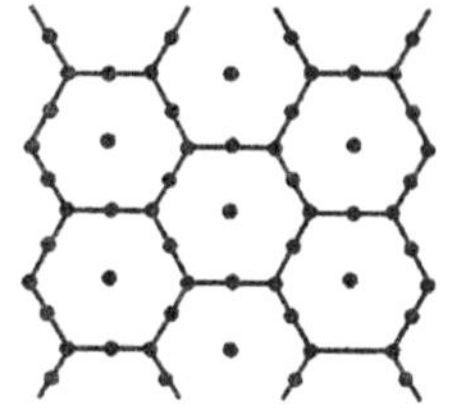

Transportating principla
K=4

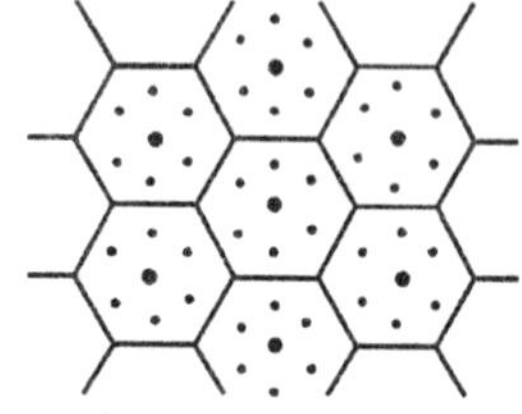

Administrative principla
K=7

Diagram - 5

One of the most important characteristics of a central function is that it generates spatial interaction, through the movement of men, materials and ideas between the central place and the complementary region surrounding it. The rarer the function, the higher the range of the interaction.

Each centre has its complementary area and from the centre emanate the centrifugal or distributive functions and from the complementary areas to the centre gravitate centripetal activities or activities of collection.

Thus there is two - way inter - dependence and interaction between the centre and the complementary area. A continuous process of centripetal and centrifugal interactions takes place between the spatially dispersed settlements and their nearest nodal centres containing bundles of different services and facilities. Advantage levels of the nodal points differ. Hierarchies of the centres and services differ. All these differences determine the interactions and interdependence.

Concentric Circles of the Market Versus Hexagons. The "k" Values

The *'k'* value is the total number of settlements of a certain order served by a central place of the next higher order. It is the total number of settlements served by the central place.

There are three types of *'k'* values assigned by Christaller.

1. The marketing principle *'k'* value which is equal to 3
2. The transporting principle *'k'* value, which is equal to 4.
3. The administrative principle *'k'* value which is qual to 7.

Then there is frequency of occurrences of different levels. In case of the marketing areas, this frequency will go in geometric progression of:

1: 3:9:27: 81: 243 and so on.

Marketing Principles and 'k Value

Christaller conceives that there are six hamlets at the corners of the hexagon surrounding the village. Since a hexagon is divided into three parts (see hexagonal diagrams), each village serves 1/3rd of the 6 hamlets i.e., 2 hamlets.

Adding to them will be the village itself and the 'K' value becomes 3.

A town serves *3* villages and hence 6 hamlets. The central place of the next higher order (city) will serve 3 towns or 9 villages or *27* hamlets

Thus the number of *centre* are successively lower order levels in the hierarchy follows the geometric progression.

In the scheme of Christaller, each central place is surrounded by six lower order places which are situated at the vertices of the hexagon, When the original central place Is surrounded by six other central places of the same order, the first order trade area of each of the lower order places is competed for by three of the first order places. Therefore, each first order place can depend upon the full first order trade area from itself and one third of the first order trade area from each of the six lower order

This market principle is called the '*k - 3*' pattern, because it has the trade of (itself) and six times the one - third (6x1/3 = 2) of the trade of the other areas. Thus, the frequency of occurrence of different levels of market areas follows the geometric progression of 1: 3: 9: 27: 81: 243 and so on, at successively lower levels of the hierarchy.

Transportation Principle and 'k' Value

This is also known as the 'principle of traffic'. If several habitations lie on a route, then the route will be efficient and cheap. Sub - centres should be on the route to the centre., (See diagram of the transportation principle). A hamlet is shared by two villages.

Since a village is surrounded by six hamlets (each hamlet being si mated midway between two comers of a hexagon and lying on the straight line connecting two villages), each village serves (1/2 x 6) 3 hamlets. Adding the village itself, we get 'k' value or transportation principles as 4.

The sub - centres in the Christaller's scheme of things have "dual loyalty". The traffic principle leads to a hierarchy which minimises the distance between the sub - centers and the main centre, with as many important places as possible lying on one traffic route between main centres.

The Administrative Principle and 'K' Value,

This principle emphasises that each centre should have complete control of the six surrounding areas and no divided allegiance exists. No power sharing between lower and higher order centres is permitted. The centre governs itself also arid hence the 'k' value is 6 - f 1 = 7.

Critical Evaluation of the CPT

Appreciation

CPT is an abstract model but there is no dearth of abstract models in any subject. There is no doubt that there is a hierarchy of settlements and functions and that there is interaction between various places to avail or supply functions and facilities, It is also true that the entire space will be covered by the producers and retailers of goods and services, 'They will either reach out to people or people will have to move to central places to avail functions and facilities.

One can also plan allocation of functions and facilities for orderly distribution of functions over space. *Central functions and centers have a minima (threshold) and a maxima (range).* The minimum is the break-even point where average revenue equal the average cost (AC=AR). In arid region a minimum population/income level is necessary. The maximum limit i.e., the range depends on a host of factors like population density, city size, price of the service of commodity, income distribution, distance and transport costs. The range is well explained in terms of the circles and hexagons.

In Christaller's scheme of things, the threshold and range together determine the number and size of central places supplying each service. Corresponding to the hierarchy of centres, there is hierarchy of services and facilities. The essence of his CPT is that the whole area is covered with the help of hexagonal service areas.

According to Christaller, there is "crystallisation of the 'mass' around the core and then gravitational pulls (or agglutination tendencies) develop in favour of the central places. More and more functions are added to the central place and new functions get stuck to the mass. The place is 'central' in relative terms only.

Certain things have to be done keeping in view the existing hierarchy of the settlements, while in other cases the centres are to be upgraded through improving the infrastructure and manufacturing facilities.

The small, intermediate and big towns/cities have interaction of the type Christaller had explained. They transmit and absorb ideas also. Regional planners can plan the most satisfying central places.

Critical Observations

The 'k' values are arbitrary, Christaller obtained his values by locating as many hamlets as he wanted so that they conformed to his 'k' values. That there are 'k' values cannot be denied but no sanctity is to be attached to the figures he gave, though geometric progression can also be admitted.

In the words of Richardson:

> "There have been many criticisms of central - place models. Their beautiful regular patterns so easily disintegrate when the homogeneity of space assumptions are dropped. The location of manufacturing industries and other economic activities serving national or international markers distorts the hierarchy, or even ignores it. Specialisation of function within a size class is also a serious disturbance factor. The CPT model is static and cannot shed much light on the dynamics of urban growth". (R & UE p. 329)

8

Losch on Central Place Theory or 'Ideal Economic Space of Losch

I: Differences between the approaches of Christaller and Losch.
II: Losch on location of agricultural and Industrial Activities.
III: Losch on CPT forms.
IV: Losch's "Ideal Economic Space".
V: Critical evaluation.

Differences between the Approaches of Christaller and Losch

Christaller believed there is hierarchy of settlements but Losch emphasized that there is *continuum of settlements.* The orderly hierarchy of settlements around central place is not accepted by Losch. Losch incorporated more realism and flexibility into Christaller's rigid hierarchy. The rigid 'k' values are not accepted by Losch,

While the Christaller's version is appropriate for the *tertiary activities, Losch's version is more, appropriate, for the secondary activities.* Christaller's approach is purely an explanation of the service elements in spatial structure, whereas that of Losch could be said to be more an explanation of the spatial distribution of the market - oriented manufacturing industry.

Christaller assumed homogeneous plain but Losch studied an area of USA which was not homogeneous.

Christaller proceeded from "macro to micro centres", while Losch proceeded from "micro centres to macro centres or from lower order functions to higher order functions.

In the Christaller's model central, places of the same size provide the same functions but in Losch's model central places of the *same size may provide different Junctions,* The 'k' values are variable and hence the level of functions performed by a central place is not determinate.

Though Losch also considers hexagonal patterns in the space being the most satisfactory, the possibilities of triangular or square patterns or even, conic patterns are admitted. In Christaller's model there is a strict hierarchy with hexagons of the same size for all central places of the same order and bigger hexagons of higher order will include one full lower order plus a part of the other lower order hexagons; in Losch system all markets are not of the same size,

Loschian landscape is more diversified and hence complex. His model is more practical than that of Christaller, Loschian hierarchal concept leads more to continuum rather than distinct tiers of the central places of Christaller because Losch's (a) centres are not of the same size, (b) do not provide the same type of services, and (c) higher order places provide lower order functions at *differing intensity.*

Losch on Location of Agricultural and Industrial Activities

According to Losch the population and agricultural activities are distributed like polka dots over the space and hence, their location is area, Location of industrial activity is PUNCTIFORM.

Population gets so distributed that it has proximity to food as well as industrial production. There are crop gradients of agricultural production according to geo - climatic and economic conditions. The agricultural production is said to a punctiform city. Punctiform industry is distributed for selling to a really spaced customers. Industrial production is agglomerated but at several places.

Agricultural production is in a area but rural settlements (farm houses, shelters for cattle) are punctiform. Losch says it will be better if farm houses are laid in hexagonal form on a 60° lattice.

Non - agricultural activities are located (or should be located) in such a way that high transfer costs for agriculture are not involved. *If there were to be economies of scale only, and* no transport costs, then all the activities would be located at one place. If *there were to be only economies of transport,* and no economies of scale, then all the activities would have got to be located at every inch of the space. Obviously both types of economies are available in differing degrees at different places and locations are dispersed, but some .are agglomerated at some places.

Losch incorporated the demand aspect, in the 'least cost approach' for location of economic activities. When the 'least cost approach' was combined with the 'market analysis approach' the main result was the emergence of *the concept of "ISOTIM"* or a contour line of equal delivered price.

In Losch's model there are different delivery prices of goods. Loschian combination of the 'Least cost approach' with the 'market area approach' *belongs to the realm of 'partial equilibrium setting'*. It is not general equilibrium analysis.

Losch even incorporated conditions of non - competitive markets through overlapping markets. Maximisation of profits, occupation of all space, equality of price and average costs, minimum - size market areas, and indifference, lines delimiting the boundaries of market areas were essential features of Losch,

Losch did not believe that the 'least cost approach' is optimum also. Losch emphasized that location decision depended on the availability and price of inputs and on the differences in commodity prices at alternative locations. After the location has been accomplished, it is the entry of the firms which affects the pattern of prevailing prices of inputs and outputs. Through these inter - relationships, the pattern of spatial price differences and the location of economic activities are simultaneously determined.

The 'general equilibrium approach' to location is not as dynamic as the partial equilibrium approach because there is scope of incorporating local differentiations. Partial equilibrium approach to location was adopted by O. Englander, H. Ritself, Palander and Hoover also. Walrasian general equilibrium conditions are irrelevant because transport costs are not zero.

Losch on CPT Forms

Losch also believed that hexagons are ideal *but they do not exist in space.* If there is competition amongst the producers, then new producers will enter and they will cover the entire market space in equal regular hexagons. There will be no area which will not be served. Honeycomb hexagons minimise the total transport costs. The size of the hexagon will depend upon demand and supply conditions, the transport costs and other costs. Since people do not require one commodity but several, hexagons *for each commodity will be of different sizes.*

Losch emphasises that in order to produce the maximum number of goods and services at the minimum cost, *the aggregate distance between the settlements should be minimum,* and not merely the route kilometre distance.

In the Loschian model, the production of lower order goods is located in each central village in a region having the ideal triangular hexagonal pattern of '*acentral*' villages with hexagonal service area boundaries.

In the Loschian system:

(A) All goods and functions requiring threshold of settlements between 1 and 3 basic hexagonal market area would be located in "k=3" system.

(B) All goods and services of which settlements threshold requirements range between 3 and 4 basic hexagonal market areas would be located in "k=4" network.

(C) All goods and services with settlements threshold demand between 4 and 7 basic hexagonal market areas would be in "k=7" network.

All these hexagonal systems are then superimposed and rotated around the highest order centre until there is maximum coincidence or agglomeration of goods and services at the centre.

In the economic landscape of Losch there are City poor sectors' where minimum threshold concentration of activities is found, while in "city rich sectors' maximum concentration of activities is found.

There will be *locational couplings* e.g., rectified spirit industry is coupled with sugar industries, as the former will use the molasses released by the latter.

There will be 'nesting also' i.e., on the network of lower order there will be superimposition of the network of higher order central places. The *satellite ratio or nesting* is variable and not constant i.e., large centre may or may not contain lower order industries. Thus the size distribution of urban centres in a region is more continuous than in Christaller's rigid hierarchy.

Losch on "Ideal Economic Region"

Losch also gives a model of his own which is not intended to replicate the real work. *It refers to an ideal economic region that should be or could be.*

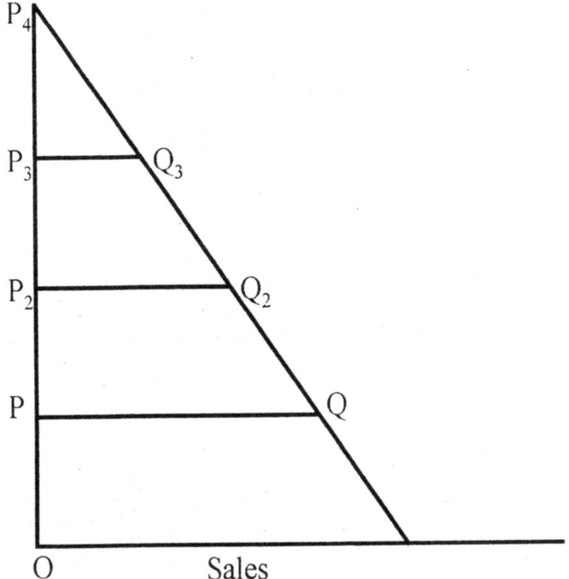

Fig. 1

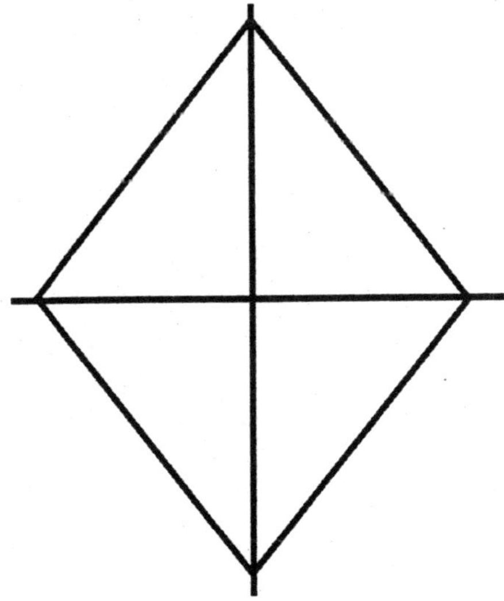

Fig. 2

He assumes (a) unbounded homogeneous plain, (b) no transport barriers, (c) ubiquitous raw materials, and (d) transport costs proportional to distance only.

The general economic principle of price being equal to cost of production is true 'at the factory gate only'. Costs rise due to transport costs as the distance is to be covered (in his diagram costs are shown on vertical axis and demand on horizontal axis).

First we illustrate how rising transport costs reduce the demand.

In the diagram above, *P* is the point of location of the factory. At this place the price charged is OP and the quantity sold is *OQ*. As the producer wants to sell in the distant markets, costs of transport get added to the cost of production and they are to be covered. Thus farther from the place of production we have (let us say) three points where the price becomes OP_2, OP_3 and OP_4. At the next

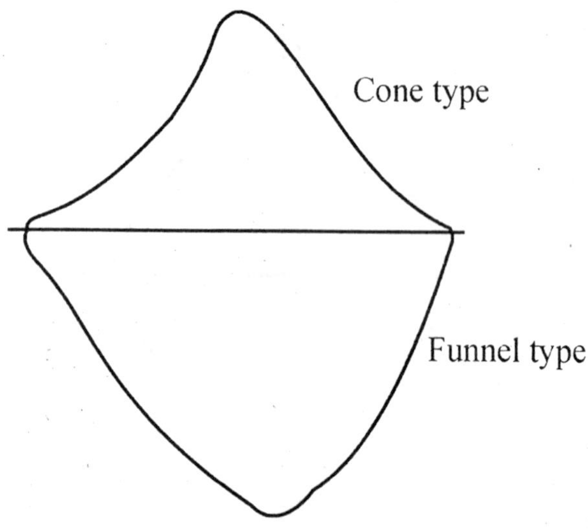

Fig. 3

two prices the demand become lower i.e., OQ_2 and OQ_3 while at OP_4 price, the demand becomes nil. Joining P_4 and Q, we get the demand curve which can be extended to the horizontal base line also.

We get the trianage PP_4Q the area boundary for the plant.

Losch then turns the triange and rotates it around the axis. It is then smoothened to obtain market area and the price range.

In the above diagram, we have four trianagles. *[These are independent triangles and have not been drawn to measure to conform to the old triangle. The outer lines smoothen the triangles.]*

In the diagram we represent the price on the vertical axis and the base represent the market area or sales. *The sales area is a circle of the radius p i - .e., the price.* Sales area is in all the four directions. Losch preferred to represent it with a cone and we have *smoothened the area.*

Markets will be around a centre and in the circular form, will be covered. Triangles made smooth.

The Cogwheel Arrangement

Losch also believes that hexagonal arrangement is the best as It covers the entire space. However, the sizes of the hexagonal nets will differ with commodities, economies of scale and the cost of transport. Hexagonal arrangement, besides covering the entire space, minimises the cost of transport also.

Hexagonal nets are to be thrown over the space; there are production centres and the nets are to be so thrown that there should be six 'full' sectors and six 'empty' sectors just like in a cogwheel. This arrangement will minimize the total transport expenditure without sacrificing access to market.

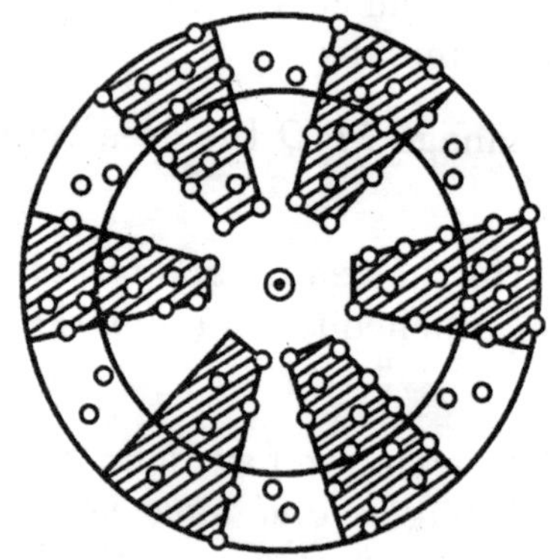

Fig. 4: This the 'ideal economic region'

A cogwheels pattern around a big metropolis will take form. Around the centres there are *price funnels* of different deepness. Price funnel shows that if price is low, market will be wide and at a certain high price there will be no market, Prices determine the distance upto which the commodities can be sold. In the illustrations of Losch, the price funnels break up the landscape so completely as to make meaningless the concept of local price levels'. No simple deductions can be made, therefore, about the comparative advantage, migration of factors, or purchasing power

Losch writes about *price waves* also. As the prices change the demand and supply of inputs and outputs change, which bring further changes in the prices. Some prices go up while some other go down; they constitute the ups and downs of the waves and since the prices go up and down at different rates, the heights of the waves differ. Flatterning of price waves is deceptively like the dying out of the multiplier.

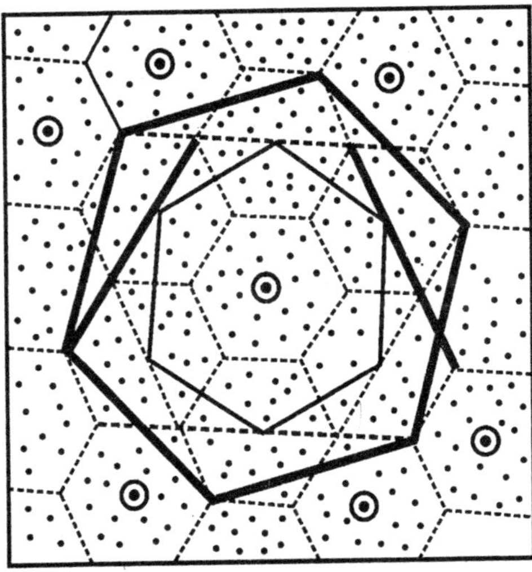

Fig. 5: Loschian Landscape, Overlapping Trade Areas.

Inter - industry concentration is emphasized in Losch's model. Larger centres will develop at considerable distance from each other. The essential features of the model are that the producers have enough space to locate and locations occupy all space. Competition for locations eliminates abnormal profits. Supply and market areas become small, therefore. *Market area boundaries are drawn so that consumers located at the boundary are indifferent among the alternative nearest suppliers. There may be (say) two or three, depending upon whether they are located on the side or at the vertex of the hexagon.*

Critical Evaluation

Losch's model is considered much more comprehensive model of location in comparison to all the models developed earlier. In the words of Richardson:

> "His theory was the first to describe the basic principles of spatial analysis as a set of equations, and to interpret the space economy in terms of monopolistic

> competition, His conditions of equilibrium were: maximisation of profits by each producer, occupation of all space, equality of price and average costs, minimum - size market areas, and indifferent lines delimiting the boundaries of market areas."
>
> "Losch was one of the first to discuss the 'regional policy related to location'. He accepted that a competitive spatial equilibrium may not be socially optimal, and market intervention could be directed either to modify the impact of market forces or to help bring about a free market."*

Losch builds up the whole structure of the space economy including systems of region upon a framework which starts from the market area of the individual firm. Losch analysis uses tools of traditional economics, like maximisation, pure competition, partial equilibrium and simultaneous equilibrium. *Discontinuity of the hexagon sizes and the rotation of hexagonal network were the ideas given to us by Losch and they attest to the genius of Losch.*

Criticism

Uniform population densities, uniform gradient, uniform quality of transport and uniform cost of transport over the entire space are some of the assumptions which are incorrect and mutually inconsistent with the 'concentration thesis'. If population densities are heterogeneous, then the regularity of the identical hexagon nets is disturbed. Losch introduces modification. The hexagons become smaller with proximity to cities because markets are denser there. According to *hard*

> "Similar reductions in market area size are found adjacent to major transportation routes. For the same reasons it is difficult to maintain the hexagonal shape, and irregular polygons — frequently approximating rectangles — tend to develop."*

* Regional Economics: A Reader, pp. 7 & 11.

The equal area hexagon as suggested by both Christaller and Losch are not likely to take shape in real life. *Isard* has pointed out that though Losch retains the hexagon, it is not consistent with some of the implications of his solutions. Losch postulated uniform distribution of consuming population but his model indicates varying degrees of concentration of activities and functions at different central places. As a result of this, market areas would assume rectilinear or rhomboidal shapes.

Since there is neither uniform population density and since consumers need not buy from the nearest shop, there are deviations from the central place hypotheses. Central places are bound to get distorted with the differing population densities, It is surprising how some writers while busy calculating the differing population densities, could assume uniform densities. Different goods have different variable tributary area populations. It is impossible that area boundaries are always bisected. Centres which are normally of the same level of hierarchy will offer different bundle of services as the tributary populations differ. Neat hexagons are myth.

Losch model is unsatisfactory *in* several respects. If production of an industry is concentrated, why were the cost differences at alternative sites neglected? If there are nodal points of production and nodal points of labour market, how come they be there under the assumption of uniformly distributed population? The position is that even today the general, theory of location is explained with reference to transport cost differences but of uniform surface !!!,

*Though regional economists Christaller and Losch gave well researched regional spatial structure models,** they were, however, more deductive than inductive in nature,

* See: Isard (1956) *Location and Space Economy*, p. 272. Richardson quoted I sard in *"Rural Urban Economics"* p. 74.

Christaller's model had the limitation that it was largely based on the service functions and Losch included agricultural and industrial activities also. Christaller's neat hexagons were made overlapping by Losch and realism was introduced. The CPT is generally *static;* it explains what is but fails to highlight how the CPTs evolve and shall change in future. In complex settlement structures CPT loses its significance. Yet all said and done the economics of hierarchy of functions, hierarchy of locations of manufacturing, hierarchy of settlements, the minimum thresholds and the market ranges are very important concepts.

We can conclude in the words of Richardson:

> "It is true that the analysis has weaknesses: the incompatibility of uniform population distribution assumptions with the hierarchical pattern of settlements; the under - estimation of industrial agglomeration economies: the neglect of interdependence between sectors, *Nevertheless, it is beyond dispute that no regional economist or location theorist could afford to neglect Losch's work."*

9

Sargant Florence, Edgar Hoover, Polander, Greenhut, and Isard on Industrial Location Richardson on Location Constants Locational Preferences General Equilibrium Theory of Industrial Location Hotelling Principle

Sargant Florence's Theory of Industrial Location

Sargant Florence as a critic of Weber's Theory of Location, maintains that it is wrong to trace relation of location to the areas and it is important to trace the relationship with population, its distribution and other things relating to population,

If there are a few industries only in an area, it need not be "industrially backward" if the population density is very low. Therefore, the opposite of this is that in a thickly populated region, even concentration of a few industries may not make the region "industrially developed".

Florence gives us two measures: (1) Location factor or Location Quotient, and (2) Co-efficient of Localisation.

Location Factor or Quotient: It is an index of the degree of concentration of an industry in a particular region. It gives the degree of concentration of a particular industry in a particular region. It can be calculated with the help of two ratios:

(a) the percentage of workers of the industry in question found in the region under consideration; and

(b) the percentage of all industrial workers found in that particular region to the total industrial workers in the country.

The first is divided by the second. (See next chapter).

If the quotient is 1, the location factor is unity i.e., the industry is evenly distributed over the whole country. If the location quotient is 1+ (greater than 1), it shows higher than national concentration. If the location quotient is less than 1, it means that the region has not got its due share.

The location quotient can become different if the region is redefined in any other sense than administrative. LQ differs from area to area..

Coefficient of Localisation is the sum of deviations for regional percentages of workers in a particular industry from the corresponding regional percentages of workers in all industries. It will be a single figure for the industry and for the country as a whole. It refers to the industry and not to a region. It refers to the tendency of attraction or repulsion exercised by the existence of a unit or units of an industry in a region for other units of the industry. It measures localisation of an industry in any part of the country.

Location Quotient: Calculation of

1. If the total number of workers employed in all industries in the 20000 thousand;
2. If the total number of workers employed in the country in industry is 2000 thousand;
3. If the total number of workers employed in region is 8000 thousand;
4. If the total number of workers in j industry in region is 1000 thousand; then

(A) Percentage of workers in; industry to all workers in that industry in *n* region will be:

$$\frac{1,000 \times 100}{2,000} = 50\%$$

(B) Percentage of workers in N region to total industrial workers in the country;

$$\frac{8,000 \times 100}{2,000} = 40\%$$

Location factor A/B = 50/40 = 1.25

Since the *LQ* is 1 +, it means *j* industry has higher share in the *N* region.

Coefficient of Localisation

Zone	Total/Nation workers'000	j Industry workers'000
South Zone	6000	1000
East	4000	2000
Western	8000	500
North	2000	500
Tolal	20000	4000

Regions	% workers in reg. to all the country		Reg. % of workers in j industry in region to all workers in that industry	Deviations
Southern	30	–	25.0	+ 5 0
Eastern	20	–	50.0	- 30.0
Western	40	–	12.5	+27.5
Northern	10	–	12.5	- 2.5

Sum of positive deviations, negative ignored = 32.5

Coefficient of localisation $\frac{32.5}{100} = 0.325$

Not Significant: Less than one (1).

This industry can thrive in various region.

Coefficient of Localisation can be calculated as under:

(a) Calculate the percentage of all workers found in each region;
(b) Calculate the percentage of the workers of the industry in question in each region,
(c) Calculate the deviations of b from a (positive) and add up.
(d) divide the sum so derived by 100.

The end result is coefficient of localisation. High, medium and low coefficients will be found for different industries. Then their concentration and dispersal can be found. High coefficient means high concentration (low dispersal) and vice versa.

Critical Evaluation of Florence's Analysis

Florence has given us important statistical measures. The verbal explanation of the reasons for concentration and dispersal will also be necessary. He uses the work force as the indicator with which to measure the concentration and dispersal and it is not altogether satisfactory. Capital investment and output concentration or value adding are more important.

Florence takes administrative regions as the regions for calculating the concentration or dispersal. He does not take economic regions or natural regions for the study. An erroneous result can be found. If the industries are highly capital intensive, then low employment figures will prove dispersal, which will not be correct inference. The government measures which encourage or discourage the concentration and dispersal are not studied. Concentration and dispersal are good in their own places if they conform to the national socio-economic policies.

Yet Florence's measures are of great help in assisting and understanding the existing state of industrial concentration or dispersal.

Edgar Hoover's Theory of Industrial Location

Hoover attempted to combine Weber's treatment of the influence of raw materials with Fetter's market area analysis', the main result of which was the *concept of isotim* or a contour line of equal delivered price. Hoover gave a theory of location making use of "margin lines". There can be random elements in location decisions that undermine the value of deterministic maximization models. Hoover admitted such possibilities but asserted that random locational choices also can ultimately lead to efficient location patterns as the process of competition gradually weeds out the poorly located firms. Hoover in 1948 wrote in details about the significance of route layout, junctions, and long-haul economics. In Hoover's economics of location there was economics of relocation also and his views are more dynamic incorporating the effect of perfect competition. In his words:

> "Competition, in so far as it prevails, will reward the well-located enterprises and shorten the lives of poorly located ones. Even if new establishments were 10 be located purely by guesswork or whim or by sucking pins into a map at random, and if they were never relocated, some semblance of a reasonable pattern would still emerge as a result of competition."

Hoover took into account the costs of production and cost of transporting the output (cost of transporting the inputs to the manufacturing unit are included in the manufacturing costs), separately.

It is true that the cost, of transporting output over distance increases, but not always proportionately. It can go down per unit because of the economies of hauling long distances. The burden of loading and unloading is higher on hauls of short distances. If this is the case then possibilities of wider markets are created. If because of the differences in the gradient, per unit costs increases somewhere, the market cannot become wide.

If the cost of production/extraction goes up due to diminishing returns, the possibilities of competition over long distance get reduced. If the increasing returns are obtained, per unit costs go down and markets become wide.

If economies of scale/manufacturing and transport, are high, markets can be wide. However, in the long run they both rise and margin lines of market are to be determined.

If the increasing returns are obtained, then the cost per unit keeps on declining. The market widens and at *lower price.* The following diagram shows this:

Margin lines will turn upwards after the point of increasing return takes a "U" turn i.e. decreasing returns apply. Then the market widens only if the consumers are willing to pay more. They will pay more, unless some other producer is prepared to offer at a low prices.

We show cost/price on the vertical axis and market area in distance on the horizontal axis. If mineral is extracted at point *0,* and the cost of production is *x,* then the market range will be *OX.* As the cost of production rises due to higher demand, then the cost or the price will become *y, and* for selling upto OY market, the price will be *Oy.* The rise in the cost is inclusive of the cost of production and higher cost of transport. In any case, (even if there is less than proportionate increase in either cost) the transport gradient is represented by the horizontal lines, and with points extending upto *x,y,z* for *OX, OY* and *OZ* markets. If the points *x', y',* and z' are joined we get the margin line.

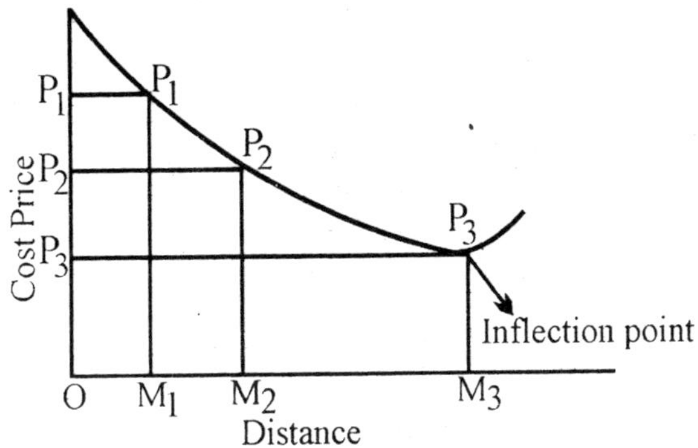

As the producer produces more, the cost of production goes down and price also goes down. The market widens. The producer earns higher total profits due to higher output effect. This continues till the point of inflection of costs.

Fig. 1

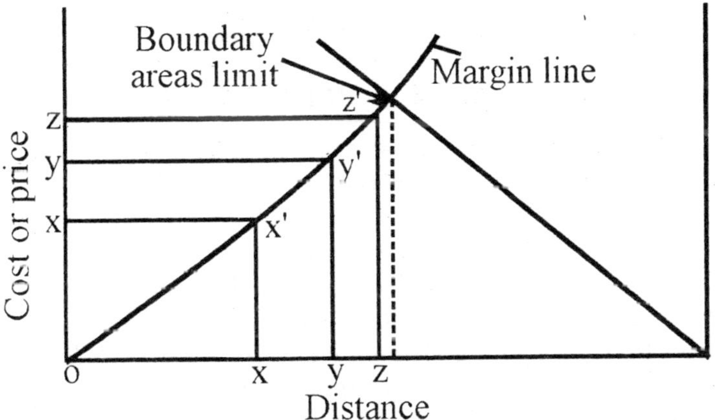

Fig. 2

If there is another source of mineral extraction, at centre *0'* then on the inverted horizontal axis facing *0* (because they are competitive), a similarly drawn market margin line intersects the market margin line of *0* centre. This is *E* point. At this point the delivered price of both the centres is the same. On all other points the delivered prices differ. *0* centre cannot transgress to the right of this point, while 0" centre cannot transgress to the left of this point.

In the words of Hoover

> "A situation in which margin lines rise steeply away from the point of extraction will encourage other producers to set up in intermediate locations to serve areas with relatively high delivered price, but if delivered price differs little with distance from the point of production, a small number of producers will tend to supply large market areas".*

POLANDER ON LOCATION

Swedish economist Polander wrote in 1935 about the factors which determine industrial location. His is also a contribution to the 'market area approach'. He is in the company of Fetter (1924), Hoover (1937), Hyson (1950), Greenhut (1952), and Losch (1955). Polander rejected a 'general theory of location'. *Polander emphasised the importance of linking economic development with location theory to understand the dynamic processes influencing the choice of the initial site and adaptation to change of the individual firm.*

Polander opined that societal development is a historical process. At any given point of time there exists an inherited physical structural framework. A plant which is already functioning cannot be dismantled and relocated elsewhere as high opportunity costs are involved. The market boundaries of a plant, are determined by the fixed plant

* E.M. Hoover: *"Location and Economic Activity"* McGraw Hill Co. 1948.

costs (costs of production, presuming constant returns to scale) and variable transport cost, a function of distance. The methodology may differ but in essence the conclusions are the same as in the Hoover's analysis.

Initially he assumed a linear market. When the assumption was relaxed, market area boundary becomes a line *(termed as isotante)* which is the locus point of points where the delivered prices from both the producers are equal and the gradients of delivered price can be seen as inverted conical surface with an apex directly above the point representing the factory.

GREENHUT ON LOCATION

This is an integrated approach in which location is not a function of just one variable. The 'least cost approach', can *be* valid only when the demand is distributed uniformly over the space. If the demand differs in various pockets of the space, industrialists may prefer to locate their plants where their sales are maximised, even though the cost of production may not be the least. The entrepreneur is concerned with total profits which need not necessarily be a function of low cost only.

Polander, Hoover., Losch, Fetter, Hotelling, Joan Robinson, Chamberlain, Lener and Singer (who wrote about monopolies oligopolies, monopolistic competition and imperfect competition), had (what is termed in Regional Economics) the 'market area approach'.

The punctiform markets of Weber are not considered relevant for maximisation. Many producers function in their semi-monopolistic markets, protected by transport costs burden that would fall on their rivals if they want to come to the territory of the 'limited monopolist'. The delivered price to consumers varies with the cost of overcoming distance from the factory. The manufacturer exercises monopoly control over that section of the market which he can supply at a lower price than his rivals. The spatial patterns of plant location and market areas is thus a product of variations from place to place in demand and of the locational interdependence of the firms.

Melvin Greenhut considers that not only the cost of production and the nearness to market count in the location decisions but three other factors are also important:

1. Cost reducing factors i.e., chances of achieving economies of scale and scope;
2. Revenue increasing factors, including government concessions; and
3. Purely personal reasons.

Greenhut has taken Marshall's analysis as basis for location decision. Transport costs matter in location when they constitute a good proportion of the total costs. Otherwise not the revenue maximisation but profit maximisation is the aim and the entrepreneur simulates such a location point and locates there.

ISARD ON LOCATION

Isard is an important name amongst the regional economists. He made historical surveys of the development of regional economics. He is also known for making use of the gravity concept and retail trade applications in his 'income potential model' and studied the spatial influence that one region can exert on another. Isard studied in details the economies of (1) location (ii) industralisation and (iii) urbanisation in juxtaposition. Isard integrated the inter-regional trade theory with location theory and also integrated the 'least transport cost approach' with the 'market area approach'. His work is ecclectic in nature.

Isard made important contributions in 1956, 1960 and 1969 to the theories of 'location in space economy' and 'methods of regional analysis'. He pointed out that there are always advantages and costs involved in choosing locations at different places. "Principle of substitution" comes to the rescue of the prospective locator. Isard takes the help of the game theory for developing his theory of location. As we know (a) buyers play game with fellow buyers to take advantage of prices/commodities, (b) sellers play game with fellow sellers to corner greater chunk of the market and to have a bigger share of profits, and (c) buyers and sellers play game with each other — buyers trying to maximise their use-values and sellers trying to maximise their exchange values. Locating the plant is a part of the game of securing advantage — all things considered together. Perhaps the game can be played under the supervision of a competent authority — might be the government or a techno-economic expert.

> *(Many of the theories of regional economists get out of tune with reality when we consider that now a days there is the problem of shortage of space also. In the regions of least cost, there may be no space, left for location or the government may not permit the same.)*

Since the games are not constant sum games, location decision remain uncertain. Location decisions are very complex now. In the words of Isard:

> "Clearly, game theory strikes at the heart of this situation. The several participants are the several units of production. Whether they be new units with whom no relocation costs are associated or existing units confronted with relocation costs, they interact engaging in various forms of collusive action. The bargaining which ensues is complicated not only because of the innumerable coalitions which are possible but also because of the different scales of agglomeration which are potentially feasible for each unit of production."*

* Game Theory, Location Theory and Industrial Agglomeration" Walter Isard in Richardson's. Reader, pp. 42-54

Isard makes some suggestions (while simulating several options of location of a hypothetical industrial unit). The regional planner should have a veto power to give final verdict in favour of or against a location plan. No location decision should make another region worse off. There should be such locations that we get *mutual improvement sets through 'incre-max' procedures.* From the "zone of incremax", the total profits will fall if location is outside a zone of maximum advantage. Two regions can also find a zone a cooperation in the matter of location. Isard says:

"Weberian analysis still contributes relevant analytic elements to what a modern-day agglomeration theory must contain. However, the game element must also be a basic component of such theory. It is essential that we understand fully both the conflict and cooperative elements present in the interdependent decision situation associated with any given agglomeration problem. And we also must have in the background theory which states under what assumptions on action spaces, outcome spaces, preference functions, objective and guiding principles can we project that 'rational actors' will take decision which lead (or do no lead) to agglomeration. Then, of course, as regional planners we must try to set up these conditions so that motivated individuals will out of their self-interest achieve the agglomeration goals we have in mind."*

Richardson on Location Constants with Reference to Centres

The words 'location constants' were used by Richardson for pre-historic nodal points. As we know, there are some such cities or concentrations of resource - oriented industrial installations which are to be taken as given. Most countries had some nodal points of economic activity even before industrial revolution started there. In due course of time these nodal points can develop into big centres or may

* Isard: in Richardson's *op. cit.*, p. 45.

degenerate into minor settlements, as new industrial points and agglomerations emerge elsewhere. Location constants are those nodal points which become indelible. In real life situations we find many nodal points unevenly distributed ever the space.

These location constants (related to centres) determine the spatial structure of the economy. Many urban centres developed as concentration centres of resources activity (mineral extraction etc.).

There is no universal tendency for the leading metropolis to be located near the centre of gravity of the economy. The 'market area model' of Loschian hierarchy does not hold good in all cases. Centres may not be located in such a manner that the transport costs are the least from all the surrounding locations. Those who plan economic activities in the centres which are already existing since quite a long time, have to adjust their operations in such a manner that their total costs may be less or if they cannot be do so, then they will have to manipulate the demand conditions. If the centre is to be taken as given, there is no choice of locating economic activities in such a manner that the transport costs are minimised. Then the transport costs themselves will have to be taken as given.

If the centre has to be accepted as given (location constant) then many factors and costs become 'dead weights' that are to be carried along. A port town is a location constant; an old administrative centre is also a location constant.

If there are several location constants, then the space cannot have the neat hexagons. Those locational constants are fixed locations that act as a focus for the agglomeration of population. In effect, they provide a few reference points in the space economy that would pre-determine the subsequent structural changes.

According to Richardson, locational constants, which

reduce the freedom of locations and make them bound, are of three types:

(i) Immobile natural resources e.g., deposits or a deep water harbour.
(ii) a long established city e.g., administrative centre of military town or a chance location,
(iii) Particular sites.

The concept of locational constants has been discussed by Richardson with reference to the location of cities and not with reference to industries.

Richardson avers that historically evolved patterns of urban settlement impose constrains on further development. The fact that the location of some cities is pre-determined (due to spatial irregularities and good natural sites as well as to historical factors) makes it much simpler to assign locations to the others, but it does distort the actual from the theoretically predicted spatial distribution.

The concept of locational constant was put forward by Richardson to point out that the Central Place Theory of Christaller and Losch are unrealist for all cases. The .spatial structure in which region is taken as homogeneous and the location of the centres as being evenly dispersed in terms of population as well as income is unrealistic.

There are only a few new cities or towns that can be planned from scratch. Most of the towns that we see around us have developed on the old sites. Hence we cannot find the smooth and un-differentiated surface. New development takes place at the old nodal points and many things are taken as given.

Regeneration and degeneration take place around these locational constants or old nodal points. Locational constants have several important functions in urban and regional analysis. According to Richardson, these are as under;

1. A general model of spatial development, by fixing some key locational co-ordinates, can be developed on realistic lines.
2. Instead of wasting time on the imaginary and absolutely archaic and abstract model of location, a realistic spatial pattern can be predicted. One cannot expect to find on the land surface the lattice networks of the Loschian Model.
3. We have to take it for granted that the spatial structure of the economy will be irregular and distorted and we have to make best out of this situation. Locations planned *ad novou* in hexagonal pattern can be shown only in abstract models of some theorists.
4. These locational constants affect the number and the relative size and spacing of urban centres in a region which in turn influence the intra-regional spatial distribution of industry and population and, may alter the total agglomeration pull of the region.

According to Richardson, these locational constants are the reason why all centres do not crowd together into one giant, centre.

In some cases new nodes can emerge: some planned ones and some unplanned ones. If rich deposits of a valuable mineral are found in a virgin territory, new centres can emerge. A new habitat can be planned after reclaiming a ravine type area. A new capital city can be constructed. Shifting villages may be organised into a good-sized village where sedentary economic activities can be practised. New areas can be taken up for horticultural development or for the development of any other activity and a new township may be developed.

According to Richardson, the locational constants are

immobile and they impose constraints on agglomerations. These constants are fundamental for understanding the dispersion process. The existence of transport costs on goods, services and the movement of people explain why these fixed locations attract other services. When they do, new centres of agglomerations may not come up easily.

More light can be shed on the spatial pattern of production of different goods and of the generation of services also when these goods are classified hierarcally according to the size of the market areas over which the goods and services are traded. Commodity and service hierarchy can be explained with the locational constants. Lower order goods restrict the scope for agglomeration since these must be produced locally. Hence many goods and services have to be supplied at all centres regardless of the size.

If the actual spatial pattern of locations of centres and industries is to conform to the abstract pattern, which is the construct of the academicians, then there have to be planned new centres to reduce the influence of the locational constants. The old centres cannot be 'dismantled"; they can be improved. It is really quite difficult to so plan the development of the centres that they conform to the text-book patterns drawn by some regional analysts.

The General Equilibrium Theory of Location

General equilibrium theory of price or of location is difficult to construct. Richardson, for the same reason, wrote:

> "The search for a satisfactory general equilibrium model of location has been *unsuccessful.* To achieve progress it is usually necessary to *trivialize space.* The problems raise some interesting issues *for the amusement* of the high priests of economic theory, but the *practical value is limited.* Readers primarily

interested in the policy relevance of regional economics may skip this topic".*

Actually any change in the locational adjustment should lead to endless readjustments throughout the space economy. Regional development itself is endless disequilibrium and locational equilibrium in regional space becomes difficult to conceive. In their *models of maps and atlases* some regional analysts argued that "market concentric circles" are actually break-even areas and in order that (a) all areas be served and (b) normal profits be available to all, there should be hexagonal areas *equal to circles !* Since regional growth is disequilibriating, to overcome the intractability of the problem, *inter-regional trade models* were attempted. These models assume fixed production and consumption locations, resources patterns and transportation networks, and constant technology.

In effect, they freeze the spatial structure of the economy and then seek to determine equilibrium prices and commodity flows. Thus, they abstract from locational influences. At best, they are special cases of a general location theory either where transport costs are zero and all inputs and outputs are perfectly mobile (a one-point Walrasian general equilibrium model) or where transport costs are zero commoditics are freely traded but factors are immobile.**

Regional economists studied the location of the firm and its market territories. At best they studied the influence of location of the firms nearby and their market areas. Entire space cannot be covered. Conversion of this limited partial equilibrium economics to general equilibrium economics is far from easy.

Losch tried to develop a *general theory of location, which he called 'ideal' but it remained quite unreal in*

* *R.U.E.*, p. 75.

** *R.U.E.*, p. 75.

practice. In his model, (a) all space exhausts through hexagonal superimpositions, (b) price equals average costs so that all firms earn normal profits, (c) market areas are of minimum size, (d) producers locate optimally, and (e) market area boundaries are stable. Thus even inter-regional trade can be taken into account However, even this model is not satisfactory:

> "This model neglects locational interdependence and agglomeration economies within industries. The model can cope with *inter* industry but not with intra-industry agglomeration. Also the population concentrations that result from inter-industry agglomerations will disturb the locational conditions. The model says nothing about the inter-relationships between commodity and factor movements.*

Actually locational equilibrium could result in the clustering and/or the dispersion of plants rather than the regular dispersion of the Loschian model. A general equilibrium model for a region is quite difficult to construct because the region is ever in a state of dynamism— much more than the closed economy of the country, if we want to so treat it. General equilibrium model determines prices mutually but in the regional general equilibrium model there are pre-determined prices coming from outside, Many regional economists used complicated algebra, geometry, econometrics formulations and maps but succeeded in obfuscating the issue. General equilibrium model assumes relocation, if need be. But this choice is available to firms. Households cannot have relocations options ! Verbal explanations can be more realistic than the general equilibrium models presented in mathematical language.

Locational Preference; Locational Constants with Reference to Industries

There are location constants with reference to industries

* Richardson: *R.U.F.*, pp. 77-78.

also. It is a well known fact of industrial development, that some industries got located at a particular place for no particular reason e.g., brassware industry at Moradabad or glass bangles industry at Firozabad. It was not the compulsion of the proximity of the raw materials there. There were no specific advantages relating to supply of power or creditor of transport facility. Some skilled labourers started their ventures there and the early start got a momentum. This momentum of an early start led to agglomeration or concentration. Now prospective entrepreneurs in the same line have to establish their units there only.

It is also seen that some centres acquire goodwill for the manufacture of certain types of industries. Discerning consumers prefer drugs manufactured by 'standard companies', frequently located in big cities. It is seen that even though the manufacturing units are located in the interior areas, a big city is chosen for headquarters address, if the new pharmaceutical unit cannot be located at metropolitan centre.

Entrepreneurs have preferences for certain centres where they can get all inputs of development as also lead a good life in an advanced centre of development. Sometimes the entrepreneurs have to prefer a centre which all others prefer. Losch also acknowledged this:

> "The mathematical determination of the optimum transport point, for example, is infinitely more impressive as a solution of the location problem but also incomparably *less* accurate than the statement that an entrepreneur, all things considered, will establish his enterprise at a place that the likes best".

Such preferences lead to location constants with reference to industries. Location agglomerations are promoted by inelastic demand, negatively sloping marginal cost curves, and low transport costs. *Uncertainty* reduces plant size owing to a reduced willingness to risk capital.

Diminishing returns to management decisions also force the same situation. To minimise risks entrepreneurs should establish new industries at the urban agglomeration sites. This reduces the 'friction of space' and uncertainly. Risks of peripheral locations are reduced. Better innovations are available at agglomeration points and, therefore, economies of scale are reaped in larger quantities. Profit position becomes secure. Even relocation of some firms is done not far from the centres of agglomeration. New industries imitate the behaviour of a successful. *Peer group* and even in the absence of external economies there may be tendency a agglomerate to reduce uncertainty.

Locational Interdependence and Hotelling Principle

It is not necessary that entrepreneurs should always be locating their plants where internal and external economies are the highest so that they can have least cost situation. How often do we see in real life that the new units are located where the entrepreneurs can closely watch the polices pursued by the competitors. Spatial differences in production costs and marked variations in demand may even be disregarded when oligopolies try to pry into the affairs of the competitors and locate their units where they will keep an eye over competitors. By locational interdependence we mean that the location decision of a new plant may be affected by locations chosen and policies pursued by its competitors.

H. Hotelling (1929) in his "Stability in Competition",* made certain assumptions to develop his theory of locational interdependence. (1) He took two or three firms only, (2) took market to be linear rather than areal and (3) costless and instantaneous relocation. Hotelling argued:

* *Economic Journal* Vol. 39.

> "Duopolists would agglomerate at the centre of a linear market even though this maximized rather than minimized transport costs because only with agglomeration would there be no incentive for one of the firms to jump over, and secure a larger share of protected market."*

When there are a few firms a question arises whether they would disperse and share the market in a monopolistic way or would they cluster to keep an eye over the rival? If two firms are already located apart from each other and the third firm locates near any one of the two firms, will the third firm also relocate the plant near them? Will the firms cluster from dispersed position or disperse from the clustered position? Even more fundamental is the question whether the firms will try to optimise and enjoy semi-monopolistic positions in space or will be actual distribution itself will differ from the optimum condition, because the rivals are to be closely watched? Will the old producers *'hop over' (according to the hopping over hypothesis)* to be near the rival *Lerner and Singer* argued that in such situations there will be more 'instability' then stability. Both tendencies can be seen — of locational interdependence and of independence (for optimisation)..

It can be found that some entrepreneurs prefer to locate their units in such a manner as to create a monopolistic type market for them; others want to be near the competitors rather than being away. While we see tendencies towards agglomeration as also towards dispersion, the *hopping over sequences' are* not admissible because the costs of relocation cannot be wished away: they are not only positive but heavy indeed.

The hotelling principle of Hotelling is actually examining the cases of agglomeration. These points were emphasised.

Hotelling	*Dispersion*
1. When the demand is inelastic	When the demand is elastic and cost reduction is a necessity.
Higher prices can be charged from customers.	
2. Low transport costs. .increase	High transport costs which costs over distance.
3. Tied resources.	Ubiquitous resources.
4. Uncertainty forces new entrepreneurs to by near the rivals.	Certainty of getting demand
5. Least cost places. Higher production costs elsewhere—more than the savings in the transport costs.	Highest demand places.
6. High population density	Low population density
7. *Same, price everywhere.* If same prices are charges from all customers (e.g., prices primed on medicine bottle), It is discrimination against nearby customers. If possible then hotelling.	*Different prices* If people of different places refuse to pay the same price as persons of other places pay, then dispersal.

10

Location Quotient

DERIVATION OF COEFFICIENT OF SPECIALISATION FROM LQ • COMPARATIVE ADVANTAGE AND LOCATION LABOUR COEFFICIENT • COEFFICIENT OF SPECIALISATION • LOCALISATION CURVE

Coefficient of Geographical Association; Indices of Dissimilarity and Segregation of Occupation Coefficient of Redistribution, Population Concentration; Coefficient of Differentiation

Location quotient (LQ) is used for measuring the relative specialisation region in selected industries. Employment is conventionally used as unit of measure. Total employment in the country becomes the reference variable in comparison to which employment in a selected industry is studied. The findings of regional and national levels can be compared.

Employment in a selected industry is related to total employment by means of a simple ratio compulation. Then the ratios at the regional and national levels are compared by means of another ratio computation. Thus, the location quotient is the ratio of these ratios.

LQ demonstrates a region's share of employment in a particular industry. Sometimes it is used as a *Self-sufficiency ratio* also. The base that may be used for the computation purposes can differ from region to region and problem to problem. It can be used to compute the employment in primary, manufacturing, construction or any other activity.

Various Methods

One way of calculating the LQ is as under:

$$\frac{E_r}{TE_r} \div \frac{E_n}{TE_n}$$

E_r is employment in industry in region

TE_r is total employment in the region.

E_n is employment in industty in the nation

TE_n is total employment in the nation.

There is another method also:

$$\frac{\frac{E_r}{E_n}}{\frac{TE_r}{TE_n}}$$

The above expression actually means:

$$\frac{\frac{\text{Employment in industry in the region}}{\text{As a fraction of emp. in industry in the nation}}}{\frac{\text{Total employment in industry in nation}}{\text{As a fraction of total emp. in the nation}}}$$

Here E_r and E_n refer to employment in industry in the region and nation respectively.

TE_r and TE_n refer to total employment (reference variable) in the region and nation respectively.

We can take examples: (If employment in industry and total employment is expressed in thousands):

	Emp. in Industry		Total Emp.	
MP	150	E_r	260	TE_r
India	10000	E_n	*24000*	TE_n

One way:

$$\frac{150/260}{10000/24000} = \frac{0.577}{0.416} = 1.385 \text{ or}$$

$$\frac{150}{260} \times \frac{24000}{10000} = .577 \times 2.4 = 1.385 \text{ or}$$

$$\frac{18}{13} = 1.38 \qquad \frac{3600000}{2600000} = 1.38$$

Other Method:

$$\frac{150/10000}{260/24000} = \text{Any one} \quad \frac{0.95000}{0.01083}$$

$$\frac{150}{10000} \times \frac{24000}{260} \quad \text{or} \quad 0.015 \text{ x } 92.3$$

$$= 1.38 \qquad \text{both } 1.38 \text{ or so}$$

Under certain assumption, location quotients may be interpreted to indicate relative location specialisation in particular industries and thus to service as a proxy indicator of such industries as are under study.

Location quotient is thus a statistical devise for measuring the relative specialisation in selected industries in a region. It measures the degree of concentration of an industry in a particular region — or the regional concentration of a given industry compared to the total national specialisation in an economic activity.

Industries which show high LQ in a region show concentration effect and this concentration constitutes the industrial base of the region.

Industries which show low LQ show that the industries are dispersed in the region or have low concentration here. Alternatively this will suggest that the concentration is elsewhere.

LQ identifies one or more sets of inter-related industries in which a region is specialising. Specialisation will show that all those Weberian factors which lead to location of specialised industries in a region, are available in plenty in the region — raw materials, skilled labour, power, strong demand base (wide market), and other scale economies which bring cost advantage. High LQ will show high linkages effect also.

Different regions will show specialisation in different industries and the LQ will be an index. Some arithmetic inferences are obvious. The LQ can be equal to, greater than, or less than 1. In these cases the degree of specialisation of the region is naturally equal to, greater than or less than the national position.

LQ, if more than 1, will naturally show that in that particular industry, the region will have comparative advantage and that this industry can be the export industry of the region. A regional import industry will be expected to have a location quotient of less than 1. A local service industry would be expected to have a location quotient equal to one.

Location quotient is one technique which can demonstrate a region's share of employment in a particular industry. It can also be used as a *self-sufficiency ratio.* As the regions are different or problems differ, the base of calculating the LQ also differs. One way of putting the calculation of LQ is that *numerator represents the region's percentage share of total employment in industry. The denominator will represent the region's percentage share of the total national development in the concerned activity.*

LQ is the product of the division of numerator by the denominator. For example if in MP.:

(a) the employment in mining as percentage of total employment in construction in India is equal to 10% (numerator); and

(b) the number of persons employment in the primary sector as a percentage of total employment in the primary industry in India is equal to 7.5% (denominator); then

10% ÷ 7.5% = 10/7.5 = 1.3

Similarly if the State's total in manufacturing employment accounting for by the steel industry is 12.5 per cent and the percentage of national total in manufacturing accounted for by the steel industry is 7.2 per cent the LQ will be 12.5/7.2 or 1.7 : Good position.

If the value of the LQ is less than one, the region's share in that particular industry is *less than fair* or *less than proportionate.* If it is equal to one, the State's position exactly duplicates the nation's position. If the LQ is more than one, the region's share is *more than fair* or *more than proportionate.* The LQ shows the dominance of a particular activity *of a sector* in the region's structure of that sector. The LQ along with other industrial location techniques can be used for greater understanding of the industrial structure of a particular region, and its capacity to export.

LQ which measures relative specialisation of a region in a particular industry to the total national magnitude can also help us in understanding the industrial structure of the industrial economy of a region. If time series data are available, LQ enables us to compare the position of the region over the time period. Low LQ is an indication of the dispersal of industries and high LQ in a region shows concentration and this may be due to comparative advantage of location.

Since the data about the number of workers employed (employment) are commonly and readily available, LQ is generally calculated with reference to employment variable. However, any other variable can also be made reference variable e.g., (a) output, (b) value-added, (c) capital investment, (cl) gross profits, (e) total wage-bill etc. Usually the total employment becomes the reference variable.

The overtime position can be compared with the help of the LQ. In the previous example the LQ for one particular year (now made the base year) was calculated as 1.385 Using the same technique we can compare the positions in two years.

	Employment in x industry		*Total employment*	
	1980	*1990*	*1980*	*1990*
MO	150	400	260	520
India	10000	12000	24000	36000

$$\text{For 1990:} \quad \frac{\frac{400}{520}}{\frac{12000}{36000}}$$

$$\frac{.76}{.33} = 2.30$$

The LQ has further improved. We can also say:

(a) A high LQ suggests the industry to be export industry.
(b) A low and less than 1 LQ suggests that the industry may not provide sufficient output and it will be import industry;
(c) If the LQ one it suggests a local service industry.

Using the same technique the LQ can be used for comparing the *inter-district position also vis-a-vis a State.*

Using different variables, the technique can be used to find out the (i) relative per capita income positions (welfare and distribution study) or share in manufacturing also.

This very simple technique can become basis for different types of studies. It throws light on the *relative* position — whether the region has concentration (greater than 1) or is a loser in dispersal scheme (less than 1) or is in more or less the same position as the nation (=1). Any characteristic can be chosen as proportion of urban or rural population to the total population. In India one good use can be made about the concentration of scheduled caste or scheduled tribe population in certain pockets as compared to the country as a whole. Suppose we want to find out the concentration of scheduled caste population in a sub-region. Then:

$$LQ_i = \frac{P_{ij}}{P_i} \div \frac{P_i}{P} = \frac{P_{ij}}{P_i} \times \frac{P_j}{P}$$

P_{ij} = No. of persons in they *jth* category (SC) in area i (sub-region);

P_i = Total population in all the categories of area *i*

P_j = Sum of persons of category *j* in all the n areas i.e., population of region under category *j*.

P = Sum, of *P*. in all the area i.e., total population of the region in each category.

If persons belonging to SC ans ST category (P_{ij}).

In a State are 2 crore out of the total population of the State (F), of 6 crores, and the population of the SC and ST persons in the country is 16 crore (P), while the total population of the country is 80 crore [P], then the LQ for this characteristic will be:

2/6 : 6/80 = .3333 ÷ 2 = 1.6665

i.e., there is 66 per cent extra concentration in the State of the persons belonging to *j* category.

The researchers can find different location quotients for different things e.g., for Soyabean in *MP;* for cement production in *MP;* for Transport equipment production in *MP;* or for food production in MP vis-a-vis the country.

LQ can be computed for any level of disaggregated economic activity i.e., crop-wise agriculture or any sub-activity-wise. It can also be calculated for the sub-regions. In some cases the reference variable can be anything else than the national average i.e., the State average or position in parent region. The reference variable will differ as our needs are different. For a service LQ, the appropriate reference variable might be population. The reference variable can be number of households rather than population if the service is related to households than to population e.g., supply of cooking range. This reference variable can be median household income also. When the analysis is oriented towards productivity considerations, revenues, (or value-added, or unit-output measures) could serve as reference variables.

When the LQ is being used as tool in linkage investigations, employment or output in a linked industry might be appropriate reference variable. LQ can be calculated for the diverse things as these:

(i)	movie seats	per 1000 persons;
(ii)	mid-wives	per 1000 child-bearing women;
(iii)	cold-storages	to area under horticulture.

LQ can help highlight regional relative inefficiencies and it can focus on the potential import substitute or products with export - expansion potential. LQ can give us an idea about which industrial activities require concentration or dispersal and about which industries further detailed study is necessary. The study is very useful in the context of linkages analysis, economic: base analysis, input-output analysis, mix and share analysis. LQ can be computed with regard to any reference variable. It can be computed for different times or for areas. Not much time, money or manpower is required for this because not much elaborate data are necessary.

However, far reaching inferences should not be drawn from this. It is only a rough and ready indicator. Much will depend on the selected variables of specialisation and reference variables as also on the choice of the area. Different regions differ in tastes, needs, levels of income family sizes, nature of resources, labour practices etc. and thus LQ should not be used to compare various things which have obvious inconsistencies.*

Derivation of Coefficient of Specialisation from the Location Quotients

This can show the degree of concentration of industry in a particular region. This method measures the extent to which the distribution of employment by industry in a region *deviates from the national pattern.* The coefficients of specialisation can be estimated as follows:

1. *Numerator* represents the ratio of employment in industry in the *region* to employment in primary/manufacturing/construction/service sector in the region.
2. *Denominator* represents ratio of employment in a particular industry *nationally* to employment in

---

* Isard: *Op. cit.,* Ch. 7.

Avrom Bendavid: *Regional Economic Analysis for Practitioners. Praeger Publishers* 1974.

T.W. Buck: "Shifts and Share Analysis —A Guide to Regional Policy" *Regional Studies* IV, 4, Dec. 1970.

primary/manufacturing/construction/ service sector in the nation.

The numerator is subtracted from the denominator to arrive at coefficient of specialisation. If will values between 0 and 1 without any regard to positive or negative sign. If the region has an industrial mix identical with the nation, the coefficient would be 0. If all the employment in a region is nearly concentrated in one industry, the value of the coefficient would tend to be 1.

1. Suppose the ratio of employment in agriculture in Madhya Pradesh to employment in primary sector is .74 and the ratio of employment in agriculture to employment in primary sector in the nation is 0.61: then *numerator is 0.74 and denominator is 0.61:* Then: 0.61 – 0.74 = 0.13 ± signignored.

This coefficient will show the extent to which the economy of Madhya Pradesh in relation to the country is specialising in agriculture.

The LQ throws light that if a region is more specialized than the nation in the production of a particular good, then it "exports" to other regions. *However, a theory of exports cannot be built on LQ because it assumes that the pattern of demand in each region is identical to that of the nation, that productivity per worker in each regional sector is the same as in the national industries, and that the nation is a closed economy. LQ cannot be used for developing international trade theory'.*

The Comparative Cost Principle of Specialisation and Location

This principle is fundamental yet simple. Intact it can be said that all subsequent developments in the theory of inter-regional and international trade are additions and alterations in this principle.

Isard, the famous regional economist, considers this of greater profound importance than various coefficients curves and indices. He wrote:

> "It should be noted that the principle of comparative costs is superior to the labour coefficient, coefficient of location, coefficient of specialisation, index of diversification or the localisation curves. This is because the former is analytical and basic while these coefficients give a limited description of a measure." *op. cit.*, p. 233.

If two regions/countries possess absolute advantage in costs i.e., produce both the commodities cheaper (taking two-country and two commodity model) then one country will specialize in the production of that commodity in which the comparative advantage is greater.

Per unit

Country	*Wine*	*Cloth*
Porguta! (costs in S)	80	90
England (costs in S)	120	100

It can be seen that Portugal produces both the things cheaper but the comparative advantage is greater in wine. Its cheapness is 33.33 per cent in wine and 10 per cent in cloth. The deamess of England is 150 per cent in wine and 111 per cent in cloth. Hence Portugal should specialize in the production of wine. It should leave the production of cloth to Britain. In this case it is not Britain which will exercise the first choice about specialization; it will specialize what is left to it by Portugal. The fundamental principle is *specialize (and export) in the production of that commodity in which the comparative advantage is the greatest* Thus the other commodity is to be imported and the principle is

$\frac{40}{120}$ (i.e. 120-80) = 0.3333 x 100 = 33.33

$\frac{10}{10}$ (i.e. 100-90) = 0.1 x 100 = 10.00

import that commodity in which the comparative disadvantage is the least. If wine were to be left by Portugal, then its comparative disadvantage would have been the highest and comparative advantage in cloth would have been the lowest. The opportunity cost of specialisation (equal to the income of the next best alternative) should be the least. This is the principle of individual specialisation also (a doctor can be a good compounder but he engages a compounder so that he can concentrate on the best suited activity. This is the reason why a botanist engages a gardener).

Haberler in his 'opportunity cost theory of international trade' emphasized that specialisation should be partial in case of production being under decreasing returns (which usually is in the long run). His other essential point was that international trade will take place only when the international terms of trade are higher than the domestic terms of trade.

Heckscher and Ohlin (pronounced OLEEN) argued that the comparative advantage should be in prices and not merely in costs. They also argued that inter-regional or international trade takes place when differences in the international terms of trade and domestic terms of trade (also known as barter terms of trade, domestic exchange ratio, or domestic rate of transformation) differ because of the differences in the factor endowments. They argued that the comparative advantage in costs/prices can be secured only when (i) abundant factor is used intensively and (ii) scarce factor is used sparingly only where imperative. In other words countries rich in natural resources can export resource rich goods (minerals); countries rich in labour resources can export labour - intensive goods and countries rich in capital and technology can export capital - rich goods. In their system (i) partial specialisation leads to full employment of labour and natural resources and

(ii) complete specialisation leads to their partial under-utilisation.

Once the line of manufacture in which the comparative advantage is the greatest is identified, the projects have to be located in the area of least cost. It can be argued the other way round also i.e., if the export industries are located in the area of least cost, they can secure comparative advantage in prices in international trade. Specialisation alone can promote export and increase income propagation. Least cost location for specialisation and export was emphasized by all classical and neo-classical economist writing on national (inter-regional) and international trade.

The loss in importing things dearer from outside can be got compensated by diverting capital, labour and natural resources to the production of that commodity for which a person/region/country is best suited. *Comparative advantage will be secured by locating the industries where the raw material, labour, capital, organisational personnel and infrastructure facilities abound.* The principle of comparative advantage had been the over-riding principle of location of economic activities in the past, till the governments of various countries stalled intervening. Now the erstwhile socialist countries too will allow location on the principle of comparative advantage.

Labour Coefficient

The labour coefficient measures the advantage of cheap labour in a region. Cheap labour has a pull effect, when the advantage of cheap labour is sufficient to outweigh any locational disadvantages. The lowest average labour cost per unit of commodity establishes the existence of advantage of cheap labour.

As is well known, low per unit of cost of labour is not the result of low wages but of higher productivity. High wages, if they induce higher productivity, can reduce, instead of increasing, the cost of production.

Weber developed the concept *of Labour coefficient.*

In his words;

> "It is the ratio of the labour cost per unit of product to the locational weights of that unit. The locational weight is the sum of the required weights of localized raw materials plus product."

High labour coefficient means higher productivity of labour and this will lead to savings in the labour costs. In such cases, the disadvantages which result from not locating the industry in the minimum transport area may be exceeded by the cost advantage in real payment to labour.

The industrialists can calculate the savings *on labour wage bill* as a result of the high labour coefficient if figures of output, persons employed, wages paid etc. are available with him. As against this advantages, the disadvantage in locating an industrial unit in cheap labour area and incurring additional costs of transportation can also be calculated. The locational weight per unit of product, multiplied by the transport rate and net additional distance involved in location away from a minimum transport area gives the additional disadvantage in costs.

Savings on labour account should exceed the losses on transport account, then only the labour coefficient is significant for location decisions. If labour coefficients between two regions are identical, then transport cost advantage and advantage in other types of costs become important. Various regions can be ranked in terms of labour coefficients and it can be a good indicator of the comparative advantage, but only when juxtaposed with other indicators.

Coefficient of Localisation

> "The coefficient of localisation is a measure of relative regional concentration of a given industry compared

to some national magnitude such as population, land area, manufacturing employment or income."

Any base denominator can be taken e.g., employment. We can compare the (a) percentage distribution of employment by region in a given industry, (b) with the regional percentage distribution of the total national manufacturing employment (also known as percentage distribution of the base magnitude).

If we suppose that there are four regions where the percentage of employment in industry; is 20,30,35,15 respectively and (b) percentage of total employment in the country's manufacturing employment is 15, 20, 30, and 35 respectively, then the differences will be:

5, 10, 5, and(-)20.

The sum of positive *OR* negative differences is 20 and divided by 100 it will give the *coefficient of localisation as 0.2,* which is for all the four regions.

When the value of the coefficient is zero [0], the geographical association is complete and when the value is one, no geographical association exists.

If the denominator is population, or the area or income percentage, then it is not necessary that the coefficient value is the same.

If there is low coefficient of localisation, then it means there is more dispersal than concentration (low concentration), and further diversification in various regions is possible. Since the industries are not tied, new units can be located elsewhere also.

Coefficient of Specialisation

While the coefficient of localisation measures the concentration of *one* industry in a region, the coefficient of specialisation measures the degree of *overall* specialisation in the regional economy, considering *all* the industrial groups. *The opposite effect of specialisation is diversification and hence we can construct the index of diversification also from the coefficient of specialisation.*

Because of the differences in the natural resources, — labour skills, capital endowments, demand, and socio-cultural conditions different regions differ.

(A) Same industry is differently distributed over regions; and

(B) Different regions have different concentrations of different industries/economic activities.

Territorial division of labour which was discussed in great details by the founder of Economics — Adam Smith — is based upon over all regional differences. Some industries are known by regions and some regions are known by industries. Some industries thrive only in certain regions. There is nothing which prevents carpet industries being developed in Madhya Pradesh but there is no labour like Kashmiries here. Bangles industry is technically a footloose industry but it is concentrated in Firozabad or brass work industry is localised in Moradabad. The specialisation of Bengal in jute industry is due to natural factors — jute grows there and since jute has low value in large bulk the industry is to be concentrated here. Thus there are 'tied' specialisation and specialisations just by 'accidents' or chance. The industry of specialisation becomes the *basic industry* for the region — which generates higher income and employment through higher production and exportable surpluses.

If a few industries provide almost equal measure of employment in a region, then none of the industries is 'basic' and there is no specialisation in the region. If one industry provides 45 percent of the total employment of the region and the rest of the 55 per cent employment is provided by (let us say in equal measure) by 11 industries, then specialisation is clear. There can be two industries of specialisation — both of them providing 35 per cent employment each and the rest of the employment is dispersed in several industries then specialisation can be said to be in two lines of manufacture.

Some regional analysts developed 'index of specialization' (opposite of it 'index of diversification') on the basis of the difference between (a) minimum requirement in an industry and (ii) actual employment. For example if the minimum requirement of employment in iron and steel industry is 10000 workers but the region has 30000 workers, the coefficient will become 3 but conventionally coefficient of specialisation is between 0 and 1.

If all the employment of the region is concentrated in a single industry, the coefficient will be 1.

If the region has a proportional mix of industry and identical with the country, the coefficient will be 0.

> *Coefficient of specialisation measures the extent to which the distribution of employment by industry groups in a region deviates from the national distribution (or sub-region from a regional distribution).*

The method of calculation of the coefficient of specialisation can be as under:

(A) *Numerator:* It is the ratio of employment in industry in question in the region to employment in primary/ manufacturing/construction/ service industry in the region.

(B) *Denominator:* It *is* the ratio of employment in the industry in question (same as in the numerator) nationally to employment in primary/ manufacturing/ construction/service industry in the nation.

To calculate a coefficient of specialisation, the numerator

is subtracted from the denominator, without regard for sign, yielding values between 0 and 1. If the region had a mix of industry identical to that of the nation (or sub-region to region), the coefficient would be 0. Alternatively, if all the employment in a region is concentrated in a single industry, the value of the coefficient of specialisation would approach 1.

Numerator Denominator: 0.05 (50000/1000000) Coefficient of specialisation: 0.125 Not significant.

Item	*Region*	*Nation*
Emp. in j industry in region	35000	50000
Total emp. in Manufacturing	2,00,000	10,00,000

Numerator: 0.175 (35000/20000)	0.175
Denominator: 0.05 (50000/1000000)	- 0.050
Coefficient of specialisation: 0.125	———
Not Significant	0.125

(Crore persons)

Item	*Region*	*Nation*
Jute	2.0	2.2
Agri. Emp.	2.5	32.0

Numerator: $2 \div 2.5 = 0.800$

Denominator: $2.2 \div 32 = 0.06875$

Coefficient of specialisation: 0.80000

High degree of specialisation. - 0.06875

= 0.73125

It would be much better if this coefficient is calculated with reference to *value-added rather than with reference to employment* because it is possible that employment may be high in one line of economic activity but income may be quite depressed.

Narrow specialisation or territorial division of labour is termed in regional economics as *burst type of economies.*

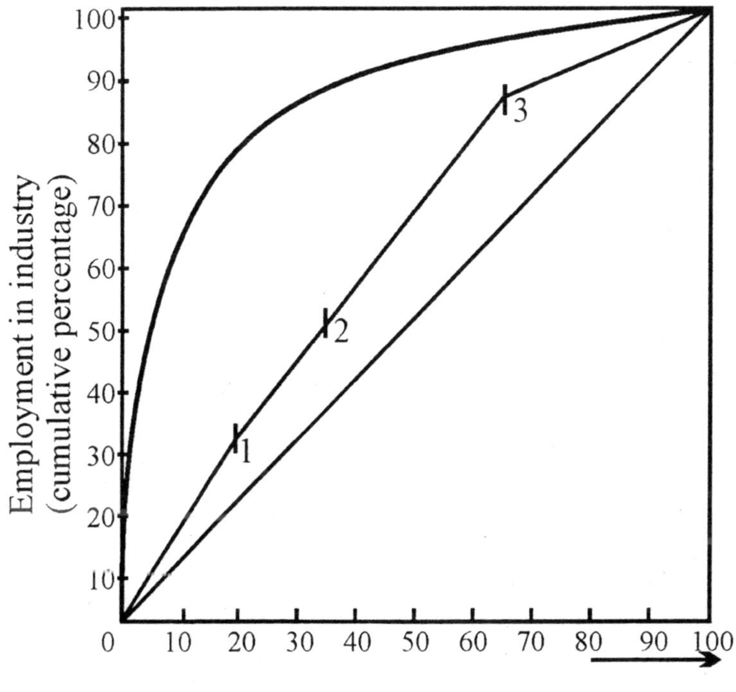

Fig. 1

From the defence point of view or from the point of view of economic self-sufficiency it will be highly desirable if (unless it is a deterministic compulsion due to natural endowments) there is as much diversification as possible.

Localisation Curve

In a box diagram, we can draw a line of 45° which will show that a given industry is located or distributed regionally exactly the same as the base magnitude (or denominator distribution), whatever it may be — population, State domestic product, employment. In such a case the location quotients will all be unity.

To plot this curve, the location quotients of different regions have to be found. Then on the basis of the values of the LQ, the regions are to be ranked. A curve is to be plotted on the basis of the cumulative totals of the rank-percentages. If A, B, C and D regions have location quotients of 1.33: 1.5: 1.17: 0.43 respectively then B, A, C, and D become the rank orders. Their percentages are 30: 20 35: 15 and the cumulative totals to be plotted will be:

30: 50: 85: 100.

They will be plotted on the vertical axis with reference to the percentage of the country shown on the horizontal axis.

There can be a "power coefficient", a "fuel coefficient", or any other type of coefficient for a region — industry by industry. All these coefficients will have a numerator — the average cost of the specific resource input per unit of output, of product; and as a denominator the locational weight associated with the unit output of product. The combined coefficients decide the locational advantage. If a region possesses advantages of cheap labour and transport disadvantage. The weights of the numerator will have to be decided and the combined advantage should be greater than the combined disadvantages. It is the basic principle that those coefficients will decide the location which give the net advantage.

Coefficient of Redistribution

The coefficients of localisation for the two time periods

are compared; then the deviation is calculated. The resultant figure is the coefficient of redistribution.

This can be done for population distribution between States. In each census the population that lives in a State is a certain percentage of the population of the country'. These percentages vary in each census — mostly due to net migrations. Taking one percentage distribution as the base, the deviations of the other percentage distribution can be computed. *Summing up of all positive OR negative deviations, yields a figure which, when divided by 100, can be designated as the coefficient of redistribution.* If the coefficient is zero, it means there is no redistribution; if it is one, then it means complete redistribution.

Eminent *demographers* Hauser and Duncan and Hoover and Florance calculated several coefficients taking different numerators and denominators.

Coefficient	*Which measures*
1. Coefficient of geographical association	Share of employment in manufacturing — industrywise
2. Index of dissimilarity in occupation	Occupational pattern of different States
3. Index of segregation of occupation	One special occupation versus all occupations in an area. Relationship of "One to total"
4. Coefficient of Redis- and redistribution	Share of population in the country change there of between two censuses or, the share of gain-fully employed person: to dependents
5. Coefficient of population concentration	Statewise population related to area
6. Coefficient of differentiation	Share of ethnic groups of population e.g. Hindus versus Muslims: or SC ST in total population

11

Mix and Share Analysis Shift and Share Analysis

Mix analysis is like studying the cropping combinations. There can be three seasonal cropping combination viz., kharif season (sowing in rainy season), rabi season (sowing in winter season), and *Zaid* crop season (sowing in summer).

We can study the overall mix of crops in the total output crals + pluses, which become foodgrains. A part of it, if given to animals will be feedgrains. Various aspects can be examined.

Production:	physical measures of crops.
Outputs:	Sum total of all crops, season-wise, then year-wise, both in terms of physical production and then in money values.
Productivity:	Outputs ÷ area in acres/hectares.
Value-Productivity:	Out puts x prices = money values.

Employment is the most important variable of mix analysis in a nation and in various regions.

David B. Creamer in 1940s and Perloff in 1960, illustrated these concepts.

E is for reference variable employment–

One important practice of studying the mix is to understand the difference between the (i) expected growth in employment and (ii) actual growth in employment, between

(a) Nation and Nation
(b) region 1 and region 2
(c) nation and regions.

We write

G for growth
A for actual
N for nation
R for region

Then

(a) GEN – GAN
(b) GER_1 – GAR_1
(c) GEN – GAR_1

We can write them as under also

Gne – Gre
Gna – Gra

Mix analysis studies *structure;*
Share analysis studies *change in* structure

With reference to regional economies, following position are good

GER_1 > GEN
GAR_1 > GAN

That will mean that the region is doing better than the nation. *It must have been a region of modern sunrise industries and high productivities.*

Shift and Share Analysis

Usually the shift is studied between the (i) actual of something e.g., employment or income generation or production and (ii) the potential of the something on a particular date. For example we can view ex ante a 9% growth rate in GDP in January 2008, for the financial year 2008-09. The *ex post* position will be revealed only after 31st March 2009. The evaluation and enumeration may take one to two months.

The shift can also be evaluated for the actual state between two time periods. For example, the shares of primary sector in two years were an under (suppose)

2005 – 2006	2006 – 2007	percentage shift
GR 25 p.c.	24.2 p.c.	24.2 - 25 (-) 0.8

Thus the comparison can be between

(i) the actual and the expected (potential) or
(ii) the actuals of two time periods, current state with the benchmark (base year) date.

> The shift and share values are add or subtract values ± . Shift and share analysis begins with a baseline value for expected component/indicator of growth. This can be for nation/region or nation versus region.

A matrix of shift will expand horizontally as we take more time periods and vertically if we take more indicators/variables.

- If GDP is expected to grow at 9%.
- If last year's growth rate was 7%.
- If growth rate in *e*' in *i* industry was 8%.
- Then with 9% it should be 10.3% g.r. in e' (employment).
- If total employed were 10,000, then 10.3. - 8 = 2.3

should be the growth in employment i.e. 230 persons.

- If actual employment grew by 180 persons, it was short by 50 persons. It was $\frac{50}{230} \times 100$ or 21.74% less or $\frac{180}{230}$ = 0.7826 - 1 = (-) 0.2173 x 100 = (-) 21.74.
- If actual employment was of 260 addition persons, this was + 30 and $\frac{30}{60} \times 100 =$ 13.04% extra. $\frac{260}{230} \times 100$ is 113.04 = 100 = 13.04 extra.

All these things can be presented in much rigorous form. A simple thing need not be made obfuscating.

Instead of linking employment to the GDP, the employment of (say) in Tamil Nadu's automobile industry can be linked to the national automobile industry.

1. If Gra > Gre or 6-5 = + 1. We can put it : Good.
   If Gre < Gra @ 5-6 = + 1 actual rate is more by 1. This is positive
2. If Gre = Gra @ 7 -7 = 0. The position is just right.
3. If Gre < Gre @ g - 9 = +1 for region.
   Gre = Gra Region did better if the expected regional growth rate was realised.

R. Actual rates should be > than expected in N or R

Advanced regions lead in growth
Poor region lead in declaration

Nothing success like success for advanced regions. Nothing fails like failure for backward regions. Poor sectors usually record slow progress when nation is professing well. In such a case the external push is necessary. Massive investment in a good project/or many projects or activities and functions will provide the necessary stimulus and the "trigger-effect."

Balanced regional growth aims at reducing leads and lags. That actually means that the growth of a fast developing region is not to be brought down. What would have been better is that poor regions should received unbalanced (higher) incentives and investments than the already well developed regions.

The rules are simple:

- Divergence* in regional investment more in favour of the poor, will lead to convergence in incomes of various regions.
- Convergence** in investment in some regions, particularly advanced regions, will lead to divergence in incomes.

No policy can ensure complete equality in incomes, particularly inter-personal incomes. There are three modes of development.

A. *Individual mode.* Individuals as production units work for their betterment.
B. Community mode: Communities work for their common good. They solve their common problems. This is becoming rare now a days.
C. *Intervention mode* or government investments. *All* developing economies have massive corruption leakages now from the funds allocated for the development of regions, sectors and people. That is the reason why backwardness and destitution/poverty could not be ended.

Actual (ex post) growth rates are seldom equal to expected or planned (*ex ante*) growth rates if the targets fixation was over-ambitious. There is always a coveted mix and share and shift and share. Regional economies

---

* Dispersal or decentralisation.

** Concentration or agglomeration

aims at realisation being in conformity to the coveted M&S, (which are expressed in quotients/ratios/percentages). Shifts can be measured thus.

G = $R + S_d + S_p$ whereas $S_d + S_p = S_t$ total

G = Growth (say in employment)

R = Total employment in a region that would grow at the same rate as in the nation

S_d = *Differential shift or locational / regional component of the shift.* + plus - minus (whatever) difference in the region away from the nation. If regional growth in employment is 3 while in the nation it is 2, it + 1 for the region. If these figures are 1 and 2 respectively, then it is -1 for the region, locational advantages/disadvantages bring this change. It can be >< or equal.

S_p = Proportional or specialisation shift. One region may be specialising in jute/tea/bangles..... If specialisation industry grows faster/slower than nation as a whole, the +/- effects will be there.

Some calculation can be had as under.

	Nation		*Employment in million*				
Item / Sec.	*$Time_1$*	*$Time_2$*	*Percentage mix* *T_1* @	*T_2* @	*Total in mill.* *	*Percen-tage* **	*Points change in share* ***
1. Agriculture	150	120	41.7	29.3	-30	-20	-12.4
2. Industries	120	150	33.3	36.6	+30	+25	3.3
3. Tertiary E	40	60	11.1	14.6	+20	+ 50	3.5
4. Tertiary S*	50	80	13.9	19.5	+30	+60	5.6
	360	410	100.0	100.0	+ 50		00.0

*E for economic
S for social T_1 @ for time 1 and T_2 for time 2.

1. Total change in e = 410 - 360 = 50 million.
2. @@ are calculated thus (say for

   industry. $\frac{120}{360} \times 100 = 33.3$

   $\frac{150}{410} \times 100 \quad = 36.6$
3. * Total change for agriculture is 120-150 = - 30; for industry 150-120 = + 30; for TE 60-40 = 20 and TS 80 - 30 = 30 or + 30.
4. ** is calculated thus in *percentages,* $\frac{-30}{150} \times 100$ = -20%.

   $\frac{30}{120} \times 100 = 25; \frac{20}{40} \times 100 = 50$ and $\frac{30}{50} \times 100 = 60$ p.c. (all)
5. *** points change in shares

   Agri = 29.3 - 41.7 = -12.4
   Ini = 36.6 - 33.3 = 3.3
   TE = 14.6 - 11.1 = 3.5
   TS = 19.5 - 13.9 = 5.6
   ———
   00.0

Change in Total 000 because distribution of percentage mix in T1 & T2 is 100 in each case.

Exercise For the Region

Emp. in mill.

Sector	*Total* T_1	*Empl.* T_2	*Percentage shares* T_1	T_2	*Total mill.*	*p.c. change*	*Points diff.*
1	2	3	4	5	6	7	8
1. Agri	25	25	39.7	32.5	—	00	-7.2
2. Industry	20	22	31.7	28.5	2	10	-3.2
3. T.E.	8	10	12.7	13.0	2	25	0.3
4. T.S.	10	20	15.9	26.0	10	100	10.1
	63	77	100.0	100.0			00

Improvement 11% 17.5%

$\frac{77}{63} \times 100 = 18\%$

Region

$\frac{63}{360} \times 100 = 17.5$ 17.5

$\frac{77}{410} \times 100 = 18.8$

We can compare the difference in the nation with region (see column 8)

TABLE 3

		Nation		*Region*
1.	Agri	-12.4	- 7.2	Region less unprogressive
2.	Industry	3.3	- 3.2	Region in bad position
3.	TE	3.5	+ 0.3	Region Very Little Dev. 0.3/ 3.5 = 8.6%
4.	TS	5.6	+	10.1 Region very progressive

Percentage alone do not matter

Absolute figures also matter.

Total employed: Total adult population is more important

Mix or shares is shown in columns 4 and 5 of tables number 1 and 2.

Shifts are shown in columns 7 and 8 of the table 1 and 2.

Shifts between Nation and regions are ultimately best shown with commentary in table number 3 of this chapter.

Shift and share and mix and share analysis show differences between the (a) expected and the actual states between (b) nation and the region—sectorwise. The reference variable can be VAM (Value added by manufacture) or income also.

* Mix and share analysis is for a *point of time.*
* Shift and share analysis is for "*over a period of time.*"

Shifts and share analysis or mix and share analysis do not explain qualitative changes. Literacy percentages in the nation and the regions may improve but the dichotomy between the quality of (i) students of rural and urban areas, (ii) English medium school, and the language of the region, is not explained. Good students can be from anywhere but the poor students become disadvantaged. Spoiled brats of the rich can also become bad students.

Critical Evaluation

1. *Richardson is a vehement critic of this analysis and calls it*
   "a part time game for small boys with pocket calculators." (see pp. 202-06 "Regional and Urban Economics).
2. The mix and share and shift and share analyses give us growth differentials but these findings are not earth shattering. They do not throw light on the causes and consequences of these differentials.
3. Suppose the employment in any activity may be going down and more so in a region (double-drag) but the people may be migrating elsewhere in more productive jobs of high value-adding, mix and share or shift and share *figures* will not reveal the truth of something better happening. These analyses take only employment variable normally.
4. These analyses have bred scores of research papers of little consequence. M&S and S&S analyses are totally inappropriate for projections. *The so-called advantages of the technique are illusionary.*
5. Shfts cannot be stable over time. S&S analysis tells us nothing about the capacity of a region to retain

growing industries, much less how to attract them. S&S analysis had a long run yet it is *dangerous* (Richardson) as a guide to policy.

This primitive technique should be abandoned .... it is a biased and inconclusive method of analysis.

Yet we can write something in difference. We can not only study the M&S and S&S with reference to employment, but also with reference to outputs and or incomes. These analyses can be with reference to more than time period.

The nation vs. region positions can be understood with references to (i) inputs-outputs relations, (ii) sales (iii) value-adding by sectors, (iv) gross revenues vs. net earnings.

The ratios can be analysed.
Causes behind them can be
understood. One can decide
which laggard activities need
be pushed in backward
regions. Nothing is totally useless.

PART-III

Regional Flows

12

Commodity and Service Flows Vs Monetary Flows and Capital Flows

Markov's Chain Model

The Export Base Theory and the Theory of Regional Multiplier are based upon the "commodity and service outflows" or the exports of a region. It is a well known fact of life that regions and people cannot have autarky and that they specialise. Therefore, they sell the goods and services of their specialisation to acquire money and then they command the goods and services produced by others. Thus there are inter-personal, intra-regional and inter-regional flows of goods and services. *Monetary flows are reciprocal of the flows of goods and services, unless they are unilateral flows.* Unilateral flows are grants, subsidies and special loans and transfers to a region or to persons from other regions.

The commodity and service flows and the resultant monetary flows determine the consumption, savings and investment pattern of the region. The employment and spatial structure of a region is manifested in the level and pattern of inter-regional flows. A time series analysis of the inter-regional flows will not only give an idea about the exports and imports of a region but also about the interdependence and linkages between the regions. A hierarchy of market helps in the flow of goods and the degree of complementarity and competitiveness between the regions can be judged from these flows.

One great problem of estimating these flows is to obtain data. Railways, road carriers, and other transport agencies (relating to shipping, inland waterways, or air transport) can provide this data. Goods move across the 'borders' of the regions in private carriers e.g., bullock carts or on headloads also. A combination of the information obtained from the carriers, through sample survey and through complete direct counting for a certain period of time will be necessary to obtain the data. Normally much of the trading and transporting are without proper billing, to avoid the payment of various taxes and hence extra efforts are necessary to obtain as correct data, as much as possible.

The commodity and service flow analysis can enable us to know the points of origin and points of destination also. However, this can be done only in a limited way. It is impossible to maintain accounts of flows from one settlement to all other settlements. The bigger the territory about which the accounts are being prepared the less the problem, provided data are available. Tables can be prepared both for the inflows and the outflows by modes of transport.

Open borders with many regions, different modes of transport, non maintenance of the accounts by the people, suppression of the information about the trading, and transportation of goods with the help of self-owned means of transport are some of the difficulties in obtaining precise data. Many goods and services move *through* a region but not *into or from* a region. Besides a question arises viz., what is the need for maintaining detailed accounts of the movement of goods and services between various settlements, particularly when the expenditure and use of manpower will be immensely costly. These efforts can better be directed towards the production. It will be sufficient to have a rough and ready idea about the inter-State flows. Accounts of even inter-district flows will be of less practical importance.

Most of the earners would know about the 'weights' of the commodities earned by them but prices may not be known unless the invoices sent to the buyers are inspected. Goods and services sold on oral contract cannot be known.

Ubiquitous goods are transported over very short distances to the market while the specialized commodities are transported over long distances. There are certain discernible patterns of commodity flows— developed regions import more inputs and export more outputs while the volume is less in less developed districts. Backward regions export primary products and import manufactured products. Centres of great industrial activities have larger inflows and outflows to distant places. Inflows and outflows will be greater into/from those regions where population is large and has high purchasing power also. Efficiency and cost of transport will also determine the directions of flows and the volumes thereof.

Monetary Flows

Since there are unilateral and unrequited monetary transfers, all monetary flows are not opposite of the goods flows Relatives send money to dependants. Rich nations transfer funds to the poor countries; Central government transfers funds to the State governments and the State governments transfer funds to various local bodies and persons. Transfer of wealth and titles to wealth between individuals and institutions involve monetary transfers. Financial institutions also transfer funds and then there are monetary flows due to the sale and purchase of shares and debentures—which are not commodities. Thus there are capital and non-capital transfers. Since many organized financial (banking and non banking) institutions are involved, record of monetary transfers may be constructed a little bit easily than the records of the commodity and service flows. Yet, it is to be noted that transfers of the so-called black money may not be recorded and a lot of money may be carried in private carriers or on the body of the persons moving across the regions. Many a times the monetary and fiscal policy measures are to counteract the 'undesirable flows' dictated by the market mechanism. As such, not all the monetary flows also can be recorded.

Credit-deposit flows from the banks, credit deposit flows from such NBFIs (Non-Banking Financial Intermediaries Institutions like UTI or LIC), post-office transfers, transfers from the Centre to the State or vice versa, transfers of leading corporate bodies etc. can be recorded, though they give a partial picture only. Monetary flows can give an idea about the income earning and distribution pattern.

Even best of the matrix tables cannot record correctly the total monetary flows, as problems associated with tax evasion will not make this possible.

Linkages

Regions and settlements are linked together not only through network of transport and communications but also in all respects. The flow of goods, services and money is a measure of linkages. Regions have physical input-output relations. Rough and ready estimates about India suggest that about one-third of the NNP of India moves from one State to another. It is because of inter-regional linkages that spurs and leakages work in regional multipliers, of which timings of working and reversal are difficult to specify. Different regions have differing income 'generated' and income 'accruing'. If the region receives income through exports (with profit), then income accuring will become greater than income generated in real terms. Unilateral transfers make all the difference between the income accrued and the income generated. Inter-regional linkages, forged by transport and communications network, are actually the proxies for the regional dependence. The fortunes of different regions are inter — linked. Highly adverse or favourable economic conditions in one region are bound to affect other regions also, in varying degrees. These linkages undergo a change over time and the changes are not because of the causes emerging in the same region.

Outputs produced in one region are used as inputs in other regions, giving rise to *forward production linkages.* The output of one industry in one region (e.g., of steel in Chhatisgarh) may give rise to some other activity in other region (coal mining)) in Bihar, giving rise to *backward production linkages.*

If there is a textile industry in one region, there will be intense cotton growing activity in some region or in the same region. Then there will be activities related to the production and transportation of inputs like seeds, fertilizers, implements, pesticides etc. These are *upstream or backward production linkages* Further backward linkages of fertilizers can be traced and the process goes on. The textile industry will supply cloth and there will be production of sewing machines for them; or garment manufacture; of shops selling garments and so on. These activities will further require additional activities. *These are downstream or forward linkages.* However, there is no hard and fast rule about which industry or activity should be regarded as the central activity. It is the designation of an activity as 'central' which will decide the *forward and backward production and distribution linkages. The scales of operations will decide about the commercial, institutional, financial and technological linkages.*

Various centres collect and distribute /disseminate goods and services and forge strong *distributive linkages.* The direction and volume of trade determine the *commercial linkages.* Financial institutions determine the inflows and outflows of deposits and credit and determine the *financial linkages.* Various government, semi -government and private institutions are involved and their relationships determine the *institutional linkages*. Technology' is developed and transmitted from certain centres determining the *technological linkages*.

Mobility of Capital

Movement of capital does not involve those personal psychological barriers which come in the way of mobility and migration of labour. Capital moves where there are greater chances of earning profits or interest International capital movement is largely based upon the rate of interest and the currency in which the returns are available. In inter-regional migration, the quality of money is the same: only the returns differ. The cost of moving homes and hearths matter significantly in the migration of human beings but the transfer costs of capital are just bank commissions, for which concessions may be available for large transfers. Here also there is a neo-classical theory; the capital flows between regions/places will continue till the rates of interests are the same everywhere. Now this aspect loses significance where the rates of interest are fixed by the Central Bank and the commercial banks cannot offer higher rates of interest to lure capital. In case of the unorganised money lenders, the movement of capital will become related to the movement of persons because normally, the money lenders lend to the people living around them. Besides, the amounts involved are low and the money lent is usually for consumption purposes rather than for capital investment.

If the cost of transferring capital over the space is the same; if capital market is highly developed; if the knowledge about investment, opportunities is freely available; if the capital is supplied on competitive basis in all parts of the country at the uniform rates (as in the case of nationlised banks of India), then *capital flows will depend upon the profitability and expectations about profitability*

It is not the movement of capital *alone* which is

responsible for convergence or divergence. It depends upon *all* factors of production — technology, management, entrepreneurship, capital and labour. Left to itself the theory maintains that initially there will be divergence in the per capita income but ultimately there will be convergence. This is possible only when the factors keep on being mobile *till the marginal returns are the same.* In case of the capital the movement of capital will continue till the rate of interest and profits in all lines of manufacture are the same everywhere.

Capital flows are the consequence of savings. Savings differ in region to region — and more precisely with persons to persons. Somewhere there can be more savings than can be invested while at other places the requirements of the investible funds may be more than the supply of investible funds. Banks and other non-banking financial institutions mobilise these savings. The banks indirectly bring together the surplus units of the economy and the deficit units of the economy: banks are the buyers and sellers of the *use* of money. The banks create credit. Without credit, only the money proper would have been the medium of exchange and money would have been *warehouse certificates* i.e., the proxy of the goods and services produced in the *past*. Credit enables a borrower acquire purchasing power in advance before the borrower has acquired a legitimate claim over it. When credit is taken the present goods and services are commanded (purchased) not with the past goods and services (as a result of which selling, money was acquired) but with future goods and services to be produced lateron.

This is the reason that *the credit-deposit ratios differ over the region.*

People of backward regions may complain that the banks take away the savings of the poor districts to be invested in the rich districts. Thus the credit-deposit ratio is high in the advanced regions rather than in the backward regions. The bankers, on the contrary, say that this is narrow view of the whole thing. If money is invested in developing a port at a particular place, the investment should not be ascribed to that particular coastal district but to the entire region which exports through that port and uses imports made through this port.

Savings in a region depend upon the income of the people and their marginal propensity to save. The investment depends upon the resource availability, capital availability, and the desire of the entrepreneurs to invest The government projects can be located on the basis of the decision of the government, if they are of the foot-loose variety. *Private movement of the capital will continue till the marginal productivity of the capital in all lines and in all the regions is equal. The government sponsored capital movements will continue till the social marginal productivity of the capital is the same over the entire space.*

The following diagram illustrates:

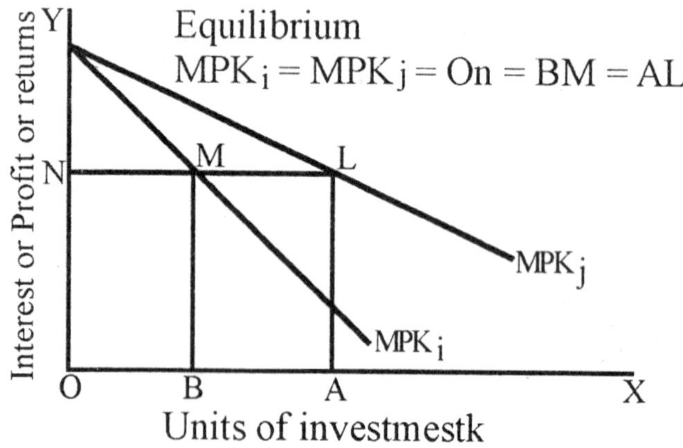

Diagram: 1

The diagram shows that the marginal productivity of capital is lower in region i than in the region j. Thus the first region receives *OB* capital while *OA* capital will be invested in the second region, which has higher productivity.

Movement of capital for investment purposes can be greater than or less than the internal savings. A backward region will receive more capital for investment from outside the region and in a planned economy such transfer of resources may be from the Central revenues and/or newly created money as a result of the budgetary deficits.

Some regional analysts have termed the neo-classical theory as being *absurd* and this itself is an absurd accusation. There may not be precise equalisation of the marginal productivity of capital in different lines of manufacture and in different regions — but the assumption was about the "long period". It cannot be denied that it is this theory which remains in the minds of investors that they do not over-invest or rush to invest where they find there is under-investment. Once it was difficult to sell even the limited number of imported watches and clocks in India. [In Bhopal where the author resides, there used to be one clock in one Mohalla! Now all rooms of the houses of even upper middle class family have wall clocks.] Then they started being sold on large scale. Thereafter, further investment in this line of manufacture stopped. Now once again new watch factories are coming up. This is because there is demand for them and if there is demand for them, the marginal returns of capital in this line increase. The reshuffling of the *risks, uncertainties and investment* go according to the expected profitability or productivity of the capital.

Marginal productivity theory never claimed that if the marginal productivity of capital declines in a certain line of manufacture, the *sunk capital* will also be transferred; futhere inflow will stop. *If possible and needed,* there will be dismantling of the fixed capital, only when all demand has tapered off and the zero demand is not expected to become positive in future.

As we have seen the capital flows on the government account aim at the equalisation of the government account aim at the equalisation of the *socio-economic marginal productivity of capital* and hence may not conform to the simple model of equalisation of interest/profits/returns.

Some writers have gone so far as to say that the marginal productivity of the capital in big and small irrigation projects cannot be equal because indivisibilities involved in the former are high (lumpy capital). This is wrong: capital investment will not be the same; marginal productivity will be the same. If the small projects have higher marginal productivity, there will be more investment in them till percentage returns from both types are *more or less equal.* One point of limitation of the neo-classical theory is that since there are *imperfections of all types,* the equalisation of marginal productivity becomes difficult even in the rough and ready sense. Uncertainties, risks, political pressures and pulls, technological changes, etc. make the equalisation of marginal productivity a difficult task. *Yet implicitly investors do follow the principle.* Some regional analysts opined that even if the profits are high in under-developed regions, the capital will not move there because the region is under-developed. The problem with such analysts is that they never were investors. If high profits are expected and there are no security and nationalisation risks, capital *will* move.

There is difference between the movement of capital for "directly productive activities" and movement of capital for the "development of the infrastructure." The infrastructure development requires movement of capital sponsored by the government and this will move not for the high private marginal returns but for the high socio-economic returns. Private capital moves to those areas and lines of manufacture where the infrastructure facilities are available. If infrastructure facilities are available and if the promise of profitability is there, there is no reason why capital should not move, unless there are administrative and tax barriers.

It is also argued that because of the high risks and uncertainties, marginal returns cannot be equalised. Risks and uncertainties add to the costs and if the returns are still higher than these costs i.e., if the returns can take care of these costs, then capital moves despite risks and uncertainties. Risks and uncertainties are there almost in all lines of investment and investors invest only if they are capable of meeting these risks and uncertainties. Capital movement takes places after these are taken into the reckoning.

Some exceptions of course can be admitted e.g., for the goodwill of the place of manufacture, the capital may move to the agglomeration centres and some entrepreneurs may transfer capital to their native places rather than elsewhere. However, here again it can be said that if the agglomerations *have greater diseconomies* than economies, capital will not move. The ghost of neo-classicism will follow those regional analysts who want to criticise neo-classicism. Some pseudo-socialists do not want to touch neo-classicism with a barge pole even when socialism failed to deliver goods because the fundamentals of supply side economics were neglected (1991 total collapse year).

If the capital movement is controlled and directed, then it will be guided by political considerations also and if it is the movement of the private capital it will be guided by marginal returns/interest/profits etc. Once again it may be mentioned that all those capital movements which apparently give the impression that they are not following the principle of equalisation of marginal returns, may be aiming at the equalisation of socio-economic *marginal returns.*

However, transfers of funds are not on the basis of the returns; but transfer of money is not transfer of *capital.* Some regional analysts have written that transfer of *funds* from the higher order governments to the lower order governments under statutory, discretionary and planned transfers are not following the principle of equalisation of marginal returns. Then what is the principle, logic or strategy behind this? None else except to develop infrastructure capital, invest in the human capital formation (better medi-care and education), and increase the productive capacities. The productivity in the backward regions is low. All transfers of funds are meant to increase the productivity in such regions: per person, per unit of land, per unit of time, per unit of inputs and in various lines of manufacture. *Funds are transferred so that they become capital.* The neo-classical theory is not about the transfer of funds which are not to be used as capital i.e., it is not about the transfer of funds which an earning member may send from a city to the family in village so that consumption needs of the family be met.

Capital movement will follow location of industry only in so far as it as still profitable. If the marginal returns of capital in all lines of manufacture or in all regions are not equal, this is none of the fault of the neo-classical theory. Infact this is what will introduce dynamism and will induce capital inflows and outflows. Capital movements will always follow the principle of returns — economic or socio-economic. The theory does not apply for transfer of all funds but to transfer of funds to be used as capital.

MARKOV'S CHAIN MODEL OF INTER-REGIONAL SAVINGS AND CAPITAL GROWTH

Regional economists argue that the study of how savings, capital growth and investment take place in a limited space have to be treated differently from national economy model.

The nation is 'closed' with reference to the region which is more 'open'. When we talk about the national savings, we lake macro figures but when these are discussed with reference to space economy, we know that certain regions are too poor to save substantially while certain other pockets of the country 'over-flow' with the savings. That is the reason why, in a free economy, rate of interest would be lower where savings abound and hence they are transferred to those regions where they are needed and command higher rate of interest. Thus it is quite common to find that in some regions investment exceeds local savings and vice versa. This is possible through the transfer of savings/capital/investible funds.

Capital formation also differs from region to region, though in a macro national study we would take one figure of "capital formation as a ratio to national income". The capital formation can be studied in real and/or financial terms.

Regional investment has several features which become peculiar to the region. In many cases investment is attracted towards *agglomerations*. Investment in backward regions can be greater than the savings of those backward regions. This is through fiscal transferences. Thus different regions can be *net debtors or net creditors*.

Regional location of investment is thus independent of the regional savings. However, if investment is to exceed the savings then extra savings should flow-in from outside (either from the foreign country or "foreign" region). High mobility of savings because of the openness of the regions is responsible for this divergence.

Regional investment decisions are based upon previous investment in the region. New 'directly productive investment' follows the investment in socio-economic overhead infrastructure/external economies. *There is a definite sequence and interdependence in investment.* Normally, as the region gets adequate infrastructure facilities, autonomous investment follows. Then imitative, supplementary, complementary and even speculative investments follow.

Markov breaks the direct link between savings and investment in a region. He emphasizes that there is *a sequential interdependence in regional investment pattern.* The regional investment pattern is usually related to some locations *which may partake the nature of the 'locational constants'.* Thus regional investment acquires a certain amount of "durability" and the spatial structure changes, but rather slowly.

Regional investment is not primarily determined by the generation of savings at a particular point but by investment opportunities (if the profit motive is supreme) or where it is ordered to be made (if social returns are important and the government decides the investment).

Markov's model is not deterministic but probabilistic. Depending upon a host of assumptions about the investment opportunities, a savings flow matrix was constructed to show how savings can flow out or flow in for investment.

Financial institutions play a leading role in deciding the investment pattern in a region. As is well known, the financial intermediaries e.g., banks and insurance corporations or unit trusts, buy and sell *the use of money.* They borrow funds from those who have surplus savings but cannot use them because they are too small or the savers are not venturesome. On the other hand there are venturesome persons, who require more money than they can save.

The financial intermediaries unite these 'surplus units' of the economy with the 'deficit units' of the economy. *In the transient region* of Markov, savings are not all absorbed or invested. Savings flow from *non-absorbing regions to the absorbing regions.* In the absorbing regions frequently, investment is greater than the savings generated by the same region. Coefficients of profitability (expected) will attract the savings. Strong agglomerations promise higher returns and the 'coefficients will be higher' in the absorbing regions. *The absorbing regions can themselves be arranged in declining order of profitability. Within these regions there will be avenues of investment which will be more profitable than others.* Thus investment will be in the most profitable line of manufacture/ activity and in the most suitable region.

Markov explains why investment has a tendency to agglomerate or concentrate. Instead of investment getting diffused, frequently it so happens that savings flow to the absorbing state and transient regions have "zero values of coefficients of profitability expectations'. *In a non absorbing or transient regions investment is either not there of is very less. It is a region which is in reversible state* i.e., in future funds can flow, there can be investment and it will become absorbing region inflow of investment and the hithertofore 'transient' region can become 'absorbing region'.

The absorbing regions become 'irreversible' for investment in fixed capital.

However, the same is not true for *hot money* flows. Hot money is that investible money which flows freely between regions/countries in pursuit of the maximum gain/ interest. It is the portfolio investment theory of international bonds *which has been presented by Markov in regional economics as the 'chain model'.*

Hot money is investment in such portfolios that it does not get sunk and can be transferred at will to different places/regions. The *chain model of inter-regional flows is for non-absorbing regions. The same region can be 'absorbing with respect to one type of investment (fixed) but transient for another type of investment (financial portfolios).* Thus all regions are transient regions for financial portfolio investments.

Each regions has (a) its own volume of savings, (b) invests these savings in the region itself and in other regions, and (c) receives savings from other regions. A cross matrix of these regions can tell us about the savings which a region has and which it distributes over other regions. From this we can deduce how much total savings come to a region.

If the construct a similar matrix after a certain interval, then we can deduce from it the *change* in the positions during the two time periods. The transient matrix will show the volume of total savings transferred between different regions.

These movements of savings can be simulated also on the basis of certain assumptions. We can indulge in an exercise in which we can 'forecast' ex ante the likely generation of savings and their inflows/ outflows between various regions. In this case the matrix will become 'probability matrix; or P Matrix.

A time may come when exogenous disturbances cease and inter-regional short term movements of funds will tend to settle down in a state of equilibrium. If new disturbances come, then equilibrium may not be reached. *Some transient investments may become fixed investments and investible funds go down but they are replenished with the new savings.* Such processes go on.

Columns show savings going to different regions. Rows show Investment, coming from different regions. For example, E region saves Rs 155 as but investment there is Rs 500 as it is a net receiver.

Rs. Crs.

1→ S↓	*A*	*B*	*C*	*D*	*H*	*Total*
A	20	30	10	25	15	100
B	80	50	10	10	150	
C	10	10	40	20	20	100
D	10	50	15	65	10	150
H	100	100	50	150	100	500
Total	140	270	165	270	155	1000

Similar matrix table can be constructed for another time period.

1→ S↓	A	B	C	D	H	Total
A	20	30	10	25	15	100
B	—	80	50	10	10	150
C	10	10	40	20	20	100
D	10	50	15	65	10	150
E	200	100	50	150	200	700
Total	240	270	165	270	255	1200

In the changed situation investment rises to Rs. 1200 as Investment in E rises by Rs 200 as out of the A region, come additional, Rs, 100 as out of the E region itself, come additional Rs 100 as.

Markov has his own terminology. Savings invested in fixed and sunk assets is 'absorbed and locked'. Such savings are 'lost' and they 'disappear'; i.e., are not available for transfer and circulation. Savings which are invested in portfolios of various types are 'non-absorbed' and 'transferable'. In case of the sunk assets, the savings-investment process is irreversible. The investment climate (opportunities, profits, interest, tax concessions) will help in all savings getting absorbed in different regions. Usually the savings will be transferred from the 'transient regions' (states) to the absorbing regions (fixed states). When all savings are utilised, the process is exhausted and an equilibrium is reached — which itself will be transient as fresh savings will emerge in net additional terms. If there is decline in savings, then less savings will flow to transient and absorbing regions. Thus increment in the capital stock is equal to the long term savings of different regions: thus,

$$dk_i = S_i + S_{ii} + S_{iii} \ldots\ldots + Sni$$

In Markov's illustrative model, only one region is absorbing. Other transient regions are contributing their savings. Thus in the absorbing regions the increment in the capital stock will be equal to the savings generated in the region itself plus savings generated in other transient regions. As all savings of the transient regions are absorbed in the absorbing region, the entire process become irreversible for that much of the stock of savings/capital.

This investment in the absorbing region is sequential in character and is also influenced by agglomeration economies. Not only the private entrepreneurs but even the financial institutions help in the process. It is not the rate of interest alone or the rate of profit alone which is responsible for transfer of capital from all transient regions to one absorbing region. Agglomeration economies and investment climate there are responsible for this.

Critical Evaluation

The most serious criticism of the Markov's chain model is that he assumes that there is just one absorbing region—the region of agglomeration. All other regions are transient regions in his models. The fact is that all regions are transient regions and all regions are absorbing regions at the same time—not fully but partially. Granted that the model is 'probabilistic' and not 'deterministic', yet it is a far too abstract an exercise.

Inter-regional flows are seldom correctly recorded, even with the help of the financial institutions. Investment in stocks, inventories, real estates are not fully disclosed. If the matrices are to be constructed on simulation basis then many experts will make their own hobby horses run wild: amok too. In the absence of any reliable data base, it will be tempting to cook figures of hypothetical values.

In Markov's model investment is the result of the availability of the economies of agglomeration. In a space where investment is being deliberately getting decentralized either because of the incentives offered by the government or because of disincentives, the basic principles of Markov prove to be wrong. Markov's model is neither a comprehensive theory of agglomeration, nor of external economies, nor of the generation of savings, nor of the transfer of savings, nor for investment.

How much long or short a chain of investment can be in different regions at different times or over a period of time? The chain can get elongated or can snap short. These factors are not analysed by Markov. The interaction of the market mechanism and the controlled mechanism can not be estimated. All that Markov said was that some areas receive more investible funds than others!

13

Migration: Typology, Interfaces, Causes, Ramifications, Models, Measurement Methods

I. Introduction, Typology and Socio-Economic Interfaces
II. Causes of Migration: Push and Pull Factors
III. Repercussions and Ramifications of Migration.
IV. Models of Migration. Models of:
(1) Ravenstein, (2) Neo-Classical Economists, (3) Raimon, (4) Fabricant, (5) Blanco, (6) Lowry. (7) Zipt. (8) Stouffer. (9) Lee, (10) Lewis, (11) Todaro, (12-13-14) Bogue. Blau and Duncan, (15) Gravity Model.
V. Measures of Migration: Direct and Indirect.
VI. Cumulative life time *versus* Decadal Internal Migration. Gross and Net; Rates of Net-Redistribution Differential Selectivity: Streams, Counter-streams.

I. INTRODUCTION: TYPOLOGY AND SOCIO-ECONOMIC INTERFACES

Migration is not a sojourn for pleasure or business; nor it is a temporary shift from one locality or habitat to another. It is a movement from one place to another for non-temporary earning and living. It may or may not combine occupational mobility that is, a persons can be vertically mobile (promotion) without involving migration and can be a migrant without involving occupational mobility.

There are three components of population change namely, births. deaths and migration. Internal migration does not change the population of the country as the international migration does not change the population of the world. National migration is largely free. [It is not free in certain States of India, though]. In USA certain regions have been marked for red Indians and non-red Indians cannot "migrate to take their lands". People leave places to seek better socio-economic prospects. Sometime they move out from very bad conditions to uncertain future at different places. Migration an important component of the change in the size and distribution of population in a country, adjusts "people to environment" while the process of economic development adjusts "environment to the requirements of the people." Half the population, that is, of women, migrates after marriage unless the husband's home is in the same town. Net internal migration (balance of in-migration and out migration) changes the distribution and structure of population of the country and of the regional settlements. Net international migration (balance of immigration and emigration) changes the size of the population also of the country. International migration is now subject to great restrictions and hence cannot alter the size of population of different countries in a big way. Both types of migration redistribute people in terms of resources, labour force participation, industrial attachment, job opportunities, housing facilities, etc. International migration now is more an instrument of policy than a product of individual initiative. Inter-regional migration is both a cause and consequence of differences in the rates of development of different regions. Structural changes in employment, income generation, savings, capital formation, consumption, investment, production, exports, imports, and sectoral composition of domestic product are both migration-inducing and migration-induced.

The highest component of migration is social that is, of brides who have to move out of their cities, towns or villages to other cities, towns or villages. There is movement from lower order habitats to higher order habitats generally but seldom does a girl of a city moves to a village after marriage, unless the family was on a temporary stay in a city as a menial or manual workers.

> Generally migration is a movement away from a pain economy to (at first) less painful economy. Lucky ones can move from pain to pleasure economy in one go. Then there is migration from one type of pleasure economy to another type, usually better. All migrations even the socio-cultural migration of brides should involve some better economic status or else that change in status or place will not be acceptable unless it is distress migration after a natural disaster.

TABLE 11

Typology of Migration

Type of Migration	Destination	Migration Selectivity
1. Rural to Rural (R-R)	Other rural habitations	* Rural Brides. * Migrants to "better" villages.
2. Urban to Urban (U-U)	Other urban habitations	* Brides * Inter-city migrants. * Migrants from lower order, urban areas to higher order urban centres.
3. Rural to Urban (R-U)	Urban centres	*[Most important type]* * Persons pushed from unprogressive to progressive economic environment. * Persons pulled by expectations for better future. * Brides: Students. * Labour for informal sector. * Most other types of migrants.
4. Urban to Rural (U-R)	Rural areas	* Frustrated migrants R-U. (Back migrants) * Persons receiving rural postings for dev. jobs. * Back to their moorings.
5. Wandering/ nomadic	Any	* Migrants from hostile eco. environment. Nomads.

6. For resource search	Site of work better resource regions	* Young pioneers * Slaves and indentured labours * Distressed/expelled persons.
7. Mass Flight	Urban centres. Places of safety Settlement areas.	* Minority and discriminated. * Suffers of calamities. * Expelled persons.

Note: Most migrants show persons selectivity.

Migration has resulted in genetic fusion of races. There are inter-marriages between black and yellow races; black and brown races; black and white races; yellow and white races; yellow and brown races and so on. *Migration becomes "influx"* when push and pull factors force a very large number to migrate. Migration adjusts "people to environment"; while economic development adjusts "environment to people".

Population growth and agglomerations: Balanced distribution of population is more a socio-administrative decision than economic. There are developed, less developed and backward regions. *Migration, if planned, will take people from the advanced regions to backward regions to provide services and human-resource-inputs to development. Planned migration can be of persons who have tradeable skills. This can be resented by the local people, unless they see in this that they are going to have higher education, tradeable skills, employment and incomes themselves. Backward regions will first have nodal centres of development, usually district head-quarters or block head-quarters further down. Mega-cities developed due to over-migration in most of the less developed countries.* Most countries can introduce system of "work permits" so as not to allow influx of people. It is first ensured that the incoming persons will have housing facilities. In countries like India housing facilities (or improvised houses of the shanty houses types) follow the inmigration of unskilled persons. Only big corporate 'houses' first arrange the residential houses and then ask their persons to come. *The governments in India failed miserably in this regard. They now do not make arrangements for their own government servants in the centres of administration, not fully now.* Even the ex-Ministers and politicians of all hues continue to occupy government quarters—that too without paying for anything. To keep the media "blind" on the issue, they provide government quarters to "journalists" of all hues. Environmental degration, of the worst type have taken place in India due to unplanned migration and almost no action for not allowing the slums to emerge and their replacement with good but small houses. Not even slum improvements are made. Money meant for the improvement of the slums usually goes down the gutter.

Migration and Poverty: Migration and Affluence/ Development: They are both inter-related. Poverty pushes persons out from a definite position of unemployment/ under-employment and low income to a position of better employment and income *or atleast a hope for the same.* Poverty is a great push factor so much so that even if the income at the new place is low it is still a pull factor. Here the old dictum "something is better than nothing" applies.

General development of the country most of the time gives emergence to the phenomenon of'enclave growth'. Erstwhile static places/regions/areas become areas of hub of economic activity. They develop the hinterland also. People remain stay put in these regions as they promise better socio-economic environment. Migration is checked. Infact some persons may move to the developing hinterland to provide services. How often do we not see a physician moving to a developing town to provide private medical services? People of other professions can also move. Initially they may keep two homes but when the income earning activities gain intensity, the person becomes tied to the place. Persons of the same activity can open many shops and establishments for various services. Others can move in. *Yet while others are moving in, some persons may move out in search of richer "pastures ".*

It can be believed that economic development will promote such migration that the unskilled persons of rural areas will migrate to urban or *rurban* areas (partly rural and partly urban) while the skilled persons may migrate to rural areas to exploit the income earning potentials that can emerge. There can be administrative postings also in rural areas of government and institutional manpower. *Even if the interface between rural and urban economy does not translate into migrations, it will certainly translate into better interactions,* for example salesmen from urban areas go to rural areas to put things with the shopkeepers. They supply physical inputs of rural development to the rural sellers. Then urban people can go to rural areas to collect their outputs at *farmgate prices.* These prices are lower than the prices that the rural people can obtain in urban markets or *mandies* but this activity saves the transportation time and charges for the rural people. The rural people who can afford to have access to urban markets will go there and not sell their products at 'farmgate' prices. Free competition offers the choice to the rural people to obtain best position for themselves—buying at the cheapest net prices; selling at the highest net price.

Balanced spatial distribution of population is possible only under the regimented socialistic regimes; in the democratic growth model based on comparative advantage principle of location of profitable economic activities, the distribution and redistribution will always be haphazard. It may solve some problems while creating new ones.

It will be in the very long run that an ideal redistribution of population can be imagined and that too in such countries as the USA, Canada, Australia or New Zealand. These countries had the advantage of migration and settlements being 'managed'. Less developed countries will always have such settlements which give proof of poverty and low quality of human life and out-migrations or in-migrations, as necessary, cannot be planned.

Factors that affect distribution and redistribution are first natural. Barren desert regions, highly forested regions, snow covered mountains, very cold and hot climatic regions, rain-forest regions will never have the population density of the plains with moderate climate. Plains will have high density and that cannot be eased out to the above mentioned areas. Those who have become used to living in the problem areas do not all leave them. People continue to live in quake-prone, in desert, mountaneous and forested areas. Their physical constitutional get up gets used to that. *[For example, people in areas of high altitude somehow develop larger lungs and hearts to take enough oxygen from the oxygen-poor air. If they come down to plains they feel the "heat" because their large hearts and lungs get more oxygen than they were used to].*

This is the reason why people continue to live in difficult areas from arctic region countries to tip of the southern hemisphere. Rich natural resources, good climate, prosperous agriculture, large marketable surpluses for industrial development and consumption, facilities for developing *manufactoring* and *manufacturing* industries, location of services of high order, network of communications, transport and adequate socio infrastructural facilities result in concentration of population in certain regions. Primate cities to mega cities all depend upon the clustering the advantages of location and habitation.

It is said that a village habitation in India used to get started if a well, a money lender and a mandir could be arranged at one place! There is a "minimum threshold" population to keep a habitat going; then there is an upper threshold of population that cannot be sustained in a limited areas. Soon the nearby water sources may be insufficient; there may be no land to develop the housing colonies even vertically. Everything may become too congested and polluted. There may be jitters of living lives in a cocoon. Over-crowding may put great psychological stress.

Inter-relationship between patterns of population and socio economic development: Though there is relationship between patterns of distribution and redistribution of population (caused by migration) and socio-economic development, it is not the only factor.

(a) A redistribution of population from congested regions to less congested regions should be in the interest of both the regions but several factors come in between. For example, Arunachal Pradesh of India has a density of 4 person per square kilometre but it will not take migrants from Bihar or West Bengal for the fear of their culture getting inundated with that of the inmigrants. Besides, the migrants too will not go to deep forested areas of different climate from the urbanised economy. If that could be possible, then the north eastern States of India could develop *provided there is massive investment in the development of infrastructure and industrial development.* The people of the Seven-sister States would *first* like this investment to come; absorb the local unemployed manpower and then may welcome the people of other States if they feel that there is good of the region without any detriment to them that the migration shall bring.

(b) The socio-economic repercussions will be good on both the regions provided there are no socio-economic tensions of the type discussed above. There will be socio-cultural interactions and the migrants and well as the migrated persons will learn good socio-cultural aspects from each other. It is expected and desired that "unprogressive" traits will be jettisoned and progressive traits absorbed. If the two groups remain in water-tight compartments then there will be tensions. *For example, the Indians who had migrated to Uganda were not inter-marrying the native Ugandans; that made the then ruler Idi Amin demand that Indian girls should marry the African boys.* On this and many other problems he turned all Indians (almost all) out of that country.

The quality of life of the migrants improves; their miseries go down. They move from positions of unemployment or under-employment to positions of employment and better employment. Their earnings increase. In the region where migrants come, they bring industry (quality of labour) and skills. There will be increase in the regional income. Migration enables the "surplus" labour to move out to places where there is relative shortage. *Environment of congested regions should improve and so should the quality of life. However, if migration streams from various sides cluster in one region / area / city, then there shall be environmental degradation in the region where migrants go.* If the migration can be planned (as was in the erstwhile Soviet Union) then the migrants do not defecate in the open; do not have their private ablutions in the open and do not cause environmental degradation from shanty houses. It *was the unplanned migration in the limited area of Bombay / Mumbai that made it get the dubious distinction of having the largest slum of the world, Dharavi.*

Agglomerations are generally industrial agglomerations. They come into existence when all things which are necessary for the location of industrial and service units are there or can be provided there. These can be (i) nearness to raw materials*, (ii) adequate power, (iii) adequate water and

* If the raw material is ubiquitous that is, found everywhere, the location of industrial units will be "foot loose" and near the markets. If the raw material is specific that is, heavy with low value as iron ore or coal, then the nearness to them will be important. That is the reason why iron and

land for sustenance and expansion, (iv) no dearth of the type of manpower needed at competitive rates, (v) adequate infrastructure facilities like roads, railways (and other modes of transport as needed), communitation, banking, medical and educational facilities**, (vi) availability of a package of concessions relating to subsidies and taxes etc.

Agglomerations attract migrants. When the agglomerations become too congested with all types pollutions, they dispel migration. Then migration cannot be sustained.

> Agglomerations bring convergence of the industrial and service units. Their convergence leads to divergence of income between these developed agglomerations and other regions around the agglomerations even though some income from these agglomerations percolates to the hinterland.
>
> Dispersal of industrial units leads to diversification of industrial development over the entire space which may get dotted with production units. Dispersal of incomes leads to convergence of incomes over the regions. In other words the differences in incomes in different regions will not be as great as they are in the unbalanced growth pattern. Dispersal of economic activities over the entire region leads to balanced growth.

---

cement plants will be near the sources of raw materials. The same applies to sugar producing units. In the following locational triangle, the location of iron plant is shown:

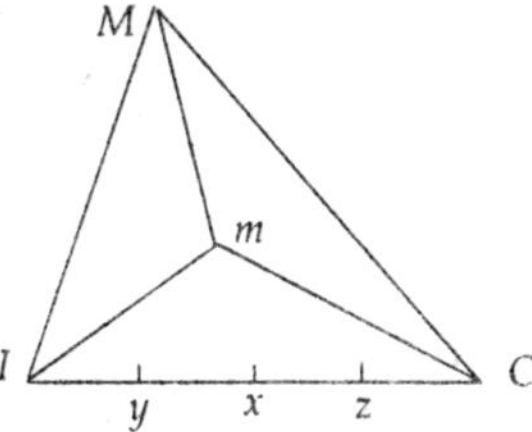

M is market, *m* is mid-point between *M*, *I* and *C*. *I* and *C* stand for Iron and Coal. It is cheaper to haul iron over long distances than coal because per unit of value, hauling of a coal wagon is costlier. So the location should be near coal at *Z*, which will leave space for coal mining also.

** These should be there *before* the location in some measure but they mostly develop to higher specialities afterwards.

Pulls and Pushes of Migration

Pushes	Pulls
1. *Unemployment, under-employment, assetlessness /landlessness in villages* are the most important push factors that force the rural people out to urban and semi-urban areas. People migrate from known bad positions to unknown *expected good* positions.	1. *Employment prospects* are great pull factors. Sometimes the migrant migrates after making sure that there is a job/work and sometimes he moves to the cities without rudder and compass and hunts for a job. Ultimately he may get one.
2. *Low incomes and people being below the mythical poverty line.* The natural consequence of unemployment and under-employment is the low income. Even if all the members of the family slog, the total income may not lift them above the poverty trap. The life with low incomes has high degrees of miseries and people naturally move out in search of less miserable life, which may lateron, with luck and labour, become a life of good physical quality of life.	2. *Higher per capita real incomes* flow from employment and higher employment intensity. Sometimes even one migrant labour may be able to earn enough to sustain the family in rural areas though at low level of living. Skilled persons get much higher incomes to improve their levels of living in a very substantial way Generally migration ensures "graduation" from the poverty level Good quality of life may follow.
3. *Socio-cullural discrimination* too forces people out *Being a 'dalit ' is so painful in India that only dalits can describe it.* People practise untouchability towards those "filthy" persons who actually remove the filth of others. Filth creaters are touchable; those who enable them to remain sanitised are despised! Only in India and some other countries persons belonging to certain castes are untouchable even when they are in clean clothes. Without migration they can hide their surnames and hope to save themselves from discrimination.	3. Urban societies are, sort of, less biased towards castes. In Indian railways who asks the caste of the pantry car hawkers/servers. Urban economies and administrative setup offer reservations to dalits and then they can afford not to mention it till they want further advantages of reservations. They need not lead the life with social stigma and untouchability being practised. [We can find in urban India brahmins shaking hands with the dalit bosses and ministers.] It is better life in urban areas with the new-fangled surnames which do not reveal the castes.
4. *Geological-Geographical reasons* like a region being prone to earthquakes, floods, draughts, typhoons can push many persons out to safe havens. However, all cannot leave because	4. *Good geo-physical features:* Regions with good climate attract persons. So do the trouble free regions of safe existences. Plains shall always have higher population density than

adverse geo-physical conditions can emerge elsewhere also. Besides people remain tied to their lands, business establishments and jobs. Other things remaining the same, people are pushed out from bad climatic regions. Hostile terrain and inadequate resource base push people out. Many countries have themselves created conditions that can lead to famines for example, low rainfalls due to felling of forests. People, who can afford, will move out.

non plain regions, unless the entire country is devoid of such plains.

Prospects of getting land, employment and other income earning livelihoods attract persons.

5. *Lack of basic facilities and amenities* push the people out. Villages lack "minimum needs components" for example, all weather roads, communi-cation linkages, medical facilities, facilities for higher education and tradeable skills, etc. *Karl Marx averred that people move out to escape from the "idiocy of the country life "*. The atmosphere in rural areas is placid, devoid of the thrills of modern life. Those who have seen that all and can afford to move out will move out to escape the humdrum life of rural areas.

5. *Presence of pleasures of life* pull persons. People migrate to cities to avail *on permanent and assured basis* facilities as better connectivity, communications, education, medi-care and entertainment facilities. *"Urbanism"* (high consumerism), *"urbanity"* (rational way of living, civilized way, but without moral decadence) are great pull factors. Prosperous farmers, therefore, start having double residence system—houses in rural as well as urban areas.

6. *Marital push* can be there in regions where people cannot find a mate. People from certain gulf countries come to India to find a mate and show themselves as "temporary migrants". Not that India has surplus girls/women. However, there is a plethora of poor girls/women who are lured by the shady persons who take such poor girls as wives; use them and then "discard" them as used "commodity", not following the civil or religious procedures. NRIs must have got an initial thrust of push; then their wives/financees got the push same way.

6. *Marital pull* makes wives go to the places where there husband work. In case the husbands cannot keep their wives with them, they are pulled back to their wives. People are pulled to places where they can have nuclear family, away from the shackles of the joint family. Young couples want to break loose from parental bonds.

7. *Political conditions* in most countries

7. *Canada, the USA, Australia and New*

have become intolerable. There is corruption all around. Salaried class is being dismantled. There is casualisation of job market.

The politicians, the bureaucrats, top officers, officials, industrialists, traders, professionals and operators of black economy, the inspector-raj departments are all (with many honest exceptions, though) mulcting the people. India was witnessing killing and deaths of poor due to hunger and *class wars, which are taking the shape of caste wars.* Tens of thousands are dying due to effects of malnutrition and poverty. The Government was (2001) sitting over 6 crore tonnes of foodgrains which would be sold in not so bad conditions but will be declared as soiled in official records. The fear of God has gone out of the hearts of the vested interest economic groups and they are pushing crores of persons, educated and illiterate alike, to positions of uncertainty. Where to go? Their position is such as of the fish in a pond when the pond infact is a net. *(Wrote a Pakistani poet "Machhli bach kar jayey kahan, jab saaraa jal hi jail* that is. where can a fish go when the entire water is a death-trap?) India is to witness soon the disintegration of middle class into the lower class.

8. *Structurally disadvantaged/ completed construction sites* push the workers away. If the mines exhaust (for example, Kolar gold mines near Mysore) then people will have to migrate. If projects are completed people have to migrate out. If the industrial centres decay, people are pushed out.

Zealand pull people because of better law and order situations, though the USA will not score much on this point *vis-a-vis* Canada.

Many Indians (the author had the first hand experience about them) who went to Seychelles opted to obtain citizenship of that island (population less than 60000 and area 21 kilometres long and 3.5 kms. wide only) because it is corruption free, crime free, dust free and poverty free country. The fact that they were cocooned in a limited space surrounded by thousands of kilometres of oceans all around did not bother then. It was a great pull effect. There are many island countries where are heaven on earth.

8. *Special work sites of special projects, new growth centres and industrial estates are attracting migrants.* Agglomerations pull, Centres of prosperity pull people with their *"mass"* that is, the sum total of all benefits.

II. CAUSES OF MIGRATION: "PUSH" AND "PULL" FACTORS

Push factors force the people out to emigrate; pull factors are attractions which induce people to inmigrate. In between there are "frictions" which do not translate all pushes and pulls into actual migration. Pushes of one side can be pulls from the other side.

Thus the same factors, if adverse, exert a push for outmigration and the same factors, if promising alluring incomes and good ways of living, become the pull factors. For some person the same factors which are pull factors for someone can become push factors for others just as some healthy persons find weather good enough for picnic while someone may be dying at the same time.

III. REPERCUSSIONS AND RAMIFICATIONS OF MIGRATION

Favourable	*Unfavourable*
1. *Employment intensity* improves or else migrants will not migrate.	1. Local population loses job opportunities; atleast so they feel.
2. *Income earning also improves in real terms* that is. after taking into account the severence of the links with the relatively cheaper living and incurring higher costs of living at the new place.	2. *Local people's "economic rents that is, higher payments* will go down. *However, total Income increases and these unfavourable effects may not actualise.*
3. *One can move away from the unprogressive and oppressive shackles ofsocio-cultural discrimination.* Many racial, religious and caste/tribe groups have to find sanctuary elsewhere with the people of their groups. The mass killing of the Jews (60 lakh of them were got murdered by Hitler) forced the world to find a home for the Jews. Millions of the Muslim and Hindus had to move away from India/Pakistan to Pakistan/India after Partition of India.	3. Migrations bring various social groups together and if thee is no cohesion, then cleavages develop. There can be violent clashes also. In Pakistan the Indian migrants, though Muslims, are still called "mohajirs" that is, the refugees. They have not been assimilated in the society and the economy. Killings are routine. When the migrant Muslims dominated the then capital of Pakistan, Karachi, they took the capital away to Islamabad. The mohajirs felt cheated.
4. *Even if there is brain drain, there is inflow of foreign exchange* if international	4. *Brain drain may seriously undermine the real production economy of the region/country wherefrom the migrants come.*

migrations are involved. The same is true of the relationship between backward and forward regions. Backward regions 'lose' their skilled and unskilled manpower but if the ties are not altogether severed, their families receive inflows of money. Kerala's economy is known as "money order" economy as the money comes from Gulf countries.	The economy of the region that receives migrants may also be seriously stressed. There can be pollution, congestion, housing shortage and distance jitters. Slums may proliferate. Crimes of all sorts may get promoted. Slums are breeding grounds of prostitution and provide easy recruits for the black economy.
5. *Redundant labour of rural areas will 5. get employment in urban/industrial and tertiary sectors and its marginal productivity will increase.* This redistribution of labour will help reduce the disparities in wages in rural and urban areas.	5. *Maldistribution of labour may undermine some centres.* Wages at certain places may become too high (which lose labour) and may get depressed where there is the super-abundance of the same.
6. New businesses and ventures start at 6. all places. Population gets redistribu-ted optimally. Then there can be dov-etailing of seasonal activities that is, per-sons can get engaged in another seas-onal work after one seasonal work.	6. *Some regions may lose young person and old persons may be left behind.* This may seriously under-mine the production in rural areas or in the areas wherefrom migrants go.
7. *National integration* aspects of migration are profound. Persons of different State of India have made another State their "home". No linguistic States of India is free from the people of other States. People get nostalgic about the places they reside. Socio-cultural affinities develop.	7. Sectarian violence may erupt. The migrants may never be able to assimilate with the local people. We can find in every big city separate associations of Maharashtrians, Gujraties, Andhras, Keralites, Kannadigas, Tamilians, Bengalies, Oriyas, Punjabies, Haryanvies, Rajasthanies and so on.
8. *As technical skills develop, there is diffusion of technology in the form of use of capital goods of high technology everywhere.* Innovations first get embodied in capital goods and then they get diffused, people move from "negative sum activities" (reducing output due to "too many cooks spoiling the business broth" or indulging in destructive activities for example felling of trees illegally to make some money or indulging in anti-social activities). They also move from "zero sum activity" doing nothing, except trading in which case additional	8. *Technological upgradation (not a very direct consequence of migration of labour but of mobility of capital and technology) can bring unemployment of the "natives".*

real outputs are not there. Sellers, who perform vital function of uniting the producers and consumers, add their own marketing margins to have a high price spread. If migration encourages "positive sum activities" of real production", then the nation gains much more.

9. *Lower dependency in rural areas, higher degree of employment intensity of those who leave and those* who are left behind, additional real output per person and transfer of money from the city-sibligings to those left behind in rural areas improve the economic conditions of those also who are left behind.

10. *Migrants infuse modern values* in the population. Contraceptive acceptance goes up. Hygienic conditions improve, sanitation can improve, if the government is not inefficient and corrupt in their activities of public *health engineering,* people can accept immunization measures and even consciousness towards nutrition can improve. Urban societies discriminate less against women. Infact in many urban societies, men complain about many females becoming "masculinized" in behaviour.

    Overall improvement will be everywhere. The period of demographic transition is less in urban areas. As ingestion of funds improves in rural areas better technologies and cropping patterns may be adopted. The rural people will get the urge to develop. There will be dynamism everywhere.

9. *Brain drain.* This is a big problem of international migration. India, for example, spends millions on a IIT graduate. Most of them migrate out of the country. (They send money for sometime but then become permanent citizens of the country where they migrated to. Then they lose their moorings and feelings for the country). This is true for others also.

10. *It is a fact of life that bad habits are copied easily and good values are imbibed very late.* People complain about the corrupting values of the migrants for example, the British and the Australians* are still not psycholo-gical chums. Separation from spouses have brought cases of marital corruption that is, adultery. It is used to be said in yester-years that a seller has a wife in every port. Children may not receive equal attention from both parents. They may have psychological depression and even adultery may increase the guilt complex. It may make life more complex with divided loyalties and all the consequences of moral slips. Many persons in urban areas have to slog worse than slave labourers. Once caught in the criminal economy of urban areas, the people have few escape routes.

* The criminals in UK used to be exiled to Australia. The people of UK used to look down upon the people of Australia. Once a boy of UK and a girl of Australia fell in love. Parents of both objected. The UK parents said "you are marrying a girl where the criminals of this country go!", while the parents of Australian girl asked "you are marrying a boy of the country wherefrom the criminals come?".

Brain Drain and Indentured Labour

The British colonial rulers took labour from India to other colonies from Fiji to Guiana, from Uganda to Mauritius infact to most of their colonies. Indian workers were relatively more skilled (even when unskilled) relative to the native labour. Brain drain is volitional and of the highly skilled persons, who, had they remained in the country, could have changed the face of the country. *The top Indian brains migrate because of the politicians and the bureaucrats; they do not allow anyone to get higher status or salary than bureaucrats.* These persons send money to their parents (but not all of them) for some years and then the brain drain means neither the persons come back nor do they send money to their kith and kins or invest in domestic industries. The brain drain can be of doctors, engineers, computer experts, experts of other fields but can be of semi-skilled persons also. *Even taking into account the higher cost of living in the Western developed countries, the migrants make 10 times more in real terms even as salaried persons. If they become entrepreneurs, then "sky is the limits ".* The opportunity gains are greater than the opportunity costs in very high way. Nobel Prize winner in Economics, Gunnar Myrdal, included this also as "backwash effects of international relations".

Specialists come from the developed countries to less developed but they do not stay back to take the citizenship of the poor countries, though there are sometimes exceptions. [Dr. West (Director General of Geology, Government of India, stayed in India to become Indian citizen and teach at Saugor (the then spelling of Sagar) University, Madhya Pradesh. Mark Tully, eminent correspondent of the BBC, took citizenship of India.]

IV. MODELS OF MIGRATION

Every writer on migration emphasized one aspect or the other or used a striking explanation of migration and thus several "models" of migration were developed. Here some better known ones only are being presented.

1. Revenstein's Model

The essential points of this model (1885) are:

(a) From the stand point of distance, the rate of migration between two points will be inversely related to the distance between two points of migration. Migration will be to great centres of commerce and industry.

(b) From the stand point of stages of migration, migration has its currents. Migration will first be to nearly places and then to most rapidly growing cities and even to far off places.

(c) From the stand point of streams of migration, the usual stream of migration is from rural to urban areas. There are counter streams also from urban areas. Other two streams of migration are from rural and from urban to urban centres.

In Ravenstein's model determinants of migration are development of manufactures, commerce and public work, climate, lack of employment opportunities in certain regions, and oppression and discrimination.

2. Neo-Classical

A host of "models" continued to be propounded which were nothing but the elaboration of the pulls and push factors of migration. *Deterministic models* explained migration in terms of some objective considerations for example, wage differentials or better income earning opportunities/expectations. *Probabilistic models* are not predictive and explain that migration may or may not) take place as a host of factors many subjective also decide migration. These factors, apart from differences in income and income earning opportunities, are attachment to a particular region/culture/language of the region or inertia.

Distance, income differential, and information about the new places are important deciding factors. The neo-classical economists propounded their migration models with reference to the *wages being equal to the marginal productivity.* They argued that if wage differentials exist, and if there is no hindrance and if the people are "economic men," then people will migrate from places of low wages to places of high wages till the wages at different places are more or less equal and so is the marginal productivity of labour at all the places.

3. Raimon

Raimon in his "model" showed that inter-regional migration of labour was strongly co-related with per capita income differentials and with differences in the availability of job opportunities.

4. Fabricant

Fabricant suggested that migration from one region to another takes place in response to *excess demand for labour* in a region *plus a barrier function* (distance, kinship ties and residential difficulties). The demand function promotes migration while the barrier function slow it down or hinders it.

5. Blanco

Blanco stressed the role *unemployment differentials* in inter-regional migration. Labour will move from that region where the incidence of unemployment is high to such regions where employment opportunities are greater.

6. Lowry

Lowry in his "model" states that people tend to migrate from low to high wage regions and from high unemployment to low unemployment regions. Migration-flows thus can bring in the "long run" and in due course of time, regional wage and unemployment rates towards unity.

Such type of functional relationship was given:

$$M_{u} = f = \frac{U_i, W_i, L_i L_j}{U_j, W_j, D_u}$$

M is migration between /andy regions;
U is unemployment as a percentage of non-agri. labour force in the respective regions;
W manufacturing wages in respective regions;
L is number of persons in non-agri. labour force in respective regions, designated.
D distance.

In equilibrium condition because of mobility of labour $W_i = W_j$ and $U_i = U_j$

The equilibrium position will prevail only when distance is not a major barrier and sufficient number of jobs (Ls) are available at *j*.

Deterministic models were propounded both on the basis of the wage differentials and distance. However, probabilistic models took both economic and non-economic factors into considerations as also measurable and immeasurable factors into consideration. Not only the monetary costs, the psychic costs, the physical distance, the social distance, the psychic gain, uncertainties, are taken into account but some precise relationships can also be worked out.

7. Zipt and Stewart Models

They talked more about the "gravitational pull" factors than about the "push" factors. People migrate even when they are not pushed out of their original places but because greater promises are held out in new places. Ecqnomic conditions may or may not be bad in the places of original residence but people prefer to settle down and raise families in big or intermediate cities. Distance was regarded by them as the major/only obstacle.

8. Samuel A. Stouffer

He considered migration a function of the "intervening opportunities" or "intervening obstacles." Positive gains induce migration and they are those gains which are anticipated at the new places where people are migrating to. These gains are compared with the possible losses, or the "negative factors." The speed breakers of migration have been presented as the negative factors and some of these factors may intercept the migrants at intermediate places.

9. Lee's Model

In this model also the "pull", "push" and "neutral" factors are analysed. There are three sets of factors; the "plus", the "minus," and "zero" sets. The balance of these sets determines whether the net outcome is positive or negative for a place. The repellent and attractive forces are thus identified. What is repellent for one place can become an attractive factor with reference to the place of destination. If the conditions at both the places are the same with reference to some variables, then for some persons these things may figure in the "zero" or "neutral" set. Migration will not be possible if there are restrictive laws, or will be limited if there are quotas and permits. Distance and transport costs may be obstacles for some but not for others; for poor persons minor problems may become major constraints.

In Lee's model, migrants are the persons who are ambitious or who cannot get any job at the place of their original residence or cannot get jobs there to suit their skills, knowledge, or aspirations; or, who do not find the total environment (rural setup; socio-cultural conditions; climate, etc.) agreeable.

In Lee's model, the *volume* of migration depends on the diversity of people and places. The volume of migration will naturally be high if obstacles are less. One stream of migration can become counter stream of an earlier migration.

10. Lewis's Model

Lewis suggests that migration from rural (subsistence or non capitalist) sector be promoted to the urban (capitalist) sector. He argued that in rural areas there is massive disguised under-employment/unemployment. Several members of a family work on a small farm because they have nothing else to do. If some of the family members are taken away from these farms, even then the output will not go down. That proves that these persons were redundant and were having zero marginal productivity. If the farm productivity improves (too many cooks were spoiling the broth), then it proves that they were having negative productivity. If the persons are transferred in an orderly manner from those works where they were have zero or negative marginal physical productivity to places/works where they will have positive marginal physical productivity, it will do good to the rural and urban economies; to the agricultural and industrial sectors; or to the nation as a whole. Less developed countries are characterized by "enclave" development—there are islands of development around a sea of stagnation.

Lewis suggests that if the government can conceive of several public works, which can be financed with the help of the newly created money, then these persons can be transferred to those works. It will be necessary that these workers be paid subsistence wage plus something extra to compensate for higher cost of living in the capitalist sector. This will be a way of development which will not be inflationary. It will raise productivity of the people as also of the capital. It will be necessary that the capitalists should be allowed to reap good profits, because they have a high marginal propensity to save and will accumulate capital. Labour intensive or intermediate technology is suggested and it is suggested that the government should ensure that there is orderly transfer of surplus manpower from the rural agricultural sector to the urban/ manufacturing sector.

In due course of time the surplus population will be absorbed. Till the rate of capital accumulation remains higher than the rate of growth in population, and till surplus population can be utilised in the above manner, growth process will be facile. When the capital accumulation catches up with population, the real wages will start rising. In Lewis model, migration is not treated as an exogenously determined variable but something which should be promoted in the desired way.

11. Todaro Model

Todaro studied all factors that induce migration. In his model *expectations* play an important role in migration and internal migration is treated as a problem for the urban areas. He writes:

> Migration today is being increasingly looked upon as the major contributing factor to the ubiquitous phenomenon of urban surplus labour and as a force which continues to excerbate already serious urban unemployment problems caused by growing economic and structural imbalancs between urban and rural areas.

Todaro explains that people migrate to (i) break up from backward rural social structures, *(ii)* to find jobs in urban areas, particularly when due to decline in rural death rates, density of population per unit of cultivable land increases, (iii) to break away from extended family, and (iv) to live in modern setting in cities. While they regards socio-cultural and demographic factors of the point of origins as "push," expected economic gains of the place of destination as a "pull."

Youngmen and women migrate for education and training, for jobs and marriages. Old and retired persons return to the places they had chosen for retired life. Unskilled and uneducated persons seeking jobs are floatsams and driftsams.

Migration exerbates the rural and urban structural imbalances. It swells the urban labour supplies, where providing a job will be a lot more costly.

According to Todaro, any economic and social policy that affects rural and urban real incomes will directly and/or indirectly influence the migration process. This process in turn will itself tend to alter the pattern of sectoral and geographic economic activity, income distribution and even population growth. Opening of public works, special programmes for employment, higher wages will attract migrants.

Todaro says:

> "There is a clear need to recognize the central importance of internal migration and to integrate the two-way relationship between migration and population distribution, on the one hand, and economic variables, on the other, into a more comprehensive analytical framework designed to improve development policy."

Todaro opines that instead of allowing people to migrate from rural to urban areas, jobs should be created in rural areas themselves. Migration of rural people to urban areas creates problems of housing and degradation of the environment due to emergence of slums.

Todaro's model explains the migration in *terms of income expected at the new places* rather than the actual income earned later on. It also depends upon the expected level of differences between real incomes and between rural and urban job opportunities. Migration to urban areas is based upon the expectations *of permanent incomes in the long run* and the migrants bear temporary difficulties in the hope of improving their future—at least in comparison to what it would have been in villages. This is the essence of his *thought process thesis about migration.*

12-13-14. Bogue, Blau and Duncan on Migrant Selectivity

They aver that migrants to large cities in developing countries are heterogenous in their socio-economic backgrounds. Migrants are usually of such age, education, occupation, risk-taking propensity that they are equipped to cope with the conditions of the city. In the early period of urbanization the migrants selectivity is higher. Migration selectivity and occupation requirements are interrelated. Migration can be highly selective with respect to a given characteristic in one area and be selective to only a mild degree, or not at all, in another area. If the selectivity of migration can vary in both pattern and intensity between different places, it is equally possible that it can vary between different places, it is equally possible that it can vary between different periods of time. Hence it is fruitless to seek permanent inflexible differentials in migration that will not vary.

Large cities accept and absorb those migrants who are venture-some and who can withstand the early tensions. Some important features of their analysis are:

1. If the degree of urbanization is low and urban size hierarchy is less developed, migration will not conform to the "stage migration model," that is migrants will not be trapped in the small centres.
2. Migrants, if they are skilled and educated, will find ready acceptance. Return migrants from large cities

on the whole will be "negatively selective" from the total group of migrants, thus increasing the positive selectivity of those whose remain in the cities.

3. Migrants to urban places are concentrated in the young adult years. Migrants to large cities are disproportionately single when compared to the populations from which they originate.
4. Migrants to large cities have higher educational attainments that the populations from which they originate. Migrants to large citis have, on the average, a higher occupational level than the populations from which they originate. Migrants to large cities are more disposed to assume risk than the populations from which they originate.
5. The lower the rate of out-migration from rural and small town areas to large cities, the greater, the selectivity. The longer a rapid rate of urbanization is maintained, the more probable a decline in selectivity of migrants from rural areas. Most of the migrants are those whose kinship groups are already in the big cities.

15. Gravity Models

This is the name given to spatial interaction and there are two basic principles to this model: *(a)* The influence of an economic force at any point in space is directly related to the size of the force; and *(b)* it is inversely related to the distance between its source and the point in question.

The use of gravity models in regional population and development planning is made to assess how an aggregate quantity distributes itself across regional space.

In the gravity models, the rich *region is conceived as a 'mass'*. The measures of mass can be many, for example, SDP, number of functions and facilities, the investment, the number of jobs.

Gravity models are social physics of Newton, They are migration economics made difficult. Reilly's Law of Retail Gravitation was one of the earliest applications of gravity models. This law states that a city attracts retail trade from an individual customer located in its hinterland *(a) in proportion to its size (population) and (b) in inverse proportion to the square of the distance separating the individual from the city center, (centre).*

The gravity models make analysis of spatial interaction among spatially separated nodes with a wide variety of applications, for example, migration, commodity flows, traffic flows, residence-work place commutation. There are both *predictive (deterministic) and stochastic (probabilistic)* interpretations, the latter being less precise but more realistic. It is emphasized that certain nodes exercise gravitational pull while the other centres may allow factors and resources to migrate/be transferred to other places due to push effect. The distance is important in these models because pulls and pushes decline with distance.

Two places are compared to two "masses" and according to the law of gravitation, *gravitational force between two masses is a function of the product of the masses themselves and inversely proportional to the distance between them.*

If a region has low SDP, low level of economic activities, low employment intensity, low income generation, low investment, less number of functions and facilities, then it can be said that it has a *low mass* and hence another region which has more of all or most of them will have a *high mass* and will attract factors unless distance constraints (in the form of costly, time consuming or unsafe transport), come in the way. Inverting opportunities can cut short the distance of the gravitational pull, that is a person migrating from a village need not land at the largest city.

Gravity declines not only as the distances increase but more probably as the costs of transport increase. It is also possible that the two places may be near but there may be considerably administrative political distance (change of state or national boundaries) or social distance (cultural or language barriers). All types of "distances" reduce the gravitational pulls.

Gravity models do not spell out how to optimize, that is they do not suggest what is to be done for what purpose. They just tell about the expected behaviour. A complete theoretical framework is missing in the gravity models. Even the complex gravity models use *weights for different determining factors but converting everything in terms of transport costs.'*

Isard has developed *Income Potential Model* on the basis of this analysis. If

i is a region;
j is another region;
Y is income;
d is distance;
z is rate of growth in income.

It is explained that if for the time being the distance factor is disregarded then if the rate of growth in j region is more than in i region, they region will exercise gravitational pull. If, however, they region is situated far off, that is there is a long distance between the two regions, the diseconomies of distance covering will overcome the potential gains of income. Just as simple as that.

In the gravity theory, the agglomeration economies or diseconomies represent the "mass," of the social physics. If the economies are greater than diseconomies of agglomeration, the region will attract and in the opposite conditions it ill repel and expel. Migration will be high if the *income density (size) and Income potential* (future prospects at a new place compared to the prospects at the old place) are high. There are some important income fronts (new and virgin regions give rise to great income frontiers) which attract people and resources and in due course of time these "income fronts are dissipated" and then migration steams thin out.

This gravity model is nothing but ordinary migration economics is new garb. Richardson wrote:

> Despite the novelty of the concepts (income fronts and, to a lessert extent, income potential), this analysis has a familiar ring to it. I would argue that it is merely the neo-classical theory in disguise.

Regional Growth Theory

The problem with many gravity models was that they tried to develop equations of migration and movements on one variable, keeping others constant. *Distance was the main friction or the main spur, depending upon whether it was long or short.* The problems become further complicated when data are not available for *all points* of migration in a region. Thus was developed the concept *of economic centre* of gravity and distances/costs were usually measured with reference to capital towns of the regions. In case of the gravity studies movement of goods between the countries, all socio-political tariff, subsidies, goods quality factors were ignored. *Distance was made surrogate of everything.*

In the gravity models, gravitational differences are due to distance differences. This theory ends in whimper ultimately.

Only some notable analogies remain: *Johnson* uses the lapse rate analogy in the interaction of movement. It is suggested that migration from a centre might be compared to the emission on a ray of light. Light is gradually absorbed by the medium in proportion to the flow per unit of distance.

In the same way migrating population may be thought to be gradually absorbed by the areas into which it moved.

V. MEASURES OF MIGRATION

Census can record whether the person enumerated at a particular place of residence had his birth place elsewhere and that whether he lived there for some time. The census can record whether the person *ever moved, or moved during the period of enumeration.* Transient population in journey or in hotels is not considered as "migrant". Sample surveys can also record the native places of the respondents. *Under the direct method* the registration authorities record the out-migration and in-migration. This would require some administrative functionary to record this for villages, tehsils, blocks, districts and the States. The census can also collect the data. The balancing equation of the growth component method of projection of population is:

$$P_t = P_o + B - D + M_i - M_o$$

this is, the population at the end of certain number of years will be equal to the population at the beginning of that period, plus total births minus total deaths and the net balance of in-migration and out migration. *Internal migration is seldom measured directly through this balancing equation because of the non-availability of the data.*

Indirect Method

There are questions in censuses and surveys concerning prior residence at some point in the past such items as: "Where did the respondent live five years ago (or any other period)? or, where was the respondent born?

As series of gross migration matrices can be constructed, one for each age and sex group. By subtraction of those departing from those entering each age/sex cell for each sub-area, a corresponding net migration table can be constructed for any or all sub-areas within the system.

Another indirect measure of migration frequently used by demographers or regional analysts is based on a residual method, •whereby the population change between two censuses not attributable to the difference bet\veen births and deaths is assumed to be migration.

To apply this method, two accurate and complete censuses are required. The individual age/sex groupings or cohorts are aged from the earlier application of survival factors; the "'expected" survivors, including the survivors of those born after the earlier census, are compared with those enumerated in the later census. The difference between the expected numbers and the enumerated numbers is assumed to be the net migration.

The migration component appears at its simplest in the balancing equation referred to earlier. Since data on in and out-migrants are generally not available, the same equation may be modified to estimate net migration indirectly, expressed as:

$$M = P_t - P_o - B + D$$

where M refers to the net in or out-migration between the two censuses; P_t refers to the population at the time of a second census; P_o represents population of an earlier census and B refers to births and D refers to deaths, during the intercensal period. Since migration is not uniform, yearly breakup cannot be given.

Annual population estimates alone (through registration system) can provide data for the annual migrants. Rates of migration may be calculated, after allocating the migrants to the individual years of the intercensal period *evenly*. Or, if they are to be *allocated proportionally,* then this should be based upon some independent estimates of net migration of all ages, prepared independently from administrative data which reflect migration.

One method is to estimate migration of a region being equal to the population enumerated minus those born in the area itself. This is immigration.

The total out migration is *the total population born in the area minus those still residents in the area.* This will give the figure of out-migration.

Net migration of a region is actually equal to the difference between-migrations and out-migrants during a time period under study minus the deaths among the immigrants.

VI. CUMULATIVE LIFE TIME MIGRATION *VERSUS* DECADAL INTERNAL MIGRATION

If a person is residing at a place but was born elsewhere, the person is taken as migrant. This definition may be taken for one generation only. However, certain problems arise. A child delivered in a city hospital will always be regarded as migrant in his native rural place! A chance birth of a child elsewhere of a permanently settled family at a particular place will make the child "migrant."

Demographers attempt to estimate internal migration from various decadal censuses. Migration by age and sex can be estimated through this "census survival method." The method of calculation is very simple.

> If population "resident" at time / and belong to age x is multiplied by the probability of survival from age x to age $x + 10$ during time t and $t + 10$, one can estimate the population surviving to age $x + 10$ at time $t + 10$.

If it is assumed that the difference between the actual population counted in the census at time $t + 10$ and belonging to $x + 10$ and the estimated surviving population at time $t + 10$ and then belonging to age $x + 10$ is due to net migration, then a rough estimate to net migration by age and sex for the period t to t +10 can be obtained.

A very simple way of calculating the net migration is to take the population of a particular age group in the base year and then, on the basis of the past growth rate, to project the population n years (say 10) hence. Then the actual population at the terminal year of the study can be compared. The difference is net migration.

> For example; if the population of a region of the persons of a particular age group in 1980 was 6,54,534 and the expected population for this age group in 1990 was 7,65,607 but the actual population of the age group turned out to be 7, 87, 77 '5 in 1990, then 22,168 children/persons were net in-migrants.

Gross and Net 'trans-humance' (migration) of the journeymen labour can be calculated. Gross migration is the sum total of immigration and out-migration. If ten lakh persons move into and another ten lakhs move out of a city, the net migration is nil but the gross migration is 20 lakhs. Data about gross migration is very important for transport planners as also city planners. Net migration is the difference between in-migration (and immigration) and out migration (and emigration) and it changes the size and structure of the population for the sub-national regions. It is net balance of international migration which can change the size of the population of the country.

The rates of net-redistribution can be calculated for different states of the country or regions of the state. This is best done by taking the figures for two different years. They can be terminal years of the census, that is 10 years apart. We can study the change over any number of years, say 50 years. The rate of net-redistribution in a state or a region will be equal to the number of persons migrated in net terms *(M)* divided by the mean population (P_n) of the *country* during the time period under study. Thus:

$$R_m = \frac{+M_t}{P_n}$$

Differential migration-selectivity.[2] It can be calculated per 100 or per 1000 of population. Any group (religious, ethinic, occupational, income, etc.) can be selected. Where M_i is the number of migrants of a particular character; M is the total of all migrants; N is the number of all non-migrants and N_i is the number of non-migrants of the same character as Mi; then

$$DM = \frac{M_i}{M} - \frac{N_i}{N} \cdot K$$

It can be seen that:[3]

Per cent		
(A)	The Different migration of people from Kerala in Madhya Pradesh is	13.00
(B)	*DM* of Punjabies in Madhya Pradesh is	7.40
(C)	Gross migration in MP to the total population is	0.20
(D)	GM of Keralites as ratio to *GM* of Punjabies in Madhya Pradesh is	175.67
(E)	Population of Keralites in Madhya Pradesh to the population of Punjabies is of the order (Thus there is greater relative representation of Keralites in the GM of Madhya Pradesh relative to Punjabı population.)	111.00
(F)	The crude ratio of out-migrations of Keralites: Punjabies	200.00
(G)	Crude ratio of In-migrations of *Ks:Ps*	150.00
(H)	Crude ratio of GA/of *Ks.Ps*	154.55

Migration Streams. Both out-migration and in-migration streams can be quantified A measure to estimate the out-migration can be

$$\frac{M_{id}}{P_o} \cdot K$$

Here M refers to out-migration: P_o is population of the 'origin'. AT constant is per 100.

This formula can be modified a little bit by adding (or deducting, as the case may be), the net change in population as a result of migration streams. We can then write:

$$\frac{M_{id}}{P_o \pm M_i - M_o} \cdot K$$

M_i-M_o refer to in-migration and out-migration and the entire term to the net change.

The ratio of 'stream' to 'counter-stream' (also the tension between the push and pull streams) can be calculated thus:

$$\frac{M_{ij}\,P_x}{M_{ji}\,P_y} \cdot 100$$

Suppose we measure the streams of migration between Bhopal and Delhi. Then with reference to Bhopal, M_{ij} is migration from Bhopal to Delhi and M. is migration from Delhi to Bhopal. P_x and P_y are populations of Delhi and Bhopal respectively. The populations assign weights to the calculations. Suppose:

M	Bhopal to Delhi	50,000
M	Delhi to Bhopal	5,000
P_x	Population of Delhi	1,00,00,00
X	Population of Bhopal	10,00,000

Then the *thickness of the migration streams is of the order of 10000:1 for Bhopal versus Delhi with reference to these two cities.*[4]

URBANISATION: GROWTH AND DISTRIBUTION OF RURAL-URBAN POPULATION IN DEVELOPED AND DEVELOPING ECONOMIES

We can better start with certain terms: *Urbanisation* simply means populations of urban centres increasing due to "population implosion". That naturally happens due to inmigration from rural areas. The natural growth rate of population in urban areas is almost always lower than in the villages and non-urban centres because of low fertility and low mortality. If the fertility-mortality of the newly arrived persons is not included (say for 10 years or so), then this can be taken as a rule or even a law!

Generally "urban" centre is one where population exceeds a certain limit (say 5000) and 75 per cent* persons do not depend upon the primary sector activities for their livelihood. Different countries can adopt different definitions.

Urbanisation, as Karl Marx said, picks up because people want to escape from the idiocy of the country life. Well said words, though they may hurt the villagers.

> *Villages in the developed economies are not much different from the housing colonies of the cities. There is rural-urban continuum in the levels of living. There is not much difference in the per capita income. The access to various urban facilities is easy. There are good roads, good communication and transport facilities and all basic and "minimum needs " as we call them in India are available there.*

If a city of say 1 lakh becomes a city of 15 lakhs in say 50 years, the reasons are that industrialisation and commercialisation must have attracted persons in search

* The present author was once talking to an Indian Professor in a University at a place (population less than 25000) near Sydney in Australia. When asked about the medical facilities, the Professor replied "we have in that 'city' medical facilities better than anywhere in India!

of jobs. The trade and service activities expand. The migration is from the nearby towns and these towns get persons from the villages. There is direct migration to big centre from the villages. Urbanisation is a tendency whereby centripetal tendencies give rise to new urban centres and the old urban centres become more urbanised.

If persons from illiterate societies become educated they move away to good urban centres. There are better medical facilities also. There are jobs and higher incomes. Urbanisation is a movement from the primary sector activities to the secondary and tertiary sector activities.

Urbanism: That term is inferior to the term "urbanity" that will be explained hereafter. It simply means adopting all the good and bad things that urban societies provide. *Urbanism is associated closely with consumerism* and consumerism has two senses. In the bad sense it is used as the demonstration effect consumption of the urban persons which sometimes make families spend more than they earn and become indebted. It can also mean taking to certain vices for example, visiting bars and dance floors, taking heady drinks, having drunken driving, eating junk food, having illicit sex relations and so on. Life is impersonal when urbanism peaks. Consumerism can also be used as a term when the consumers defended their rights as consumers.

Urbanity. This is rational living away from superstitious practices. It means rejecting the illogical in favour of the logical. It means getting not merely literate but educated; not merely educated but having tradeable skills/knowledge etc. It is supposed that urbanity will produce economic men (who pursue materialistic objectives) as well as social men (who behave as a societal persons).

> One who is urbane is having best of the combinations of cultures. Culture/urbanity explains why communities living under identical economic conditions

> differ in demographic behaviour. The degree of urbanity in groups of population distinguished them as more or less developed in socio-economic terms.
>
> Urbanity, however, is not synonym of total culture. The Chinese culture will always be different from Egyptian culture though ultimately human beings have the same traits. If people are urbane they will not think that all boys are assets; but that all good children are assets. Urbane parents discharge their liabilities to develop asset elements in their children. They do not shirk their liabilities towards their children and *cultured, urbane children (and \vell-endowed with moral traits) will not forget their duties towards their parents.*

Urbanity and culture are not mere "collections of habits". Culture and urbanity are symbolic systems erected on given superstructural and infrastructural systems. Where people have urbanity they try to develop as much as they can but they do not create social disorder.

> Persons who are urbanised without being urban can create problems.

World Urbanisation Scenario 1850-2000

In the year 1850 only three cities of the world had population of more than 10 lakhs *(See Ira S. Lowry, PDR: "World Urbanisation in Perspective 2000, PDR)* and they were London, Beijing and Paris. There were (perhaps) 110 cities with more than 1 lakh population. Of the 25 largest cities:

> 11 were in Europe;
>
> 8 in East Asia;
>
> 4 in South Asia; and
>
> 2 in North America.

Ancestors of all humanbeings were once tribals! We were all tribals once !

World Urbanisation 1850-1950

The number of large cities increased from 100 to 946 and the largest city's population increased to 1.23 crore that is of London. In 1950, 29 per cent of the world was urbanised. Only 19 per cent world population lived in cities of 1 lakh or more.

World Urbanisation 1950-2000

World urbanisation picked up a tremendous pace. Nearly 290 crore out of the 610 crore person were living in urban areas.

That came to 47.5 per cent. *This was largely because the MDRs "virtually became entirely urbanised ".The* following facts should be noted:

> The urban places are areas of dense continuous settlement whose boundaries do not necessarily coincide with administrative boundaries; they usually include one or more cities and an urbanised fringe. Nations differ in their definitions of "urban"; those differences are reflected principally in the residual category. "Other urban". For the year 2000 the UN independently projected the total urban population of each country and the population of each city that had reached 5 lakh inhabitants by 1980. (See UN World Demographic Year Books and other publications on Population).

By 2025, nearly 60 per cent of the world population will be living in urban areas, *as the urban centres get the upgraded status.* By 2025, 85 per cent of the population of the North America, Northern and Western Europe, South Europe, South America, South Korea, Australia and New Zealand will be in urban areas. *Only in Eastern Africa, China and Certain South Pacific islands do demographers expect a majority of the regional population to live in rural areas. Indian sub-continent will of course not experience that high urbanisation.*

It is to be noted that three tendencies are working simultaneously in improving the figures of urbanisation. They are (I) villages are becoming "rurban" centres and "rurban" centre are becoming urban centres, (ii) there is migration of people from the rural settlements to urban settlements (over urbanisation) and *(iii)* there is transfer/ location of urban facilities in the hitherto rural areas. That is the essense of urbanisation. Better economic lives in urban areas make people migrate to urban areas.

> UN and text-book norms differ from the norms of the statistical bureaus of different countries.
>
> In UK, Belgium, the Netherlands, (Holland or Dutchland), Western Germany (area), Denmark, Japan, Canada, Sweden, Norway and US, their statistical bureaus list urban populations between *75* per cent to even 96 per cent.

China, India and Indonesia as indeed Pakistan, Bangladesh and Nepal have great urban-rural chasm in levels of socio-economic development. The first three countries account for 40 per cent of the population of the world.

> Before 1980, China pursued a deliberate policy of restricting urban growth, refusing residence permits and ration cards to would-be rural-to-urban migrations. In addition nearly 1.7 crore young urban residents were forcibly rusticated during the Cultural Revolution (1966-1976). Consequently, rural population growth far outstripped the availability of arable land. The commune system of agricultural production offered little incentive for using labour efficiency.

In India there is unbriddled migration of the poor regions of the country to the metropolitican cities, [this macrocephalic urbanisation: See Urabanisation in India in this book]. Then emerged the slums— Dharavi is the biggest slum of the world. *India's capital Delhi is the*

TABLE 13.1

Estimates and Projections of Total and Urban Populations, by World Region: 1950-2025

World region	*Population (millions) or percent*											
	1950			*1975*			*2000*			*2025*		
	Total	*Urban*	*Percent urban*	*Total*	*Urban*	*Percent urban*	*Total*	*Urban*	*Percent urban*	*Total*	*Urban*	*Percent urban*
Northern America	166	106	64	239	176	74	297	223	75	345	267	77
Caribbean	17	6	35	27	14	52	41	27	66	58	43	74
Central America	37	15	41	80	46	58	149	105	70	223	178	80
Tropical South America	86	31	36	175	107	61	301	239	79	429	370	86
Temperate South America	25	17	68	39	31	79	55	49	89	70	64	91
Northern and Western Europe	195	135	69	234	188	80	240	201	84	234	201	86
Eastern Europe	88	37	42	106	60	57	120	80	67	131	94	72
Soviet Union	180	71	39	253	152	60	315	222	70	368	273	74
Southern Europe	109	48	44	134	78	58	152	104	68	159	122	77
Western Asia	42	10	24	85	41	48	168	107	64	271	205	76
Northern Africa	52	15	29	94	36	38	176	89	51	261	172	66
Western Africa	65	7	11	123	24	20	277	97	35	558	300	54
Middle Africa	27	4	15	45	13	29	92	44	48	170	110	65
Eastern Africa	63	3	5	122	15	12	272	77	28	537	246	46

	Population (millions) or percent											
	1950			1975			2000			2025		
	Total	Urban	Percent urban	Total	Urban	Percent urban	Total	Urban	Percent urban	Total	Urban	Percent urban
Southern Africa	17	7	41	29	14	48	55	33	60	91	67	74
China	555	61	11	927	187	20	1.256	315	25	1,475	645	44
Japan	84	42	50	112	84	75	130	101	78	132	106	80
Other East Asia	33	9	27	57	31	54	89	70	79	114	98	86
South-east Asia	182	27	"15	324	71	22	520	184	35	688	374	54
Southern Asia	480	76	15	849	181	21	1,387	466	34	1,855	968	52
Australia-New Zealand	10	8	80	17	14	82	22	19	86	27	24	89
Melanesia-Micronesia-Polynesia	3	0	0	5	1	20	8	3	38	27	24	45
World total	2,516	734	29	4,076	1,564	38	6,122	2,844	46	8,206	4,932	60

Note: A list of countries composing each region is given in each source publication. Estimates and projections of urban population for each country are based on that country's definition of "urban".

Sources: UN-CHS. 1987: Annex Table 1: UN-ESA. 1987: Table 2. Entries are based on the UN's 1984 assessment.

dirtiest capital of the Asian country. Books were written about Calcutta (Kolkata) that it is now a dead city beyond salvage. Bombay (Mumbai) has Dharavi; Delhi has slums in trans-Yamuna region; Chennai has them to be seen as one enters the city and the old Kolkata is a nightmare for the city planners. Kanpur or Kochi, all cities have most polluted zones.

> Shortage of space for buildings; limits of horizontal growth of houses; limits of vertical growth of housing projects; shortage of water; inability to dispose garbage and sewerage and sullage; and rising crimes will set the upper threshold of the further growth of cities.

TABLE 13.2

Population of the 30 Largest Urbanized Areas: World, 1950-2000

Rank in year 2000	*Country*	*Urbanized area*	*Thousands of inhabitants*		
			1950	*1975*	*2000*
1	Mexico	Mexico City	3,050	11,610	25.820
2	Japan	Tokyo-Yokohama	6,736	17,668	24,172
3	Brazil	Sao Paulo	2,760	10,290	23,970
4	India	Calcutta	4.520	8.250	16,530
5	India	Bombay	2,950	7,170	16,000
6	United States	NewYork-NE New Jersey	12,410	15,940	15,780
7	Rep. of Korea	seoul	1,113	6,950	13,770
8	Brazil	Rio de Janeiro	3,480	8,150	13,260
9	China	Shanghai	10,420	11,590	13.260
10	Indonesia	Jakarta	1,820	5,530	13,250
11	India	Delhi	1,410	4,630	13,240
12	Argentina	Buenos Aires	5,251	9,290	13,180
13	Pakistan	Karachi	1,040	4,030	12,000
14	Iran	Teheran	1,126	4,267	11,329
15	Bangladesh	Dhaka	430	2,350	11,160
16	Egypt	Cairo-Ginza-Imbaba	3,500	6,250	11,130
17	Iraq	Baghdad	579	3,830	11,125
18	Japan	Osaka-Kobe	3,828	8.649	11,109
19	Philippines	Manila	1,570	5,040	11,070
20	United States	Los Angeles-Long Beach	4,070	8.960	10,990

21	Thailand	Bangkok-Thonburi	1,440	4.050	10.710
22	United Kingdom		London	10.369	10,310
10,510					
23	USSR	Moscow	4,841	7,600	10,400
24	China	Beijing	6,740	8,910	10,360
25	Germany	Rhein-Ruhr	6,853	9.311	9,151
26	Peru	Lima-Callao	1,050	3.700	9,140
27	France	Paris	5,525	8.620	8,720
28	Nigeria	Lagos	360	2,100	8,340
29	Italy	Milan	3,637	6,150	8,150
30	India	Madras	1,420	3,770	8,150

Note: The urban places listed above are areas of dense contiguous settlement whose boundaries do not necessarily coincide with administrative boundaries: they usually include one or more cities and an urbanized fringe. The list includes all such places projected to contain at least 8 million inhabitants in the year 2000.

Source: UN-CHS, 1987: Annex Table 6. Based on the UN's 1984 assessment. See also Martin Brockerhoff in PDR 25(4) Dec. 1999.

SELECTED BIBLIOGRAPHY

U.N.O. The Consequences and Determinants of Population T Trends, 1953, Ch. VI.

U.N.O. Pop. Div. Problems of Migration: Study No. 5, 1949. U.N.O. Proceedings of the World Population Conference, 1954.

U.N.O. International Research on Migration: Misc. Series No. 18, 1953.

U.N.O. Elements of Immigration Policy. Misc. Series No. 19, 1954.

B. Thomas: Migration and Economic Growth, 1954 Cambridge.

B. Thomas: Economics of International Migration. 1958.

Brinley Thomas: International Migration, Ch. 22 in Hausar and Duncan's. *op. cit.*

HW Saunders: Human Migration and Social Equilibrium See 'Population Theory and Policy'. Ed. JJ Spengler and O.D. Duncan. Glencoe, III, Free Press, 1956.

Ch. Hamilton: "Population Pressure and Other Factors Affecting Net Rural Urban Migration", CF: Spengler & Duncan, *op. cit.*

DJ Bogue: "Internal Migration". Ch. 21 in Hausar & Duncan's. *Op. cit.* Thompson: *Op. cit.* pp. 482-499. K. Davis: "International Migration and Urbanisation in Relation to Economic Development".

Paper in World population Conference 1954, U.N.O. Report.

MV Duragen: Economic Development and International Migration UNO Report, Vol. IV, 1965 Conference.

JA Ponsioen: "An Analysis of—and a Policy regarding—Rural Migration in Development Countries.

JG Williamson: "Migrant Selectivity, Urbanisation and Industrial Revolutions", PDR, Vol. 14, No. 2, June 1988.

WB Arthur, TJ Espenshade: Immigration Policy, PDR, Vol. 14, No. 2, June 1988.

DS Massey: Economic Development and International Migration PDR, Vol. 14, No. 3, September 1988.

Myron Weiner: On International Migration. PDR, Vol.11, No. 3, September 1985.

U.N.O. Methods of Measuring Internal Migration. Manual VI, ST/SOA/Series A/47, New York, 1970.

SOME CALCULATIONS

1. Similar models were propounded by many other authors. G.W. von Leibniz (17th century), August Comte and A. Quetelet (19lh century), H.C. Carey (1858), Hilgard(1872), Ravenstein (1885), WJ. Reilly (1929), S.A. Stouffer (1940), G.K. Zipf (1941 and 1949), J.O. Stewart (1947 and 1948), W. Isard and G. Freutel (1954), W. Warntz (1959), and Roland Artle (1959).

2. Suppose we calculate this for Madhya Pradesh of which population is 5,00,00,000: in migrants from Kerala are 15,000 and Keralite out-migrants are 2,000: or Punjabi in migrants are 10,000 and Punjabi oul-migrants are 1000. Suppose the total populations of Keralites and Punjabies in Madhya Pradesh are 20,00,000 and 18,00,000 respectively and gross migration in Madhya Pradesh is 1,00,000. The differential migration for Keralites and Punjabies will be:

DA/for Kerala $$\frac{17{,}000}{1{,}00{,}000} - \frac{19{,}83{,}000}{4{,}99{,}00{,}000} \cdot 100$$

$$.17 - 104 \times 100 = 13$$

DM for Punjab $\frac{17,000}{1,00,000} - \frac{17,89,000}{4,99,00,000} \cdot 100$

.11 -0.36 x 100-7.4

3. *A* and *B* as calculated on previous page.

$C = \frac{1,00,000}{5,00,00,000} = 0.2\%$

D = 13 + 7.4 x 100 175.67%

E = 2,00,000 + 18,00,000 111%

F = 2000+ 1000 = 200%

G = 15000+ 1000= 150%

H = 17000 + 11000 154.55%

4. Bhopal = $\frac{50,000}{5,000} \times \frac{1,00,00,000}{10,00,000} \times 100 = 1,000$

Delhi = $\frac{5,000}{50,000} \times \frac{10,00,000}{1,00,00,000} \times 100 = 1$

PART-IV

Price Theory, Applied to Regions

14

Space and Price Theories: Perfect Competition

Introduction

These chapters may look like chapters of "Managerial Econ." or "Micro Econ." or "Advanced Econ. Theory."

Space *inter alia* determines factor prices, commodity prices (commodities come from the primary sector as wheat, rice, iron ore, timber, fruits etc.), prices of goods (goods come from the manufacturing sector as cars, battle tanks or TV) and prices of services (which come from the tertiary sectors.

We note down the following catch points, numbering eight.

1. *Fiat prices* charged on the *order* of the government may not be related to space. Postal articles like post card, inland or envelope are delivered all over India at the same rate. The changes for different countries do differ but the same rate is charged all over the space of that country. Here internal space becomes irrelevant for price.
2. *Factor price of land or rent* will depend upon location and demand primarily. Supply of land in due course of time becomes very scarce in urban areas, primarily in prime locations. Even in a city like Bhopal, land

which was given @ Re 1 per 4 sq. feet in a market in the periphery of the city is now crores of rupees per sq. metre in commercial areas. In metropolitan cities a three bad-room flat may be sold in 10 crores in the *new* localities. The prices can range from low to *sky-rocketing* in metropolitan cities. A tenant may have to pay 10 to 12 months rent in advance. Productivity in terms of tonnes of crops may decide prices/rents of agricultural land. Urban lands command prices on the basis of "prestigious location" and productivity in terms money." Realtors have to be monied man and most of them are reported to be "dons," who control prime lands.

3. *Wages and salaries* are more on the basis of differential skills than on the basis of location only. Rural wages are low primarily due to a plethora of unskilled or very little skilled labour. Even migration to urban areas improves the wages only marginally. The structure of wages is a function of hierarchy of skills and occupations. Some regional differences are compensations for higher costs of living. (The coolies at railway station at Bangalore/Bangaluru charge @ 100 per piece and the charges may be higher than a sleeper ticket from Bhopal to Bangalore). Political differences in space, (communist party rule in West Bengal and Kerala is scare-crow to the industrialists). Wages here can be high not due to high demand but high pressure of trade unions. Specialisation wages differ over space. Utensil makers of Moradabad have different wage structure than the pluckers of tea leaves of Assam.
4. *Interest rates differences* are less between places and very high between formal (organised) and informal (unorganised) markets. Capital is very mobile and hence interest rate differentials are less. Usurous rates of interest are changed in rural India.

Professional money lenders borrow from the nationalised banks at the caps of 15 p.c. to 18 p.c. and loan out money, mostly for consumption needs, @ 36, 48, 60 or even to 100 p.c. They charge @ 3%, 4%, 5%, per month. Interest is deducted in advance. If Rs. 10,000 are given @ 48%, then 10,000 - 4,300 = 5200 will actually be given. Regional D' and S' differences do affect regional interest rates—but in informal markets. Space dos not play much role.

5. *Profits are differential rewards in the rent of abilities*, and they are not space related. The present leading entrepreneurs had their great-grand parents or might be great-great rand parents who were tribals! We all were tribals once.* Entrepreneurs and enterprisers move to urban and metropolitan centres. It is a fact that rural activities cannot ever make people billionnaires, as the urban persons can be. The hierarchy of profit earners is in accordance with the hierarchy of the size and expertise of the entrepreneurs. Tied entrepreneurs are tied to locations in space. VAM (value-added in manufacture) is not space related as it is work-related.
6. Transport changes and space have very close relationship:

Transport costs are "ignored" for space. This is another way of saying that in perfectly competitive market prices at the centre will be equal to that in the phriphery plus transport costs**

Gradient around a centre need not be of the same time. In that care equal price will not be the same in a neat concentric circle

* A top industrialist's grand father's house had to be sold for Rs. 50/- only.

** See ahead in this chapter.

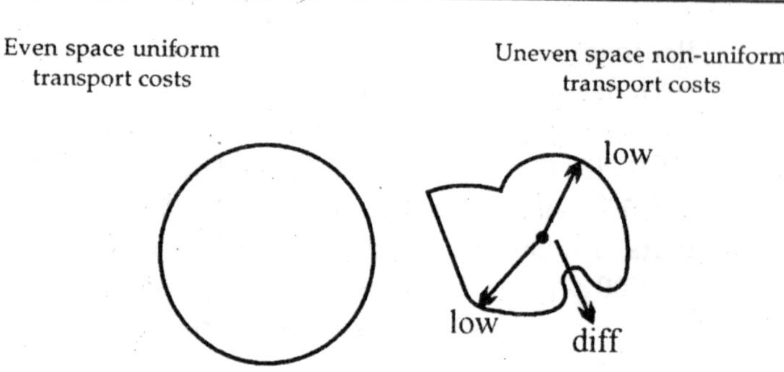

Fig. 1

7. *In monopoly price discrimination between different regions can be practised if there no seepage of the goods sold from one market to the other.*
8. *In oligopoly* (a few sellers) price discrimination may or may not be practised depending upon how close or remote substitutes the two products are. The entry level Maruti standard and the costliest car made for the very rich are "no substitutes." Transport wastages can be there over the space. Car produced in Gurgaon (Haryana) near Delhi can be transported to Tamil Nadu. A car produced in Tamil Nadu can be sent to Delhi.

Neat circles of markets in space are not to be found. Perhaps this picture appended below may be nearer the reality.

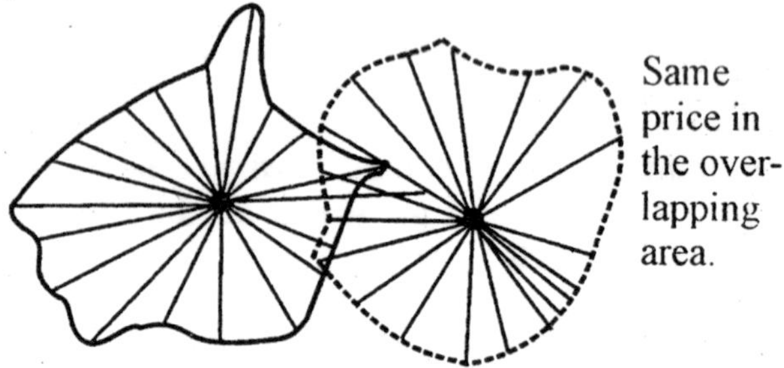

Fig. 2

We can show the inter-relationship between conditions *over the space* and examine the likely repercussions.

Sellers	Buyers	Market	State of affairs
1	2	3	4
Concentrated	Dispersed	Perfect competition	– There will be same price or AR * for all the sellers.
Tied location		Imperfect	– AR will go down for due to tied location. – AR goes down at different rates for different locations. – Transport costs will have to be low for sellers to get a competitive edge: Efficient 'transport of one's own will give edge over rivals. – If transport efficiency not available, then sellers will disperse.
Dispersed	Dispersed		– Sellers from all comers will charge the same price. – Distant producers can compete only when they have lower costs. – Or, they will have to accept a lower margin of profit. – Rent gradients will develop: Nearby lands commanding higher rents. – Improvement in transport will bring down rent of places near the market centre – Improvement in transport will provide advantage to distant producers. – Rent of nearby places will go down.
Dispersed	Central	Dispersed	– Competitiveness of Market dispersed sellers will depend upon their efficiency in production. – Markets will develop at intermediate places.

Dispersed	Dispersed		– hexagonal markets, size of hexagonal markets different for different products. – agglomeration tendencies will develop. – hexagons will get misshaped. – If products differentiated then monopolistic competition in their own hexagonal market areas. – Supplementary costs will change sizes of hexagons.
Oligopolies	Uneven	Uneven	(See Separate chapter) Super-normal profits in short period. Normal profits in the long period. Criss crossing of markets. In most markets uncertainty is the only certainty because of the dynamic changes is economic and technical conditions of production function.

* See the succeeding pages and chapters.

Even for those homogeneous commodities which are conventionally regarded as the commodities of "perfectly competitive market" different bulk rates may be quoted under different circumstances. "Free on Board" (FOB), Free on Rails (FOR.), Cost-Insurance-Freight (CIF) rates may be quoted. The sellers are now interested in quick turn-over and multiple rolling of stocks i.e., larger number of commodities sold at smaller profit margin, may still bring greater net total income. Hence not the transport cost differentials but several other considerations enter into spatial pricing.

This is not to deny the correctness of the Reilly's "Law of retail gravitation" which states that a —

> centre tends to attract retail trade from an individual customer located in its hinterland in proportion to its size (as measured by population) and in the inverse

> proportion to the square of the distance between them. (Gravity Model: See elsewhere in this book).

It is the population of the centre that serves as a surrogate for the variety of goods obtainable. In the words of Richardson:

> "The square of distance assumption is a crude way of adjusting geographical distance for the costs and disutility of travel."

In the present day market situations *price discrimination* has become common even in non-monopoly situations. Commissions and gifts given by some sellers introduce imperfection in the market of homogeneous products also in that the sellers want to promote a captive clientele. Price discrimination is actually related to *income and price elasticity of demand for the products.* Rich persons can pay higher prices and at fabulously high incomes demand for anything is inelastic at any high price. Such persons can be made to cough up higher prices. Personal discrimination practised by professionals or others is not space related. *Space comes into the picture in the form of a condition that it will be better if there is no seepage of goods between the groups discriminated whether at the same place or at different places.* A market in which one can discriminate is the one in which his rival cannot enter for various reasons, transport cost being one. Cross hauling continues despite transport costs.

A. Essential Characteristics/Features/Conditions of Perfect Competition

We generally find perfect competition in the market of commodities, provided that market is not organised and formalised. A weekly vegetable market held in towns and cities is an example of perfectly competitive market. Foodgrains, vegetables, fruits etc. are sold in such a market. But to describe that market fully we can analyse the top 10 essential features/conditions/characteristics of that market. Intense competition is not perfect competition, unless the following conditions are satisfied.

1. The product sold in such a market is *homogeneous* and need not be *homogenous.* (Homogenous is exactly the same; cloned type) *homogeneous* is 'alike' or nearly the same.) When wheat, rice, pulses, onions or bananas are purchased from such a market we do not know the name of the producer. In fact we do not even bother to know that. There is no brand name and there is no differentiation. *Grading and standardisation* can be done. For example, small-sized, medium-sized and large-sized onions can be kept apart. Rice of one variety is kept separate from the other—*kalimooch* from the *baasmati.* They are in perfect competition.

In this connection it may be noted that if baasmati rice is packaged in 1,2 or 5 kg. packets and is given a brand name, the produce no longer remains of the perfectly competitive market. *(TV is a product: rice is a 'produce'.)* The processing, packaging and branding involve activities of 'manufacturing sector'; the product becomes product of 'monopolistic competition'. [See section on this topic]

2. There is a Large Number of Producers/Sellers

Each one is of atomistic size. One single seller cannot raise the price of the product by threatening to withhold the supplies. His supplies constitute insignificant portion of the total supply. *Each producer is a price taker and not a price maker.*

3. There is a Large Number of Buyers and Each One is of Atomistic Size

No single buyer can get the price reduced by threatening not to buy. His demand is insignificant part of the total demand. *If there is some reduction in price for bulk purchase, it is not for that buyer; it is for all.* The rates for 1 kg. can differ from the rates if 100 kgs. are purchased in one go. This is not contradictory. This rate will be available to all bulk buyers. *Each buyer is a price taker and not a price maker.*

> This single producer/seller can decide how much to produce/sell at a given price. He cannot set the price. Similarly, each single buyer can decide how much to buy at a given price but has to take the price as given. Outlay* adjustments are possible via decisions about output and not about prices.

4. Demand and Supply Conditions are Elastic

The buyers and sellers are attached to the price and not to each other. (In imperfect competition a person can be attached to a particular dress-designer.) If the buyer offers a lower price, no seller will sell him. If a seller charges a little higher price, all buyers will leave him.

5. There are No Transport Costs

(This statement may look ridiculous *but it actually is a way of saying that there will be difference, in the prices in the market for the same product but these differences will be subject to the differences in the transport costs.)*

> If price at centre 'A' in a city is Rs. 20 per kg. and in another part of the city it is Rs. 19.5 a kg. There is a saving of Rs. 0.5 per kg. If the to-and-fro transport costs are Rs. 20, that means even if the person purchases 40 kg. the total expenditure will remain the same. *If the person purchases substantially more than 40 kg. there will be some saving.*
>
> But there are "time costs" in transport. Azim Premji cannot afford to waste time in availing this economy. Time is precious to him.[1]

---

* Outlay = price x output.

1. Henry Ford used to personally go to the desks of his employees, if he wanted to know something or say something. A media man asked "You can summon the highest officer in your chamber; why do you go to the desks of the lowest salary employee even?" To this Henry Ford replied "anyone who comes here wants to impress me and overstays. That means waste of my time". Time costs are thus very important

Market expands if there is reduction in transport costs per unit of value. One can go some distance to purchase cheaper gold but not to purchase cheaper potatoes because of the cost of transport. A brick used for constructing a house will be sold at the nearest places around the place of manufacture. It cannot be exported because transport and insurance charges will be several times the cost of manufacture. On the other hand, the gold-brick can easily bear such costs of transport, insurance and handling. Hence its market is worldwide.

The concentric circles of centres (say) A, B and C can overlap. In the overlapped areas the buyers can buy from any producer/seller of the circles not from outside. Reduction in transport costs per unit value enlarges the market and vice versa.

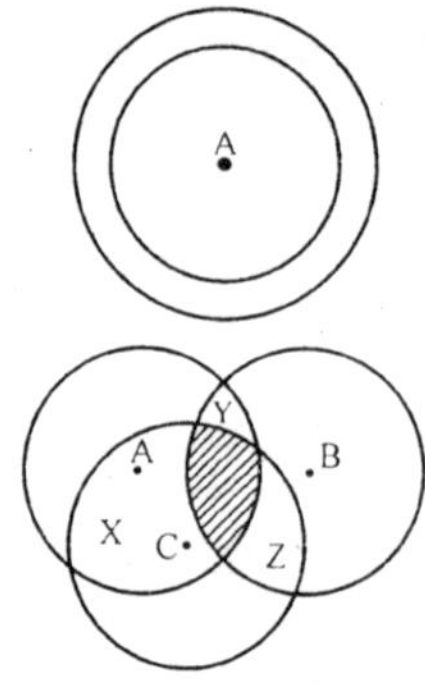

Fig. 3

Concentric circles. Market widens due to lower transport costs and vice versa.

(a) Buyers in the shaded portion can buy from the producers/sellers of 'A', 'B' or 'C' centres.

(b) Buyers of (Y) space can buy from 'A' and 'B' centres but not from the 'C' centre.

(c) Buyers from the (X) segment can buy from 'A' or 'C' centres but not from 'B'.

(d) Buyers from the (Z) segment can buy from 'C' or 'B' centres but not from 'A' centre.

6. The sixth feature which emerges from the 5th point above is *cost of production of a produce sold under perfect competition will be the same over the entire country, except the differences in the cost of transport.* This assumption is based upon another assumption that *raw materials, capital goods and factors are mobile over the space that their prices become more or less equal.*

> If in Bhopal the wage rate for the semi-skilled worker is Rs. 150 per day and in Raisen (a town 35 kms. away), the rate is Rs. 100 per day, there will be outmigration from Raisen and immigration in Bhopai. Wages will fall in Bhopai due to the arrival of workers and will rise in Raisen due to reduction in the abundance of workers. Let us say they become 140: 110 and then 130: 120 and then 125 at both the place. When this happens, there will be no more mobility as the wage rates get equalised.
>
> *[Even if this does not happen in real life, the assumption or condition or characteristic is there in the theory. It is the non-realisation of assumptions that the theory of perfect competition was discarded in favour of the theory of 'imperfect competition'. There were other reasons also...please keep on reading the entire section].*

7. The players in perfect competition are *rational.* They buy at the cheapest prices and sell at the dearest prices—provided they are competitive prices. Ultimately the buyers and sellers buy/sell at the same price for the same product/produce. Buyers try to minimise costs and maximise use-values. Sellers want to minimise costs and maximise the exchange values.

8. It is assumed that the buyers and sellers have perfect knowledge about the prices of everything and act accordingly. Mobilities of factors and movement of things will be guided by this.

9. There is no government intervention. Rules are there but regulations are not there. *It is a laissez faire system and there is complete freedom for the entry and exit of the firms.*

10. There is no queuing system in perfect competition. Price clears the market. If not, then the price changes.

B. Price Determination Under Perfect Competition—1. Two Theories: One Synthesis

These two theories were of classical economists (cost of production theory) and of the Austrian economists (utility theory). The former argued that P = CoP i.e., the cost of production; the second group argued that price = MU or marginal utility.

A. Classical theory or the 'cost of production' theory of price under perfect competition emphasised that price will be and should be equal to the cost of production in the long run; *but cost of production will include normal profits.*

Hence if we say that price is equal to the cost of production it is not a case of "no profit no loss". This is because the cost of production includes recompense to all the five factors of production i.e., rent + wages + interest + salaries + normal profits. These are given to/for land/ natural resources, labour, capital, organisation (technology included), and entrepreneur/s.

Three Questions:

(a) The critics of the theory argued that if the price is equal to the cost of production, then why do the units of the same lot sell at the different prices while their cost of production was/must have been the same?

The answer to this objection was that the price is equal not to the 'past' cost of production but to that cost of production "as it would be today". Since this will change, the price also changes.

(b) The second question was why some products may not command any price even when their production involved costs. If a study table does not sell in a society of illiterates how do we explain that?

The answer was that utility plays a part but partially only. Cost of production is from the supply side. From the supply side we take the 'scarcity element' that is represented in the cost of production. The use-values are created by to command the price or exchange value the buyers should perceive utilities.

But this was not an acknowledgement of the demand side being incorporated. It was admission of a paradox. Water has greater utility than gold but gold commands higher price and water may even be free. Thus scarcity element counts. That accorded with the cost of production argument.

(c) The third question was/is/can be that why some goods sell at fantastically high prices while their cost of production is not much e.g., a painting of Picasso? This is because such things are rare. The cost of production theory applies to normal goods and not goods of rare artistic value.

B. The Utility Theory: Austrian economists, however, gave utility theory of value. They pointed out that if a man sees greater utility in a thing, which otherwise has a very low cost of production it will command high value. On the contrary, if a commodity has high cost of production but none sees any utility in it, it will command no value. Thus utility is the true determinant of price.

General Statement of Value: (Marshall) Synthesis

Marshall, the greatest economist, who formalised the pure economics, ended this controversy for ever. He pointed out that cost of product and utility both determine value and said.

> "Just as we cannot say whether it is the upper or the lower blade of a pair of scissors that cuts a piece of cloth, when the two blades operate together, so we cannot say whether demand (depending on utility) alone or supply (depending on the cost of production) alone determines value and just as there can be no cutting until the two blades meet so there can be no value until supply meets demand—the point at which they meet in order to cut *i.e.,* the equilibrium point is the point at which market value is fixed."

Marshall combined the two views of the classical economists and Austrian economists. In fact both the cost of production and utility determine price. The cost of production sets that minimum limit below which the seller will not accept. The buyer will not pay more than what he considers the utility of the commodity. Thus, both the demand (utility) and supply (cost of production) determine price.

C. Equilibrium

Demand and Supply of Commodity and Price Determination

The demand of a commodity is a function of the utility congealed in the commodity vis-a-vis the price of that commodity. A commodity or a service is demanded because it satisfies a particular want. The more the utility, other things remaining the same, the greater the demand. The greater the demand, other things remaining the same, the greater the price. There is thus direct relationship between the impact of demand on price. The demand of a commodity goes on decreasing with the increase in price and goes on increasing with the fall in the price. Thus the demand curve of a commodity slopes downward to the right. The utility of the commodity is the highest limit beyond which the buyer will not pay.

Supply: Economics of Supply—Once Again

Supply is that part of the production ± stocks which is brought for sale in the market at the given price. Just as the demand cannot be mentioned without reference to price, so also the supply can also not be mentioned without reference to price. If the price becomes very low and does not cover the cost of production, intended supply will remain stock. *The elasticities of supplies are as under:*

Supply Response

Ability to increase or decrease the supplies as per demand. If all resources can be marshalled easily to increase the supplies as a result of increase in demand, we say supply responses are positive.

Elastic Supply

When the supply is reduced proportionately as a result of a fall in price by a certain percentage or when as a result of the rise in price, the supplies can be increased in the same proportion.

Zero Supply 'E'

When supply remains invariant in quantities and contents whatever be the price.

Infinity Supply: Perfectly Elastic 'S'

When the supplies change without there being any change in the price. This happens due to agro-climatic and natural reasons.

Highly Elastic Supply

When as a result of a small percentage change in the price, the change in the supply in the same direction is more than proportionate.

Less Elastic 'S'

When percentage change in supply is less than

proportionate in the same direction as a result of a certain percentage of change in the price.

We have the usual demand and supply curve. They intersect at point E. We drop a perpendicular from *E* on the horizontal line and get OS as the equilibrium supply. This is sold at OP price. OS is the total supply as well as the total demand.

In the informal (non-organised) perfectly competitive marketing, prices are settled after higgling and bargaining. There can be bidding also. As different lots of supplies are cleared, the price can change also.

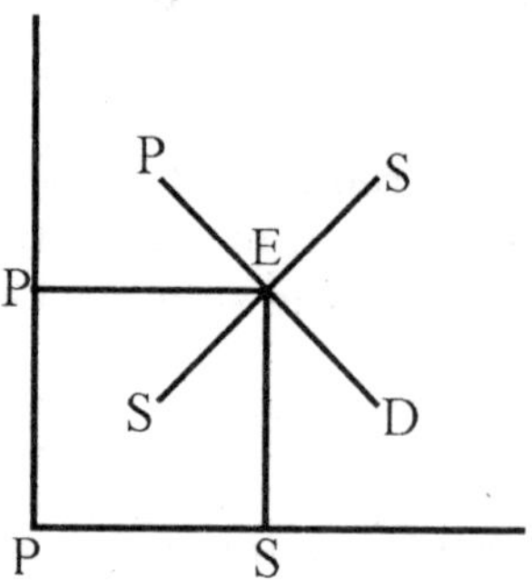

Fig. 4

Price Rs. per unit	*Demand: Unit?*	*Supply Units*
10	1000	—
12	750	250
13	500	500
14	250	750
15	—	1000

At the price of Rs. 10 the supplies are zero. That does not mean that the stocks are also zero. Stocks are withheld. *This is reservation price* at which intended supplies can be converted back to supplies. Transport costs will be incurred if the intended supplies were already taken to the market. Storage changes will also be there. There will be that notional cost of the 'loss of interest'. Hence next time the suppliers would like to sell at higher price. *In case of the perishable goods, there may not be any reservation price. In fact when there is danger of the whole lot getting soiled / spoiled, the suppliers may sell at whatever price they can get. This is 'salvage price'.* At price Rs. 13, the D' and S' are equal. We have shown zero demand at price Rs. 15; this seldom happens. Zero demand is usually due to non-price reason.

Equilibrium price, equilibrium output and equilibrium demand are not permanent. The price will change if there is change in either the supply function and/or demand function. At the new price there will be change in the demand and supplies also. The relationship is circular.

Equilibrium is of ephemeral nature. When demand and supply determine the price, we study the "law of price". When the price changes the demand and supplies, we study the "laws of demand and supply". Equilibrium disequilibrium equilibrium disequilibrium come in chain but giving different prices.

In isolation we can say:

- When demand function improves, price rises.
- When demand function deteriorates, price falls.
- When supply function improves, price falls.
- When supply function deteriorates, price rises.

When price rises, supply function improves. When price falls, supply function deteriorates. When price rises, demand function deteriorates. When price falls, demand function improves.

Price gets determined where the demand and supply

function lines intersect. This gives equilibrium price we get the equilibrium demand and output which are equal. It is a circular relationship. [Rise in demand raises the price: rise in supply brings down the price: rise in supply price raises the supply: rise in price reduces the demand. If rise in demand is the cause and rise in the price is the consequence, it is part of the law of price. If rise in supply is the cause and fall in the price is the consequence, it is the other half of the law of price. If the price rises first and demand goes down, it is the law of demand—and if we measure how much change there is in the demand as a result of the initial change in the price, it is the study of the 'degree of the elasticity of demand'. If as a result of the initial change in price, there is a change in supply it is the study of the law of supply. If we quantify this, it is the measurement of the 'supply response or elasticity'.

D. Eight Changes in Equilibrium

The equilibrium price level in perfect competition depends on aggregate supply as well as demand. Both cost of production (supply side) and utility (demand side) are important—-just like two blades of scissors (Marshall). Equilibrium price, once obtained is subject to change if there are changes in either or both supply and *demand functions*. There can be eight types of changes:

	Demand	*Supply*	*Price*
1.	Same	rises	falls
2.	Same	falls	rises
3.	Rises	same	rises
4.	Falls	same	falls
5.	Rises (provided in the same proportion)	rises	same
6.	Falls	rises	steep fall
7.	Rises	falls	steep rise
8.	(a) Falls (if both fall in equal measure, no change)	falls	price will be affected by that factor which changes more.
	(b) Rises	rises	(proportions differ)

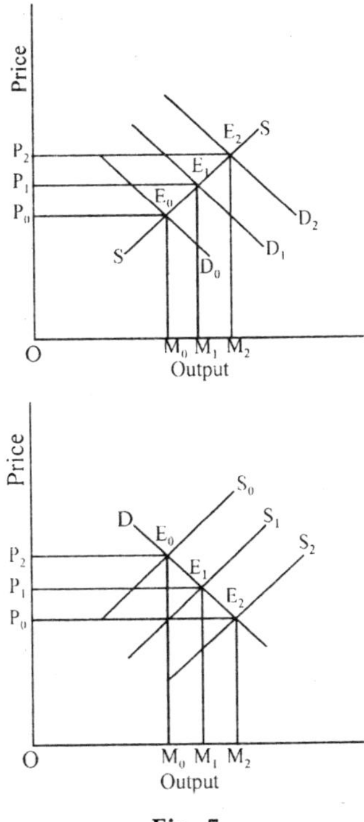

Fig. 5

Supply function same and demand function improves from D_1 to D_2 price at E_2 e.g. is higher, so is output.

- Demand function unchanged.
- As S function improves from S_t to S_2, output increases to M_2 at E_2 and price falls to

Supply function same, and demand function deteriorates (falls) to D_o, then at new e.g. E_o, output is M_o at P goes down to P_o.

- As S function deteriorates from S_1 to S_o, output falls to M_o at E_o e.g., pt. and price rises to P_o.

Price changes affected by Δ df. Price and demand change in the same direction.

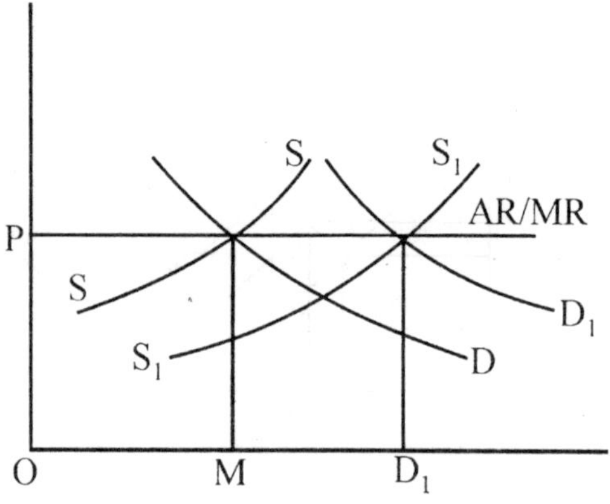

Fig. 6

- Price moves in the opposite direction of the changes in supply function.
- Both demand and supply functions so improve $(S \rightarrow S_1)$ and $(D \rightarrow D_1)$ that price remains the same. They mutually cancel that the change.
- We can also infer that if both fall equally, then also the price will remain the same.
- There will be changes in outputs only.
- Supply function improve which brings down prices S to S_1.
- Demand function deteriorates which also brings down price D to D_1.
- Both bring down the price sharply not warranted by change in output but changes in the demand and supply functions.
- We can look at the other way also from S_1 to S and D_1 to D and can prove that price rises sharply from P_1 to P.
- Here the demand function has improved from D to D_1, and so has the supply function from S to S_1. Rise

in demand function has not led to rise in price because the supply function has improve more and hence the price has fallen.

- We can look and infer the other way also, from D_1 to D demand has gone down, yet no fall in price takes place because supply function deteriorates more from S_1 to S. Output changes from OM_1 to DM. Hence price rises from P_1 to P.

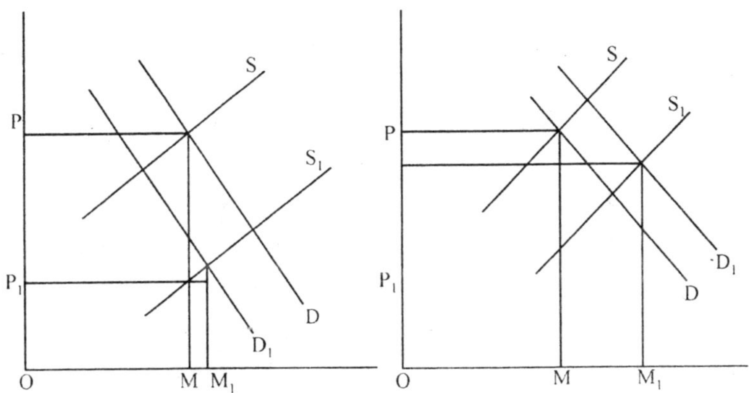

Fig. 7

E. Price Determination in the 'Short' and 'Long' Periods

The 'short' or 'long' period is not calculated in terms of the number of days, weeks, months or years. A period is 'short' if supply cannot be changed according to demand. If there is a rise in demand, the producer has to make it certain that it is of enduring nature; then he has to arrange raw materials, labour, capital and all other factors and resources. It will take time and till this is done the period is regarded as 'short'. If the demand has gone down permanently, reduction in supply will require various painful measures of liquidation. When supply can be adjusted according to demand, it becomes a long period. However, further changes in demand can again put the demand and supply positions in disequilibrium and the process of reaching equilibrium starts all over again. The process is continuous and thus we may say "long period seldom comes".

In the *very short period* spot stock is spot supply. In other cases stocks can be converted into supplies (when there is a rise in demand) or supplies can be converted into stocks (if there is fall in demand and the goods and not perishable or do not involve immense storage costs). In the long period factors of production, resources and even technology can be adjusted according to the needs dictated by demand and other conditions.

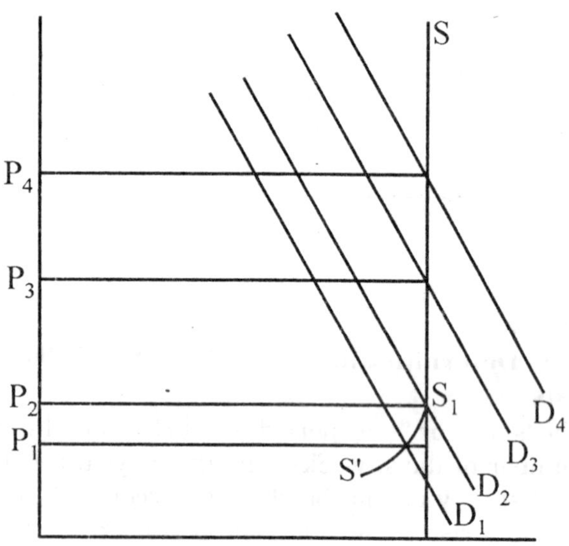

Fig. 8

In the short period, the supply curve becomes inelastic and assumes the shape of a vertical straight line. The price moves in sympathy with the demand function. As the demand function improves, price rises and as it falls price falls. In that segment of the supply function line in which there is a little bit of elasticity due to conversion of stocks into supply, the price movement in' sympathy with the demand will be less than proportionate because dampening influence of supply response is there. Thus 8,8' segment shows a little elastic supply function. Thereafter, the supply function curve becomes a vertical, absolutely inelastic. As demand function rises, price also rises in the same proportion.

Market Prices and Normal Price

Market price is the price at which the buyers and sellers actually transact their business. It is the price of the present 'moment'. Hence prices can change several times in a day, week, month or year. If daily changes are taken, there will be so many points of the height of the price that the trend rate line will be for a week. If weekly averages are plotted, we can have the trend line for month. If monthly average prices are plotted on a graph, the trend rate of normal price for the year can be found. If the prices of various years are plotted on a graph, we can have a line of the average "normal" price for (say) 15 years.

Market price is the actual equilibrium price. Market price cannot be less than the variable costs per unit but it can far exceed in favourable circumstances the average cost. In this case there are super-normal profits. They get obliterated soon because of the additional production that the firms make or because of the entry of new firms. Exit of the firms is much slower process. An entrepreneur does everything to avoid closure of the unit before it is finally closed.

> *Normal price* is a theoretical concept. It is a long term price. Long term is elusive as much as this sentence shows "cash today, credit tomorrow". That

tomorrow never comes; today's tomorrow is today next day! It is a trend rate price. There cannot be a loss or profit at this normal price—theoretically that is. If demand exerts greater pressure on market price, the supply side factors exert greater pressure on the normal price.

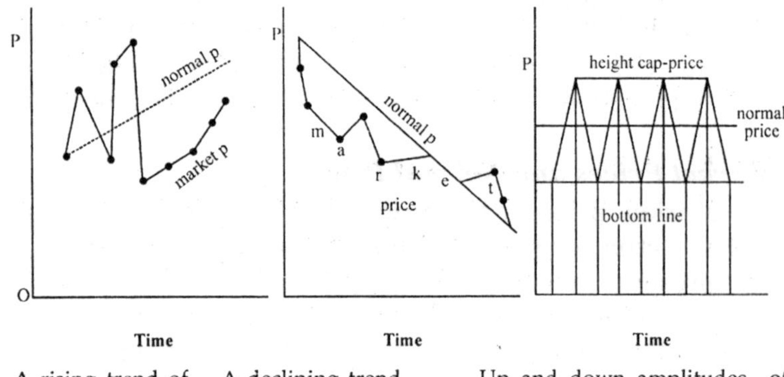

A rising trend of the normal price

A declining trend of normal price

Up and down amplitudes of market price same, hence normal price "comes out" a steady price.

Fig. 9

Above diagrams can show the positions:

In the short period above-normal profits can be earned even in perfect competition as AR can become higher than AC. Soon these profits will be brought down to normal with the entry of the new firms or increased production by the old firms. *There is a reservation price also.* It is that price which is lower than the cost of production and on which the sellers would like to convert the supplies back to stock. Instead of selling at a loss the producers can bring back the potential supplies back to their godowns and incur additional cost of storage and rent. However, this is possible only in case of non-perishable goods. Perishable goods can be sold at a loss also because holding them back means total loss. In such a case the price will be known as the *salvage price.* It is not necessary that losses are incurred on perishable goods only. In the face of falling demand or excess supply, losses can be incurred in all types of goods, as above normal profits can be reaped in case of all goods—provided there is a case of shortage of supply. *Short period price is known as 'Market Price'.*

Long Period: 'Normal Price'

In the long period, when the supply can be adjusted according to the dictates of the demand function, the price becomes equal to the cost of production, which *includes* normal profits. Since demand can be met, the changes in price become the function of the changes in the supplies. The supply function becomes elastic. In the words of Marshall:

> "As a general rule, the shorter the period, which we are considering, the greater must be the share of our attention which is given to influence of demand on value and the longer the period, the more important will be the influence of the cost of production on value. Normal price is the price which would exist in a state of equilibrium, if all the disturbing influences which are continually interfering with stable price adjustment could be removed."

In thc long run: $P = cp$

Price equal to cost of production. The cost of production can behave in three ways in the long run:

1. Constant costs under constant returns;
2. Falling costs under increasing returns; and
3. Rising costs under the decreasing returns.

The third possibility is much more realistic for the long run. However, we can study the price determination under these conditions:

Under constant returns or constant cost of production,

rising and falling demand function does not alter the per unit cost of production. Hence as the demand function line rises or falls, the price remains the same: only supply moves in sympathy. There is normal profits in all conditions; larger with larger output.

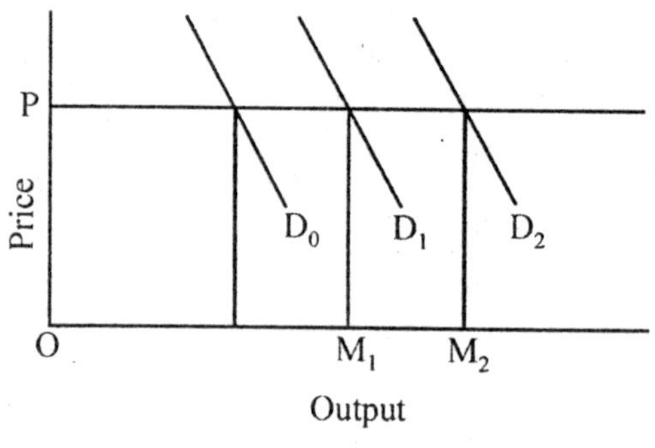

Fig. 10

Contrast Costs Rise in *a*" from D_1 to D_2 = price same. Fall in d' from D_1 to D_0 = price same.

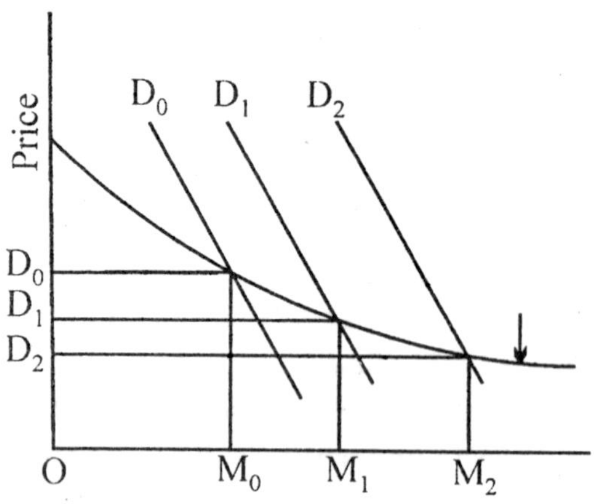

Fig. 11

If there is *increasing return in the long run,* the price will move *in the opposite direction of the change in demand function.* (A) When the demand function rises, output also rises and per unit cost goes down because of the economies of the scalc and hence the price also goes down. (B) If the demand function falls, output is reduced and the cost of production rises. With fall in demand function now there will be rise in price! Thus:

Demand function rises from D_1 to D_2 = Price falls from P_1 to P_2.

Demand function falls from D_1 to D_0 = Price rises from P_1 to P_2

This is for the industry as a whole.

The most likely situation is that in the long run the production function will be subject to decreasing returns and per unit cost of production will rise. As this happens, the price shall rise with the rise in demand function and fall with the fall in demand function. Thus:

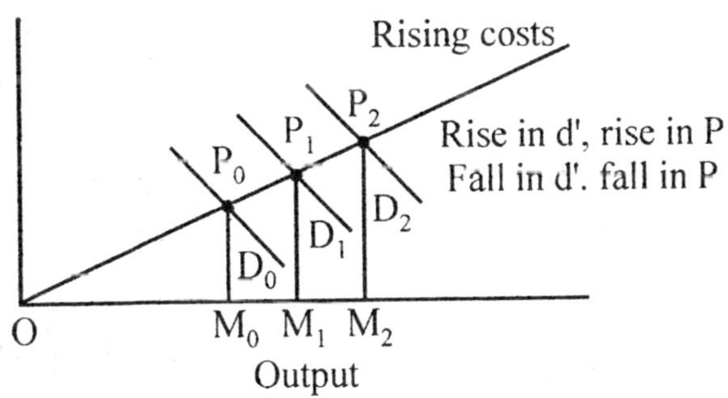

Fig. 12

At first the cost fall with the rise in output (declining AC and MC, then they may remain constant (horizontal AC/MC, and ultimately both AC and MC rise. Thus:

The MC curve cuts the AC curve at the lowest point of inflection in AC.

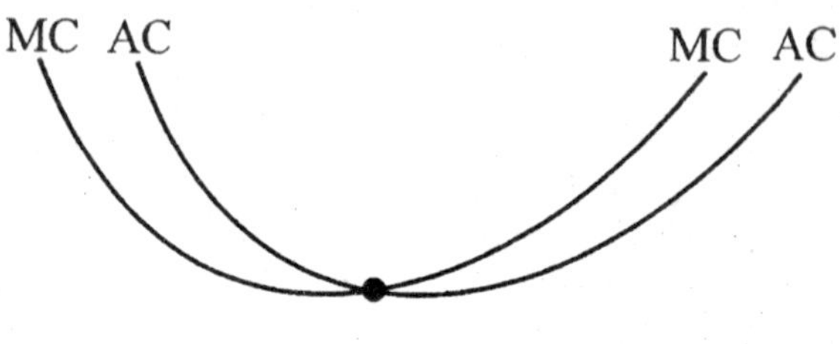

Fig. 13

F. Equilibrium of the Industry and the Firm: Short and Long Run

All industrial units or firms producing the same output in a country make the 'industry' of the country. The price, as we have seen, for the entire industry is determined at a point where the total demand is equal to the total supply. The changes in the price are due to: (A) changes in the demand function, and (B) changes in the supply function.

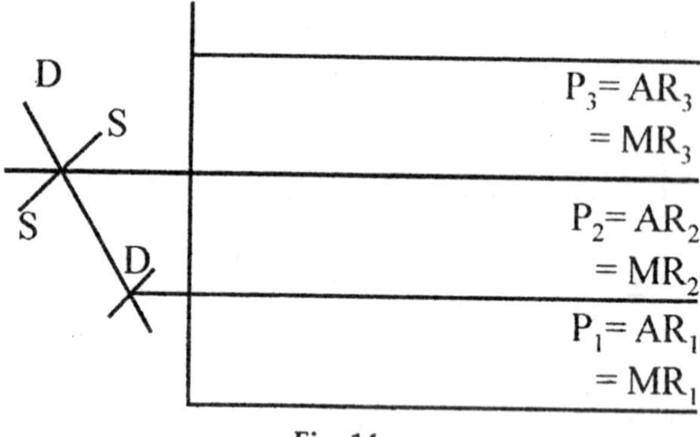

Fig. 14

Thus, there are changes in the price prevailing under perfect competition, but this is true for the industry and not for the firm. A firm cannot attract all customers by cutting the price because all others will do likewise. Hence the price comes down or goes up or all. $P = AR = MR$ for all at lower or higher levels thus:

AR and MR lines in perfect competition are horizontal to the base line and they converge on each other. They show that there is no need to reduce the price to attract the customers from the rivals. 'Unlimited amounts' can be sold at the same price. The AR and MR lines come down or go up for all. They do not slope down for individual sellers.

The essential points about the equilibrium of the industry have been studied in the previous pages. *The firm, which is a price taker and not a price maker, has to adjust the output to the given price, which comes from the equilibrium of the industry.*

1. In the short period at least the variable costs will have to be recovered. Fixed costs cannot be fully recovered in the short period. However, if the *variable* costs are also not recovered, the firm will not go into production or will stop production. As soon as the price rises, enough to cover the variable costs, it will go into production again. There is no point in producing when even the variable costs are not recovered.

   When average fixed costs are not recovered and only variable costs are recovered, there is a loss. When variable costs are also not recovered, the loss becomes more. Part of it can easily be avoided by not going into production. Fixed costs have already been incurred and thus that part of the loss cannot be avoided. *The firm, therefore, goes into production and remains in production only when at least variable costs are recovered.*
2. When the price is so high that a firm cannot only recover its variable cost per unit but also fixed cost per unit i.e., when the $P = AC$ or $AR = AC$, then the firm is in equilibrium position and earns normal profit (average cost itself includes normal profits).

3. When, because of the aggregate demand exceeding aggregate supply, the equilibrium price of the industry rises, and it is higher than the AC of the firm (which we are studying), the firm will earn extraordinary profits, which will in any case be soon wiped off because other firms will increase production. XY portion shows super-normal profits.

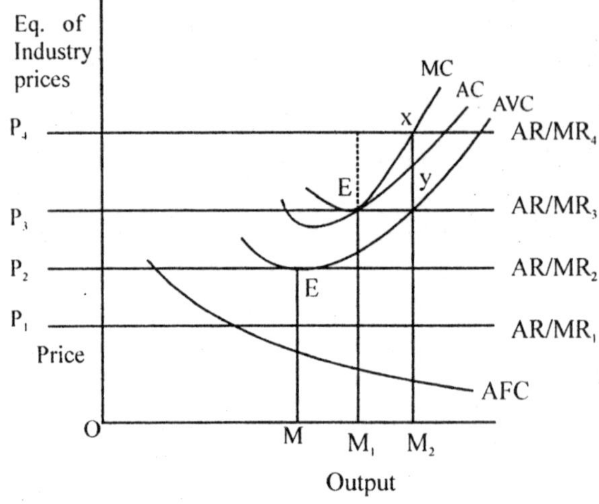

Fig. 15

In the long run all firms should be in equilibrium and earn normal profits. No firm can earn extraordinary profits because they will be shared by all the firms which increase their production. Similarly no firm will incur losses because such weakings will be eliminated. *Perfect competition is the rule of jungle, the survival of the fittest.* All firms earn normal profits in the long run. In the long run *AR=MR=AC = MC.*

- E' is the equilibrium point.
  However below the point of the price.
- E point is the "shut-down" is declining from P_4 to P_3 to P_2.

- E is *the production starting* point if the prices are moving upward from P_1 to P_2 to P_3 to P_4.

On P_1 Price no production,

On P_2 Price production *OM,* but there is loss because $AR<AC$ or *AC* is still higher than AR_2. Only variable costs are covered. OM_1 output.

On P_3 $AC\ MC + AR_3\ MR_3$. Normal profit. This is equilibrium price AR_3 or P_3 and OM_1 is equilibrium output. E^1 equilibrium point.

On P_4 $Ar_u > Ac$ so super normal profits = *XY* line.

Price in perfect competition is equal to cost of production. But cost of production of which firm spread over the space, particularly when the cost of production is falling.

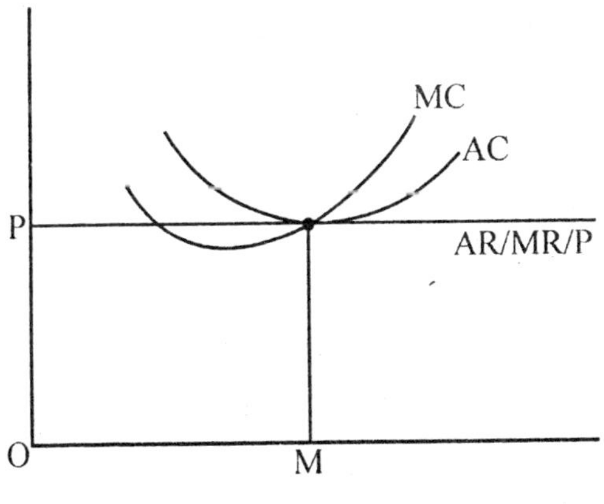

Fig. 16

Firms of perfect competition are spread over the entire space. If the price in the long run is equal to the cost of production, then what cost of production? Is it average cost of production of the industry? The solution conceived by Marshall is that is should be equal to the cost of production of the marginal firm.

G. Incompatibility of Perfect Competition and Increasing Returns of Decreasing Costs Per Unit

If the long period price is equal to the cost of production, then cost of production of which firm? Theoretically the cost of production per unit should be uniform over the entire space, subject to differences in transport costs. *But this does not happen in practice because the mobilities of factors and materials are not perfect.* Hence some differences in costs of production remain. There can be a least-cost firm and a firm with the highest cost per unit. There can be many with costs being in-between.

Marshall was of the opinion that a *"representative firm'* can be identified which can be, a sort of average firm, with average life and with average access to internal economies for average production. Such is a firm need not be very old or very new; it may of average efficiency and may be earning normal profits only.

Pierro Sraffa was the first to point out the impossibility of perfect competition and the increasing returns / decreasing costs. Any firm which has the lowest cost of production will attract all customers and as its cost of production goes down further, it will oust the competitors. It can lead to a monopoly even. If not, then to oligopoly at least.

Pigou, in this connection, gave the concept of the "equilibrium firm ". It is a firm which is in the same position as the industry. But who will search it where? Then this equality can be of temporary nature. After some time the firm in question may lose its equivalence and another firm may come in that position. It is also possible that there may be no firm which may be contracting in the same way as the industry or may be expanding in the same way as the industry. *Hence the "equilibrium firm" also does not solve the problem of* incompatibility.

Bye wanted to introduce the concept of *""optimum firm"*.

> The optimum firm may be defined as that organisation of business enterprise which, in given circumstances of technology and the market for its products, can produce its goods at the lowest average unit costs in its long run.

Brigs and Jordan defined the optimum firm thus:

> The optimum firm is a concrete possibility. It is the unit of size which the forces of competition compel all firms to approach who wish to survive in the struggle for existence.

Sraffa pointed out that under increasing returns only a few most efficient firms can survive, come what may.

Suppose there are 6 sets of 100 firms. This example is wrong because in the long run costs are equal. This is proved with this example.

	A	B	C	D	E	F
Cost per unit Rs.	6	7	9	4	10	8

Cost of production of firm D is the lowest at Rs. 4 per unit and of the firm E is the highest at Rs. 10 per unit. This is *short period situation.* Here the most efficient firm cannot under cut others by charging Rs. 4 as price because *under decreasing returns, as soon as this happen all customers will come to that firm and its cost of production will rise. As the cost of production rises to Rs. 6, 7, 8, 9 and 10 firms A, B, F, C and E firms will join the production.*

All firms will have cost of production at Rs. 10 and all can exist by earning normal profits only. In the long run because of the mobility of factors and movement of resources, the cost of production will become the same over the space. That was the explanation of price determination under perfect competition. *So throughout if the cost or price is equal to the cost of production of the marginal firm, super normal firms will produce more till the cost of production of all becomes the same.*

This *cannot happen under increasing returns or decreasing costs.* As the firm with the least cost under-cuts others, it will attract buyers and as it increase the production, its cost of production will fall further. In such cases, the competition is bound to become and *imperfect competition will ensue.* Immobilities, indivisibilities and inelasticities over the space will convert the competition to imperfect one. *Competition is perfect only when same cost rules: transport costs make competition perfect in a zone of concentric circle only.* Taxes and subsidies also give rise to concentric circles of competition.

H. 'Inter-Related Values' or Under Joint Demand and Joint Supply

The words 'interrelated values' mean value under the joint demand and joint supply. Before we proceed further we should understand the meaning of 'joint demand' and 'joint supply'.

Joint Demand

A joint demand is one which requires purchasing of one more or even more than one articles when some article is purchased. Such examples are (i) car and petrol (ii) lighter/scooter and petrol (iii) pen and ink (iv) watch and chain (v) milk and sugar. Thus. "When two or more goods are closely complementary, they are said to be under joint demand."

It should however be noted that sometimes that first commodity is a durable commodity while the other is not. Car is purchased once but petrol is purchased frequently; watch may be purchased once but the strap may be purchased every five to six months: pen is purchased once but inkpot may be purchased every month; sugar may be purchased once in a month but milk be taken daily.

It is not necessary that both should be purchased at the same time everytime.

Price Determination in Joint Demand

The problem of pricing under joint demand is a complex, but not an insoluble problem. It can be analysed under two heads: (a) jointly demanded goods where the proportions in which they are combined can be varied, (b) jointly demanded goods where the proportions in which they are combined are fixed by technical considerations.

(a) Under Variable Proportions

Jointly demanded goods are also demanded on the basis of their marginal utilities. If the marginal utility is zero and the price is positive or if the marginal utility is less than the price paid, further demand will cease. This table illustrates that:

Input Package Nos.	*Total Output Rs. Cr.*	*Marginal Output Rs. Cr.*
Benchmark	440	—
1.	500	60
2.	550	50
3.	590	40
4.	620	30
5.	635	15
6.	635	00

It is clear that even when the price is not taken into account there will be no investment demand for the 6th input-package because its marginal significance is zero.

If this demand curve for input packages is set against their supply curve, the equilibrium price can be determined as shown in the following figure (that is, Rs. 30). The equilibrium price is determined...at *P*.

(b) Under Fixed Proportions

Where the proportions of the goods jointly demanded are fixed by technical considerations, the problem of pricing becomes more complex, but, still not beyond solution. In

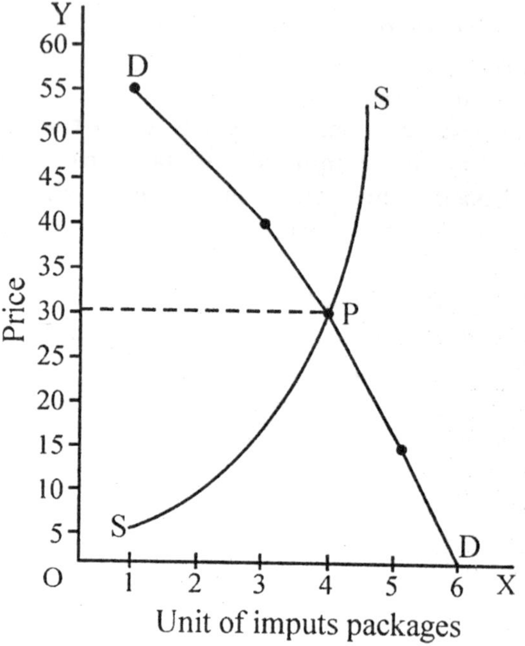

Fig. 17

the manufacture of eye-glasses, for example, the frames and the lenses have to be used in fixed proportions. Two lenses have to be fitted in one frame. This relationship is fixed and no variation is possible. The problem of pricing in such a case can also be solved by means of slightly different demand and supply curves. We have to set the single demand curve for eye-glasses against two different supply (or, cost) curves for curve frames and lenses in such a manner as to enable to determine the separate prices of frames and lenses. Let us consider the following table.

Now, if the corresponding points of the 3rd and the 6th columns are plotted on a graph and joined together, we shall obtain the supply curves for eye-glasses. If this supply curve is set against the demand curve for eye-glasses, the intersection point will determine the equilibrium price (13.50 hundred) as shown in the following figure, or Rs. 1350/-.

Units of frames manufac-tured	*Total cost of frames (Rs.) hundreds*	*Marginal cost of frames (Rs.) hundreds*	*Pairs of lenses (Rs.) manufactured*	*Total cost of lenses (Rs.) hundreds*	*Marginal cost of paris of lenses (Rs.) hundreds*	*Marginal cost of eye glass*
(1)	(2)	(3)	(4)	(5)	(6)	(7) (3) +(6)
1.	5.00	5.50	1	6.00	6.00	11.00
2.	10.50	5.50	2	12.50	6.50	12.00
3.	16.75	6.35	3	19.75	7.25	13.50
4.	24.00	7.25	4	28.50	8.75	16.00

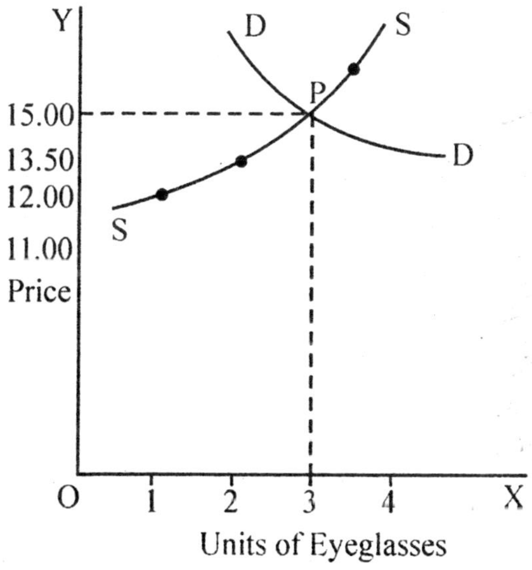

Fig. 18

Let us now examine the relationship between the prices of two jointly demanded goods, *A* and *B*. As pointed out earlier, when two goods are jointly demanded, a rise in the price of one goods will cause a fall in the price of the other. Let us suppose that the supply of *A* is reduced due to reasons, whatever. The price of *A* will go up and at the higher price, people will purchase less of *A*. As this commodity can be used only in combination with *B*, this will bring a fall in the demand of *B* as well. Consequently, the price of *B* will fall. This situation has been depicted in the following figures:

In the Fig. (a), as a result of a fall in the supply of commodity '*A* ' (this fall has been shown by shifting the *SS* curve upward to the left to the position of *S'S'* curve), the price of '*A* ' rises from *OP* to *OP'*. The reverse is the case as shown in Fig. (b). When demand for '*A* ' goes down, the demand for '*B*' also declines (this has been shown by the downward shift of the demand curve from *dd to d'd')*. The new demand curve for '*B*' intersects the supply curve (which is the same as before) at a lower point, thus, giving a lesser equilibrium price that is *OP'*.

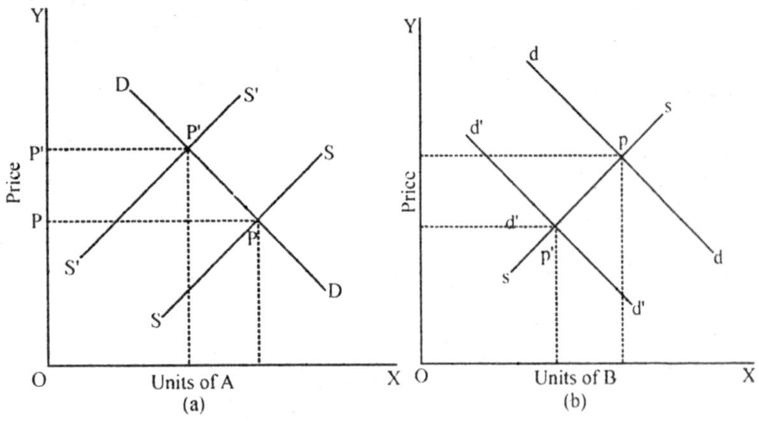

Fig. 19

Conclusions on Price Determination

Price determination under joint demand posed one problem. While the things are demanded jointly; they are not produced jointly. However, certain principles are there:

(i) If both things are having high demand (have inelastic demand) high prices will be charged for both. If use of cars and scooter is very necessary then the high price for petrol can be charged.

(ii) If one commodity becomes very dear then the demand for the other may also go down. For example, due to Arab squeeze on petrol, the prices of car went down (at least the black price).

(iii) If the other commodity is not very dear and expenditure on it is not a major item of the budget expenditure, then demand for both can be high and high price may be paid. Alternative use of higher utility will make the commodity command higher price. Availability of substitutes will depress the price.

Joint supply has joint costs. Joint products are produced automatically e.g., wheat and straw or spirit and molasses.

There two situations have been depicted in the following figures:

(A) Fixed Proportions

Let us suppose that goods '*A*' and 'B' are in joint supply and that there is a rise in the demand of '*A* '. Consequently, its demand curve. *D*, shifts upwards to the position of *D'D'* cutting the existing supply curve, at a higher point *P'*. In this case *OP'* is the equilibrium price. This is shown in the following Fig. (a):

Now look at the Fig. (b) above. As a result of more demand for '*A* ', the output of both '*A* ' and '*B'* has been raised. But, as there is no change in the demand of *B*, its price falls down from *OP'* to *OP*.

Thus in case of joint supply, good which have to be produced in fixed proportions, a rise in the price of one leads to a fall in the price of the other and vice versa.

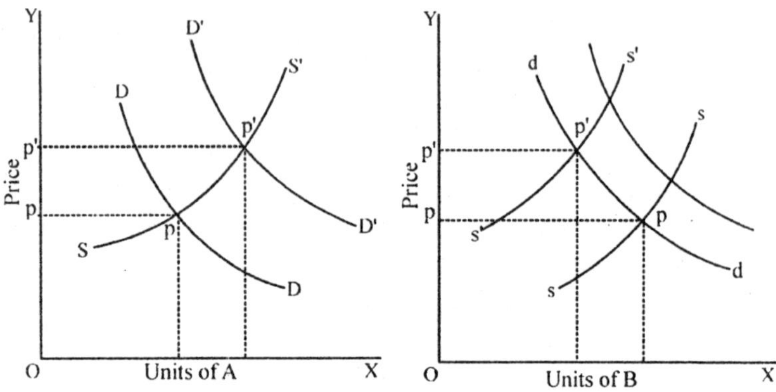

Fig. 20

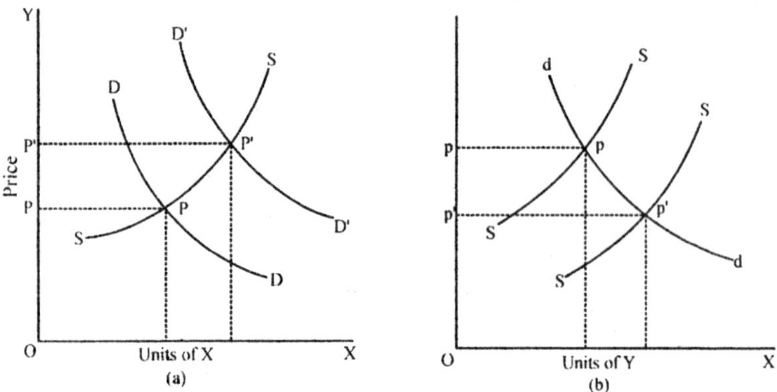

Fig. 21

(B) Variable Proportions

Suppose *X* and Y are such joint supply goods that they can be produced in varying proportions, that is, an increase in the production of one can take place while keeping the output of other constant or even lesser. Let us suppose that the supply of X can be raised by lowering the supply of *Y* a bit. If the demand for increases from *DD* to *D 'D'*, its price will go up, from *OP* to *OP'* as shown in the following Figure (a). As higher demand for X can be satisfied only by reducing the supply of *Y*, the price of *Y* will also go up, from *OP* to *OP'*, as shown in the following Figure (b).

Thus, in case of joint supply of goods which can be produced in varying proportions, a rise in the price of one commodity will lead the price of the other to a higher level or at least keep it unchanged.

Price Determination

The fundamental principle of price determination under joint supply is that "the price of the joint products must together be enough to cover their joint or combined expenses of production, but the apportionment of the total price between the two joint products will depend upon the relative demand for them and not so much upon their cost of production.

In such a case the price determination will be as under:

(i) The price of both the commodities will be so fixed that the total cost of two or more joint products will be realised from the sale of these products. It is also possible that more than the cost will be realised.

(ii) Price in each case will be determined by the elasticities of demand for these products,

(iii) Joint cost is the minimum below which the total price of these products cannot fall,

(iv) If the price of one falls, the price of the other will have to be increased so as to cover total cost.

Same principles apply for *composite* demand e.g., steel required by the manufacturers of different goods. And, for *composite supply,* which are competing goods the cross-elasticities of demand will determine the prices.

15

Space and Price Determination Under Monopoly: Price Discrimination, Degree of Monopoly Power, Public Control

A. Top Ten Features of Monopoly: Monopoly Defined Causes of the Emergence of Monopoly,

B&C. Costs and Revenue Curves of the Monopolist Steep Slopes of AR & MR in Inelastic Demand Flatter Slopes of AR & MR in Elastic Demand

D. * Break-even Technique of Determination of Price
 * Trial and Error Method of Price Determination

E. * Marshallian Technique of Price Determination: Output *f. of MC* = MR, Price *f. of AR* > *AC*
 * Chart Showing All Possible Combinations of Elasticities of Demand and Costs (Laws of Returns) and Price Determination

F. Short and Long Period Price Determination Super-normal Profits, Loss and Normal Profits

G. Price Discrimination, International Dumping Case

H. Degrees of Discrimination and Monopoly Power

I. Monopoly and Economic Development

J. Public Control of Monopolies

K. Monopoly Pricing and Pricing Under P.C. Compared [A Special Diagram Comparing the Welfare Situations Under Monopoly and Perfect Competition]

A. Meaning and Characteristics of a Monopoly

Whosoever wrote on price determination under monopoly first defined it. *We take the definitions given by the pioneers.*

J.S. Mill wrote "a thing which is limited in quantity is still a monopolised article". This was the earliest yet the widest definition ever given. *Benham* did not admit such a situation as monopoly. In his opinion "monopoly means *complete* control over the supply". *K.E. Boulding* wrote "a pure monopolist is a firm producing a product, which has no effective substitutes among the products of any firm, effective in the sense that even though the monopolist may be making abnormal profits, other firms cannot encroach on these profits by producing substitutes which might entice purchasers away from the product of the monopolist".

Marshall defined a monopolist who is a single producer and price maker and decides about the output also but who cannot at the same time charge a high price and sell more.

Chamberlin defined monopolist as the "one who has complete control over the *supply* of a *commodity, good or a service"*. Chamberlin thus took (i) production and/or (ii) supply both for defining monopoly. Besides he admitted the possibilities of there being a monopolist in the production of (i) commodity, (ii) good and (iii) service. We can use the word "product" to include all the three words which are used interchangeably in the book.

Top Ten Features of *a* Monopoly

1. There should be a single producer or seller. We are not taking into account *a petty monopolist* here like one barber in a village or one cinema house in a small town. We take a *global, continental, national and a State monopoly* atleast.
2. The monopolist is a firm as well as the industry for

that product line. A monopoly is the anti-thesis of perfect competition.

3. Thirdly, there is no close substitute of the product of a monopolist. If between two places there is only a rail link and no road link, then the railway there enjoys the status *of pure and perfect monopoly.* In most cases such a monopoly can hardly be found because substitutes are there. If air travel becomes too costly, people may go by ship even if takes too much time.
4. The buyers of the monopolist do not act in unison as they are not united. Besides they are dispersed also. If they form a union of buyers, we get a *bilateral monopoly* which situation becomes alike perfect competition.
5. Demand for the product sold by a monopolist is inelastic because the buyers cannot go elsewhere. The degree of inelasticity will differ whether the thing or good belongs to the category of luxury, comfort or necessity. Besides the degree of inelasticity will differ from buyer to buyer according to their incomes.
6. The cross elasticity of demand for the product of the monopolist becomes zero in the case of pure and perfect monopoly and very low in the case of others for which only *remote substitutes* are there. Reduction in the prices of other products normally will not affect the price of the product of the monopolist.
7. While a producer in perfect competition can sell unlimited amounts at the same price, a monopolist will have to reduce the price in order to sell more. *Hence a monopolist is one who faces declining AR and MR curves with decline in the marginal revenue causing decline in average revenue.* AR and MR curves slope down to the right in monopoly but the

degree of slopes can be flatter or steeper. In perfect competition the AR/MR lines are horizontal, converging on each other.

8. A monopolist can charge a high price for necessities. He can charge a high price for other products also but cannot hope to sell more. A monopolist selling luxury good will find *a hidden competitor*—the limited money in the pockets of the people. Hence high price and high sales combination is impossible.
9. A monopolist can keep 'excess capacity' which means unutilised capacity. That increases the overheads of the monopolist but he gets himself compensated by charging a high price by keeping the artificial scarcity in the market.
10. *Causes: Emergence and continuance of monopoly* depends upon a host of factors. *First,* it can be a natural monopoly whereby the control of the natural resources are with one company only. This right was usually given by the imperial powers to the company of their own country. *Secondly,* the monopoly can be a "legal monopoly" whereby either the government itself or any company is given exclusive right to produce. No one can have a parallel railway system in India. The same is true for the State Electricity Boards. Post Offices in India for their total functions have a monopoly. [For example courier service cannot collect savings in savings account in rural or urban areas.] *Thirdly,* monopolies emerge and function behind a patent for the product and/or process. WTO regime grants "intellectual property rights" and monopolies can emerge under this. Copyrights can also give emergence to monopolies counterfeiting of products now-a-days is infringement of IPR. *Fourthly,* a price war between oligopolies can lead to one monopolist emerging as a victor.

Perfect competition can never become a monopoly. *Fifthly,* large capital investment of a monopolist, his unique technology, the goodwill of his product and certain other things may deter others to enter the fray and the monopoly position may continue. *A selling monopoly can come in the form of a cartel.*

Monopolies are not favoured even in the USA. Anti-trust laws (anti-monopoly laws) exist there.

Then a monopoly *may be' simple monopoly or a discriminating monopoly.* If a monopolist charges different prices from different customers at different places, it is known as discriminating monopoly.

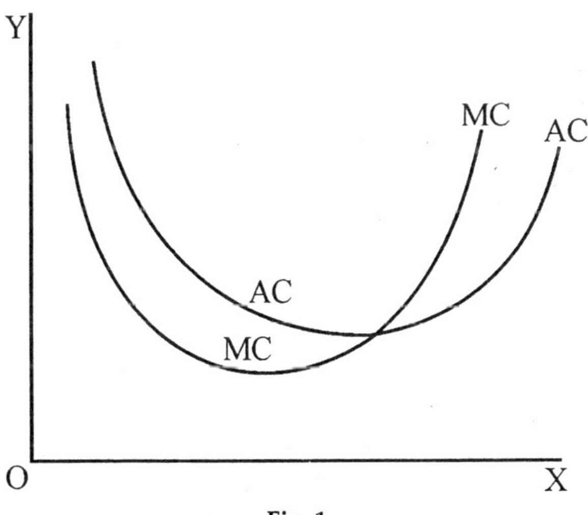

Fig. 1

B & C. Cost and Revenue Curves of the Monopolist

The cost curves of the monopolist are 'U' shaped cost curves. Other things remaining the same, as the monopolist goes on increasing his scale of production, he enjoys greater and greater internal and external economies of production. That brings down his cost of production or, in other words, the law of increasing returns operates. But ultimately the diseconomies become greater than the economies and then the law of decreasing returns will apply. Thus first the average and marginal costs will come down, marginal cost falls at a faster rate; and then the average and marginal costs will rise—marginal cost rising at a faster rate. The shape will be as under (as we have seen in the earlier chapter of this book). *MC* point of inflection of the *AC* curve.

Revenue Curves

As we have seen in the study of the characteristics of monopoly, "a monopolist cannot sell infinite amount of commodities at the same price; in order to sell more he will have to reduce his price." This will bring down his marginal and average revenue. The following table will illustrate this point:

No. of Commodity	*Price*	*Total Income*	*Average Income*	*Marginal Income*
1.	10	10	10	10
2.	9½	19	9½	9
3.	9	27	9	8
4.	8½	34	8½	7
5.	8	40	8	6

Note: (i) The price reduction given here is just illustrative. It is not necessary that the monopolist should reduce price for selling every additional commodity. In fact, it is like this: for selling, say, first 10000 commodities, he will charge, say, Rs. 10/ 'per' commodity, but for selling additional 10000 (or for selling a total number of 20000), he will have to reduce the price to Rs. 9½.

(ii) When Rs. 9½ are written against the second commodity, it does not mean that the first commodity was sold at Rs. 10 and the second at Rs. 9½. It means "if two commodities are to be sold, each will be sold at Rs. 9½".

(iii) The marginal revenue is calculated by deducting the previous total revenue from the present total revenue.

(iv) We see that, as additional goods are sold, both the average and marginal revenue go on decreasing—marginal revenue, which causes decrease in average revenue, is decreasing at a faster rate.

The curves will be as under:

AR is the average revenue curve, (b) *MR* is the marginal revenue curve.

The figures of *AR* and *MR* are plotted on a graph, it will be seen that both *AR* and *MR* lines will slope downward to the right out *MR* will fall at a faster rate.

The slopes of the *MR* and *AR* curves differ. The slopes will be flatter for the elastic demand and steeper for the inelastic demand.

Here are the two sets with two proofs.

Set *A* proves that the same amount of reduction in price will lead to greater increase in demand in case of the elastic demand and less than proportionate increase in demand in case of the inelastic demand.

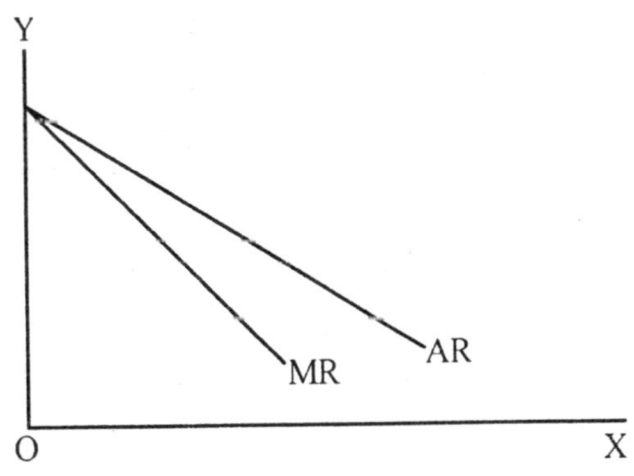

Fig. 2

AR/MR Set 'A'

PP_1 is same in both but $MM_1 > QQ_1$ for elastic demand.

Set *B* proves that to secure the same increase in demand, (i) there has to be marginal or less than proportionate reduction in the price in case of the elastic demand and (ii) quite substantial reduction in price in case of the inelastic demand.

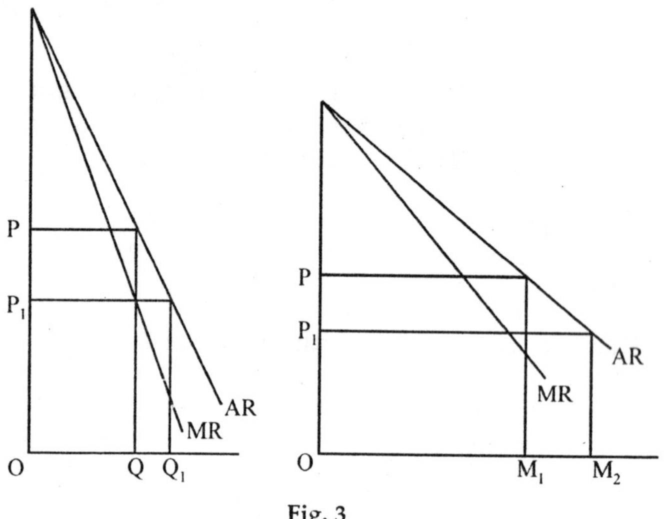

Fig. 3

AR/MR Set 'B'

$MM_1 = QQ_1$ the desired increase in demand but $PP_1 >$ Pe_1 Pe_2 for inelastic demand.

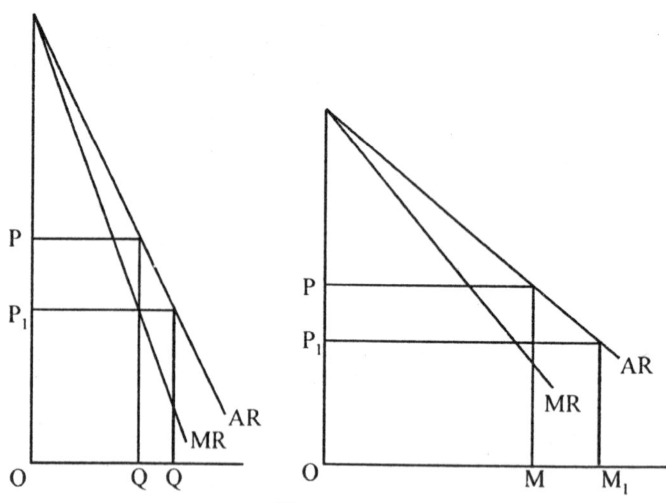

Fig. 4

In case of luxury goods, slight reduction in price will increase the demand more than proportionately and vice versa. In case of essential commodities substantial reduction in price will lead to less than proportionate increase in demand and vice versa.

The AR and MR curves can have (i) straight line slopes or (ii) can be convex or concave upwards, (Hi) or concave to the origin.

As has been seen, if we deduct from the last *TR*, the *TR* upto previous unit of output, we get the marginal revenue—the revenue earned by the last unit of the output. It is the change in the margin which induces the change in the average. In perfect competition the *MR* remains the same and hence *AR* remains the same and both lines converge.

When the demand curves are elastic, it is the case when (i) the commodity is an article of comfort or luxury and (ii) when the demand curves relate to the long period. In the long period the demand even for the necessities can be reduced if the price charged is high. Tastes and fashion can also change. Habits can be overcome.

It can be seen that in order to increase the sale, less than proportionate reduction in the price will suffice. A slight reduction in price brings more than proportionate increase in the demand.

D. Price Determination Under Monopoly

(a). Total Cost and Total Revenue Break-even Technique

This is no longer regarded as a satisfactory technique. It is said that "the monopolist will produce upto that point when the difference between the total revenue and total cost is the highest". Thus:

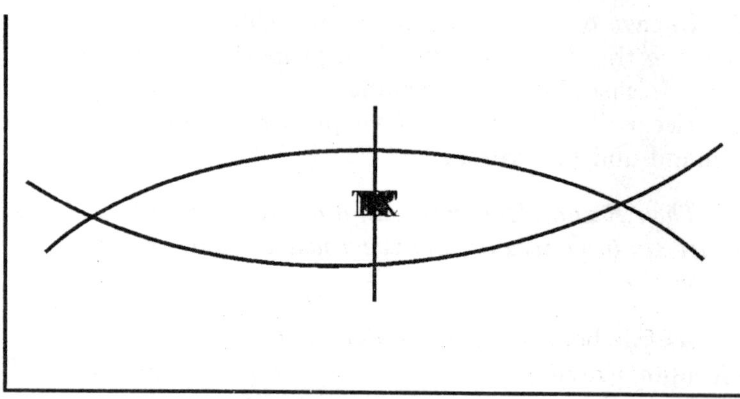

Fig. 5

In the above diagram we see:

(i) The total cost curve goes up. First it goes up slowly because of the operation of the law of increasing returns and then it increases at a faster rate because of the operation of the diminishing returns.

(ii) The total revenue curve also has a tendency to rise, but it starts coming down, when the price reduction for selling more are very substantial. This, while the costs increase ultimately, the total revenue curve will come down after the maximum possibilities of sale are exhausted.

(iii) In the above diagram the position upto the point *OM* is such that as the producer goes on producing he does not get any profit. But he produces because he has the hope that when he reaches the point *M* he will no longer suffer losses.

(iv) At point *OM,* his costs and revenue are equal. Here he just earns a normal profit. This is also known as *'break-even' point. Here the costs and revenue are even or equal* (normal profits are of course earned).

(v) As he goes on producing the revenue increases at a faster rate than the costs and thus more and more profits are earned. This continues upto the point *OM'*. Here his profits are maximum. It is said that *the monopolist will produce upto this point.*

(vi) If he goes on producing his profits increase, but at a declining rate. When he reaches *OM"*, he again reaches the break-even point. Here again his revenue and costs are equal—only normal profits are earned. This is also *break-even point.*

(vii) After that point there are only losses. No monopolist will ever produce after this.

Criticism

This is considered to be a crude method. The most fundamental objection is that why should the monopolist stop at *OM'* when he can continue to earn profit even upto *OM"*. A monopolist cannot forego that profit.

The Trial and Error Method

It is said that the monopolist may first fix a certain price. He may then try to raise it. So long as the total revenue goes on increasing he may continue to raise it. But if the total revenue starts declining he will not raise the price. He can experiment with downward cuts also. He will fix the price at such a point that gives him maximum possible revenue.

Criticism

While it is agreed that the aim of the monopolist is to earn maximum possible revenue, he will not experiment with the prices as a layman. This may be done by a small monopolist, but a big industrialist-monopolist will use the refined technique of analysis with the help of marginal cost and revenue curves.

E. Marshallian Explanation of Price Determination Under Monopoly

Marshall highlighted: *"The fundamental aim of a monopolist is not to charge a high price, nor to sell what he has produced, but to earn maximum profits."*

Maximum Profits Can be Earned in Two Ways

1. Charge a high price but for this he will have to produce less. No monopolist is powerful enough to sell more at higher and higher prices.
2. Produce large output but for this he will have to charge a low price.

Which Policy Will the Monopolist Choose? This Will Depend Upon Two Things Again

1. Elasticity of Demand

It gives *the power* to monopolist to charge a high price.

2. Lows of Returns or Per Unit Cost of Production

It determines the *willingness* of the monopolist to decide the price-output relations.

1. *If only elasticity of demand is taken into account then:*
   (a) Elastic demand — LP + HO
   (b) Inelastic demand — HP + LO
   LP = low price
   HP = high price
   HO = high output
   LO = low output

Maximum Price will be charged when he has the power

to charge and willingness to charge a high price. *Inelastic demand + decreasing returns.*

Lowest possible price will be charged when the monopolist does not have either the power or the willingness to charge a high price: Elastic demand + the law of decreasing returns.

1. *Constant returns or constant cost:* According to the elasticity of demand.
2. *Increasing returns or decreasing costs per unit:* LP + HO. The more the monopolist produces, the less the per unit cost of production and hence the greater the difference between average revenue and average costs.
3. *Decreasing returns or increasing costs per unit:* HP + LO. The more the monopolist produces, the higher per unit cost of production. Hence the monopolist can create artificial scarcity by under-utilising the capacity, known as having "excess capacity".

We can now get some combinations of situations:

1.	Very high price	Low output	Inelastic demand Increasing costs
2.	Quite low price	High output	Elastic demand Decreasing costs

In case one determining factor indicates towards a low price while the other towards a high price, the actual price charged will depend upon the *differences in the degrees of advantages / disadvantages from the relative situations.*

Increasing costs	Suggest high price
Elastic demand	Suggests a low price
Decreasing costs	Suggest a low price
Inelastic demand	Suggests a high price

In such mutually contradictory cases, the monopolist will weigh the pros and cons of the high and low prices and (may be) through a process of trial and error may find a combination of the best price-output situation which yields maximum revenue. *Theory tells us that the price output decision can be found at the equilibrium point, the fundamental principle of which is that MC = MR. The slopes of the AR and MR curves and of the AC and MC curves will precisely decide this.*

F. Monopoly Pricing Under Constant Returns: Constant Cost

Since the production function is neutral to scale i.e., the per unit cost of production remains the same irrespective of the changes in the quantum of output, it is no guide to the monopolist. Hence he will adjust his price and output according to the *slope of the AR/MR curves or the degree*

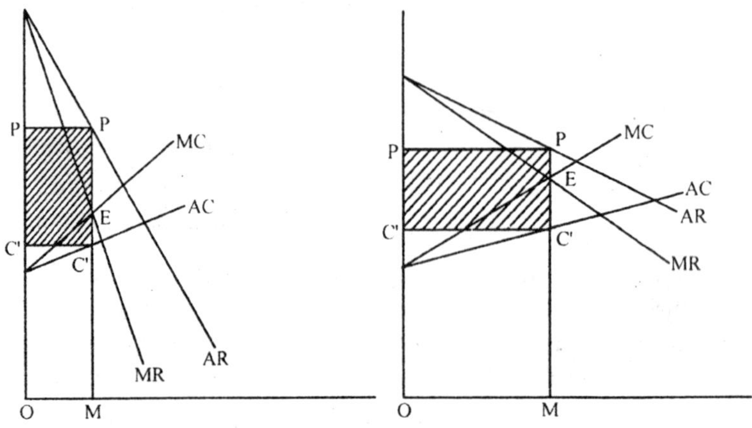

Fig. 6

of elasticity of demand. Higher price can be charged in case of the inelastic demand (with low output) and higher output will be produced and sold if there is elastic demand (with low price).

The explanation is as under:

1. Equilibrium level output is where *MC* = *MR*. *EM* gives *OM* equilibrium output.
2. The *EM* line is extended to *AR* because price is equal to *AR* or price is *AR*.
3. The price per unit is *MP* or *OP;* this line is cut by the *AC* line at the same point *E* and hence per unit cost of production is *MC'* or *OC'*. The *C'P* is the profit per unit of commodity.
4. Super-normal profits are earned per unit of commodity since *AR* is greater than *AC* and the total profits are equal to total output multiplies by the profit per unit. The shaded rectangle *C 'C 'PP* is total profit.

Short Period Monopoly Pricing

Increasing Returns Cases

The most likely short period situation is of (A) Increasing returns (decreasing costs) and (B) Inelastic demand.

We may also admit the case of elastic demand because it generally depends upon the type of commodity and a monopolised luxury good will have elastic demand all the same, even in the short period.

We can show price determination with the help of two diagrams of short period situations: both showing falling cost curves *(AC* and *MC)* and *AR* and *MR* curves of differing slopes— steeper ones for the inelastic demand and flatter ones for the elastic demand.

Here also the fundamental principles are the same viz., the equilibrium output will be one where $MC = MR$. The equilibrium output will be sold at a price corresponding to a point on the *AR* curve and this *AR* will be higher than the *AC*, thus enabling monopolist to earn super-normal profits.

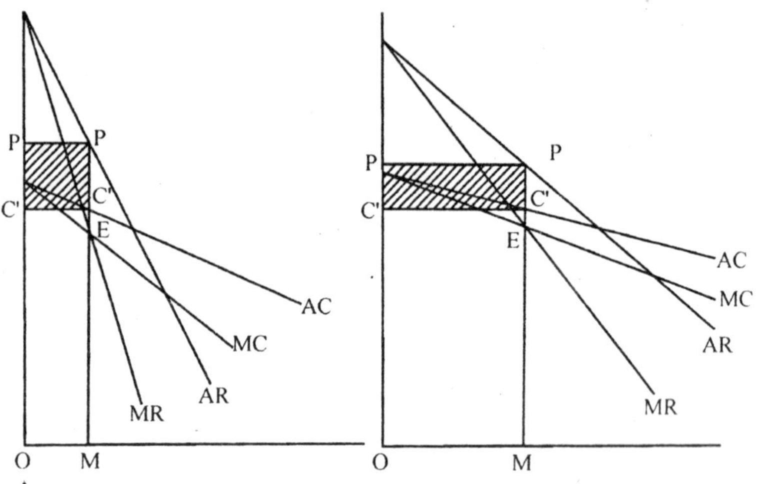

Fig. 7

In the above diagrams the equilibrium point is *E*. *ME* is extended to *AR* to find out the price. The point where the *AC* cuts the price line shows the price per unit and the remaining portion of *CP* as the profit per unit. As usual the shaded rectangles show the total super-normal profits equal to extra profits per unit multiplied by the total output.

Output is higher in case of the elastic demand and price lower. Price is higher in case of the inelastic demand and then output will be relatively less.

Long Monopoly Equilibrium

Decreasing Returns (Increasing Costs Case)

In the long run diseconomies of scale become higher than the economies of scale and diminishing returns start being obtained. Diminishing returns can be postponed but not avoided.

New techniques, innovations, increasing the scale and scope of production, efforts to economise give only temporary respite. When decreasing returns set in, the marginal and average costs rise—the former more so.

In the long run the demand for the product of the monopolist can partake the nature of high elasticity. Close substitutes can develop or the buyers can learn how to buy less of it at higher prices. Consumer resistance can develop. Hence the demand becomes elastic and the *AR* and *MR* curves become flatter.

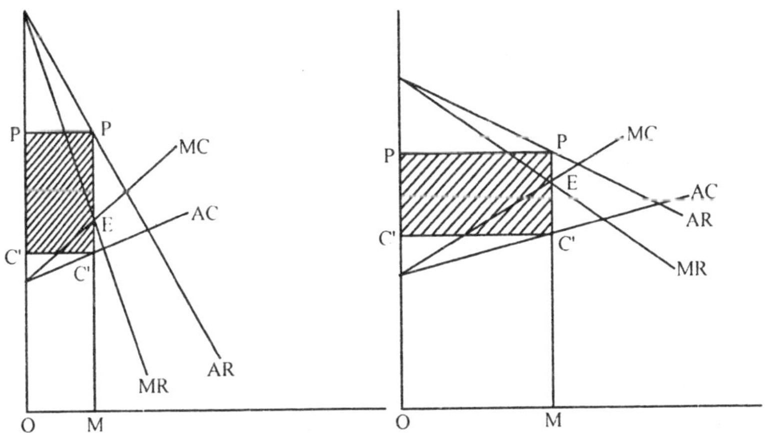

Fig. 8

However, even in the long run demand can remain inelastic if the commodity produced by the monopolist belongs to the regime of the 'pain economy' i.e., is very essential.

The market situations and equilibrium can be depicted thus:

1. Equilibrium point of the rising *AC* and *MC* lines and steeper or flatter *AR* and *MR* curves is the same where *MC* = *MR* i.e., at E.
2. The line to the horizontal baseline from the—X point gives the line *ME* and it is extended to *AR* to obtain the price *MP* or *OP*.
3. *PM line* cuts the *AC* line at *C'* and *MC'* and *OC'* becomes the cost per unit. Therefore, *C'P* becomes the profit per unit.
4. Profit per unit of commodity multiplied by the total output *OM* gives the total abnormal profits. The abnormal profits emerge because *AR* is greater than *AC*. Output is higher in elastic demand condition while price is higher is the inelastic demand condition.

What is equilibrium of the firm is also equilibrium of the industry under monopoly. A monopolist determines his own price and output but cannot keep both of them high; the buyers indirectly permit him either to charge a high price or to sell more. A monopolist will not stop producing as long as *MR* is greater than *MC* and cannot continue to produce if *MC* becomes greater than *MR*.

A monopolist fixes the price at such a point that the elasticity of demand is greater than one. If it is less than one, it means the total revenue will fall with an increase in the output. The MR will become negative at the level when elasticity of demand is less than 1. MC, *on the other hand cannot ever become negative.*

In the short run also the monopolist will keep the price as much as the variable costs are fully covered and profit is made. Costs mismanagement (non-optimum size of the plant or utilisation) and consumer resistance can create situations where a monopolist earns only normal profits or even incurs a loss. These are *exceptional* situations. *A loss is incurred -when AC is greater than AR and normal profit is earned when AR and AC are tangent.* In these cases the diagrammatic presentation can be as under:

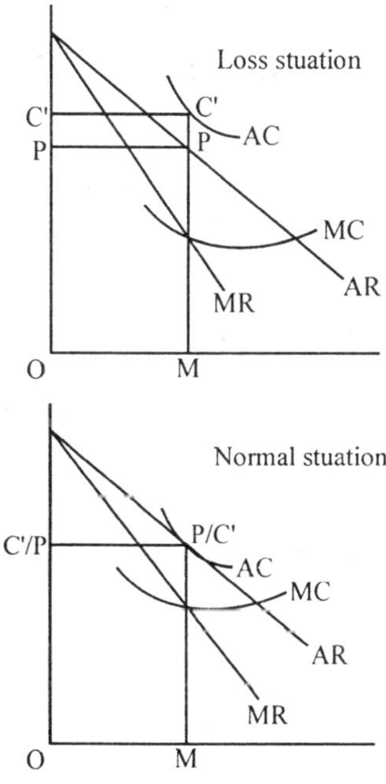

Fig. 9

G. Price Discrimination

Elasticity Factors: Spatial Factors

Price Discrimination may be defined as the setting of two or more prices for an identical product. (Stigler). Price discrimination is charging different prices for the same product or the same price for the differentiated products.

Mrs. Joan Robinson defines discrimination as "an act of selling the same article produced under a single control at different prices to different buyers".

If the railways charges different rates for 1 *AC,* II *AC,* Chair *AC*\ I, and II classes it is *not* a case price discrimination because (i) people pay different prices for differences in comforts as also for (ii) keeping themselves away from other categories of travellers with whom they would not like to or cannot travel.

Charging different prices for different packages where the prices are not in strict proportion to the weights (200 gm. toothpaste tube may not be double as costly as 100 gm. toothpaste tube) is also *not* discrimination because economies of packing may be transferred to the consumers. The goods have to be the same.

The essential condition for discrimination is the difference in the *elasticity of demand.* In the words of Mrs. Joan Robinson:

> "The sub markets will be arranged in ascending order of their elasticities, the highest price being charged in the least elastic market, and the lowest price in the most elastic market."

This hierarchy *need not be spatial in character. It can be obtained in the same city.*

Higher prices can be charged from the very rich persons because they have enough money to buy anything at any price. In case the demand in inelastic higher sources can be charged *Space comes into the picture that there should be no 'seepage between various categories of buyers.* If tea is served on the deck and in the I class cabins of the ship at different price (difference being not in the quality of tea but the mode of service), then discriminating price can be charged only when the buyers on the deck do not buy it cheap and sell it to the consumer of I class cabins at higher prices (but lower than what is charged by the management of the ship.) The discriminating prices *cannot exceed* the transport charges otherwise the buyers of place 'A' where the lower prices are charged can sell to the buyers of the place 'B' where higher prices are charged.

Price discrimination is easy where the monopolist renders personalised services e.g.,; an advocate can charge higher and lower fees from the rich and poor clients. When commodities are supplied on special orders or when bulk orders are received, discriminating prices can be charged. Ignorance and inertia of the consumers (they may not be aware of the discrimination or may not like to protest) can facilitate discrimination.

Price discrimination is practised between different *economic markets, rather than between spatially separated markets, unless the spatial separation is itself a cause of economy differentiation.*

Some regions may be generating higher incomes because of differences in the natural endowments. In this case the monopolist can charge higher prices from the people of the region on the principle of "what the traffic can bear", i.e., as much as possible.

If a monopolist has five different plants in five regions of thc country, manufacturing the same commodity and charges different prices because of the differences in the cost of production it is *not* discrimination. If from one central point, the goods are to be sent to different places and there are C.I.F. (cost insurance and freight) charges to be incurred, which are added to cost of production and prices adjusted accordingly, it is also not a case of price discrimination

Price discrimination based on the differences in *use* of the commodity is discrimination e.g., electricity may be supplied at a cheaper rate to the farmers for irrigation pumps, while it may be supplied at a higher rate to different types of industries. Here the space is not important because in the same city the households and the industries can be supplied electricity at different rates.

The price discrimination between *two economic markets* which may or may not be spatially separated markets can be shown with the help of the following simple diagram:

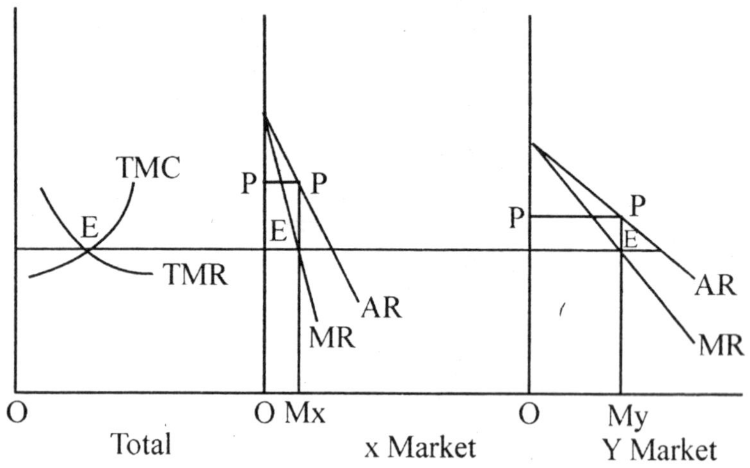

Fig. 10

The output for all the markets is produced in one plant and hence the cost of production of all commodities sold in different markets is the same. This output will be so sold that the marginal costs and marginal revenue of different markets are equal.

The equilibrium output determined in the first part of the diagram (A) is to be distributed between the two markets, according to the paying capacity of the two markets. In the

X market the demand is inelastic and hence we have steeper *AR/MR* curves. In the *X* markets, the demand is relatively elastic and hence the *AR/MR* curves are flatter. Higher price is charged in the *X* market and lower in the *Y* market. The equilibrium outputs in the two markets will be where *MC* (total) is equal to the *MR* (of the individual markets), at points E_x and *Ey* .

The word 'discrimination' usually invites adverse comments. However, *price discrimination practised by monopolists goes to the favour of the poor. The poor have elastic demand and hence a lower price is charged from (hem. The rich have inelastic demand and hence a higher price is charged from them.* The monopolist's discrimination for uses can be based on social aspects also e.g., charging lower rates for electricity used in irrigation. *Discriminating monopoly prices by the public sector monopoly can be approved not only from the accounting point of view of maximisation of profits but also from socio-economic utility and welfare points of views.*

Dumping in Spatially Separated Markets

Dumping is done to drive away a competitor from one market by selling not only below the price of the competitor but if need be even below of cost of production. Even the loss can be incurred which may be recovered from other markets and/or from the market where dumping was resorted to, after the competitors were driven away.

Dumping is malific discrimination. Discriminating prices are charged for maximisation of the revenue: output may or may not increase much. In the words of Mrs. Joan Robinson.

> "It is possible to establish the fact that the total output under discrimination will be greater or less than under simple monopoly according as the more elastic of the demand curves in the separate markets

is more or less concave than the less elastic demand curve; and the total output will be same if the demand curves are straight lines, or in any other case in which the concavities are equal."

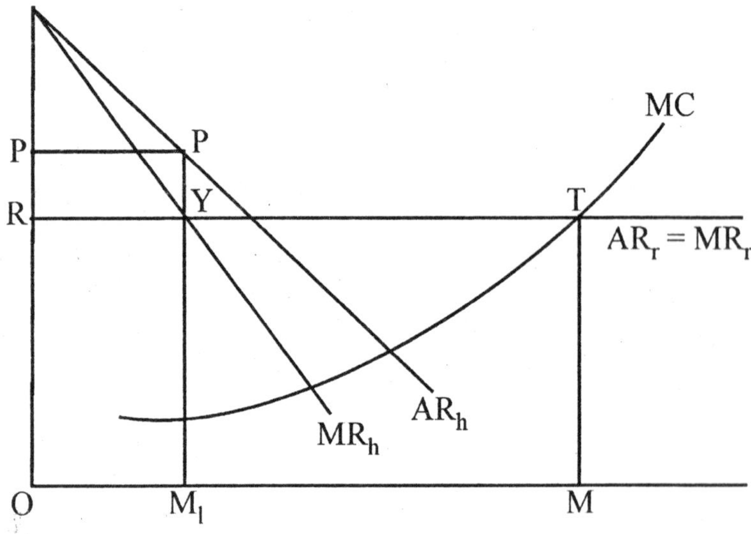

Fig. 11

If there is monopoly in the home market and perfect competition in the foreign market, then in the competitive market a competitive price will be charged. The price charged in the home market will be monopoly price and higher than the *AC*, but in the foreign market the price will be lower than in the home market but efforts will be made to have equal *MR* in both the markets. *If this itself is good enough to the competitors, the monopolist will dump without incurring the loss, if the AC is covered but the AC of this firm is lower than the AC of other firms. In other cases AC can be lower than the AR in the home market but may be higher than the AR in the foreign market, provided AR itself is lower than the prices charged by the competitors.*

In the above diagram, the horizontal lines show AR_I/ MR_I: the average and marginal revenues of the foreign markets. Since the market is competitive the prices are the same for all.

2. The output produced for the home and the international market is the same hence has the same *MC* curve. *The equilibrium output is where the MR is equal to the MC of the total output.* This output is to be distributed between the national and international market.
3. AR_h and MR_h are declining as they pertain to the monopoly situation in the home market. The MR_f and MR_h are equal at point Y and both are equal to *MC* as point T is on the same horizontal line as *Y*.

Out of the total output *OM, OM'* is allocated for the home market and sold at a high price *OP* which is higher than the dumping price *OR*. The output disposed off in the dumped market is *MM'*.

If there are more than two international markets for dumping, for more than two national sub-markets for price discrimination, the output allocation and the prices charged will follow the same principles as adumbrated above.

H. Degrees of Discrimination

Pigou has given three degrees of discrimination. *First degree of discrimination:* The monopolist charges such a high price that no consumer's surplus is left with the buyer. He charges as much price as is within the power of the buyer to pay. *Second degree of discrimination* refers to such price discrimination that some consumer's surplus is left with the buyer. *Third degree of discrimination* means that the market is divided in such a manner that each is charged according to his group abil ty. In other words, the consumer's surplus to different groups of people is not mopped up.

Is Discrimination Harmful or Beneficial to the Society?

It is not correct to say that discrimination is harmful to the society whatever sinister meaning the word 'discrimination' may convey to the people. The principle of discrimination is based on the principle of 'ability to pay'. The monopolist charges a high price from those who can afford or are willing to pay. In this way he can charge a low price from those who cannot afford a high price or are not willing to pay much. It is also possible that the monopolist may provide the benefit of charging low price to the poor and may recover the 'cost' from the rich persons. If he does so, he is beneficial to the society.

Another advantage that can be reaped by the society and to the monopolist is that the discrimination makes it possible to create maximum demand for the product of the monopolist. This will help monopolist reap the advantages of the large scale production. In other words, discrimination will make it possible for the monopolist to make the law of increasing returns applicable.

However, if the sole aim of the monopolist is just to mulct the consumers and to fleece them, then discrimination will not be beneficial to the society. It will be beneficial to the monopolist only.

Degree of Monopoly Power

The degree of the monopoly power depends on many things. Most important factors are, whether the commodity produced is a necessity or otherwise, whether the consumers are rich or poor, whether the amount spent on the monopolised article is the small part of the budget or otherwise, whether the demand curve is inelastic or otherwise, whether there is any resistence from the consumers or society, whether there is the fear of the intervention from the government or not. The greater the elasticity of demand the less the power of the monopolist.

We know that the price in monopoly market is above the marginal cost and thus the abnormal profits are earned. The greater the abnormal profits, the greater the power. There is a formula:

$$\frac{P - MC}{P}$$

The greater the value of this formula, the greater the power. In case the value is zero, there is no monopoly. (This will happen in perfect competition).

I. Monopoly and Economic Development

Evils

Monopoly is seldom beneficial for the economic development, at least when we take the socio economic point of view. The aim of the monopolist, as we have seen, is to maximise his aggregate profits. He may frequently produce less than his optimum capacity. This will increase the price of the commodities and thus the interests of the consumers are harmed.

Then this also reduces the demand for those resources that the monopolist employs in his production. Employment will not be provided as much as could be. This depresses the prices of the raw materials and also the wages. If the monopolist enjoys the 'monopsony' in the factor market and monopoly in the product market, gives him advantages in both the market. He pays less and charges more.

The monopolist creates the socio-economic inequalities. The monopolists frequently and indirectly support the politicians and political parties. The politicians become the mere puppets and tools in the hands of the monopolists. Then keep the poor, poor. These are the socio economic evils of monopoly.

Advantages

However, certain economic gains of monopolist production are apparent. A monopolist will organise his production in such a manner that he achieves maximum economies. He invests in large amount so that he achieves many technical economies. He standardises production practices and achieves lowest cost per unit of output. He achieves economies of management and utilises the talents of best skilled workers. Since he provides his own finance or can secure the required finance, he can secure financial economies also. He can extend his market and can achieve marketing economies.

Conclusion: While it is conceded that the economic organisation of the monopolist may be such as to bring forth for him optimum degree of private economies, it is not necessary that he will provide benefits to the public also. Economists distinguish between 'private and social' economic gains. From the socio-economic point of view the monopolist may be helpful for socio economic development of the country.

Public Control of Monopolies

Control of monopoly has become a function of the Government. Even in the United States of America, combination* are not looked upon with approval. In India there was a Commission which studies the concentration of monopolistic power. It examined the production plans so as not to allow this concentration to grow. It also examined policies of such monopolistic houses to see that they do not harm the interests of other producers. Now it is disbanded.

Prof. Arther Cecil Pigou, the celebrated English

Economist, wrote at length in his world famous book "Economics of Welfare", as how to control monopoly. Pigou believed that the presence of monopolies is injurious to the consumers and the public in general. He suggested several methods for the public control of monopoly. First, we can use Indirect Methods and if they do not work, then Direct Methods can be used.

Indirect Methods

First, Anti Trust Laws may be passed. These are the laws that will be passed by the government that no person can from combinations so as to form monopoly. But the sellers may make informal price-fixing agreements, *i.e.,* they may make secret agreements of charging a high price in unison. In other words, they may not actively compete amongst themselves.

Second, the government may make the producer compete with one another. If some monopolistic producers secretely work as monopolies then the government can ask them to compete. But the producers can roadblock the attempts of the government. The producers may charge different prices but may so allow the rebates and other concessions that it may in effect come be the same price. Bogus independent companies may be floated. Such methods, therefore, cannot be completely successful.

Direct Methods

When indirect methods fail, the government may resort to direct methods of control of monopoly. Pigou lists four such methods. They are:

(i) Establishing a Buyers' Monopoly

The government may help the buyers to form a buyers monopoly. The monopolist will not then be able to charge very high price from the consumers.

But the ultimate consumers are so many that they

can hardly combine. In fact it may become a monopoly of wholesale purchaser who may also side with the monopolist.

(ii) To Do Adverse Publicity to the Working of the Monopolist

It is pointed out that if the public becomes hostile then it may give adverse publicity to the working of the monopolist. But the public or the government will hardly be able to know the correct position of the profit and costs. The monopolist may itself so put his position before the eyes of the public as to appear innocent. Now-a-days this may not be sufficient.

(iii) Price Control

This is the most powerful weapon in the hands of the government. First, the government may resort to indirect price control. This means that while the government will not fix any price, it will just not allow "charging of an unreasonably high price". The interpretation of what is reasonable or unreasonable may be left to a body of experts.

If this method also fails, the government will have to study the cost-prices structure of the monopolist and then fix the maximum price. *This is known as the direct price control.*

(iv) Public Operation in Industry

When all such methods fail, the government can take over the monopolies and operate the industry as 'public enterprise'.

Distinction Between the Monopoly Price and Perfect Competition Price: Is Monopoly Price Always Higher?

There are several distinctions between the monopoly pricing and the perfect competition prices. They are:

(i) In perfect competition the firm and industry are

separate; but in the monopoly the same firm is the industry also,

(ii) In perfect competition, the firm is a price taker and not a price maker. In monopoly the firm can fix its own price and decide about its level of production also,

(iii) In perfect competition the price is equal to the cost. But in monopoly the price is more than the cost (i.e., the *AR* is greater than the *AC)* and thus the monopolist always earns abnormal profits. Abnormal profits can be earned under perfect competition only for the short period,

(iv) In perfect competition *AC*= *AR MC* = *MC,* but in monopoly only *MR* = *MC* are equal. *AR* is higher than *MR, MC* and *AC.*

It is said that the price in monopoly is higher than the price in perfect competition, but such a statement is meaningless. When there is no perfect competition we cannot imagine an 'imaginary price' that would have been there had perfect competition been there is that line of production! However, one-thing can be said that it is not in the interest of the monopolist always to charge a high price. In case the demand is elastic and the law of increasing returns applies, the monopolist may charge a low price also.

Monopoly and Perfect Competition Compared

- Consumers' surplus. Gain, As D' or AR segment is above the price. Higher utility than price.
- Loss as D/AA at a lower position than P. Thus D is < P or utility less than price.
- MP-P-E-CP are super-normal profits of the monopolist.
- OMP price is monopoly price.

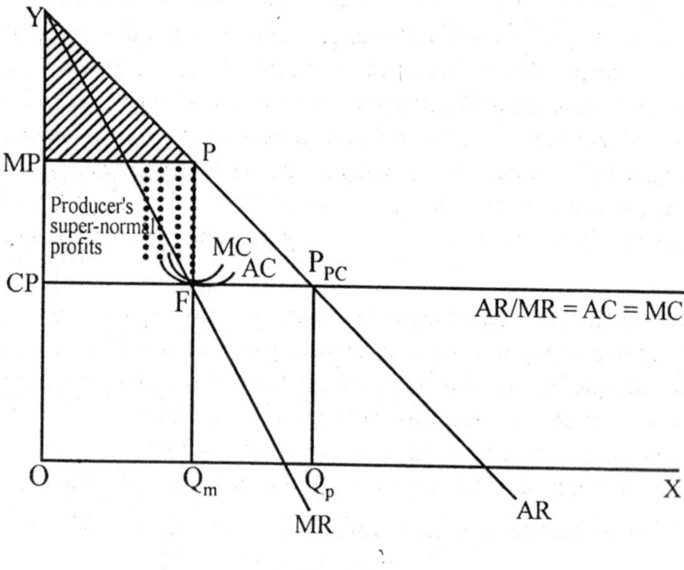

Fig. 12

- OCP price is perfect competition price.
- Had there been p.c. all space over the line of CP would not have provided extra profits.
- At point *EAR* = *MR* = *MC* = *AC.*
- At point *E* in monopoly only *AR AC.*
- CP-E-P-MP could have been part of consumers' surplus, had it not been taken away as the super-normal profit by the monopolist.
- This is one additional point to prove that p.c. is better than monopoly.
- Monopolist does not sell beyond OQ_m. In p.c. production could be OQ p.c.
- AR and MR extended below OX just to show them explicitly in the diagram.

16

Space and Price Determination Under Imperfect Competition

DUOPOLY, MONOPOLISTIC COMPETITION, OLIGOPOLISTIC COMPETITION, KINKED DEMAND CURVE, PRICING UNDER GROUP LEADERSHIP

A. Definition of Imperfect/Monopolistic Competition, Top Ten Features of Imperfect Competition, Wastages in Imperfect Competition

B. Price Determination Under Imperfect Competition
   - Under Duopoly without Product Differentiation
   - Under Duopoly with Product Differentiation
   - Under Oligopoly without Product Differentiation
   - Under Oligopoly with Production Differentiation [Conditions without product differentiation convert into perfect competition : Hence not elaborated.]

C. Price Determination in Imperfect Competition under Different Laws of Returns (Situation Inverse in Changes in Costs) and Different Degrees of Elasticities of AR and MR

D. Price Determination under Oligopolies Illustrated with the Help of Diagrams
   - Case of Increasing Returns and Both Types of Elasticities of Demand
   - Case of Decreasing Returns (Increasing Costs) and Both Types of Elasticities Curves of AR and MR

- The Normal Profit Case: The Loss Situation

E. Kinked Demand Curve Equilibrium
The Case of "Group Leader Leads and Others Follow"

F. Diagrammatic Illustration of Price Output Equilibrium After Incurring the Supplementary Costs

G. Game Theory and Oligopoly[1]

A. Features or Characteristics of Imperfect Competition

All conditions of the market other than that of perfect competition and monopoly are of imperfect competition.

There can be following main groups:

(a) *Duopoly*—i.e., two producers with or without product differentiations in theory but with product differentiations in practice.

(b) *Oligopoly*—There are 'a few' producers only and they produce highly or substantially differentiated products. "A few" in practice should mean less than 10—but there can be an oligopoly of 12 even if we are considering the world as a whole.

(c) *Monopolistic competition*—Here the producers are many. *The main thing that distinguishes "monopolistic competition "from "perfect competition" is the existence of differentiated and branded products.* No one know how many matchbox producers are there in India with different brand names.

Pierro Sraffa wrote his famous article, "The Law of Increasing Returns Under Competitive Conditions" and proved in that the two are incompatible. He elaborated how the assumptions of perfect competition do not hold good in all conditions and in some cases partake the character of "a myth". Thereafter, Hotelling, Pigou, Robins, A.A. Young, Robertson, Shove, Harrod, Kahn, Mrs. Joan Robinson, Chamberlin, JK Mehta, Kaldor, AJ Nichol, White,

Boulding, Bain, Clark, Knight, Lewis...made important contributions.

> Mrs. Joan Robinson and Chamberlin stand out as the most outstanding. What Mrs. Joan Robinson calls imperfect competition, Mr. Chamberlin calls "monopolistic competition". Mrs. Joan Robinson's elaboration includes the contribution of Chamberlin. Other writers tried to popularize the following words and the theories related to them. But they could not attract the attention.
>
> (a) Impure competition.
> (b) Non-perfect competition.
> (c) Limited competition.
> (d) Partial monopoly.

Top Ten Features of Imperfect Competition [They also Prove the Less Relevance of Perfect Competition]

1. Differentiated Products

Producers of goods bring their products with different qualities, logos, brands and at different prices for different income groups. Cars, mopeds, motor-cycles, TV, computers...all have intra-product differentiations, i.e., one brand of car differs from the other brand of car. Over a period of time, the car of the same name can have a different looks and features.

> Product differentiation can be real or imaginary. *Mrs. Joan Robinson gave an example, which is of no importance in modern times,* (a) There can be two restaurants one with real good stuff and the other not with such quality stuff. This is real differentiation. There can non-real 'imaginary' differentiations also.
>
> If the quality of food is the same in the two hotels but in one hotel male waiters are there and in the other there are female waitresses, *"then all husbands accompanied with their jealous wives will go to that*

hotel in which male waiters are there. On the contrary all bachelor boys will go to that hotel in which there are female waitresses. Advertisement, publicity and propaganda create illusions about which one is superior. [It looks ridiculous that wearing a particular brand undergarment or vests or banyans can make a person most powerful as certain leading actors of Indian cinema show in advertisements].

2. Buyers Attached to the Products

There are many similar products and they are patronized by different groups of buyers according to their income, tastes and preferences. Customers get attached to the brand rather than to the price. In other words, even if cheaper varieties of competitive goods are there, the customers will keep on purchasing the goods to which they become attached, for example, some persons prefer yellow level tea only.

3. Price Elasticity of Demand is Less Than One

Producers in imperfect competition have to lower their prices in order to sell more. Hence the AR and MR curves slope downwards to the right. The degree of inelasticity is less in comparison to monopoly. The AR/MR lines are not horizontal as in perfect competition. If the oligopolists are selling luxury goods, the steepness of the AR/MR curves will be less; they will be flatter but with downward declining slopes.

4. There Can be Attachment to the Sellers Even

This leads to imperfections in the service market. People prefer their own surgeons, lawyers, architects, physicians, hospitals, beauticians, barbers and tailors. Thus for personalised services, different prices can be charged. A handsome vendor (vender) may be preferred by the vendees.

5. The Cross Elasticity of Demand is There But Not Very High

In perfect competition it is infinite. In monopoly it is zero. In imperfect competition it is in between. The buyers do not act in unison. They do not show as much attachment to the price as to the brand and producer.

6. Indivisibilities are High in Imperfect Competition

Oligopolies are no ordinary firms of the economic size of perfect competition. As we saw earlier in the chapter on increasing returns/decreasing costs, "indivisibilities" are lumpy investments which cannot be invested in bits and pieces. Either there has got to be full investment or none at all. *The power of the oligopolies is in direct proportion to the power of 'overcoming indivisibilities'*, i.e., making those huge investments in one lump.

Non-neutral returns to scale give rise to imperfections. Imperfections can lead to deterioration of the conditions of some. For example, Lambretta scooter and a few other like it based on the same technology are gone. There were many mopeds also. Fiat car of old model is no longer manufactured. There were indivisibilities involved in them but the infrastructure had to be dismantled.

> Non-neutral returns to scale, if leading to increasing returns, will establish oligopolies. Maruti and Hyundai, for example, are doing well. Daewoo lost ground and now Ford is struggling. Its parent headquarter lost over $ 1 in two months i.e., $ 6 b, in a year if press reports (May 2005) are to be believed. *Bigness is not always a passport to victory. Small car manufacturers showed that. They solved the problem of space and parking. A big car carries the same four persons as the small car.*
>
> Rationalisation, upgradation, innovations, relative cheapness and relative conveniences will enable the oligopolistic firm to move ahead.

> *Overcoming indivisibilities will require one additional capability also i.e., of sustaining before the break-even point is crossed.* The costs are always higher than the revenue before the break-even point. Losses are there. But ahead in time horizon there are promising profits. Only those firms which can keep on going can become oligopolies.

Even monopolies advertise to create demand. *Monopolies and oligopolies incur supplementary costs to increase the degree of inelasticity of demand for their product.* In simple words these costs are incurred so that the buyers buy more and remain stuck up with the products of the oligopolies and not go to the rival oligopolies. *Monopolies and oligopolies are notorious for mulcting the customers as well as the labourers.* They may pay more but they take the nerves of the employees out of their bodies![2]

7. Entry of the Firms is Free but not Frequent

In perfect competition the entry of the new firms is unrestricted and so is the exit. Inefficient firms cannot survive. In oligopolistic market, we do not have a new firm entering into car manufacturing each day. A lot of money, a lot of product differentiation and still greater courage to invest are necessary.

8. Producers are Independent but Their Fortunes are Not Independent

The firms in oligopolistic competition have to keep an eye on what the rival firms are doing. If a firm announces price reduction, most others may have to follow. In practice, they follow a "group leader". If one producer brings new changes, others will also introduce the same. If out of six car producers, five have power steering, it is scarcely possible for the sixth not to provide that facility. Innovations are constantly being introduced to beat the competitors. Independent price policy is there; but in name only.

9. Buyers are Not Rational Nor Perfectly Mobile

Buyers need not always be well aware of the price differences. Besides how much time can they devote to get all the information from everywhere. Even in the purchase of cars, one goes to the nearest dealer in big cities. Buyers can be lethargic and inert.

10. The Costs Curves are U-Shaped and the Revenue Curves (As we saw earlier) are Downward Sloping to the Right

The shapes of the "U" shaped costs curves may not be such that the MC and AC of two firms converge on each other. Their slopes will differ over time periods and for different lumps of production.

The AR and MR curves can slope downwards very gently in one case and very sharply in the case of the other firms. *There is no single case of imperfect competition, but a whole range or series of cases representing progressively more and more imperfect competition.*

Wastes of Imperfect Competition

There are supplementary costs and wastages of cross-transport. A car manufactured at Delhi, is purchased in Chennai, while a car manufactured in Chennai is purchased in Delhi. Cross transport costs increase the selling costs but they are borne by the customers due to their brand preferences. *It is to be noted that the more the competing firms indulge in aggressive advertisement to lure the customers, the more the customers will have to pay higher prices.* Afterall the supplementary costs of selling are also to be recovered from the customers. Transport costs may or may not be barriers to marketing of goods of imperfect competition. They certainly are in perfect competition.

Unemployment ensues under this system as a lot of potential employment remains ungenerated, as in the monopoly.

B. Price Determination Under Imperfect Competition

There are many types of imperfect competition. *The main study is of the "group equilibrium under oligopolies with product differentiations"*. We will study that in details:

(a) Duopoly without Product Differentiation

This is a very improbable situation that the second producer who breaks the monopoly of the first, should come to the market with exactly the same type or homogeneous product. The chances of his coming up with *homogenous* product are still less. If that happens, the situation will get converted into perfect competition.

(b) Duopoly with Product Differentiation

There can be four situations. First, they may agree to share the market and be monopolist in their territory. Secondly, they may compete with price war and one of them may succeed in ousting the other. There will be monopoly once again.[3] Thirdly, they may amalgamate to become one producer once again. Fourthly, they may remain independent but may divide the market after the ruinous price war.

(c) Oligopoly without Product Differentiation

This is a very unlikely situation—almost totally unlikely. If at all there emerges this type of market situation, it will sooner than later get converted into perfect competition.

(d) Oligopoly with Product Differentiation and a Group Leader

Price determination will be like monopoly, (a) There *will be one thing'*. The AR and MR curves will not be *very steep,* (b) Secondly, there can be kinked demand curve situation and the *game theory may be in full play*. We discuss the above II(b) and (d) situations.

(e) Price Determination under Group Equilibrium in Oligopoly

(a) If There are Constant Returns or Constant Costs

See the diagrams in the chapter on monopoly. The price determination and the diagrams will be similar. Price will be determined according to the elasticity of demand. *Super-normal profits will be there.*

> If elastic...low price and high output.
>
> If inelastic...high price and low output.
>
> *All that is to be seen is that the AR and MR curves are not very steep.*

(b) If There are Increasing Costs or Decreasing Returns

There will be super-normal profits, *but the AR and MR curves will not be steeper.* In this chapter on and after p. 331.

1. Fix point E where MC = MR.
2. Draw a perpendicular from E to X axis to have OM equilibrium output.
3. This equilibrium output will be sold at a price corresponding to AR. Hence take ME line to AR. That becomes OP or MP price.
4. Spot the point where PM line is intersected by the AC line. Mark it as "C" point. MC is cost per unit. The remaining portion CP is the profit per unit. C-P-P-C rectangle is the area of super-normal profits.

These steps were seen earlier also.

(a) If elastic demand + IC ... "mid-way" price.
(b) If inelastic demand + IC ... *very high price and low output.*

(c) When the Law of Decreasing Costs or of Increasing Returns is Applying, then :

* With elastic demand — prices will be kept low and the output will be kept high.
* With inelastic demand — prices will be kept a little high but since output is also to be kept high, the price hike will not be steep to take advantage of the inelasticity of demand.

(d) Loss Situation

This has been demonstrated with the diagram *(and the same was done in the case of monopoly),* whereby we show the AC curve being above the point where the ME line meets the AR line.

(e) Normal Profits

This has also been shown with a diagram in this chapter and the diagram is the same as that in the monopoly. The point lies where the ME line meets the AR curve and at the same point of P, the AC curve is also tangent. Other Salient Features:

1. *In monopolistic competition, the tendency to move towards normal profits will come early than in oligopolistic competition.*
2. Selling costs and cross-transport costs put additional burden on the customers. It is theoretically possible on this account that if the monopolist is not incurring these costs, the monopoly may prove less burdensome than even oligopolies. *Only when price rivalry is there,* can the oligopolies be less burdensome than the monopolies. *Once the selling costs are there, they become like fixed costs.*
3. If the selling costs increase the demand and increase in demand leads to increasing returns, then the per unit cost of production will go down. If the oligopolies are selling luxury goods, the prices charged will be lower.

4. *The conniving oligopolies (like OPEC)* are dangerous. They refuse to compete. They can decide to keep the production down and/or not indulge in price war. Informative, persuasive and dissuasive advertisements can all be part of the game—the game of sham competition. *So far there had been no price war between the car producers or motor cycle producers of India.* Their prices are rising and rising, even when the costs of inputs are not rising. The labour laws have lost their teeth. Over-work is taken from the workers and hence labour compensations are not causing cost-price hike.
5. Oligopolies are not good bet for increasing employment in the country. They too can behave like monopolies. They can be slow in innovations. *[The engine of the Bajaj scooter is on one side. This imbalance has always resulted in easy skidding. Tens of thousands of riders lost lives but the company did not innovate to centrally mount the engine. The company can argue that persons died not because of tilted engine weight but because of over-speeding and not wearing the helmet.]*

D. Pricing Under Imperfect/Monopolistic Competition

The prices charged are on the basis of 'what the traffic can bear'. There is a sellers' market in this case. The market will criss-cross the geographical territories. Only some buyers may really be exercising a choice in which case the relatively less rich may go in for the cheapest model. Price determination will be on the pattern of monopoly pricing, with AR and MR not being very steep.

Oligopolistic Competition

Oligopolistic group consists of a limited number of sellers who produced differentiated or non-differentiated goods. The situation on non-differentiated goods will ultimately lead to perfect competition and is not a real oligopolistic situation for the long run.

The number of firms in case of the oligopolistic group is limited yet they cannot charge the monopoly price because goods produced by them are near substitutes. There is no possibility of a tacit or open agreement between them about price, output or about market sharing. However, in recent years it is seen that they form "Producers Association" and avoid price wars between them. In the short period such oligopolistic firms earn super normal profits even with their relatively (compared with monopoly) flatter AR and MR lines as the oligopolistic firms keep AR above AC. In the long run firms will earn normal profits as AR and AC become tangent.

Oligopolies act like *warring firms* and we can use military analogies. (K.W. Rothschild suggested their use). They have 'price wars', 'aggressive sales campaigns', 'marketing strategies', and 'industrial espionage'.

The rival oligopolistic firms may be quite strong and now-a-days we find that they prefer to lead a quiet life and not compete vigorously. Normally the oligopolistic firms keep their prices *sticky downwards.* If they find that there is release of purchasing power in the market (say because of the rise in the money supply, government spending, release of dearness allowance to the employees, declaration of bonus), they even hike the prices. As the market slackens after the boom, they do not bring down the prices. In the face of demand resistance, the oligopolists introduce some 'side gifts' with their products rather than reduce the price. The oligopolists do not want to "spoil" their market.

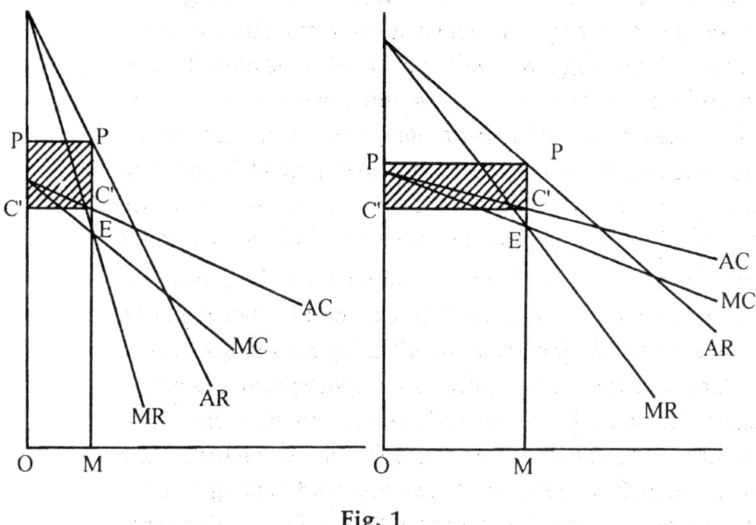

Fig. 1

Oligopoly pricing under increasing returns with 'elastic' and more elastic demand or AR/MR curves.

In the above diagrams the equilibrium point is *E* where *MR* = *MC*. *ME* is extended *to AR* to find out the price. The point where the *AC* cuts the price line shows the price per unit *OC* or *CM* and the remaining portion of *CP* as the profit per unit. As usual the shaded rectangles show the total super normal profits equal to extra profits per unit multiplied by the total output, CPP'C.

Output is higher in case of the elastic demand and price lower. Price is higher in case of the inelastic demand and then output will be relatively less.

Long-run Equilibrium

Decreasing Returns (Increasing Costs Case)

In the long-run diseconomies of scale become higher than the economies of scale and diminishing returns start being obtained. Diminishing returns can be postponed but not avoided. New techniques, innovations, increasing the scale and scope of production, efforts to economise give some respite from the inevitable.

Pricing under imperfect/Monopolistic competition follow the compulsions of declining AR and MR. As the demand goes up due to a rise in population, rise in income, rise in export demand etc. then old firms can expand or the new firms can enter.

The possibilities of cut-throat competition are less because there are so many throats to be cut! This is not possible for a single producer. Destructive competition through price wars is not a distinct possibility in imperfect competition. *In some rarest of the rare cases if one seller in the imperfectly competitive market finds a weak seller of the similar product (as it goes in monopolistic/imperfect competition), then price discrimination may be resorted to so that the rival is harmed (ousted, if possible).* Yet the chances are rare

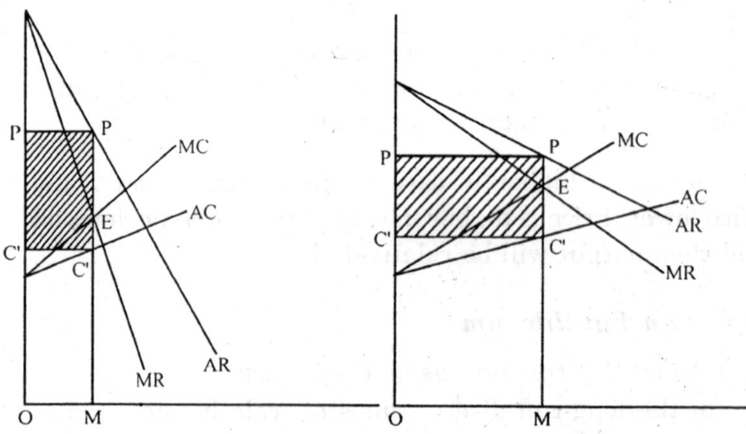

Fig. 2

because others will see through the game and will start competing with the predator firm. In this game the firm which was to be attacked may get respite. Because of the 'Associations' of the manufacturers now-a days unfair and unethical competitions are becoming lesser.

In the long-run we will have decreasing return and with elastic and highly elastic *AR* and *MR* curves we show hereafter the equilibrium conditions giving super-normal and normal profits, thus:

In both the cases above:

1. Equilibrium = MC = MR.
2. Eq. output = EM
3. Eq. price per unit = Op or MP
4. Eq. cost per unit = MC' or OC'
5. Eq. profit per unit = PM C'M = PC'
6. Total revenue = OM x OP = OPPM.

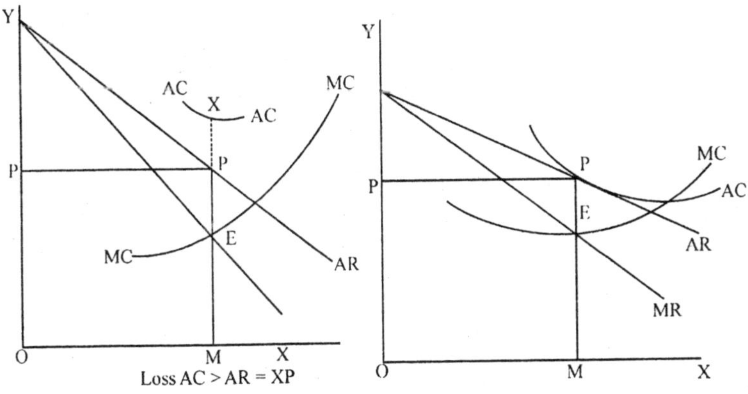

Fig. 3

7. Total costs = OC x OM = OC'C'M.
8. Total profits = C'PPC' = TR-TC.

Perpendicular on X from E. ME extended to touch AR at P. Where the AC line cuts the MC line. (Price-cost per unit, both).

Total Revenue = Price x O

Total output x per unit cost

Equilibrium output = *MR* = *MC*

Equilibrium price = Corresponding to eq. out put *OM* at *AR* = *MP* or *OP*

If *AR AC* Super-normal profits.

If *AR* = *AC* Normal profit.

In the long run *Oligopolies with the same products* will find that their *AR* and *MR* lines have become horizontal to the base line. The price situation can become akin to the perfectly competitive market. A price war *in case of the non-differentiated products* can bring down the price to a low level where only normal profits are earned, as in the perfect competition. Oligopolies now-a-days do not indulge in price wars. They rather connive to keep the prices sticky downwards.

Oligopolies with product differentiation. 'A few' firms produce differentiated products and the situation is still not of 'imperfect competition' (in that situation the number of firms will become quite substantial).

Prices are not equal because of the product differentiation but they do not differ much because the products are close substitutes. Some firms keep the prices of their products high— to give the impression that the products are better. This is possible for a *price leader* only. 'Dalda' was a brand name. It became so popular as to sound as the generic name for hydrogenated edible oil. Hindustan Lever was the group leader for this product. Hero Honda is group-leader for motorcycles. Elasticity of the demand for different products differs but it is not unit-elastic. Differences in prices do not induce the buyers to buy the cheapest brand/ model. The *AR* and *MR* curves of ail firms will be flatter with varying slopes.

Monopoly agreements will not be possible nor the cut-throat competition situation likely to emerge. Markets will not be shared equally. There will be crossing of the territories for none is respected for the rivals. The determination of price and output of the oligopolies with product differentiation can be presented with the help of long period monopoly diagrams.

Prices under oligopolies are sticky downwards. If there is resistance from the consumers and they reduce their demand at higher prices, the oligopolists (acting though cartel type associations, as in case of the OPEC—Organisation of the Petroleum Exporting Countries) will rather cut the production that cut the prices. Oligopolies may start giving some 'gifts' with their products but will not reduce the prices. Thus prices are made sticky downwards.

E. Kinked Demand Curve

Paul Sweezy of the USA, and Hall & Hitch of U.K. developed this concept in 1939. These are two important points.

(a) If the rival oligopolies are selling at a particular price (average, sort of), and one them decides to increase the price others will not follow. If all oligopolists but one oligopolist (whose equilibrium, let us say, we are studying) raise the prices but "our oligopolist" does not raise the price, his sales will automatically increase. It is not our object of study here as to why others decided to increase the price.

(b) If rivals reduce the price, 'our' oligopolist will also

have to reduce the price. If "our oligopolist" reduces the price rivals follow suit when it is a case of price cut but not when it is a case of increasing the price.

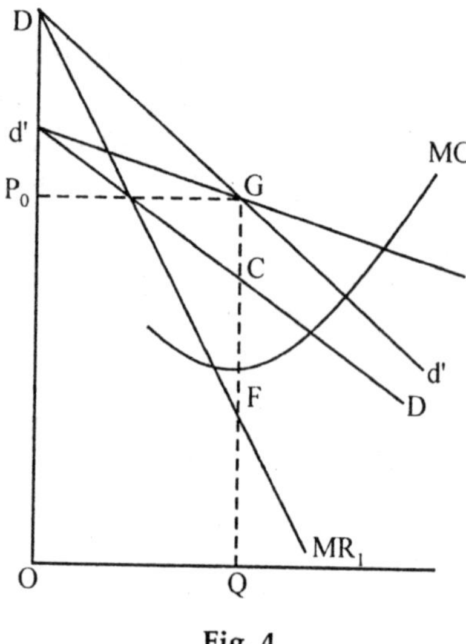

Fig. 4

The kink position in the *simplest way* be explained thus:

1. Suppose our oligopolist is producing at *OG* or *OQ* output at *OP* price.
2. From this point there are two *AR* curves available to him for raising the price. One is steeper and the other is flatter. Obviously it will not be possible for him to go on the steeper path. This curve of less elastic demand is elusive to him. If at all he can raise the price he will go on the flatter curve, provided all follow him. If he alone goes on this line, he loses the sales very substantially. Hence this is flatter.
3. After *G* point, again there are two curves—one of steep fall in price and the other slow fall in price. If oligopolist so decide to cut the price, our oligopolist will also have to follow suit. If it comes to reducing

the price, he will have to reduce the price sharply. Thus the *actual demand or AR path which an oligopolist follows is flatter above G and steeper after G.*

4. The corresponding *MR* of the earlier portion has been shown with a thick line. There is a sudden drop. It *is known as the 'gap', 'drop' or 'hole'.* At the upper point of the vertical MR the demand must have failed to fall. Hence the line dropped vertically. Then there is *MR* corresponding to the steeper *AR.*
5. The steeper demand curve line is that line when all oligopolists react to changes in prices *both ways.* Since they do not remain on this line in the upper segment, it is not *AR* line for all over the entire range.
6. The flatter line which is left of G and above *G,* is flatter shows that if the price is raised *most* customers will be lost.
7. Kinked demand curve incorporates the assumption that price cuts are followed while price raises are not. Below the kink where there is steep fall, it is shown that the sales of the whole oligopoly groups can be expanded through price cutting.
8. *D'C* is the *MR* corresponding to *DG* or *ΔG;* marginal revenue corresponding to steeper *ARI* is *DMR* or *ΔMR. For the entire kinked demand curve dGD* or *ΔGD the marginal revenue curve is "dC-gap-(drop or hole)-MR.*

Kinked demand curve or *AR* situation is real to those conditions where because of the demand depression, the oligopolistic firms decide to cut down the prices suddenly and substantially.

Kinked Curve During Boom

In the boom condition opposite things apply. (A) If one oligopolist cuts the price, others will not follow; if one raise the price, others will follow. (B) If they want to raise the price, the price can be raised sharply since it is a boom condition. (C) If they want to boost the market by cutting the prices (for higher sales), they can now reduce the prices only slightly. It will suffice. The kinked demand curve will take the opposite shape, thus:

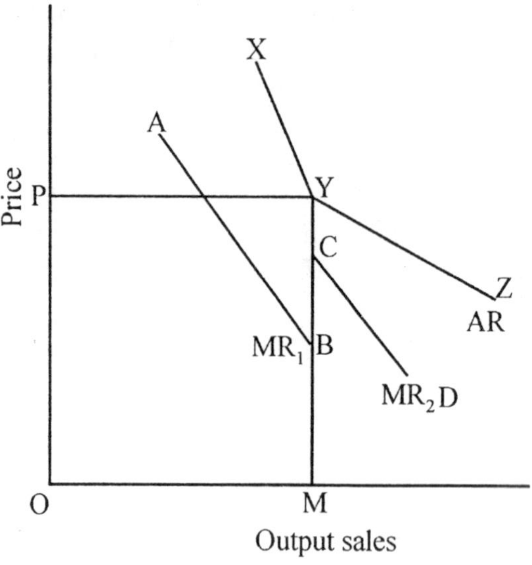

Fig. 5

- XY_2 is kinked *AR* for boom conditions.
- *AB* and *CD* are corresponding *MRs* for XY and Y_2.
- BC upwards is the 'gap'.

Equilibrium: And the Kink, in Normal Conditions of Competition

(a) If *MC* passes through the gap, there will be no reason to alter the price.

(b) If the *MC* is high and rising and passes above the upper point of the gap, there will be reason to raise the price. This is a situation of inflation and all oligopolists will have to raise the price.

- The following diagrams are of the kinks during the normal times.
- During depression also the kink will be of the same type. Shown in bits the positions will be:
- During boom if the group leader raises the price, others will also raise the price. The D' curve will be less elastic. When the boom ends, the D' curve will become elastic. The steep *AR* will become flatter.

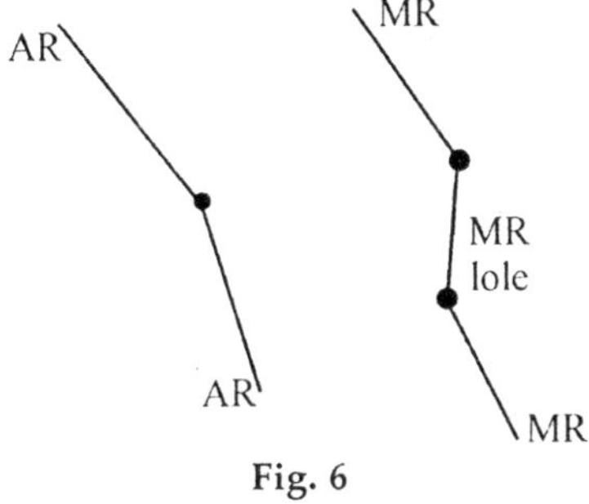

Fig. 6

- Hole drops in normal times and depression.
- Hole rises in boom.
- *The* price is not raised in any condition, so long as the *MC* curve is moving up and down the hole.
- *MC* curve will pass through the hole.

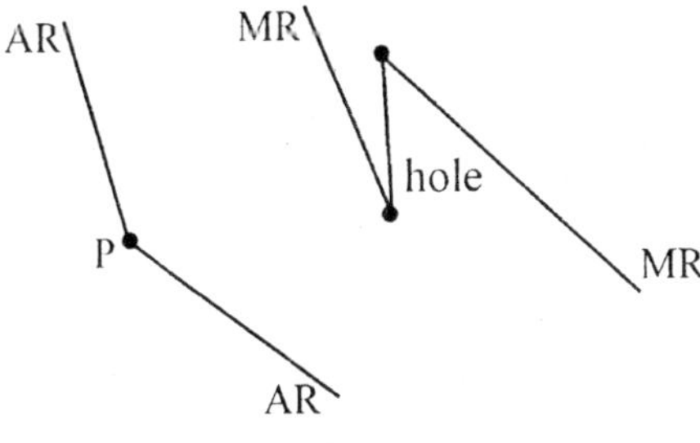

Fig. 7

Please read these three paragraph mentioned below carefully :

What happens when the MC rises within the hole of MR?

The essence of the kinked demand curve is that when the group leader increases the price, other oligopolies may not increase the price. But when the group leader reduces the price, all oligopolies will reduce the price.

The second important fact that made Paul Sweezy to explain his theory of kinked demand curve was that there were cases when the price remained the same even when the incremental or marginal costs of production were going up or down. The oligopolist may not increase the price for the fear that others may not increase their own price and he may be the lone producer to do so. He will lose market.

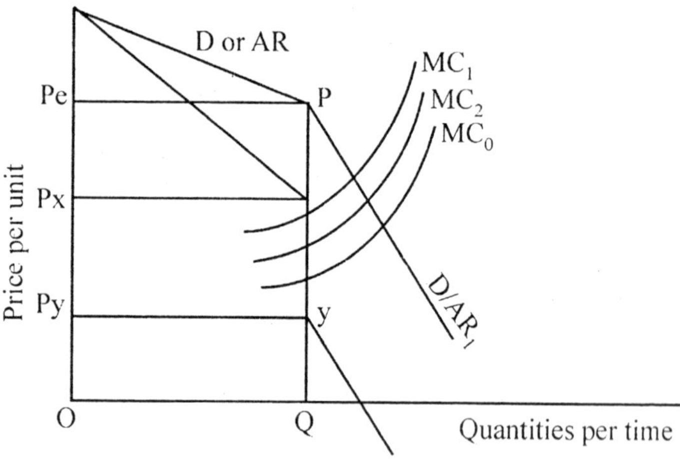

Fig. 8

Hence if the marginal costs rise within the hole or the drop in the marginal revenue curve, the price will be kept at the same level. Because if price is raised, there will problem of losing the sales. Hence the profit margin may go down: but so long as it is there, the price can remain stable.

Now note the following:

1. We see that the prices of products sold under oligoploy remain the same for considerable period of time. Various models of Maruti, for example, can have the same price for many months. In some cases, some oligopolies may have the same price for years together.
2. During this period the marginal costs do change. Yet the prices are kept constant. Lesser profit *margin* can be accepted. The total profits should be positive and, if the circumstances permit, be the same or more.
3. See the *AR* curve. From its starting point to the point P it has a steep (elastic) slope. Thereafter there is the steep fall (inelastic demand). *This shows that after the point P a steep fall in price will be necessary to sell more.* It also means that others will join in reducing the price. It can become a price war point.
4. *Price will be set at a point where the AR curve gets kinked. If price is reduced further, others will follow.*
5. *Dropping a perpendicular from P on x axis, we get the OQ equilibrium output. Price sets the output.*
6. As was seen in the chapter on demand, a sharply falling demand curve means that in order to sell a little bit more, there has got to be a substantial reduction in price. This also means that substantial reduction in price will be necessary to sell more. Hence why reduce price substantially to sell a little bit more. *Hence price remains stuck up at point P.*
7. As is known, there is a corresponding *MR* curve to *AR* curve. It remains below the *AR* curve. If *AR* is falling it is due to falling *MR*. Hence the rate of fall of *MR* is higher.
8. With this type of sudden fall form flatter to steep,

Paul Sweezy found, the *MR* will fall vertically.[4] This is a hole. After a point the *MR* curve will fall like *AR* curve i.e., steeply. A point will come when the *MR* will become zero. It being shown as "negative" is just the extension of the line in the diagram.

9. The hole in the *MR* is the lowest point. It is the lowest point over the entire vertical space. Equilibrium point is there where *MC* cuts the *MR*.

10. Price remains the same even if *MC*1, goes upto *MC*2 and then to *MC*3. *MR* is equal to all the *MCs* because the value in the 'hole' is the same for *MR*. This is the common portion of *MR*.

 Q.E.D.: Proved

Firms in oligopolistic market can have rising marginal costs still the price may not be increased, provided the marginal costs are rising "in the hole." Supplementary costs are oligopoly equilibrium.

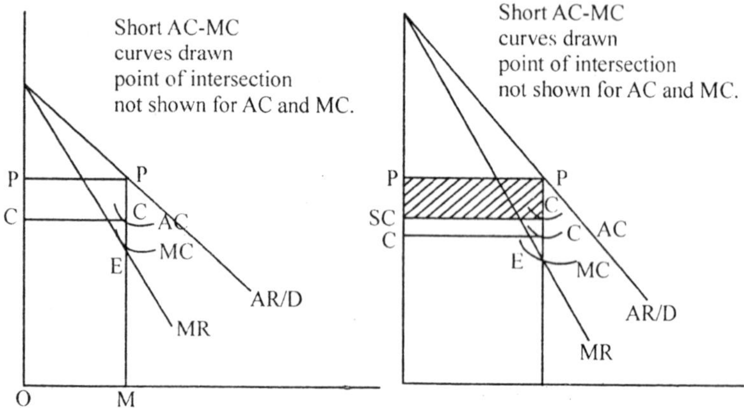

Fig. 9

1. We have shown that supplementary costs increase after advertisements *OSC* instead of *DC,* as in the second diagram below. Now the *OSC* becomes the *ATC*—average total costs and is higher than *OC*.
2. We have also shown that after incurring the supplementary costs, the demand curve becomes higher.
3. With *AR-MR* lines and with *AC-MC* lines (which were have not shown till the point of intersection in the diagram to keep it less congested).
   (a) Equilibrium at point E, Eq, output as OMS.
   (b) Equilibrium output is higher after supplementary costs as demand increases.
   (c) However, the price is also higher at *OP* in the second diagram compared with the first.
   (d) The rectangle *PPCC* is of lesser area than *PP, SC, SC*. It means that the price, costs, outputs and profits all increase after incurring the supplementary costs.

F. Game Theory and Oligopoly

KW Rothschild in 1947 gave the idea about the game that is played in monopoly price determination. We use such words that are used in a war e.g., (i) price war, (ii) industrial espionage, (iii) marketing strategies and (iv) campaigns for sales maximisation etc. *Paul van Neumann in 1950 and Mogenstern in 1953 developed the game theory, as it is today.*

> Wars are 'games' that are *not* carried on to such an extent that the two warring nations get completely destroyed—no persons or no properties left.
>
> The same way the oligopolies fight price wars but not to the extent of destroying themselves in trying to destroy others. The essence of the 'game' is that the oligopolies take decisions after studying what is going on in the rival firms. ["Pure theory and

Oligopoly", was published in "E:onomic Journal" in September 1947: KW Rothschil l].

Neumann and Morgenstern later on made the combined presentation in 1953. Since it is a game, there should be players. *If we extend the model we can have the following points about the games that are played in the market.*

(a) There is a game between sellers and sellers who would like to have more and more of buyers patronizing them.
(b) Then there is a 'game' between buyers and buyers who would like to have the best at the cheapest prices, beating other buyers.
(c) *The most important game is between the sellers and the buyers.* There is higgling and bargaining in the informal market. The seller quotes a high price, knowing full well that he cannot get that price. The buyer offers a very low price, knowing full well that he cannot buy on that price. Then the buyer makes a move of 'acting' to go away, looking back waiting to be called by the seller at the reduced price. The seller expects that the buyer will offer a higher price. Ultimately the price is settled in between the upper and lower limits but not exactly at the mid-point. It can be anywhere. *This happens in informal markets e.g., vegetable markets.* In case the vegetables are packaged and sold at the fixed prices (as in western countries), there cannot be higgling and bargaining.

But the game theory was developed for oligopoly and that too under some assumptions:

1. Not all members of the oligopoly in one line of production are taken into account. Only two producers (say car producers) are studied.

2. They are non-cooperative and, therefore, are competing intensely.
3. They indulge in *zero sum game* i.e., profits of one are equal to the losses of the others. It is like tossing a coin. Heads one wins and the other loses (with reference to tails, it can be explained the other way round also. Depends upon what is called first [4,5,6,7,8]

Since oligopolies produce differentiated products the war game cannot be carried on till but one go. Even if it is a duopoly one will get completely obliterated. If both produce non differentiated products, the model will get converted into perfect competition. If both are producing differentiated products (which they will do if they are prudent), then product preference of the buyers will keep them there. Price-wars can result in losses (we had seen all the possibilities about it in the section on duopoly.)

> Several response tables can be constructed to show that if one raises the prices, how much the other will raise or what will happen if the other one does not raise the price at all. There can be three responses: (a) one reduces the price, the other one reduces by the same margin, (b) the first reduces the price, the second one reduces the price by a higher margin; (c) thereafter the first one reduces by still higher margin. Can they go to zero?

There can be high pitched aggressive advertisements and cross movements in each other's "territories". *The big oligopolies are not fools to play the "games". They now "connive" to mulct the buyers. OPEC is an example where the producers cut the production if the prices fall. They do not indulge in price war. They believe in hiking the prices. If they could they would take the prices to the "sky ".*

Extending the game farther, we can say that the buyers play game with the producers to minimise payment obligations (prices) and get things of better quality, including good after sales service.

The producers play the game with the buyers to get maximum revenue from them. Producers want to charge "rent element" (extra payment due to transient scarcity period) from the buyers. The producers will not hesitate to fleece the customers. They can sell things of a few paise at the rate of many rupees (cosmetics and confectionery items). *[All cartoon series offer "prizes " if so ... many coupons are collected for...].* Producers do not hesitate in dumping the goods of number 1,2,3 or 4 grade technologies even when goods of grade 6 (suppose the highest grade) are available.

> *Game theory is about the game of outguessing the rivals and calculations of effective action plan.* WJ Baumel.

Buyers play game with the buyers if there are shortages and there are rationing and controls. Then the buyers try to corner the permits. Bribes become common. This too is a game.

> All players who play games are assumed to be rational, economic men who take best alternative routes to maximise profits. They are supposed to be intelligent enough to devise defensive systems and to take their organisation to the optimum level of efficiency and competitiveness. Those who indulge in price wars and costly advertisements also know about the total costs of present and future. The players cannot dictate terms to others about the game. They watch the strategies that the others adopt. There are no set rules. Only government interventionist laws can be brought into.

The present author would like to assert that in the modern day times the game theory has done a *sheershashan.* It is now up-side-down. The game between sellers and sellers is over. They connive and refuse to indulge in price wars. There is no price war between Hyundai, Ford, Maruti and Tata car manufacturing companies. In fact they keep on periodically hiking their prices, giving rise in the cost as one reason. The timings of the price hike can differ by a day or two and the percentages can also differ. *The game theory is now an assault on the consumer. Only consumers' self-defence can halt that assault. Another things that sets the limit to the assault of the producers is the limited money in the pockets of the potential buyers. If there are no limitations of money in the pockets of their clients, the saturation or satiety levels of their wants for the things of oligopolists stop the multinational oligopolies in going slow with their "games "..*

Inflation Related Prices (Sometimes Presented as "Prices in Practice" and/or "Strategies")

> We have studied, "prices under perfect competition", "prices under duopoly", "prices under oligopoly", "prices under monopolistic competition", "prices under monopoly", "joint demand and joint supply prices"...
>
> We have also studied the "market and normal prices", "reservation versus salvage prices". Some others discuss those states of prices which can be there in inflation.

Price-Price Prices! These prices are *of macro economics* rather than the micro economics or managerial economics. Price of a good or a factor may be at a point *X*. There is no change in the demand and supply condition of that good or factor. Hence its price should remain the same.

> However, if other prices are increasing the producers of our *X good and X* service will find that they are getting the same prices or profits but they have lower purchasing power in the market. Other prices have gone up.
>
> Hence they should produce more to have the same old levels of purchasing power or should *mark-up their price.* That will enable them to acquire the

same purchasing power.

Mark-up prices are cost + prices.

Demand Pull Prices

They are those rising prices which are due to rising demand from the market. Two other things are associated with this. The demand is rising because people have more purchasing power. That purchasing power is increasing due to increasing money supply being cornered by a microscopic minority of the economy. *The pull of demand does not come from all but from a few selected groups.*

Cost-push Prices

They are naturally those prices which are linked to costs. In this context *they have always been associated with the rate of increase in wages being higher than the rate of increase in the productivity of labour due to trade union pressure.* Those days are gone. Some cases of positive wages of high level while the productivity is low can be found in public sector units.

Multi-product prices are also not something different to deserve separate blow-up of discussion. *If the price determination of onion, potatoes, mangoes and oranges is shown on the same elongated X and Y axes with different demand and supply curves,* we will get separate prices. It will, however, be illegitimate extension of the technique. If the products of the *same band* have prices differing in such figures as "'thousands" and "lakhs", there will be additional problem.

Verbal explanation of cross elasticity and different diagrams are simple and correct also.

Cap (peak load) and through (bottom line) prices too do not deserve a separate section. If the prices are set through higgling and bargaining they will touch the highest possible spot before taking a *n* turn (opposite of the U turn). Similarly prices do not sink to zero. They take a reverse *U* turn from the *n* turn. Upper and lower limits are set by the supply and demand conditions themselves as also by the cross-elasticities.

> It is sometimes seen that *prices are kept high or are hiked to keep away the customers in the times of shortages. However, no price has ever touched the "sky".*
>
> There are regulatory authorities which can intervene to decide the peak load prices. The buyers will oppose. The authorities will come up with various types of demand, subsidy-taxation packages to help those lines of production where prices have hit rock bottom. *This will not be done for the dying line of production or the sun-set industries.*

Skimming prices are taken in the early stages of marketing of a new product, (even new arrivals of seasonal vegetables command skimming prices), as in Swift car.

Penetration prices are usually prices with discounts to capture new markets or to increase the width and depth of markets.

Maturity prices are those when the product no longer remains new and when most of the potential buyers have the product. Then the prices reach a plateau.

Salvage prices can be taken for the product which is going to perish.

Daewoo motors went bankrupt in Korea even as its subsidiary in India was in rosy health. When the new of the collapse of company reached the market, people stopped buying new Daewoo cars. The old purchaser were worried. The General Motors took over. It was advertised that the spare parts will be made available through "cannibalising" i.e., using the parts of a car for different cars. So far the old car owners are running on roads smoothly. It is hoped that the revival of car may be round the corner.

> The chapters 19,20 and 21 have all the basics. One need not get lost in the new coinage of words for prices here.

NOTES

1. It may be noted at the very outset that the principles of price determination and the diagrams for imperfect competition are almost the same as that of monopoly.
2. Calcutta (now Kolkata) Tram Company incurred *"monumental losses"* in its very first year, so much so that the case was referred to the headquarter at London. The permission of the headquarter was necessary to decide whether to continue the service or disband the same. *The loss was of Rs. 500 (five hundred only) in the first year at that time'!*
3. The author remembers a near duopolistic situation of childhood around 1944. There were two sweetmeat "producers"'/sellers and they used to *prepare jalebies* in the morning. The rates were very low—just 32 paise per kilogram i.e., half a rupee per *"ser"* (which was 90 p.c, of the kg. *The rupee at that time used to have 64 paise divided into 16 "annas", each "anna" being of 4 paise. There used to be 192th part of the rupee also i.e., "pai", and it used to command purchasing power.* One day one seller decided to sell cheaper and reduced the price. All children who used to buy their *jalebi* breakfast left the other seller. The other seller reduced the price by a higher margin next day. That day all the children went back to the other fellow. The price war continued. Children were flocking to buy more and more and the sellers had prepared themselves for the same. They had prepared the necessary dough a day before. They brought "loud speakers" for playing music. They had festoons and small paper flags in their shops. It became a big *tamasha. Then they announced free "dispensations " of 4 pieces to each!*

   When the matter did not settle even at that, they climb down from their shops and banged each other's head with fists. *That brought them to senses!* Loudspeakers and festoons were removed. Old rates were charged. *Once again the clients went in indifferent manner to either of them.* They shared the clients!

Cournot's hackneyed example of two springs of 1838 (167 years old) not reproduced.

4. Readers can ask why the additional output at the same MR does not give a horizontal line.
5. Joan Robinson, 1969. Economics of Imperfect Competition, NY. Martin Press.
6. E. Chamberlin, "The Theory of Monopolistic Competition", Cambridge, Mass. Harvard University Press. 1962.
7. Jv Jeumann and O. Morgenstern 1953. 'Theory of games and Economic Behaviour. Princeton, JN.
8. O.S. Shrivastava, Principles of Economics, Sraffa and JK. Mehta quoted there.

SELECT REFERENCES

1. A. Marshall, *Principles of Economics,* London.
2. Joan Robinson, *Economics of Imperfect Competition,* London.
3. E.H. Chamberlin, *Theory of Monopolistic Competition,* Cambridge'.
4. R. Triffin, *Monopolistic Competition and General Equilibrium,* Cambridge.
5. AW Stonier & DC Hague, *A Text Book of Economic Theory,* Longman.
6. HC Paterson & WC Lewis, *Managerial Economics,* Maxwell Macmillan International Edition.
7. GC Stigler, *Organisation of Industry. Price Theory.*
8. GJ Stgler, *"The Kinky Oligopoly Demand Curve and Rigid Prices. Journal of Political Economy.* Oct. 1947.
9. JW Friedman, *Oligopoly and Theory of Games,* Amsterdom 1977.
10. P. Sweezy, *Demand Conditions under Oligopoly, Journal of Political Economy,* Aug. 1939. Cf. Paterson & Lewis: *Ibid.*
11. J. von Neumann & O. Morgenstern, *Theory of Games and Economic Behaviour,* Princeton, 1953.
12. EF Birgham & JL Pappas, *Managerial Economics,* Hindsdale.
13. E. Mansfield, *Managerial Economics.* NY.
14. D. Salvatore, *Managerial Economics,* McGraw Hill.
15. SC Webb, *Managerial Economics,* Houghton Mifflin, Boston.
16. AC Pigou, *Welfare Economics,* Cambridge.

17. A. Koutsoyiannis, *Modern Micro Economics*, Quoted earlier in the book.

18. GJ Stigler, *Theory of Price*, London, MacMillan.

19. Paul Samuelson, *Economics*, NY.

20. O.S. Shrivastava, *Principles of Economics*, JPN Meerut, *Regional Economics*, Aumol, ND. Formulating Models for Regional Development Part V Dynamic Models of Regional Growth

PART-V

Dynamic Models of Regional Growth

17

Formulating Models for Regional Development

Some regional analysts insist upon "national development through regional development only" and made national economic development a besieged deity. However, regional *economists* would simply insist that *all sectoral development programmes should have a desirable spatial dimension.* Sectoral development takes place over a space and it is needed that allocations should be equitably distributed over various regions. We have also seen that now a days the national and regional planners recognize the importance of giving more attention to backward regions and depressed ethnic groups. However, their development would require that national income should grow through a balanced development of the sectors. The question is not of choosing between growth or equity but of ensuring growth *and* equity. The "clientele development approach' i.e., the development of the targeted groups (e.g., people below the poverty line in India), cannot succeed unless the sectoral development programmes have a desirable spatial allocation system. Only when we can ensure that we can say that 'economics of poverty' is not due to 'poverty of economies'. We have to have" inclusive growth", as it is called now.

Present day economists are concerned with increasing the rate of real development, improving the physical quality of life of the people, and reducing unemployment). The problems of development are manifold like having a balance between the production of capital, intermediate and wage goods ; a balance between the primary, secondary and tertiary sectors, and greater attention to hitherto neglected regions and groups of people. If the chasm between various regions and groups of people is to be reduced, it will be imperative that the size of the national cake (GNP) be increased first because a welfare state cannot be established in a pauper state. The authorities incharge of development cannot afford to neglect regions but regions cannot be treated as nations within a nation their development has to subserve the dictates of the goals of national development.

Theories and Models

The theories and models of national and regional development are ways of expounding a strategy or philosophy of development. The theory is 'descriptive' in nature while the model is expressed in precise mathematical symbols and relationships. Classical economists wrote on all economic problems, particularly related in increasing the national income (they called it 'wealth') of the country. Their views on development were neither well integrated theories nor models but had fundamental truths of enduring value.

Not only the inter-relationships between economic variables and economic development are discussed in these theories but even non-economic variables are and can be discussed. A theory includes immeasurable and measurable (but does not measure them) variables and thus can be very comprehensive; it can discuss the problems of a closed or an open economy and it can be tailor-made for different economies. A theory of development is a model of growth presented in an implicit manner. After the models of Harrod and an Domar became popular, the writings of earlier economists were re-read and re-intrepreted to fit in the framework of growth models. The ideas were the same: they were only presented in the mathematical language.

A model is a set of causal relationships and makes the growth rate a function of some crucial variables. The relationship is not verbal— much less verbose—, but precise. It can tell us that if the rate of saving is a certain percentage of national income and there is a given capital output ratio, a certain growth rate can be realised. [National income Rs. 1000 b. : savings income ratio 20%: capital-output ratio 5:1, then savings will be Rs. 200 b and divided by 5, they will yield output of Rs. 40 billion which is 4% of Rs. 1000 b. Thus growth rate is 4 %

A Model is explicit in quantitative terms and it summarises the functioning of an economy in the form which is precise. It conceives *ex ante* the future functioning of the economy which depends upon the status and behaviour of some crucial variables.

We can demonstrates (Harrod's Equation)

$GC = S$ G is per growth rate.

$G = \frac{S}{C}$ C is capital - out ratio.

S is savings income ratio.

If the national income of a country is $ 100 b, and saving are $ 25 b, the S/Y ratio is 25/100 or 1/4 or 25 p.c,.

The S is $\frac{S}{Y}$ ratio. If the saving are 15 b, out of $ 75 b, then

$\frac{15}{75} \times 100$ = S is 20 p c, or 20/100.

C is measure of productivity, If an investment of $ 8, give us production of $ 20 b, the productivity is 25% $(\frac{20}{80} \times 100)$ CoR is opposite of productivity, ratio 25:100 or 1: 4, c is 4: 1 i.e., capital - output ratio.

Now if C is 4 and S is 20 then

$$G = \frac{20}{100} \div C \text{ or } \frac{20}{100} \div \frac{4}{1}$$

$$= \frac{20}{100} \times \frac{1}{4} = = \frac{5}{100} \; 5 \text{ p.c.}$$

If we want to double the growth, then either the value of S should rise or of C should fall. More saving are required less capital should be required for the same out-put. Or same out-put should require less capital

$$G = \frac{50}{100} \div \frac{4}{1} = 12.5$$

$$G = \frac{20}{100} \div \frac{2}{1} = 10.0$$

$$G = \frac{30}{100} \div \frac{3}{1} = 10.0$$

and so on.

A model spells out the specific propositions e.g., the Vakil and Brahmanand Model presented on the eve of launching the Second Five Year Plan of India, emphasized that Gandhian strategy be implemented in India. In that model growth is a function of higher employment; higher employment is a function of mass production of wage goods consumed by the masses; and the production of wage goods is a function of production near the masses with labour intensive technology i.e. low COR. The government of India implemented instead the Feldman model in the form of Mahalanobis model in which establishing basic industries of high capital intensity was considered necessary for laying the foundation of long term economic growth.

Many variables are treated as 'fixed parameters' in

the models. This is done to reduce the number of variables so that the simultaneous equations of the model are manageable. Model building has become quite common now a days. Late Professor J. K. Mehta once wrote *"We are all becoming model builders today"*. Prof. Haberler wrote:

> Not only mathematical blueprints, but full blown econometric models relating to individual countries or even to the whole world, with constants and parameters statistically evaluated, are pouring from single scholar's studies statistical laboratories like automobiles from the assembly lines."

There is no explicit mention in the models that savings should be increased, or population should be controlled, or that savings be institutionalised and converted into capital, that there should be increase not merely in financial investment but in real investment, or that the government should have a right mix of various policies. Such constraints are not present in most developed countries wherefrom the models of development pour in. There is no mention about the right technology as it nearly always there is.

An economic model is a statement of relationships among economic variables. Its purpose is to illustrate causal relations among critical variables in the real world, stripped of irrelevant complexity, for the sake of obtaining a clearer understanding of how the economy operates, and in some formulations, in order to manipulate it. The statement may be set out in prose, in geometric form, or in mathematics. A model is an organized set of relationships that describes the functioning of an economic entity, whether it be household, a single industry or a national economy, under a set of simplyfying assumptions. A theoretical model consists of certain hypotheses concerning the causal inter-relationships between various magnitudes or forces and the sequence in which they react on each other.

Once the objectives of planning or planned development

are given by politics, economics provides models as how to achieve them. The model determines the values of different variables (savings, investment, exports, prices, consumption etc.) that help achieve these objectives. A model tells us (or should tell us) what could happen rather than what had happened. Models were presented to show that if certain conditions are created, steady growth can be sustained and capitalism need not run down.

Economic models have some parameters (constants) and some variables. These parameters are sometimes natural and sometimes the result of the decisions of producers and consumers. Parameters constitute the framework within which the variables operate. When we assume the equilibrium of these variables, we study a static economy. When we study how the variables vary, we embark upon the study of dynamic economy or problems of growth and development.

We start with some assumptions about the behaviour of economic units. These are then cast in mathematical moulds i.e. they are made to speak the language of mathematics. Once they are thus transformed, mathematics is allowed to have its way till the equations are simultaneously solved. The result, in terms of mathematical symbols, is reconverted into economic relationships. We do this in the same manner as a physicist changes sound waves into radio waves and then reconverts them into sound waves. A model of economic system shows the relationships between some fundamental and broad forces. These forces are macrodynamic forces of supply and demand side that change the income of the society.

Here is an example of Domar's most important equation:

"Report of the First International Economic Conference of Economists" ed. DC Hague.

Papers by : Erich Schneider : Haberler : Kindleberger from the above, p. 161, and 40.

J K Mehta, Economics of Growth P 4.

$$\Delta I \cdot \frac{1}{\alpha} = I\delta \quad \text{or} \quad \frac{\Delta I}{I} = \alpha\delta$$

Here Δ depicts change ; I depicts investment, a stands for marginal propensity to save and 5 stands for potential social average investment productivity. Domar shows that steady growth will require that productive capacity (Iδ) should equal demand (or increase in ΔI. I/α) The equation emphasizes that effective demand and productive capacity should increase in balance and at accelerated pace. This requires that investment should grew at an increasing absolute rate or at constant compound interest rate, equal to the propensity to save (α) times the inverse of capital co-efficient (δ)

A model is thus a theoretical as well as applied form of the functioning of the economy. A model is the epitome of the desired functions of the economy. The hypotheses of the model can be proved or disproved and rejected. A model is good if it leads to optimisation under the given circumstances of the country/region.

In a static model, the variables are converted into constants or it is presumed that the constant change at a constant rate. In such simple models the behaviour can be predicted easily. Static models can be used for short period and/or for limited objectives.

Dynamic models of economic growth/development/ fluctuations allow the assumptions to be relaxed. The assumptions are relaxed one by one.

Models for the closed economy are static in comparison to the models for the open economy. A region is always open but there are models treating the region to be closed. No nation is ever closed to the outside world, yet we have models for 'closed economies'.. Naturally for the models for open economy, the number of variable increases. A model cannot snap link with the past. If the capital - output ratio in the past had been increasing and reached (say) 6: 1, it will be wrong to make calculations on the basis of a COR of 5: 1. Unless there are very definite plans for increasing productivity and unless there are sound reasons to believe that productivity can be increased the capital output ratio should not be reduced because newer machine are costlier.

*Domar Model emphasiser that demand and supply side should be equal but at higher and higher levels.

Demand Side

$$\Delta D = \Delta Y \cdot \frac{1}{MPS}.$$

Substituting $\cdot \frac{1}{MPS}$ with α (for MPS) we get

$$\Delta D = \Delta Y \cdot \frac{1}{\propto}$$

Here it means that the change in demand is equal to change in income but only as much as is consumed deflated by what is saved, what is saved is not consumed. ΔY is equal to $\Delta I \cdot \frac{1}{\propto}$

The Spply Side

S = I. δ, supply is equal to investment multiplied by productivity ratio. All investment is *not* supply. If investment of $ 100 b, has 25% productivity then $ 100 b, $\frac{25}{100}$ or $100 \div \frac{1}{4}$ = $ 25 b. will be supply.

Investment I is on both sides

$$\text{So } \Delta I \cdot \frac{1}{\propto} = \text{(should be) } I\delta$$

Dividing both sides by I and multiplying by $\cdot \frac{1}{\propto}$ we get

$$\frac{\Delta I}{I} \cdot \frac{1}{\propto} \cdot \propto = \frac{I}{I} \delta \propto$$

$$\frac{\Delta I}{I} \cdot \frac{1}{\not\propto} \cdot \not\propto = \frac{\not I}{\not I} \delta \propto$$

$$\frac{\Delta \not I}{\not I} = \delta \propto$$

Change is investment $\left(\frac{\Delta I}{I}\right)$ is /should be equal to prospensity to save $\propto$ time the inverse of change in investment productivity multiplied by the multiplier should be high.

Suppose productivity is 25 p.c., of I i.e. capital out-put ratio is 100; 25 or 4;1, and suppose also that S/Y is 12 ; p.c., p.c,. Now I should be equal to S. Thus 12% of \$ 150 b, i.e., \$ 18 b., should or invested.

At 4 :1 COR \$ 18 b $\cdot \times \frac{1}{4}$ = \$ 4.5 b. will be additional output

$$\$\ 18b \times \frac{25}{100} = \$\ 4.5\ b.$$

\$ 4.5 is 3% of \$ 150 b. The value of $\propto$ is $\frac{25}{100}$ and the value of δ is $\frac{12}{100}$. So $\frac{25}{100} \times \frac{12}{100} = \frac{1}{4} \times \frac{6}{50}$

or $\frac{6}{200}$

$$\text{or } \frac{3}{100} \text{ or 3 p.c.}$$

In calculating the likely outputs from an investment, models should take into account the different gestation periods of different projects in sectors. When 'leads-and-lags'-effects are incorporated in the model, the model becomes more complicated. (Goods received on credit from abroad give a lead in the availability of real output : lags are due to gestation periods of investment). Long gestation periods create 'goods gap' while the higher productivity and low gestation waiting make the inflation (triggered off by rising investment), self-liquidating early. Models can deal with partial relations only : general relations of one economic activity with all other economic activities are difficult to concretise even with the help of computers.

Aggregate Models

These models deal with production, consumption and investment as single aggregate and apply to the entire economy. They are used to determine possible growth rates in national income, the division of the national income between public and private consumption, investment and export as also the required volume of domestic savings, or foreign assistance needed. Assumptions are then made about saving-income ratio (on the basis of the marginal propensity to save and consume), Input requirements of various factors (or assumptions about production function), including imports, requirements of capital (on the basis of output-capital ratio depending upon the choice of technique), increase in output and national income (based on the assumptions about productivity gains or about the capital-output ratio).

Estimates of capital, investment are made and income targets are set on the aggregate basis. The whole economy may be broken into different sectors and then total investment figure is allocated amongst these sectors on the basis of priorities. The resulting rise in sector income and employment can be projected constantly with assumed priorities and overall targets.

Constraints are always taken note of viz..., (i) consumption can increase, (ii) unfavourable change can occur in demographic structure, (iii) limitation of capital and /or labour can be felt, (iv) foreign aid, capital or loans may not come in requisite quantity etc. Alternative projections can be made on alternative set of assumptions. That model will be best suited of which assumptions tally with the actual data or change in data.

Sectoral Models

Sectoral models are formulated on the basis of narrowly defined problems (compared to the aggregate models), such as how to optimise the cropping pattern in the country, while trying to increase the overall agricultural output.

What starts as a sector development exercise ultimately culminates in having national and inter-regional dimensions. If outputs of agricultural sector are to be increased, then there should be planning for water harvesting, distribution of irrigation water, production of pesticides, fertilizers, farm equipment and big machines. Crop protection devices, storage/warehousing and transportation facilities, supply of credit, supply of electricity are to be provided. There will be other inter-sectoral linkages. Power development itself will depend upon (say) coal mining, tapping hydro-power resources, or developing other alternative sources of energy. Coal mining depends upon steel industry and it depends upon coal mining. It is a very complex world.

Sectoral models will not be realistic unless they are prepared in juxtaposition with other sectors and have a regional dimension also. Inter-sectoral outputs extend over different regions. Inter-sectoral and inter-regional targets can be realised only when there is coordination between various State governments, which will ultimately boil down at integration at the national level. No regional or sectoral plan can be prepared in non-national perspective. Only small sub-sector plans can have a narrow area of application where one can operate in a, sort of, closed economy.

All sectoral models have spatial dimensions and all spatial models have sectoral implications. If they are not integrated at the national level, there will be inconsistencies and fissiparous tendencies. There will be considerable wastages: non-realisation of the targets or over-realisation of the targets and ultimate chaos unless sectoral and regional plans are integrated the national levels. As such sectoral models have to take all these points into consideration.

Sectoral models are also based upon a host of *ceteris paribus* assumptions. If others things are taken as a given, a sectoral plan for (say) increasing the oilseeds yields can be prepared. Sectoral models concentrate about the sector they are charged with and are based on the assumption that there are no constraints. The primary object of a sectoral model is the rational allocation of resources between the sub-sectors.

It is a common practice to first prepare an aggregative model and then to spell out the sectoral and regional dimensions. The other way much better is to prepare the disaggregated regional/sectoral plans and then to aggregate them, taking into account all the national constraints. If sectoral and regional plans are well integrated we have a good national model. The people at lower order centres, levels of administration and sub-activities do not have adequate knowledge about the macro issues. They can at best help in highlighting pressing local problems and may provide details about the capabilities of the sub-regions and sub-sectors. Integration at the apex level is a must.

A model is for future but it is to be based upon past experiences. Lessons taken from the past are to guide in future planning. Models of planned economies were near perfect If a steel plant was to be erected not only complementary outputs were planned but even the movement of the trains carrying inputs to the plant site was planned. Prices could be kept constant because they depended upon the fiat of the State and not on demand and supply conditions. *Ex ante* targets used to be realised *ex post* also. Later this planning lost to market mechanism.

A model of economic development for an unplanned economy is just suggestive or probabilistic. Nothing can be said about the realisation of the targets. Prices keep on changing and because of them the investment programmes have to be changed, which further change the prices. It is a truly volatile world beyond the confines of a predictable model. However, on the basis of the input-output relations and performance of various sectors in various regions of the country, one can do some sort of projections about the future behaviour of the sectors and the economy.

In most countries there is wide chasm between the development of the primary and secondary sectors, or between rural and urban areas and between leading and lagging regions. Comparative cost principle dictates that leading sectors be developed more, while the equity considerations require greater attention be given to lagging sectors and areas. Now a days there is growing consensus that the 'unbalanced growth strategy should be made to do a "sheershashan" i.e., this time it should undo the past imbalances through unbalanced investment. Sectoral leads and lags are to be anticipated over a time period and necessary corrective measures should be planned in the development strategy. As the sectors take the lead, their output should be utilized and equal purchasing power should be available with the people of the other sectors : for the lagging sectors there should be efforts to increase the productive capacity. Due to long gestation periods in the sub-sectors Not only goods for final consumption and inputs are denied to other sectors, but inflationary pressure is also exerted. It will be very essential that those sub-sectors which provide goods and services for the masses should not suffer from lags. Good sectoral planning also will require good central authority. Money lead and goods lags create run away inflation

Regional Models

Now a days the sectoral development plans are to be made relevant to specific areas. If the nation has a target of increasing food production, it will be sufficient if it is secured anywhere. All increase in agricultural output, if taken from (say) Punjab, Haryana, Western Uttar Pradesh or Coastal Andhra Pradesh will not satisfy the criterion of over-all efficiency *and* equity. In the event of distress the cost of transporting foodgrains from deficit areas to surplus areas will be costly in monetary and non-monetary terms. *In India the green revolution was not 'red' (communist) at the same time. However, it remained limited to certain crops, certain pockets of the country and certain sections of the rural kulaks.* It is necessary that 'regional' and 'clientele' approach to development be also integrated i.e., increased output from development be also integrated i.e., increased output of foodgrains be obtained from as wide area as possible and that all categories of farmers particularly small and marginal farmers should also reap benefits of higher production.

It will also be necessary that 'social accounting, be introduced in the plan in that the poor also get entitlements i.e. acquire reasonable incremental purchasing power.

It would be a narrow modelling business if a plan for the development of a region is based upon the 'export base theory' only. It is true that a region can import as much as it can export — if unilateral transfers are not taken into account. Sufficiency in basic necessities is of prime importance and the production of basic goods in the region can provide prime-moving activities as well. Regional plan models are and should be based on regional resources (both natural and human) and should incorporate in them special schemes of tackling area-specific problems.

A regional growth model which is spelled in mathematical language will ignore many facts of life. It will not be able to incorporate the waste of the resources and exploitation people of the backward regions by the people of advanced regions. Goods of the backward regions may be purchased at low prices; producers of these regions may receive unfavourable terms of trade. Savings of the backward region may be transferred to advanced regions; benefits of some special programmes of development of backward regions may be reaped by the in-migrant population in the region; real surpluses may leak out to other regions.

Many archaic macro-dynamic models cannot be applied to the regions. There is no place for *laissez faire* type fiscal and monetary neutrality for the models of regional development. Backward regions suffered open or tacit neglect in the past; now there has to be an open bias in favour of them. The problems are not of precise mathematical jugglery of some variables but of changing whole socio-cultural politico-juridial superstructure. The input-output relations that may be worked out by the planners or regional model builders may prove to be false. Issues of economic development of a region can never be treated in a mechanical manner. The inflows and outflows of a region will certainly follow market mechanism but the government will also have to ensure that planned inflows flow in and outflows flow out. Government support will be necessary for backward regions before some models can be formulated. Macro economic models are generally prepared on the assumption of non-intervention by the State but models for the development of regions will have to be framed only when desired government support and intervention are assured. Yet assistance to the backward regions and people should ensure maximum development of the sectors in conformity with the general principles of market mechanism.

A regional growth model has to take into account the resources (real and monetary) that would be available from within and that can come from. Some real, financial and human resources have to be transferred 'by force' i.e., ordered to be part of the regional development plan e.g., experts in government service may be transferred to background regions.

A regional development 'model' cannot take into account such things as resistence of the trained and skilled persons to go to backward regions or the opposition of the local people about not admitting the 'foreigners' in their regions. A model handles the known quantities that can be mathematically measured.

The smaller the region the greater the role of exogenous factors and resources in the development If the region is big enough, a comprehensive model can be reasonably predictable for the 'external' effect can be minimal. However, it is to be remembered that not even the nation can afford autarky and a region has it to sell its specialised output and import those goods in which it has no specialisation (and hence is not producing or producing only in small quantities). These relationships are to be incorporated in models of regional growth.

A region where territorial division of labour is very pronouced, will depend upon other regions for depend upon 'internal strength', while the 'export base theory" emphasises that regional growth is a function of exogenous factors. Regional growth models based on either of these theories will speak partial truth only.

What is true for the nation is true for the region as well— economic development depends on economic and non economic factors as also on the balanced development of the three sectors. *The regional differences arise because of the differences in the location of facilities, functions and industries. Differences in the quantity and structure of investment and differences in the diffusion of technology further aggravate the problems.* Models of balanced regional development cannot be prepared in isolation.

Every region cannot prepare a model in which what is happening about the model building in other regions is disregarded. This exercise is also be integrated at the apex level.

"The supply base theory of regional modelling" takes the above mentioned things into consideration. Regional growth is regarded as a function of natural resources (or infusion of resources from outside), skilled manpower, capital investment and diffusion of technology.

"The Demand Base regional growth model" is the Keynesian variant. It regards regional growth a function of increase in effective demand/ absorption. Rising consumption (without undermining the capacity to export) and rising investment and exports increase the income of the region, provided leakages in the form of hoardings and imports do not negate the gains. Favourable balance of payment of the region with other regions increases the growth rate of the region. Rising real exports are 'leakages' for 'real consumption' but are additions for the regional incomes. Imports are additions in the real consumable/ investible resources but are leakages in monetary terms. Since the growth rate is calculated in terms of money, exports are additions and imports are leakages. The income of the region should not leak out for purchasing the less necessary goods of other regions or for investing in other region The leakage of manpower, real resources, real capital

to other regions may bring income today but will reduce the *growth potential of the region for future.*

The Keynesian type of models for regional growth emphasize that consumption expenditure both of the private and government sectors should increase for the regional goods ; investment of the government and private sector should increase in the region ; and exports of the region should exceed the imports of the region. *Obviously all regions cannot do this unto other regions because other regions would be trying to do this very thing unto other regions.* A regional model cannot be constructed and implemented without the knowledge of the central authority. *All regions cannot have favourable balance of payment at the same time.*

When we discuss the problems of developed versus the less developed regions, the less developed regions have very little chance of exporting more to the developed regions and that too on 'favourable terms of trade' and hence left to themselves the backward regions cannot withstand the developed regions. *A regional model has to be prepared with full knowledge and consent of the national planning authority and should integrate the supply as well as demand base approaches——more so the supply side approach.*

Flows of factors and resources between the regions depend upon the price differences and the ability of a region to buy them and ability of the region to sell them. Backward regions do not possess comparative advantage in low cost of production and cannot sell unless it comes to selling a product in which the region has a natural advantage. When it comes to buying the backward regions do not have enough purchasing power. Thus through a national plan, which should have proper regional dimension, the productive capacities of the backward regions are to be raised. If sectors develop in the regions they produce goods and people acquire purchasing power. A regional model of development cannot be prepared in isolation, not related to the overall development of the sectors in the nation. Depressed regions can offer higher wages, higher rates of interest, or higher prices for factors/inputs only if the central authority puts purchasing power at their disposal through fiscal transferences or subsidies. *Unless the physical, technological, and financial support are coming from the nation, a regional model cannot even be prepared, much less implemented.* Packages of concessions for backward regions and penalties for advanced regions (in the form of concessions and higher taxes respectively) become part of the model building leading for the regions. The models of development of regions require that the decisions taken at various regional levels are not contradictory.

18

Input-Output Analysis Consistency

The input-output table is a disaggregated model for regional development, or a base for the same. The total production is sub-divided by industry and we can derive an inter-industry matrix from the flow of goods and services from one production sector to another. I-O analysis involves double disaggregation : national aggregates are broken by industry and by region. I-O table throws light on inter-regional trade as well as on inter-regional production.

The I-O table shows the flows of goods and services from a sector of the economy to all other sectors of the economy over a specified time period. Its rows and columns show two-way interdependence of different sectors in regions or country.

The rows of the table give the distribution of the output of the sector, while the *columns* represent the production structure of a sector. The outputs of different sector require inputs which come from other sectors in the form of raw materials. The outputs of various sectors are used as inputs in other lines of manufacture as also as goods for final consumptions. Outputs to be used as inputs in one sectors remain intermediate goods only. Some outputs are only intermediate goods and never goods for final consumption, while other outputs become goods for final consumption only. Steel ingots will remain inputs for other sectors while fountainpens become outputs for final consumption. The outputs for final consumption are those which are used for private or public consumption or for exports. The I-O table provides systematic description of this inter -dependence among different sectors in the region/ economy where outputs produced by sector are distributed into other sectors that use them as input in their production process.

The I-O analysis owes its popularization to Wassily Leontief (1905-1999). He once tried to find out what will be the effect of reduction in the output of strategic arms on the USA economy. He found that war-goods industries are more input using than input supplying. Thus it was found with the help of this table that other industries will be benefited if there is a reduction in the production of strategic arms in USA.

The input-output table is a system of accounts prepared for an economy which examines the linkages of its different sectors as they combine to produce gross output for the nation or for the region, as the case may be. "Perhaps the most important contribution of an input-output analysis to area planning is the element of forecasting that it brings to bear on the process. For if the total output of a particular industry is distributed among all the other sectors of the economy (including consumers and export) in a known proportion, it should be possible to calculate a table of coefficiency which would show the effects of a given increase of output of one industry on the purchases of all others." *

This kind of definable relationship or *'chain reaction'* spelled out in an input-output grid can be useful to the regional planners. I-O model gives the picture about how the output from each industry or sector is distributed to each of the other industries or sectors and also the distribution of inputs per unit of output from all others.

These relationships or coefficients are expressed in the form of a square table or matrix. Columns of the table are outputs and the rows of the table are inputs. We also show each row figure as a percentage or fraction of its column total so that each figure records the proportion of input needed from each sector (rows) to produce unit output in each particular sector (columns).

When we study the outputs in the appropriate columns 'extra inputs of knowledge' are yielded and we can know how many inputs are needed from all sectors which contribute to that sector's output. These extra inputs to the sector are actually themselves outputs of the contributory sectors. The first process is repeated to find out the second round effects, sector by sector. These will branch out into further third round input requirements and so or..

The data requirements but I-O tables that can be made to look simple are enormous. The I-O analysis at planning level languished because so much expenditure and labour are required. There are lags in the use of data and collection of data quality and analysis very. *It best I-O relationships are snap-shot relationships and cannot be and should not be used for future planning.*

> This is not to say that the entire economics of I-O analysis is useless. It is a good guide-post in a jungle (of the economy).

Activity	*Inputs to Agri*	*Inputs to Manu*	*Inputs to Tertiary*	*Final Demand*	*Total output*
Agriculture	5	15	2	68	90
Manufacturing	10	20	10	40	80
Tertiary*	10	15	5	00	30
Labour	25	30	5	0	60
	50	80	22	108	260

* Tertiary, Transport/and or any other activity can be taken as a proxy.

I-O relations can be studied for hundred of activities/ industries. Only computers can handle them.

A short input-output table can be of three columns and rows even. Suppose one ton of steel requires 3 tonnes of coal and one ton of coal requires 0.1 ton of steel. This relationship can be shown as under:

Industry	*Coal*	*Steel*
Coal	0.0	3
Steel	0.1	0

- Suppose a country wants to produce 200,000 tonnes of coal and 50000 tonnes of steel. In producing coal/ steel will be used and in producing steal, coal will be used.
- If 50000 tonnes of steel is to be produced, then 50000 x tonnes of coal will be used: i.e., 150000 tonnes.
- In producing 200,000 tonnes of coal, 200000 x 0.1 = 20000 tonnes of steel will be used.
- For 200000 tonnes of coal, 20000 tonnes of steel will be used @ O.I per tonne of coal and only 30000 tonnes of steel will be left against the target of 50000. That means that 20000 tonnes of steel used in the production of coal will have to be produced in period 2.
- Similarly use of 150000 tonnes of coal in the production of steel will require this quantity to be produced in period 2. However, in period 2 again, the steel and coal will be used in the opposite production of coal and steel. Whatever, is thus used will have to be produced in period 3. This process will go on.
- The processes will continue till the targeted amounts of steel and coal are available in net terms i.e., not to be used for production again.

- The quantities in net terms are desired either for consumption or for exports or partly for both.

We can show how these rounds will require inputs of coal and steel respectively.

Round	*Coal*	*Steel*
1.	200000	50000
2.	150000	20000
3.	60000	15000
4.	45000	6000
5.	18000	4500
6.	13500	1800
7.	5400	1350
8.	4050	500
9.	1620	405
	497570	99595

- Of 497570 tonnes of coal, 300000 tonnes were used in production of steel and hence 197570 tonnes were left in net terms. The production could be taken to 10th round.
- Of the 99595 tonnes of steal, 50000 tonnes were used for the production of coal, leaving the output of 49,595 in net terms.

Input-output tables/economics ignore one most important thing which no other economist (other than, the present writer) has taken into account. Many production lines have indivisibilities i.e, small amounts cannot be produced. We cannot produce half a car. Lumpy and indivisible investments are necessary for further production. Hence capacities may not be possible to be created for (say) the balance 415 tonnes of steel in two or more time periods.

Usually a thermal power generating plant, for example is of 210 MW. If suppose 420 MW electricity is to be produced, we cannot just have only two plants of 210 MW. There is that PLF involved i.e., the plant load factor. The thermal plants are to be shut down for the maintenance and repairs. If the PLF is 60 p.c., that means 40 p.c., capacity is not used. Hence 40 p.c., additional capacity is to be created. Forty per cent of 420 MW is 168 MW. But there is no plant for 168 MW. A 210 MW plant is to be erected. This will generate 126 MW of the electricity at 60 p.c. PLF. Now there are two options first, the shortfall of 168 126 = 42 MW be allowed to remain or another plant of 210 MW should be erected. Two plants will have PLF of additional unused capacity of 84 MW. They will - generate @ 60, p.c. 252 units of electricity as against the *required* 42 MW. Hence we cannot have I-O relations that give the same outcomes as planned.

Two Region Matrix Can Show a Few Things

Region of Residence	*Region of Production*	
	A	*B*
A	0.75	0.28
B	0.25	0.80

The above says that 75 p.c., of the jobs and income to Region A residents and 25 p.c., to the residents of region B, of the region B, 20 p.c., go to region A and 8 0 p.c. to region B, Bigger matrix table can be there.

I-O tables can show physical output or their money values, Linear input function or constant returns to scale and no substitution between input are assumed. There is no shortage of capital or capacity and prices of output are the same there are also assumed. The I-O model shows relation of the region with other regions.

Uses and Importance of Input-output Tables

As seen earlier the input-output table shows the interdependence between sectors of the regions. The final demand of various sectors is linked with the corresponding output levels through the input-output table. The total effect of the increase in final demand of a particular sector on the production of other sectors can be obtained with the help of input output analysis. The direct and indirect requirements of primary inputs corresponding to the increase in final demand of the particular sector, can also be worked out.

The importance of the input-output table depends upon the correct and comprehensive data. Input-output tables can be used for targeting of the plans. We can work out (a) for given outputs how many inputs will be necessary and from where, and (b) how given outputs can be used to become goods of final consumption and inputs for other sectors.

An equilibrium level of inputs and outputs can be worked out for the economy/region. Sectorwise final demands; sectorwise input requirements; sectorwise inputs availability and if the required matching is not there appropriate strategy or technology mix can be worked out.

- Isard. Walter ct al., Methods of Regional Analysis: An Introduction to Regional Science MIT Press 1960.
- Leontief. Wassily W., Input-Output Economics. 2nd ed., New York: Oxford University Press 1986.
- Miller. R.E.. Karen R. Polenske and Adam Z,. Rose. eds.. Frontiers of Input-Output Analysis. X.Y.: Oxford UP. 1989. [HB142 F76 1989/ Suzz]
- Polenske. Karen Advances in Input-Output Analysis. 1976.
- Rappoport, Paul N.K.J. Rodenrys, and J. II. Savin, Energy Consumption in the Transportation Services Section, research for the Electric Power Research Institute, 1979.
- US Department of Commerce, Bureau of Economic Analysis. Regional multipliers: A user handbook for regional input-output modeling system (RIMS II). Third edition. Washington, U.S. Government Printing Office. 1997.
- Implan A software tool used to perform input-ouput economic impact analysis

The input-output model provides estimates of sectoral outputs which are consistent with each other. The model serves as an aid in the allocation of investment to achieve projected sectoral outputs. Regional input-output models help in regional allocation of resources. Being a general equilibrium approach, it takes into account the entire economy and its components.

These exercises are based upon linear function. This linear model postulates a relationship of proportionality between inputs and outputs. The inputs are assumed to be in constant proportion to the levels of output; or, to put it differently, the outputs are assumed to be in constant proportion to the level of inputs.

For the time being the substitution between different inputs (including the factors) is disregarded. It is presumed that they are used in the same proportion. Fixed input-coefficients of production are assumed.

I-O tables give us results which are valid for the *short-term only* since it cannot be assumed that the relationships between sectors (implicit in the coefficients in the matrix) will be stable through time. In fact, everyday experience tells us that they can change every month.

"Informed estimates", "experts projections" etc. are more reliable. Despite there being several techniques for demand forecasting, precise estimates for all sectors/regions/ activities become difficult

Forecasts for the country are easier than the forecasts for the regions. The tasks of converting the outputs into employment potentialities are not easy. We need productivity coefficients also.

J. Brian McLoughlin has aptly remarked :

"Having said all this, the reader may despair of ever using input output methods or may wonder why

> they are referred to here at all. They are mentioned because of their conceptual elegance and great practical potentiality in regional economic analysis and projection."

Alden and Morgan write :

> "The input-output analysis adopted for a single region can be extended to provide an inter-regional and inter-industry input-output matrix whereby the impact of changes in one sector of a region upon sectors in another region can be assessed. *Complex analysis would require use of computer facilities.*

A number of problems face the user of input-output analysis, problems which are both conceptual and technical; while the technical problems of data availability are gradually being overcome, many problems of methodology may be expected to remain. Amongst these might be included the choice of regions, the choice of a set of industries or sectors, the validity of constant input coefficients, use of the input-output approach for prediction, and regional variations in the behaviour of final buyers".

Limitations

Input output tables can be prepared if the industries are not multi product industries. The production functions are assumed to be linear in the input-output analysis, but in practice they are not: they are either increasing or decreasing cost functions mostly. Input-output tables assume that there are no 'external economies' but they do matter differently for different firms, though theoretically they should be available to all in equal measure. Input-output tables take 'fixed supply areas' hence 'stable trade coefficients' and in turn 'stable relative prices'; the last assumption being very far from reality. All regions are taken as complementary and non-competitive which is not a fact of life.

McLoughlin: *Op., cit.* p. 204.

Alden & Morgon : *Op cit.*, p. 244.

Input output tables are "snap-shot static picture" and inappropriate for long-run investigations. They are not tools of dynamic analysis.

Richardson wrote:

> "The two-fold disaggregation makes it very difficult to give region input-output models empirical content. The data requirements are very heavy, and in particular statistics referring to inter-regional flows of goods are in most countries almost impossible to obtain except via very costly industrial survey methods. Empirical application is only a *faint hope* unless we make restrictive, often heroic, assumptions".

Input output tables are important conceptually because the inter-sectoral and inter-regional relationships and interdependence becomes clear, even for the point of time, but the practical application for model building cannot be carried too far.

Richardson further wrote:

> "Given the present level of information and the costs incurred in obtaining the knowledge needed for an efficient inter-regional input-output matrix, we should not be too optimistic about the fruits of inter regional input-output research in future."

Richardson is of the view that pursuit of too precise quantification is less important than the detailed in-depth qualitative analysis of the problems and state of affairs of the region and the programme strategy can be chalked out and implemented without mathematical sophistication. However, this is not to say that no calculation be made about the physical and financial inflows and outflows.

We do not need a model of regional development only; a philosophy and a strategy are also needed. Regional growth is not a matter of numbers.

In the words of *Miernyk;*

> "The major disadvantage of a regional input-output table based on direct survey data is that its construction is expensive and time consuming. But if time and money are available and if the selected sample businessmen in the region are willing to cooperate in providing detailed data on sales and purchases the model can be used for making long, range, consistent regional forecasts. Before discussing such forecasts, it will be useful to emphasise the differences between a regional and the national model by a direct comparison"
>
> [*Ibid.*, p. 169]

Many types of data can be disaggregated from the national accounts e.g., data about various industries, agricultural output, traffic generated in different States (or even points), power generated, credit disbursed etc. and it would be better to strengthen the data base, rather than discard the input-output analysis. Inter-sectoral, inter-industry and inter-regional relationships in a consistency framework provide us important knowledge for projections also. If some analysts find fault with the assumptions of

I-O tables, he can substitute his own assumptions and derive new projects with a relative small expenditure of time and money.

Inter-regional shifts on the output are more uncertain than shifts on the inputs side. In the early stages a region may be exporter of raw materials and as it develops, manufacturing develops and exports include manufacturers in larger proportions. Exports of raw materials decline, inter-industry transactions rise, and the new intermediate processing sectors will export products with more value added. An important task of regional analyst will be to anticipate and simulate such changes.

Richardson : "Elements of Regional Economies" pp., 142-143.

Under such circumstances it will be better to have views of the industrialists, marketing experts, of persons who know about investment and location rather than rely on the strait-jacket mathematical projections.

> "Those who have a preference for rigorous models that completely avoid judgmental influences will do well to steer clear of regional forecasting"
>
> [Miemykp. 175 *Ibid*]

Thus regional input output analysis is a good guide but it is not a law of economics.

Various coefficients needed are not easily available, particularly the import coefficients. The obsolescence in old industries and the new innovations which change the technology, change the input coefficients and I-O models are not equipped to cope, with the dynamics of such structural changes.

National input coefficients may be irrelevant for the region and calculating the same from the industrial survey of the region may be cost—not worth the results that are to be obtained. *Location quotients have been used* for that; but that will be putting LQ on a very high pedestal.

A trade sub-model is very necessary to be integrated with the input output model if we are to understand dynamics of input-output relations. However, here also because of the paucity of data about external coefficients, there are difficulties. *Somewhere the regional economists have to discard quantifying everything.*

A presentation in the form of a matrix analysis can predict or show the effect of one activity of a region on others. These effects are of vital importance to the consumers, investors and the government/planners.

> Input-output analysis was considered essential for physical planning. It was necessary to know that for

achieving a certain target of any output how many inputs are necessary and from where. The outputs of one industry become inputs in others. Some outputs are also used by consumers and by the producers themselves, Wheat produced by farmers is used by them (for self consumption) by other consumers and by many industries which use flour for manufacturing n number of items. Then if we want to know how much coal will be necessary for producing steel, we also have to know how much steel will be necessary for producing machines that dig out coal or transport coal.

It is never-ending study of the cross relationship.

Wassily Leontief left the then USSR and became citizen of the USA. USSR collapsed for many reasons. One was they debated too much and were fond of beating each other with their ideological sticks- even when the stick was of the same variety. Secondly, they produced too many war goods to be at par with the USA though their resource base did not permit that. Thirdly most workers used to be dead drunk with their heady vodka and, fourthly (we keep the list short), they attached too much importance to the preparation of the input-output tables rather than leaving the work to the market.

In free economies, the producers of steel place orders for necessary inputs with the suppliers of inputs. They in turn do the same. The chain goes on. No one knows what others are doing except those in close complementary or competitive relations. Market functions blindly but not arbitrarily. It *is* like a magic box. A handkerchief is inserted from one side and the rabbit comes out of the other side. The mechanism is concealed in the box. Similarly the demand and supply requirements are inserted from

---

Those who want algebraic and mathematical presentation can consult a book on Statistics or on Quantitative Techniques.

—See also Wikipedia, the free encyclopedia.

—SC Shrivastava and VS Singh's paper on Inputout analysis in a special book published by the UP Govt., on Regional Methods and Planning.

> one side. The outputs-prices come out of the otherwise. With trial and errors and with leads and lags, the supplies match the demand.

Consistency

The foundations of consistency models were laid down by the physiocrats , one of whom (Hutchison) was teacher of Adam Smith, the father of economics. The constructed a table showing circulation of money. They called it Tableau Economique. It showed how money circulates from one sector to other and back, one by one, that the amounts of payments involved are unequal. The physiocrates were enamoured with that. They wrote:

> "Even since the human race existed there had been three great inventions, one of the money the second of the printing press and the third of the tablean economique.

Consistency deals with circulation of money vis-a-vis the supply and demand of commodities goods and services. Demand and supply should be equal for all C.G.S. In communism, this was enforced. Market can equate this but there are "costs", excess supply means lower prices to supplier. Excess demand means higher prices to be paid. Shortage and suppliers do not (should not) exist in consistency model. Physical relations of I-O table are presented in terms of income in consistency model. I-O tabler are cross-sectional and ground us against inconsistency. Now planning cannot ensure that market mechanism can secure that with luck and by chance.

Consistency assures such related activities which do not have isolated spatial demensions. All variables become mutually consistent in a consistency model. Unless consistency requirements are prejudged, the feasibility of the targets cannot be determined. Realisation of the targets becomes difficult because inputs required for the targeted outputs may not be there. Infact as the inputs are outputs of some other sectors, we can say some outputs cannot be produced because some other outputs are not there.

We can put it in a different way also. If new houses have been constructed then three things can happen (i) new houses remain unoccupied because people do not have purchasing power, (ii) people move to new houses and old houses are vacated, and (iii) both old and new houses are occupied and people now have more space to live in. The third condition is of consistency, while the first two conditions are of inconsistency.

We can say that if purchasing power has been created but production capacity is not there, then there will be inflation ; if production is there but purchasing power is not there, deflation will result. There has to be balance between the two. *The purchasing power as well as the productive* capacity are created by investment. Lack of any one of them requires more investment. It is necessary that there should be consistency between income generating and capacity generating investment for the development *of the regions or the nation.*

Consistency in planning depends upon price stability. In an economy where factor and commodity prices are changing very fast, all calculations go awry.

Physical consistency means there should be consistency between inputs and outputs at physical level. Production of certain number of metres of cloth will require certain physical quantity of yarn, among other things.

The physical consistency of inputs and outputs can remain the same even in the face of changing prices if the supply side constraints are not there, but in the regimes of changing technological conditions, consistencies will be disturbed. As there are new innovations, technical relations cannot remain neutral. Scale and scope of operations change. Changing prices bring changes in the relations of inputs and outputs and substitutions take place. As wooden doors become costly, steel window frames and ply door *Formulating Models for Regional Development* panels or synthetic materials door panels may become necessary. Constant disturbances in the supply and demand conditions of various commodities and services change the requirements of consistency situations. Planning physical consistency at national level is easier than at regional level, unless the consistency is for lower order functions and for goods which use local resources. Consistency problems are as difficult as the problems of constructing (and realising the results) regional input-output tables are.

Physical consistency in the regional growth models is also a function of financial and management consistency. Regional models are multi-level models and cannot be autonomous but part of the whole system because of the vertical and horizontal linkages. If these linkages are weak and tenuous, consistency will not be achieved.

The talk of optimum vertical and horizontal linkages is a pet subject of arm-chair planners but *complete* integration is difficult to be realised. Yet all efforts are to be geared to achieve as much as possible.

The physical consistency *is a chain order consistency in physical terms*. Targets for higher agricultural outputs will require more fertilizers, water, irrigation accessories, implements, tools, machinery, pesticides, transport and storage bins, wires for barbed-wire fencing etc. To produce them we require capital goods and inputs. These capital goods may themselves require such outputs as iron, coal, power or other raw materials. Mining itself will require more capital goods and steel output for them. A whole chain of inputs, raw materials, capital goods etc. will be required. Without strengthening the service base of finance, transport, communications and even medical, education and training facilities higher outputs in various sectors are not possible. These physical consistencies are required to be achieved in domestic production, with imports, if necessary.

If there is difference between the levels of development of rural and urban areas or between the primary, secondary or tertiary sectors, lack of consistency is not proved. The levels of income and the rates of growth need not be the same. What is needed is that the growth rate in (say) coal industry should be in consonance with the demand from (say) steel and other industries, railways, and domestic users etc.

The balancing of such nature as of wage goods versus capital goods; or of outputs from different crops; or between raw materials of agricultural origin and their demand from the secondary sector; or inputs of the industrial origin to be used in agriculture and their demand in the agricultural sector should not be inconsistent with each other. Sectoral and regional planning can have a high degree of consistency with appropriate investment and locational decisions. Right locations of right sized economic activities and facilities help in the realisation of the consistency objectives. Short and long term physical consistency objectives are to be reconciled. It will not be correct to meet the short period needs of domestic fuels by cutting down forests as it will be disastrous in the long run.

Because of the collapse of communism and inefficient performance of the public sector in general, regional economists will now rely more and more on the "market friendly economies". The politicians and bureaucrats sleep too much; only Adam Smith remains awake always!

Financial consistency is needed for internal and external price equilibrium which can make possible (or lack of it can mar) the realisation of physical consistency targets. It is an economic verity that what is physically impossible, finance alone cannot make it possible. Yet it can also be said that what is physically possible should not be difficult simply because finances are not available. There should be mutually consistent incomes for lighting consistent quantities.

Only when financial resources are put in the hands of the backward regions they can command the inputs of development. Finance and credit are to be made available to the producers of the inputs of development. Adequate flows of finance/credit are necessary both for creating productive capacity as also for putting purchasing power in the hands of the potential buyers. Various stages of economic activity — production, storing, transporting, distributing, trading and final use — are to be supported with finance in a consistent way.

The economy has 'deficit' and 'surplus' economic units — households, firms and government The 'surplus' units have money but do not know how to use it or cannot use it in directly productive activities because the amounts are too small. The 'deficit', units have plans to use money but do not have adequate money. Banks and other non-banking financial intermediaries unite these two sets. They borrow temporarily the 'use of money' to be lent to others and make profits from differential rates of interest.

It will be an ideal situation if all the finance demanded by the 'deficit units' is supplied by the 'surplus' units. Since this cannot happen, more particularly within regions, the finance has to come from 'outside' — through deficit financing and from external borrowing. These amounts should be consistent with the performance of the physical sectors or else there will be danger of inflation or stagnation. Financial consistency too is not possible unless matched by physical efforts.

The goal of finding all inputs (physical and financial)

from within the economy/region is a good one but cannot be achieved in most cases and that is the reason why real and financial resources are imported from outside the country/region. Similarly all the production of the country/ region cannot be absorbed (or cannot be allowed to be absorbed) by the country/region and exports are to be made. A consistency, which will meet the approval of the economists and people, between consumption needs and providing exportable surpluses is to be ensured. The consistency requirement is that the total outputs be equal to the total uses of the outputs. The same applies for the services.

Leontief could never introduce full spectrum of dependence relations in a market economy. Dr. Mohd Osman Gani a pupil of Leontief, recently prepared tables of dependency in terms of payments consistency analysis, which explore the consistent plan of buyers and sellers. This he did by decomposing the I-O tables, Consistency aims at integrating micro and macroeconomics. It aims at balancing monetary outflows and inflows of sectors It deeds with circulations of money vis-a -vis the movement of goods. Market makes all findingings less relevant in the next second, however.

See Wikipedia p. 7. of I-O model, Jan, 2008 updated.

19

Regional Economic Base Theory and Regional Multiplier: Regional Economic Fluctuations/Cycles

1. Regional Economic Punctuations.
2. Economic Base Theory and Equations.
3. Regional Multiplier.
4. Evaluation.

The natural and human resources of the region, the nature and extent of employment, the quantum of distribution of income differ from region to region. Not only different regions have different degrees of opulence and poverty but there are fluctuations in the economic activities also. There are spurs of development and there are speed-breakers of development of regions.

A favourable balance of payment (exports exceeding imports) will increase the employment/income of the region in a multiplier way while an unfavourable balance of payment (imports exceeding exports) will mean loss of jobs/income. In the long run the region cannot import without exporting, unless the government makes unilateral transfers of resources in its favour. Economic Base Theory, and the Theory of Regional Multiplier explain these relations. Differential multiplier and input-output relations are also part of this type of study. Economic Base Theory and the Theory of Regional Multiplier emphasize the importance of developing those industries which can export to other regions. The importance of those industries/activities which provide goods and services for self-sufficiency in the region was not emphasized.

"Economic Base." Theory is explained in terms of *employment* while the Multiplier Theory is explained in terms of *income*. However, both the theories later on started including both employment and income in the discussion and no compartmenialisation remained.

Daly and *Hoyt* developed the measurement of economic base (export industries/activities) in the 1940s. Subsequently, it was linked with the regional multiplier theory in the form of regional 'export base theory' developed by North and Tiebout in 1950s. *North (1955), Tiebout* (1956), *Perloff, Dunn and Muth* (1960), *Thomas* (1964), and *Bolton* (1966) developed these theories to explain growth and fluctuations in regions.

Regional Business Cycles

Development in one region has cyclical sensitivity impact on other regions. If a broader view is taken, then it can also be said that the development in one region of USA will have impact on other regions of other countries also. Similarly development in one State has impact on the development of not only the border States but other States of the country as well.

Economists realise that unbalanced growth leads to lop-sided development and some *'soft spots'* develop and the strategy of the balanced growth is infact designed to reduce the cyclical sensitivity in regional growth. Isard wrote:

> "A development policy for a region should consider the cyclical implications of such a policy. Other things being equal, it is generally more desirable to develop

an industrial mix whose cyclical tendencies tend to balance out or atleast do not intensify each other".

Generally *heavy and basic* industries have profound impact on regional markets, employment and income and they generally become the basic industries for the purpose of the study of regional multipliers. Regional multiplier effects naturally bring fluctuations in other activities and these fluctuations travel to wholesale and retail markets also. Imports and exports of the region determine/and are determined by the interegional income flow patterns.

National and regional business cycles are not independent of each other. It is certain that a nation in the grip of business cycle phases of great magnitude will find that there are impacts on the income and employment generation of all regions, though in different degrees. National business cycle can he said to be the weighted average of the regional business cycles. Investment in various types of activities, sectors, sub-sectors, types of outputs, etc. have bearing on the economics of regions. Changes in the monetary, commodity, service, traffic and unilateral flows are the cause and consequence of the regional multipliers. *If regional economy is more open and more sensitive to business cycles, the auto-correctives are also easily applicable in region.* Yet it can also be said that the intervention instruments are generally applied with reference to national rather than regional problems.

The nature and extent of unemployment and under-employment differ from region to region and while the macro policies of employment generation may be good for the country as a whole, there will be need for tailor-made employment policies for the regions. Differing rates of employment and under-employment/unemployment in different regions, induce migration. Migration changes the nature and extent of construction activities, service functions and production patterns. These changes have profound influence on the regional income and regional business cycles. Regions get involved in problems and get out early or late. Different regions have different amplitude, duration and periodicity of business cycles—triggered off by different causes and brought under control with different policy packages.

Inflationary or deflationary impulses are generated somewhere and then they travel to other regions/sectors/activities. Thus there are (a) inter-regional flows/cycles, (b) inter-sectoral flows/cycles, (c) region to-nation cycles, (d) nation-to-region cycles, (e) region-to-region cycles and they all require understanding before there is programming to tackle them. Yet there may be some sectors; sub-sectors, regions, sub-regions and groups of persons who may remain insensitive to upward and/or downward swing.

Schumpeter (and there are many others who have) studied the problems of business cycles. There is autonomous investment to start the clustering of activities. Imitative, defensive (by the old), supplementary, complementary and competitive investments follow. Outbursts of investment in certain sectors/regions leads to changes in other regions/sectors. They may acquire explosive cyclical nature. Massive investment in extractive industries will send waves of multiplier effects as structural exhaustion of resources will bring sudden loss of activities in some line and then shock waves will travel to other regions/sectors. *In this connection it may be mentioned that attempts to study the business cycles with reference to regions without reference to the sectors and sub-sectors will be fruitless.*

Isard has written well on this:

> "Great industrial concentrations emerge in the favoured regions, which in turn generate mass production economies and still greater extension of the market areas of the best locations, and hence still further selection between superior and inferior

> sites, trade centres and nodes. When transport facilities penetrate new space, new resource deposits become economic to exploit, which may lead to revolutionary changes in the world supply of primary goods. Such opening up of new regions and capitalizing opportunities for profitable local operations starts a process of expansion for the whole economy wherein all regions may gain and be stimulated into expansion, although to different extents. In the new region, opportunities for export cause an influx of new labour from other regions. The settlement and urbanisation phenomena in the new region entail the creation of a host of other economic activities, both residentiary and import replacing. Social overhead investment is required in huge amounts and is largely imported. All this in turn affects other regions, their patterns of export, their industrial structures, their rates of growth etc., the particular manner in which any one region is affected depending on the ways in which its resources both directly and indirectly complement the resources of the new region".

This would necessitate the study of regional cycles and regional multipliers more seriously so that inter-regional linkages are known.

Most backward regions remain insulated against regional cycles because the linkages with other regions are tenuous. If there is decline in industrial outputs of various industries, agricultural sector (rural areas) will be adversely affected only in so far as the demand for some raw materials of agricultural origin goes down. But if there is shortfall in some raw materials of agricultural origin, then some directly related industries will be gravely affected. A decline in the exports (or rise in the imports) will reduce the value of regional multiplier and thereby regional employment and income generation.

In the capitalist economics business cycles cannot be avoided ; they are like earthquake adjustments. The nature and extent of the demand for various industrial products undergo ups and downs and cyclical fluctuations follow. If the region heavily depends for its income on the export of one or two commodities and if the 'external' demand for such commodities goes down, the region will experience a serious depression. A sudden rise in the demand, provided the supply responses can be positive i.e., production capacity can be geared to produce more to end depression or even promote boom. Many regional analysts who studied multiplier effects of industrial exports with reference to certain cities/regions also came to such conclusions. *Industrial composition of the region, and the regional shares determine the regional multipliers.* Williamson, Berts, Neff and Simpson also studied the problems associated with regional multipliers. Simpson wrote:

> "On the up-turns, the expanding regions usually lead and the contracting regions lag; while on the down turns, the contracting ones lead and expanding ones lag."

This is to say that developed regions gain more during the upswing while the backward regions lose more during the downswing the disadvantage is to the backward regions on both the occasions.

Export Base Theory of Regional Growth and Regional Multiplier and Regional Cycles

In any national economy, there are seldom such regions which are self-sufficient. No region probably can progress on the basis of its output of goods and services and the demand for them. External demand sustains the region's activities and the region can export. A region cannot produce all the inputs of development itself and hence imports also. A region is much more 'open economy' than the national economy. Exports which bring additions to the income (leakages in real terms) have multiplier effect on the regional employment and income generation, provided import function (imports are leakages in financial terms and additions in the real terms), is constant function of income.

Therefore, the rate and direction of growth of a region or a city are determined by its exports to the "rest of the world", including other regions of the country. *Export industries therefore become 'basic' industries and other industries are treated as 'non-basic' and the development of a region on the basis of exports is known as "export base effect".* This is export base theory and the exports have subsequent multiplier effect. *The ratio of basic employment (or income) to the non basic employment (or income) is called the base ratio.*

As is well known the monetary flows are the counterpart of the goods and service flows, unless the monetary flows are unilateral. A region can earn as much as it can export its goods and service unless the central authorities send special grants to the region. Income from the tourists expenditure is in fact income from "exports of goods and services" bought by the tourists. The non-basic industries are also important: they are called non-basic only in the sense that they are not export industries. Basic sector is directly related to exogenous demand while the non-basic sector is related to the exogenous demand indirectly through the basic sector. There is constant interaction between the basic and non-basic activities and they increase in size and composition. The total employment and income increase in a multiplier way. If one basic job leads to three jobs in the non-basic works, then the base ratio will be 1:3 and every decline or rise in the basic job will lead to decline or rise in three jobs. Thus the multiplier will be *4*—total of both.

The regional multiplier theory is also based on the "export base" theory, which states that the growth of a region depends upon the growth of its 'exports' industries. This theory suggests that it is expansion in demand external to the region which is crucial in determining growth within the region.

North and Tiebout made important contributions in the development of the theory. *North* wrote:

> "It is the pull of economic opportunity as a result of the comparative advantage in producing goods and services in response to demand in outside market which attracts productive factors in a region, leading to its rapid growth."

Tiebout recommended the *'minimum requirement technique for* developing the economic base theory. Many regions similar to one under the study can be selected. For each such region, the percentage distribution of total employment or income among the various industries is computed. Then, for each industry, the percentages attributed to it in the various selected regions are ranked by order of magnitude. A minimum requirements profile, comprised of the lowest ranked value for each industry, may then be drawn up that covers all the industries represented in the study region.

It is believed that in a certain region, the industry must be having the smallest proportion of the total of the output of that industry. Here the size of the industry should be of the minimum requirement size. It then serves the local needs. From this it follows that basic employment or income in the study region is the sum of employment or income in excesses of the minimum requirements level in each industry. Because the regions selected for comparison may include some in which truly unusual and irrelevant factors are at play the minimum requirements level might be set at some arbitrary rank other than the lowest for each industry. However, the problem of finding out 'similar' regions or determining 'minimum requirements' are not easy to solve. Personal discretion of the researchers may be too apparent.

TABLE 1

Industry	*Employment*	*Income*
Basic		
1		
2		
3		
4 etc.		
		Cut-off point
Non-basic		
1		
2		
3		
4		
5		
6		
7		
9		
10		
11 etc.		

Non-basic activities will naturally be more

Export Base Theory Equations

There are several ways the 'export base theory' equations can be presented.

$$K = \frac{sdE_b + dE_{nb}}{dE_b} \quad \text{or} \quad K = \frac{\Delta E_b + \Delta E_{nb}}{\Delta E_b}$$

Here

dE_b change in employment in basic industries. $= \Delta E_b$

dE_{nb} change in employment in the non-basic industries. $= \Delta E_{nb}$

or

$$K = \frac{TE}{BE} \quad \text{or} \quad \frac{10\ \text{m}}{4\ \text{m}} \quad = \quad 2.5 \text{ million}$$

This gives us the total employment in the region (basic + non-basic) divided by the employment in the base or basic industries in the region. This will give us *multiplier of base employment.*

Thus the multiplier can be calculated for the *total* or the *increase* in employment. The first will measure the position at a point of time in aggregate terms while the other will present a time profile.

We require two service ratios for these. (1) First, the proportion between total employment in a region's basic (export) and non-basic (local) activities. $E_b : E_{nb}$

(2) Secondly, we require the proportion between the increase in employment in basis activities and increase in employment in service activities.

The formula:

$$K = \frac{dTE}{dBE} \qquad K = \frac{\Delta T_E}{\Delta B_E}$$

is also known as time-lag effect. The base multiplier is the function of change in total employment divided by the change in basic employment. If historical time series of base multipliers over a period of three-to-five years periods can be calculated, the time lag is incorporated. Such a technique can be useful for 'projection' purposes also as against the use of base multiplier for descriptive purposes at a point of time. This will describe the past also. *However, it should be remembered that it is said that "the only purpose economic projections serve that they make look the weather forecasting much more respectable."* Multiplier period are practically unknown.

The next important issue to be thrashed out is to designate the activities as 'basic' and 'non-basic'. *If the LQ is high for a particular industry, it is basic industry.* In other cases, a survey or an over-riding proof can be used. A district famous for mass scale mining and export does not require any elaborate mathematical exercise to prove that the activity is basic. *Location quotient which was calculated earlier, can also be calculated thus :*

$$X \quad \frac{NEI \cdot RET}{TNE}$$ [Calculated with reference to employment]

or

$$X \quad \frac{NYI \cdot TRY}{TNY}$$ [Calculated with reference to income]

X location quotient.

NEI National Employment in Industry,

RET Total regional employment.

TNE Total National Employment.

NYI National Income in Industry.

TRY Total Regional Income.

TNY Total National Income.

Total basic and service sectors can be computed by applying the LQ formula to every industry represented in the region. The sum of the positive difference between actual and X values is the total for the basic sector, and all remaining employment is non-basic.

Another simple method can be used. If the population of a region is 6% of the nation, but if more than 6% population of the region is engaged in any particular industry, then the industry is basic.

According to the Economic Base Theory, the *total employment is equal to the base multiplier multiplied by the base employment.* If the unit of measure is chosen (employment, income or output), then the next step will be to identify the industries in the basic service sector. Then E,Y, or O in each sector must be tabulated. Once this is done, the base ratio and the base multiplier can be computed. If the base multiplier is computed on an industry-by-industry basis, then the same can be very useful for evaluating estimating the impact of an expanding or new industry in the region. It can also serve as the foundation for estimates of future demand, essential to the work of physical, public service, private enterprise, economic and other planners and as the basis for estimates of basic jobs that must be created in order to reach target levels of total regional employment. Used only descriptively, the base ratio and base multiplier can provide valuable insights into the nature of the regional economy through inter-area and inter-temporal comparison.

Economics of Regional Multiplier

Multiplier measures *'by how many times a particular crucial variable under study changes as a result of some other determining variable'* Keynesian multiplier, for example, measures by how many times the employment increases as a result of change in consumption. It can also measure (or actually measures) by how many times the *national income* changes as a result of a change in the *consumption.* This consumption related to several variables e.g., income, prices, expectations about change in prices, tastes and fashion, and the relative share of the national income going to the rich, middle and poorer classes— relatively speaking. The multiplier is not the function of just one variable: but of several.

Variables which provide 'spur' effects to national income are increase in consumption (because one person's consumption becomes another person's income), change in investment and change in exports— all increasing.

The depressants of the national income are 'savings' and 'imports'. Savings are vital for capital formation and investment but 'savings' in Keynesian economics are just 'hoarding or withdrawals from the circular flow of national income'. Savings are not *to be maximised but 'optimised'.* Too much of savings will reduce the capacity of the people to save in the next time period, because this year's "over-savings" will mean lower consumption, lower demand, lower output, and hence reduction in employment and income in next time period. A nation which saves too much will find that it cannot save much in the next time period. If a nation consumes nothing but bread and water in any year, it will find that the economy is ruined because no one will be able to sell anything, except those who are associated with the production/distribution of bread and water. These savings are to be institutionalized and canalized into investment and then they go on to increase the 'absorption' in the country and hence the effective demand. Out of the production comes the capacity to export and thus C + I + X (consumption + investment + exports) increase the income in a multiplier way.

Savings and imports (S + M) reduce the income propagation and that too in a multiplier way. Multiplier therefore becomes the function of the tension between the slopes of the C + I + X on one side and the slope of the S + M on the other side. However, when the income increases in a multiplier way it is a case of "nothing succeeds like success" (more so when interacting with the accelerator), and when the multiplier works in the downward direction (alone) "nothing fails like failure".

The basic difference between the Economic Base Theory and Regional Multiplier Theory is that the multiplier, calculated in money terms (as compared with employment in the Economic Base Theory), is much more akin to the short-run Keynesian income type multiplier of macro-economics. It incorporates the effects of 'imports' and 'taxation also, which are leakages, along with 'savings' (which is a leakage of closed economy multiplier).

One simple way of presenting the regional multiplier is :

$$K = \frac{1}{s + m + t}$$

K is multiplier.
c is marginal propensity to consume.
m is marginal propensity to import
t is marginal rate of taxation.
s is marginal propensity to save.

As has been demonstrated, the regional income increases because of the increase in consumption + investment + exports. Exports are the function of investment and supply responses also as they are of external demand. Investment is possible only when there is effective demand for consumption and investment. Investment will require savings also. Savings are withdrawals from the circular flow of national income and hence are leakages. If they are hoarded only, they will bring deflationary impact. However, if savings are institutionalized and then canalized into investment, the regional/national income will rise.

Imports of any one region are 'leakages' for that region but they are exports of some other region. When the 'other region' exports, its income rises and that additional income may 'leak' in the form of imports from the region under study. Thus the exports of the region under study will rise. There are impact and reversal effects (feedback effects) of exports. Multiplier can work in both the directions.

In any economy :

Y= C+ S + I

This is to say that the income can be disposed of as consumption + savings + investment.

However, if the savings are not converted into investment, then next time period's income will go down . It all savings are invested then

Y= C + I

Region base theory or regional multiplier calculated in income terms proves nothing that base industries one good or better.

K = $K = \frac{1}{s+m+t}$ We have some nomendacures.

Prapemitier : percentages.

c	– Consumption	s =	Savings
x	= Exports	m =	Imports
t	= Taxation	I=	investment,

We now take three examples of three regions.

	A	B	C
Total Y =	\$ 150 m.	\$ 150 m.	\$ 150 m.
c =	60 m.	60 m.	120 m.
x =	50 m.	50 m.	—
m =	50 m.	—	—
s =	30 m.	30 m.	20 m.
t =	10 m.	10 m.	10 m.

Region A

$$\frac{1}{s+m+t}$$

$$\frac{1}{\frac{20}{100}+\frac{33.33}{100}+\frac{66.7}{100}} \quad \text{or} \quad \frac{1}{\frac{60}{300}}$$

$$\frac{1}{1} \div \frac{60}{300} \quad \text{or} \quad \frac{1}{1} \times \frac{300}{60} = 5$$

K value is 5

This region exports and gets necessary inputs.

Regions B

$$\frac{1}{s+m+t} = \frac{1}{\frac{20}{60}+\frac{6.67}{100}}$$

or

$$\frac{1}{\frac{26.67}{200}} \quad \text{or} = \frac{1}{1} \div \frac{26.67}{200}$$

$$\text{or} \quad \frac{1}{1} \times \frac{200}{26.67} \quad \text{or} \quad 7.45$$

This region exports but does not import. Can we say that this region is better off because import " leakages" are not there. Infact this region must be foregoing use of vital inputs for consumption and investment.

Region C

$$\frac{1}{s+m+t} = \frac{1}{\frac{13.33}{100}+\frac{6.67}{100}}$$

$$\text{or} \quad \frac{\frac{1}{20}}{200} \quad \text{or} \quad \frac{1}{1} \div \frac{20}{200} = \frac{1}{1} \times \frac{200}{20} = k = 10$$

We get K = 10. This region does not export and does not import. Its marginal properties to consume to high (hence s is low). This *seems* a self-sufficient region. But, the self-sufficiency must be rudimentary i.e. consumption may be elementary. There is misplaced emphasis on *m* and *s* being leakages, is and consumption; *s* are invested rather than handed = (S = I)

This simply means that income propagation in a closed economy is the function of consumption + investment i.e., absorption.

Thus C + S = C + I or S = I i.e., all savings should be converted into investment.

It should be noted that all consumption is not a function of Y or income. It depends upon a host of other things like prices, incomes, income distribution, taste and fashion, taxes and subsidies (disposable income) etc. *But a certain part of consumption will he there even without income.* This is rather true of individuals than for the nation as a whole. Yet in the macro-economics of multiplier we show consumption function as:

$$C = C_a + C_y$$

In the diagram there will be a *intercept in the C + 1 line, consumption alpha being the function not related to income.* C_a is the amount of consumption expenditure that is not a function of income and *c* is the fraction of income that is spent for consumption. This fraction *c* is the marginal propensity to consume which can be depicted as dC/dY.

Therefore Y = C+ I is correct, but we should rather write:

$Y = [C_a + C_y] + 1$

As seen earlier multiplier is :

$$K = \frac{1}{1 - MPC} \qquad \text{If MPC is 80 p.c.}$$

or $$K = \frac{1}{MPS} \qquad \text{MPS will be 20 p.c.}$$

$$\frac{1}{\frac{20}{100}} = \frac{1}{1} \div \frac{20}{100} = \frac{1}{1} \times \frac{100}{20} = 5$$

$$Y = \frac{(1)}{1 - c} \cdot [C_a + 1]$$

Multiplier can be explained with diagrams also. The effect is shown when the ΔY or incremental income effect is greater than C + I either under constant production function or under increasing production function. $\Delta (C + I) \angle \Delta Y$.

As the income increases, both consumption and savings increase but in absolute terms only. In relative or percentage terms MPC (marginal propensity to consume) goes down and MPS (marginal propensity to save) goes up.

	See in Rs.		*Per cent*	
Y p.m.	*C*	*S*	*MPS*	*MPS*
1000	100	—	100	
10000	9000	1000	90	10
50000	40000	1000	80	20
100000	60000	40000	60	40

Savings are withdrawals from Y stream. Savings are taken here as boardings which are not invested but are kept as idle balances. What is saved does not go back to the economy. High K is the function of high MPS, or low MPS. MPS = 1 - MPS; here 1 is for Y. Rich persons have high savings; poor have low or negative savings (loan).

- upto OY income C is > Y and the gap L is loan.
- upto OY-OY_1 C = Y i.e. 100 p.c. and no savings.

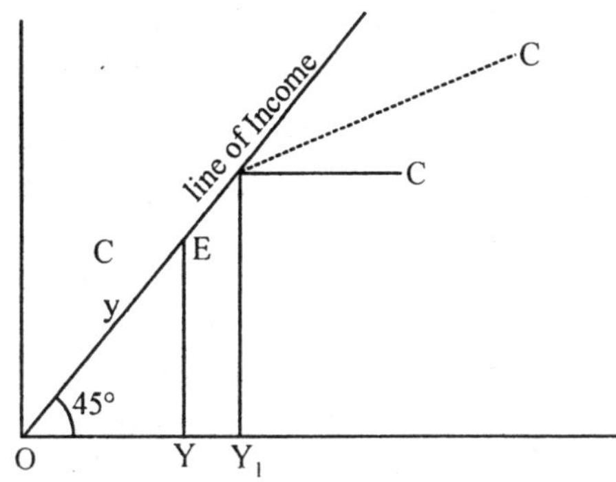

Diagram: 1

- from E to E_1 C = Y condition remains.
- from E_1, Y is > C. C line is shown flat it could have been shown as < as rising also.
- Gap between Y and C is SR or saving/surplus.

In the last two diagrams of this chapter we show K to be higher with lower S/Y and lower with higher S/Y.

K is not instantaneous: It is period K

The theory of multiplier collapses if S are not boardings. If S are invested i.e. if S = I then the savings are not withdrawals or leakages from income propagation. If C+I is 100 and K is 2 or MPS is 50 p.c then in period will to go the market.

1	——	100 + 50
2	——	25

3	——	12.5
4	——	6.25
5	——	3.125
6	——	1.563
7	——	0.782
		99.219

K = will be related in upto 9 period

Savings rise with Y (involuntary). They rise due to the exercise of 8 motives of savings also (voluntary savings).

(3) Efforts should be made to reduce the involuntary savings which cause the demand lag. Keynes pointed out that the basic problem with developed economies is that there are a lot involuntary savings; people do no have to abstain to save. Savings are an automatic function of the rising income. There are voluntary savings as well which people save for the following eight motives:

1. Motive of precaution — for bad times and emergencies
2. Motive of foresight — for those times when income may be low.
3. Motive of calculation — to earn interest.
4. Motive of improvement — to buy consumer durables.
5. Motive of independence — to avoid borrowings.
6. Motive of enterprise — to earn profits.
7. Motive of advance — to enlarge venture levels and
8. Motive of provision — to bequeath property to children.

As a result of the declining MPC and rising MPS the consumption and income consumption curves will partake the following nature.

The consumption curve should be shown with an intercept. We take Rs 50 billion as the minimum consumption needed for survival and it can shown that people will consume even if the income is zero. Otherwise they will die. (Of course this cannot apply to the entire country but only to some persons). Segment "a" of the income consumption curve (diagram shows this type of start. Thereafter segment 'a' shows that consumption is equal to income. From the point T income is higher and MPC starts declining. The gap between y (income) and c (consumption) is S, which will cause "money lag" or "deflationary gap", segment V Saving are withdrawal from the circular flow of income and reduced the national income in the next time period. From this point onwards segment "c" becomes backward sloping income consumption curve, y is income, 'b' is consumption V is gap and 'c' is ycc.

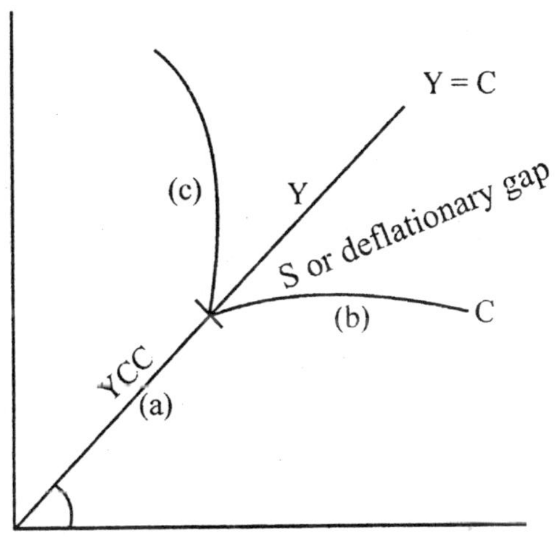

Diagram: 2

(4) Savings become ' hoardings' if they cannot be put back in the economy in the form of consumption or investment. Hence the initial efforts should be to increase consumption because it has 'multiplier effect'. And unless the savings are invested in "real investment", they will partake the nature of 'hoardings'.

In the Keynesian system the economic problems are not due to "lack of good" but due to "lack of markets".

There is no goods lag but money lag or purchasing power lag. It is most desirable to nip the evil in the bud. If MPC starts falling, initial efforts should be to increase the consumption itself. There can be subjective measures of increasing consumption i.e., through advertisements, publicity and propaganda, new demand can be created. Objective measures will be to (i) grant *tax* concessions to those who have high MPC, (ii) to tax the rich and incur public expenditure on those services because of which the persons with high MPC can divert their consumption to other items, and (iii) to control monopoly profits and incomes of the sinecures (who have low MPC and high MPS).

(5) If consumption is raised, there will be multiplier effects and these effects should be facilitated to be realised.

Keynesian multiplier, which is a closed economy multiplier, (exports and imports are not included in the analysis as 'spurs' and leakeages' respectively). It measures: how much initial changes in consumption ultimately affect the income Multiplier can be presented thus:

$$K = \frac{1}{1-MPC} \quad \text{or} \quad K = \frac{1}{MPS}$$

Higher the value of multiplier, the less will be the need of initial investment to secure a targeted income. If multiplier is 2, and the desired income is \$ 200 billion, then it will be secured with initial investment \$ 100 only.

Consumption and savings are as under the K will be

75%	25%	$\frac{1}{1} + \frac{25}{100} + \frac{1}{1} \times \frac{100}{25} = 4$
80%	20%	$\frac{1}{1} + \frac{20}{100} + \frac{1}{1} \times \frac{100}{20} = 5$
40%	60%	$\frac{1}{1} + \frac{60}{100} + \frac{1}{1} \times \frac{100}{60} = 1.66$

Example can be Multiplied* than C - C1 + C1 distance

(i) 50 b, constant c/y line with intercept of minimum consumption.

(ii) 80 b, constant c/y line

(iii) saving lines start with negative Rs 50 b. S line is lower s/y function line S line is higher s/y function line.

(iv) As c rises to $C_{1,}$ + I_1, then income propagation increases from Y_0 to $Y_{1,}$ and it is > than the distance between C $C_{1,}$ + $I_{1,}$. This is k effect on S'.

(v) On higher C + I line and lower S line income propagation of y_2, y_3 is so much more.

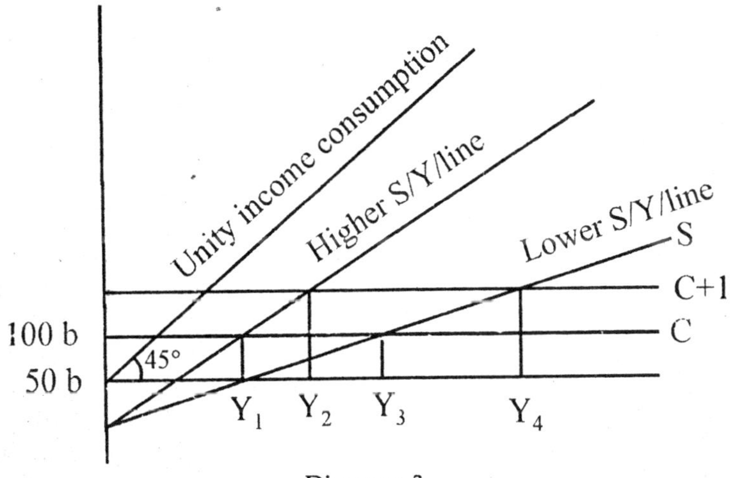

Diagram: 3

In the following show the diagram we show the consumption plus investment as the rising function of income. This does not contradict the earlier position that MPC has a tendency to fall, the C + 1 line can be a rising function due to rising investment effect. *Here the* diagram will show that the multiplier effect will be still *higher.*

- SS is the savings function line. It is negative upto point y income,

- consumption + investment intercept starts with Rs. 50 billion.
- since income is zero at point O, the consumption is positive at Rs. 50 b. , therefore the saving are negative at Rs. 50 b.

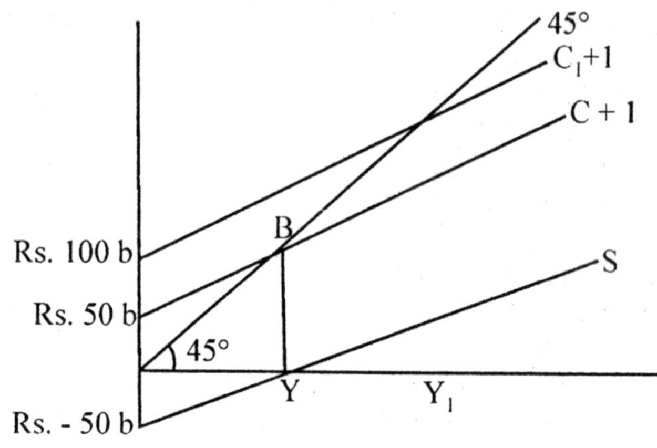

Diagram: 4

- *A question can be asked that how at zero income the consumption and investment be positive. This assumption can be made at micro level when a person can beg, borrow and steal.* At macro level this is not possible unless the economy is rudimentary i.e., people consume what the find rather than what they produce e.g. , in jungles.
- at point B there are no savings : savings are negative to the left of this point and positive to the right of this point.
- with C +1 consumption curve, the interection of this line with 45° line gives OY income.
- with higher C_1+ I_1, line, the income propagation will become y_1,.

- $Y\ Y_1$, is the multiplier effect, which distance is higher than between $C + I$ and $C_1 + I_1$

The two principles stand :

(a) Income propagation will be higher on flatter SS line than on steeper one.

(b) Income propagation will be higher on rising C + I lines than on flatter C + I lines of constant function of Y.

Old consumption line, it intersects the 45° line at point E, this is the equilibrium level of income and it is equal to a multiplier times autonomous consumption plus investment. It can be seen from the diagram that income propagation shown on the horizontal base line is higher than the distance between C line and C + I line.

Evaluation

As seen, there are three approaches to regional business cycles: (A) the industrial composition or the industry mix analysis, (B) the economic base or export base theory, and (C) the inter-regional multiplier. Industry mix analysis takes the industry mix of the region in isolation while the inter-regional multiplier, as the name suggests, takes it in the inter-regional perspective. Industrial composition analysis does not reveal the inter-industry linkages.

The 'economic base' analysis is considered too aggregative and the distinction between basic and non-basic is quite blurred.

1. There are exogenous and endogenous causes of fluctuations and therefore several measures become necessary for controlling regional fluctuations in employment and income. Stabilisation of agricultural output and a steady increase in the real output can ensure stability in the rural sector because bulk of

the income there is generated by agriculture. Real development measures (development of irrigation, checking soil erosion, improving the fertility of the soil, high yielding variety seeds etc.) can ensure this. *Stabilisation of agricultural prices destabilises the agricultural income. At constant prices, the income falls with the fall in output in bumper season.* Steady production and supply of inputs also become necessary.

2. Fiscal transferences—grants and subsidies—greater public expenditure in infrastructure development, tax concessions and greater supply of credit are other instruments that help regional stabilisation. These measures are to be implemented in a discretionary counter-cyclical manner.
3. Industry-mix should not be too concentrated on a few agro-based industries, otherwise regional employment and income will vary according to the crop performance : as would have happened in the past when Bengal was too much dependent upon jute industry. Diversified mix of industries should be located in regions so that regional income does not depend upon the exports primarily.
4. Regional flows of commodities and services and hence monetary flows are not easy to record. The 'frontiers' of the region are open and no administrative machinery records where the goods are taken to or brought from—not completely in any case. Railways and carriers can supply the data, provided they keep a correct record.
5. It is difficult to calculate the production, savings, consumption (more so the components of consumption which are based upon the production of the region and of other regions), investment (from the inputs of the region and of other regions). The problems

are further compounded at the suppression of incomes—and this problem is ever present at national, regional and local level. The overall basic service ratio at any one time is quite likely to be inaccurate as a basis for computing a multiplier value.

6. Regional economist *Vichita* observed that multiplier values computed for periods less than 10 years in length show a range of variations wide enough to render them virtually useless for purposes or prediction.
7. The export base theory places too much importance on the exports. "Home" consumption, investment and production may also make a region rich and thriving. Exports to "foreign countries" and to "outside regions" do not have the same significance. The non-basic activities may expand independently of changes in exports e.g., migration into a region induced by non-economic factors may lead to more non basic activities without expansion in exports.
8. It is to be noted that multipliers work only when there is excess capacity and less than full employment. In less developed countries the basic problem is to create capacity and here the multiplier becomes of limited importance.
9. One *great shortcoming of the economic base theory is that the propounders did not discuss the (i) impact effects and the (ii) reversal effects of exports. If a region exports too much and earns high incomes, a time is bound to come that the region will start demanding the goods produced by other regions and then the incomes will leak out.* This is the essential part of the theory of export multiplier which was not specifically analysed by these regional economists

with reference to the regional incomes and fluctuations in them.

In their system as the income flows from outside, the needs of the region are met by the non-basic activities of the region itself.

If a region exports and has multiplier effect on the income generation in the region, some other region must be importing and losing the income and multiplier must be working in the downward direction. These aspects were not specifically emphasized. Imports *as leakages have been incorporated in the equation but the effects are not elaborated.* It looks quite odd for some regional economists to suggests that "leakages to other regions should be plugged", as if these regions are separate nations. Narrow parochialism follows from the abstract analysis. What may be a sound recommendation with reference to a nation, becomes impractical and wrong from the point of view of a region. It will not be sound to suggest that the exports earnings should "not be dissipated on imports from other regions and on transfers to other regions".

10. *It is to be noted that the smaller the area, the more the chances of economic activities becoming 'basic'.* A petrol pump is 'basic' for a village where it is located in a road side, but 'non-basic' for the city or district. A hotel is basic function in a small town, but not for the area of which people avail that facility. At the urban level, many functions become service and non-basic; and at the national level, the majority of activities are non-basic with a relatively limited export sector. It is not the basic activity alone which is the 'prime- mover'. Then it is the presence of the non-basic facilities and functions that makes the coming up of the basic sector possible.

Then basic and non-basic activities keep on getting reshuffled—exported goods may be demanded locally; locally demanded goods may be exported also; and some goods may be consumed in the region as well as exported. Non-basic activities keep on getting promoted without any direct impact of the basic activities.

11. Imports are not leakages only; on them depends the productive capacity and the future capacity to export. There are *import replacing-imports.* Import replacing imports are also growth promoting—a thing not recognized by the 'export-based theory'.
12. The theory was developed with reference to backward regions, yet it fails to emphasize the importance of increasing the real supplies and real efforts. Exports from a region, if they are at the cost of sacrificing minimum consumption, will not promote development and welfare of the masses of the region.
13. The theory talks about increasing the *volume* of exports. Higher income from exports can be a function of the *improvements in the 'terms of trade; also*— the ratio of export prices to import prices. More income can be earned by reducing the cost of production, by securing better prices, by improving the quality a little bit but by charging proportionately more and so on.

This is not to reject the *idea* completely. Rising exports from a region do help.

Regional and national growth rates are too complex to be attributed to one single variable e.g., exports in the case of regional income. It is too simplistic to say that non-basic activities are a certain multiple of the basic activities and the too added together and divided by the volume of basic activities income will give the export base multiplier.

Inter-regional dependence is presented as something undesirable i.e., it is a leakage. Export base *theory remains a two-region model because all other regions are, treated as the 'rest of the world'.* There are scores of internal and external causes of regional growth. Exports are the function of exportable-surplus and they are in turn a function of the production. Production function of the region depends upon a host of natural, economic, non-economic, socio-cultural and administrative factors.

Exports depend upon the productive capacities—human and non human; and they all depend upon the investment—real and financial. Regional growth is *generally sponsored* i.e., is the result of government assistance.

Exports do not automatically lead to even 'economic growth' much less to 'economic development and improvement in the physical quality of life'. Exports of oil from middle cast countries in the past increased the personal wealth and welfare of the feudal lords. The common people remained by and large poor and backward. Backwash effects of exports can lead to immiserisations of the country of vital resources get drained out. It was only recently that democratic urges made the rulers invest in the development programmes for the people.

It is also possible that exports of real resources of the region may denude it of them and the region may become poorer. Many mining regions become wastelands. A policy of subsidizing exports of a region to other regions will promote inefficiencies. The importance of basic industries *will depend not on the employment only but on the wage-bill, which will determine the income and then the income elasticity of demand for various goods and services.*

20

Macro-Dynamic Growth Theories Applied to Regional Economic Development and Regional Planning

[Some Important Points at the Outset]

Regional economics is essentially a micro economics because region is a micro space. Macro-economic models cannot be applied to regional growth. They can be adapted and not adopted. Even if a region of a country is bigger than another country, the region will remain a microcosm and models of macrocosm cannot be applied in toto.

More dynamism is possible in a region than even in a country, A region can record a high rate of growth even when the country as a whole may be in static position. That means some regions are decelerating. Deceleration is not a state of staticity but we do not take it as a state of "dynamism". Dynamism is something positive.

There exists in the theory of regional economic development, *a* gaping desideratum. A region is not a closed economy and hence in a state of openness. Allocation of resources as desired is important for regional growth. The structure of

---

See Richardson RE Reader p. 98-99.

Richardson, Elements of Regional Economics, p. 45-47.

O. S. Shrivastava's book on "Economics of Growth, Development and Planning", explains all important macro-dynamic models in details.

Here the most relevant ones are presented

See also the chapter on Convergence and Divergence.

production and the livelihood have got, to be dynamic. Dynamic elements are to be ensured in (i) location and agglomeration, (ii) mix and share, (iii) shift and share, (iv) input-output relations, (v) infrastructure development, (vi) management of exports for ensuring higher regional multiplier of growth. Regions can develop without exports but not without government help.

> If a nation is recording the growth rate of 8 p. c., the backward regions should record more. That is to be ensured. This is dynamism. *Solow* emphasised the role of technology for this. Speedbreakers are to be removed. Spurs are to be put in place. Regional economics is not aggregative like some macro dynamic models like that of Harrod but disaggregative sector-wise and activity wise, Infact impact on different groups of persons is also to be seen.

What are Dynamic Models as Applied to a Region?

Regional models of development or theories of development [models are in mathematical form and theories are spelled out in words even if both say the same thing], are dynamic if they emphasise that the regions should develop at increasing pace. There is *no* need for the developed regions to halt their development but to establish such linkages that the poor develop along. It is for the intervention mode of the government that the backward regions come nearer the developed regions. The tasks of combining the (i) individual mode. (ii) community mode and (iii) intervention mode introduce dynamism.

Computable general equilibrium (CGE) models use economic data to estimate how an economy might react to changes in policy, technology and other external factors. CGE model is also known as AGE {applied-general equilibrium, model). The regional dynamic model are neo-classical in nature and Meade's model is the best of them, as the economists of the west say.

The regional models have the same essential elements

as the national dynamic models. In the national models it is assumed implicit) that capital, technology, trained, labour, infrastructure etc.) are all there. In the dynamic regional model, their importance is expressed *explicitly*. It is acknowledged that there can be constraints on the production front and that they should be removed.

> Input-output model is a dynamic model of regional growth. If we say that the mix and share or shift and share of the region should conform to the theory of structural development of the sectors, the discussion becomes dynamic in nature. *Export base, model is a dynamic model, emphasising, that exports should increase at increasing rate to enable the region to import on its own.* Regional dynamic models developed by the then socialist economists were based upon doing away the capitalist system. Since the collapse of socialism, the laissez faire economists insist that only free play of market mechanism can ensure dynamism.

In dynamic regional development models we study how a tax policy, or a policy of subsidising certain activities or the policy of development of infrastructure will affect or should affect different identified regions differently. That is based upon data. Recursive effect is the essence, of dynamism. That takes into account what will happen due to the effects of different policies in future.

Macro Elements in Regional Growth Models?

A region by its very nature is spatially a micro region. A country assumes the macro identity. Bhutan's national income is a macro variable, the same way as the national income of India is a macro variable. The state domestic product of Gujarat is a micro variable even though it may be higher than the national income of Bhutan.

> The macro variables of the country affect the development of a region. Investments in ports and harbours provide benefit to that State/region also

> which is land-locked i.e. has no coastline of a sea/ ocean. The variables of the regions added together in full make up the national variable. Macro-economic dynamic models apply to the country and not to the region unless we find out how the change in national variables affects a particular region.

Macro-economic dynamic models take only national income, as the variable on which the affects of incremental investment (in percentage terms) gives us a growth rate when divided by the capital output ratio or the inverse of the physical productivity of investment.

> The regional growth models have got to be disaggregative. We have to find out the income that accrues or should accrue or can accrue from different activities, functions sectors, sub-sectors and facilities. What happens where, how much and how are the issues of vital concern for the region. Regional capital output ratios differ. The C-O ratios differ activity-wise also. We cannot take one COR for one region as is required in the macro models.

> In any regional model the employment is to be evaluated activity wise. Production, outputs, productivities and value-productivities are to be studied activity-wise as well as in relation to the sub-regions of the region.

Macro-dynamic models are aggregative, particularly those which were formulated for the developed countries. Harrod-Domar models stand out as the most important. No constraint of capital, technology, trained and adequate manpower or no socio-economic stumbling blocks or speed-breakers were taken into account in the macro dynamic models.

> This cannot be done in regional models, particularly when the regions differ in the levels of economic development. Macro-dynamic growth models are mostly demand sided. There are now supply-side

> macro dynamic growth models also. Regional models have to incorporate in them both supply side and demand side variables. Nothing can be taken for granted.

1. Classical Models and Regional Development

These were *laissez-faire* models. The spatial and inter-personal differences were not wide. Adam Smith did take into account the backwardness of regions and cited the example of Bengal. Ricardo brought space into discussion when he propounded the rent theory. Differential wages in his model were also spatial in nature. Malthus saw inter-regional differences in fertility and he considered high birth rates as the most important, if not the sole, cause of backwardness.

> Classical economists felt shy of advocating the interventionist mode of development of regions. They did not recommend massive and concerted public investment for the development of the backward regions and people.

They were for higher savings and capital formation, and frugal consumption. They were for low rates of interest and wages so that investment could be made wherever it was cheaper in absolute and comparative terms. They believed that whatever is good for the producer is good for the country or region. Theirs was supply-side economics. They believed in the "percolation" theory i.e., growth fanning out to other regions. They believed that in due course of time there will be vertical (in-depth development of scale) and horizontal (widespread and development of the scope of growth). Market will take care of the under-developed space. Just as we draw water from a well and the water around the space comes to fill the gap (no hole is left wherefrom the water was taken out) so also the investment will fill the empty under-developed spaces to the advantage of all.

2. Neo-Classical Economists of Pre-Keynesian Era

Two economists stand out. First was Marshall, the father of micro economics, and the second was his student Prof. Arther Cecil Pigou. Keynes was also the class-fellow of Pigou but he lateron propounded his own model. They wanted to increase the material production and through it the national income. Physical production is more important than rise in income due to services, Mill also believed in this. Then they advocated government intervention, but of mild type only, in ensuring the fair redistribution of income for the economic welfare of all. They wanted fair wages to be paid. They wanted that more developmental efforts be directed towards the "mean streets" i.e., the habitats of the poor not merely in a city but in the country-side also.

They believed that regions and people develop best when physical productivities increase and factor payments are according to their marginal significance/productivities. They wanted decreasing returns to be arrested. They wanted increasing returns in production and for that external and internal economies were to be created.

JB SAY's DYNAMISM was Par Excellence — Both for the National and Regional Economies

JB say was one of the three most important immediate follower of the trinity of the classical economists viz., Adam Smith, Malthus and Ricardo. Two fellow travellers of JB Say (France) were NW Senior (England), and von Thunen (Germany). JB say was as dynamic as Domar. Domar's dynamism, was much more explicit and complete than that of Harrod.

However, the Domar model was infact the reiteration of the JB Say's "Law of the Market." The conclusion that emerges from the "Law of Market" is the ultimate dynamism of the growth model.

First point was that "supply creates its own demand". If there is excessive supply, prices will go down and demand function will improve. The supply function will deteriorate or the supply responses will ensure that production goes down. The adjustment shall continue till the demand and supply become equal. There is no problem of glut in the model of JB Say.

Second point is that "demand will create its own supply" and that is the corollary of the first point. If supply responses are less than necessary to meet the demand, the prices will go up. At higher prices, demand function will deteriorate and supply function shall improve. Once again the two will come in balance.

How soon this can happen will depend upon the dynamism of the economy. In Say's dynamic economics "over production, is a condition when, all the producers in sum produce "TOO 'LITTLE'" . It is not "too much". If cloth cannot be sold even when people require them (or may be half naked) it means that the potential buyers do not have the requisite purchasing power. This purchasing power is to be put into their hands. They should produce something else and sell and acquire purchasing power. Over-production in line of manufacturing is infact under-production In other lines of manufacturing.

This is the best macro approach and this is the best dynamic approach.

Classicism is the Bible of the liberal bourgeoisie. The classical model presented a stadial view of the development of the society occurring through the exercise of self interest (not selfishness) of the economic men. In the classical system, the society develops blindly but not arbitrarily.

"Invisible hand" i.e., the changing and free prices give indirect direction as to in which sectors and regions investments should be made or manufacture lines.

3. Marxian Macro Dynamic Model of National, Regional and Peoples Development

This failed model is of no importance. Marxism ultimately proved a system of slogan-mongering and hurling abuses at the producers. The Marxists killed people in crores in their own countries for expressing dissent. Poverty continued and it was acknowledged by the governments after the fall of socialism or after relaxation from the rigorous centralised planning that 40 p.c., population was under abject poverty. The communist economies were show-case economies a part of the country was shown to the foreigners as if only wealth and health were outcomes of socialism.

> The party leaders leading army and police personnel, the bureaucrats and some from party cadres were multi millionaires. The President of a country got tunnels and tunnels of under-ground living dug with well-stocked provisions (food and other essentials) yet was killed.

Socialist model envisages abolition of private enterprise and every productive activity to be nationalised. Everybody's business remained nobody's business. Work-shirkers and lazy persons emerged. False data was presented. Socialist sent criminals to their most under-developed regions for development socialists were associated with violence and debating.

> It is true that a lot of development did take place in the erstwhile socialist countries. But that was 10 years work done in 50 years. Lopsided regional development remained

Centralised planning emphasises public sector interventions taking care of the backward regions and people. But in due course of time most of the public sector units became examples of low productivity and massive corruption.

4. Keynesian Macro-Static Model of Development for Regions

Keynes (to be pronounced as if written as CANES), was the father of the 20th century "new economics". It was infact the development of the Malthusian theory of "effectual" demand which Keynes called "effective demand". Keynesian model was macro in nature but was not dynamic. It was for developed economies and not for backward/developing economies, much less for a backward region. It can, however, be converted in dynamic model.

Keynesian Model Can be Presented in 10 Catch Points

1. Economic development cannot be secured if the economy is left completely to laissez faire nor to State-socialism. It can only be managed through State-capitalism of interventionist public expenditure.

2. As the economies grow the absolute consumption and savings go up but in relative and percentage terms the propensity to consume falls and propensity to save rises. Savings are withdrawals from the income stream and savings are treated as "hoardings". There are voluntary savings (due to various decisions of the people) and involuntary (due to rising income effect, whereby a lot of money is saved even after meeting all consumption needs fully).

3. Consumption should be tried to be increased through various methods. If that is done, then the increase in consumption will have multiplier effect. (See chapter on "export base theory of regional development" or on "regional multiplier"). If the desired income is \$ 100 b., and the multiplier is 2, then investment of \$ 50 b., will secure that income (50 *x* 2 = 100). If the multiplier is 4, then investment of only \$ 25 b., will secure that (25 x 4 = 100).

4. Not all the deflationary gap (Y-C=S) can be thus filled. There are incomes with the government which collects

taxes. Hence private and public investment should be raised. For this the liquidity preference should be reduced i.e., people should be encouraged to part with their liquid funds so that the rate of interest falls. A lower rate of interest will promote investment.

5. Liquidity preference cannot be reduced merely by persuation. Hence another way of reducing the rate of interest is to increase the money supply. This is entirely in the hands of the government. Marginal efficiencies of capital (profit expectation) should be high

6. Government can create new money. New money is money for pump priming (when a water pump takes air, a little water is put in the nozzle of the pump; then the pumps starts functioning). Newly printed money is income creating finance. Money should be spent on public investment.

7. Public investment should be in those lines where social marginal returns are higher than the private marginal returns like irrigation schemes, road construction, construction of ports and harbours, opening hospitals and schools, afforestation, sanitation improvement etc. These activities will generate employment and money will reach in the hands of those who have high marginal propensity to consume i.e., the working class. This is more relevant for spatial development.

8. Rent and other unearned incomes should be taxed, out or brought down to a low percentage of the national income. There should be euthanasia of the rentier (slow mercy killing). That will reduce the propensity to save.

9. The wages should not be cut to reduce cost of production. That will reduce the purchasing power more. If wages are 10 p.c., of the cost then to reduce the cost of production by 5 p.c., the wages have to be brought down to half (5 p.c., is 50 p.c., of 10 p.c, of the total costs). The

producers will get advantage of 5 p.c, only but the purchasing power of the workers will be reduced by 50 p.c, If the labour is a large percentage of population (In the UK 85 p.c., of the national income goes to the workers), demand will suffer a serious fall. Supply will not be lifted fully. There will be glut and depression.

10. Development can be sponsored where the private investment cannot fill the gap. The taxes should be progressive but not radically progressive so much so that the initiative of the producers is sapped. Public expenditure should be progressive —more for the benefit of the poor, but should not promote indolence.

> Developed countries should give money to the developing economies. That will be to the advantage of the rich countries. The poor countries will use the money to import. The rich countries can export. Here we can draw a lesson for regional planning. If the rich regions advance credit and other facilities, the poor regions can import from the rich regions. In other words, the effective demand can start emanating from the poor regions.

The operations of public debt should be progressive. Bond holders should be poor. The government should make available such savings schemes or bonds that the poor can subscribe. The interest receivers would then be the poor. The payment of interest should be from the revenue that is collected from the rich by way of taxes.

Bondholders Receivers of Interest	*Payers.*	*Effect.*
Poor	Poor	Very regressive
Rich	Rich	Neutral effect.
Rich	Poor	Criminally regressive.
Poor	Rich	Progressive.

***HARROD DOMAR MODELS** explain that there are conditions for "steady" (knife-edge path)* growth and that *once there is deviation from the path of steady development, there will be disequilibrium on either side — inflation or deflation.* In their models disequilibrium is self-perpetuating rather than self-correcting. *Similarly, in the words of Richardson:*

> "The attainment of equilibrium conditions in one region may alter the requirements of equilibrium in others, and this will have further repercussions on its own growth rate.. .:Whether or not there will be a tendency to steady growth depends on whether or not inter-regional flows of capital and labour are equilibrating."
>
> (E.O.R.E. p. 49)

The economics of regional mobility of resources, capital and labour (neo-classical theory) will have to be incorporated to explain the disequilibrium in the regional growth.

From the H-D models, as we will presently see, higher regional growth will depend upon (a) higher regional savings, (b) lower regional capital output ratio, (c) net *capital* imports leading to rise in regional savings, capital formation and investment, (d) net regional immigration of labour [if region is deficient in labour] and outmigration [if the region is surplus in labour].

If the regional savings are less than then required regional investment, capital can be imported (loans can come); and export earnings can increase the savings. In the models of Harrod and Domar, savings are not 'hoardings' but capital.

Harrod-Domar models were born as a result of the "marriage of the 'multiplier' with " accelerator'! They assume full employment.

These models are based upon certain *assumptions:* (1) It is presumed that there is no problem of the lack of savings in the economy and thus of capital. (2) Natural resources and efficient labour supply are available. (3) Price level, interest rates and capital-output ratios are constant i.e., productivity of the capital is constant. (4) They are *laissez faire* models and hence assume fiscal and monetary neutrality also; i.e., government does not manipulate fiscal and/or monetary tools to help someone at the cost of mulcting someone else. (5) It is also assumed that government does not pursue any open income policy which would regulate any factor payment. (6) Lags and leads are ignored and their economics is instantaneous; *expost* investment and *ex ante* savings are equal. All capitals arc, lumped and depreciation is ignored. It is also presumed that all persons would like to reach the desired equilibrium levels. Initially a closed economy is presumed and then it is opened up.

Non-mathematical Description of Harrod Model

Like the classical economists, Harrod believes that *real growth is real development* and that it depends upon the real natural resources, real savings, real capital, real investment and real efforts. In a dynamic economy, hump savings (savings for precautionary motives), inheritance savings (savings to bequeath to the dependants), and corporate savings (for speculative motives : investment and further development) all increase. *Savings in Harrod Model are not taken in the sense of hoarding but as those which can be designated as capital.*

The rate of growth in Harrod model is equal to the savings ratio divided by the capital output ratio. Therefore, if a higher rate of growth is desired, the savings ratio should go up and/or the capital-output ratio should go down [or the productivity ratio should go up].

Harrod assumes that each increase in output provides the basis for further increase in output (hence income) in the next period. The chief mechanism is by reinvestment of part of this increased output through additional savings into additional investment, capital-output ratio assumed to be constant.

There is an *actual* growth rate at which the economy grows. Then there is *warranted growth rate* at which the entrepreneurs (in total) desire to grow. Lastly, there is *natural* growth rate which cannot be zero or infinity but of which maximum is set by natural resources (their discovery raises it) and manpower. Only when *all the three rates equal, there can be the steady growth rate.*

This is the steady growth path or knife edge path of economic development.

Then the system will be steady. If the system is not steady, then it is unsteady. There will be booms and slumps and they will be further strengthened.

Once there is deviation from the knife-edge path, it cannot be arrested. If the movement is towards inflation, it will hit the ceiling and if there is deflation it will hit the bottom. The ceiling is provided by the natural rate of growth and the bottom is set by the minimum rate of savings below which people will not save. (Some hump and inheritance savings will always be in positive in net terms]. There are no centripetal tendencies but only centrifugal forces that cause the system to deviate farther and farther from the required line of advance.

The Three Crowth Rates

The Actual Growth Rate :

$GC = S$ or $G = S/C$

G is dY/Y

S is S/Y

C is I/dY a capital- output ratio.

Then:

$$\frac{\Delta Y}{Y} = \frac{SY}{I / \Delta Y}$$

$$\frac{\Delta Y}{Y} = \frac{S}{Y} \cdot \frac{\Delta}{I}$$

$$\frac{\Delta Y}{Y} \cdot \frac{I}{\Delta Y} = \frac{S}{Y}$$

$$\frac{I}{Y} = \frac{S}{Y}$$

$$I = S$$

If the savings are \$ 80 out of \$ 1000 and productivity of the capital is 25% i.e., an investment of \$ 100 in capital leads to an output of \$ 40 i.e., the capital output ratio is 100 : 25 or 4: 1, then:

$$\frac{80}{1000} \times \frac{1}{4}$$

will work out to 1/50 or 2% growth rate. If the growth rate is to be raised to 4% then the savings should becomc \$ 160 or the capital output ratio should become 2:1, which happens when productivity doubles or less capital is required (half) for the same output.

Warranted Growth Rate

It is that growth rate which satisfies *all entrepreneurs in sum.* The output demanded is equal to the output produced. Full capacity is utilised. All other growth rates are unwarranted. The problem with this growth rate is that individual producers do not determine it and actual growth rates differ because different producers gear up their efforts to reach the warranted growth rate in unco-ordinated way. If the actual growth rate is equal to the warranted growth rate then the producers can invest as much as they want to earn a desired level of income.

$$G_w = s/C_r$$

In the above equation the expression w is for warranted growth rate and C_r is the capital required for the warranted growth rate. Thus there is warranted capital output ratio for a warranted growth rate.

Natural Growth Rate

It is that growth rate at which the economy can grow at the maximum rate. Naturally, if the labour supply becomes more efficient or increases, or there is resource discovery, or technological improvement, the natural growth rate will also increase. It is the uppermost limit. No country can grow at a rate which is higher than the natural growth rate, unless it is starting from a slump. Resource discovery and all other favourable changes lift the ceiling upwards.

There is an upper limit for the growth of a region also. However, the actual growth rate in a region can be higher than permitted by the natural resources. This is possible only if resources (real and financial: technological and human) are transferred from other regions. In that case the ceiling of other regions will come down.

Deviations : Inflation and Deflation

Inflation

This will happen when:

$$G > G_w$$

$$G_n > G_w$$

(Normally one would think that if the entrepreneurs want (say) 8 % growth rate but the actual growth rate is 9%, then they can bring it down and there will be depression. What compels them to grow at a higher rate that they do not want and consider unwarranted? Harrod's explanation is that in such a case the entrepreneurs, acting in isolation find that the actual capital has fallen short of the warranted capital and there will be further capital accumulation.

Hence ordering of capital goods will take place which will lead to boom/inflation.

Deflation

This will happen when G_w is greater than the G_n; then the entrepreneurs get depressed because they want to grow at a higher rate but the limits are set by natural resources.

As the warranted growth rate exceeds the natural rate, that is, the rate that the economy can ensure under the given constraints, there will be depression. Growth of investment cannot make full use of saving, and this results in the society suffer from chronic over-accumulation of capital.

This will produce excess capacity, rising inventories, bankruptcies and the attendant unemployment. Under these conditions, there will be over-loading of enterprises and chronic unemployment for a long time. In that event, Harrod says, the correct policy will be to reduce the rate of saving, which also reduces the Gw.

Conclusion

Harrod model shows that there is a *unique knife-edge line of growth which is determined jointly by technological and other considerations of investment, per unit of increment of total output* Only if producers keep this line, they will find that on balance their production in each period has been neither excessive not deficient.

On the other side of this line is a 'field' in which centrifugal forces operate, the magnitude of which varies directly as the distance of any point in it from the warranted line. Departure from the warranted line sets up an inducement to depart further from it. The moving equilibrium of advance is thus a highly unstable one.

Harrod defines over-production as a situation" *in which actual growth has been below* thr warranted growth i.e., a condition of general overproduc ion is the consequence of producers *in sum producing too little.*

(This is nothing but JB Say's famous market theory which tells us (a) supply creates its own demand, and (b) thus demand creates its own supply and (c) if there is over-production in one line of manufacture, the cause is that people engaged in other lines of manufacture do not have enough purchasing power to lift the supplies, and hence they should acquire it by producing *more of the goods of their line of manufacture.* If shoes remain unsold, yet millions of people go barefoot, it is a paradox which can be solved not by producing less shoes but by enabling the shoeless unemployed and under-employed persons to produce more goods/ services so that they can acquire purchasing power to buy shoes.")

The only way in which this state of affairs could have been avoided would have been by producers in sum producing more than they did. Over-production is the consequence of production below the warranted level. Conversely, if producers find that they are continually running short of stocks and equipment, this means that they are producing above the warranted level."

Harrod Model and Less Developed Countries Regions

It will be necessary that $S = S_w$ if deflationary and inflationary conditions are to be avoided in a region. If Technology *is being introduced and it is being diffused in regions, then the equation can be modified:*

$$G_w C_r = S - d$$

Here d is technological change. It technological change is capital saving, then c-o ratio will be reduced and the value of d will be negative i.e., it will increase the growth rate by having a favourable impact on savings.

Inter-regional Trade

The balance of payment effect can be incorporated in the equation in this form:

$$GC = S - b$$

Here b is the foreign trade (with reference to region/country). A favourable b.o.p, will have favourable effect on s and the income will increase due to multiplier effect, as in the Keynesian system.

Harrod model emphasises that the rate of growth of output should be greater than the rate of growth in income (that is how exportable surpluses are generated), and that the prices of the factors of production, other than profits, should increase at rate lower than the rate of growth income so that a cost advantage is secured.

Harrod model has borrowed the wisdom of JB Say, the philosophy of the classical economists, more particularly from Ricardo, and the neo-classical theory of marginal physical productivity of factors being greater than marginal revenue payments. Harrod model uses the post Keynesian jargon and expression.

Harrod model is not a relevant model for a less developed country, much less for a region. It is too aggregative and too *laissez faire* in implication. Regional growth in less developed countries has got to be sponsored and savings, capital, investment and resources are to be transferred under the directives of the planning agency. Political neutrality with regard to fiscal, monetary and income policy is unacceptable. We cannot wait for the auto-correctives of the Harrod model but the deviations have to be regulated and controlled through deliberate action.

The Capital Stock Adjustment Model of Domar

Domar's model has the same assumption as that of Harrod model. His conclusions are also the same. *Domar also insists that the economy must grow at the simple geometric rate i.e. or at the compound rate.* It is necessary that the investment of today must exceed savings of yesterday! That is the true dynamism and before this happens again tomorrow, they should for some time become equal also. This can be done for yearly growth rates.

The economy should grow at the growing rate. *Investment should grow at an increasing absolute rate (or constant compound interest rate) equal to the propensity to save (alpha) times the inverse of the capital coefficient (sigma).* $\Delta I/I = {}_{\alpha}\delta$ (See balancing equation ahead).

It is not sufficient to increase purchasing power: matching production capacity should also be generated. It is the investment which generates production and employment (purchasing power) and hence it occurs on both sides of the equation in Domar's model.

Domar says that both unemployment and excess capacity in industries (idle labour and idle capital respectively) are undesirable but because of the humanitarian considerations, unemployment is more dangerous, while some excess capacity may be tolerated (as in old and technologically decaying industries excess or idle human labour is not to be tolerated. *Domar's supply adjustment effect was classical in nature and he was truly a disciple of JB Say, but in emphasising that the problem of unemployment of labour is more important than under-utilisation of the capital, Domar was advancing the Keynesian line.*

Equations

Equations of Domar model emphasise that the demand and supply sides of the model should be equal or the purchasing power and production should match. These demand and supply sides can be elaborated as under:

The Demand Side

Demand is a function of income and the change in the demand is the function of change in income. Change in income is itself a function of change in investment multiplied by the multiplier. If income increases by $ 1000 and MPC is 45%, then MPS will be 100% - 45% = 55%. Multiplier is equal to: C = consumption S is savng.

$$\frac{1}{1\text{-MPC}} = \Delta Y \text{ - MPC} = \text{MPS.}$$

or K= 1/MPS

Reciprocal of MPC (Marginal propensity to consume) is MPS (marginal propensity to save) and this saving is not demand. Only that part which is consumed and hence sent back in the circular flow of the national income, can create multiplier effect. In his model change in demand (dD) is the function of the change in income [dY].

Change in income is equal to the change in investment, multiplied by the multiplier. Hence : denoting MPS, with $\propto$,

$$dY = dI \text{ . 1/MPS or } \Delta Y = \Delta I \cdot \frac{1}{\alpha}$$

The Supply Side

Supplies are that result of investment multiplied by the potential average productivity. If investment is Rs. 100 and productivity rate is 25% i.e., COR is 4 : 1, then supplies are equal to Rs. 25.

Hence S = I.δ δ denotes average productivity.

The Balancing Equation

Demand should equal supply. Then

$$\Delta I \cdot \frac{1}{\alpha} = I \cdot \delta$$

Dividing both the sides by I and multiplying by ∝ we have:

$$\frac{\Delta I}{I} = \alpha\delta$$

Domar gives an example to make the things clear. If productivity is 25% of the investment of capital output ratio is 4: 1, the national income is $ 150 billion per year and saving rate is 12% per year of the income, then to maintain full employment, it will be necessary that the investment should also be equal to the savings i.e., 180. Thus investment necessary will be 12% of $ 150 million, which comes to $ 18 billion. Now this investment of $ 18 billion will increase the production by $ 4.5 billion i.e., 25% of the same @ 4:1 capital output ratio.

Thus increase in production of $ 4.5 billion is 3 % of the former income of $ 150 billion. The same 3% is obtained if we multiply ∝δ of which values are

$$\frac{12}{100} \cdot \frac{25}{100} = \frac{3}{100}$$

or 3% per annum.

Further Conclusions

1. If there is excess capacity, but matching purchasing power has not been generated, then there will be deflation.
2. If investment generated purchasing power but matching output is not coming due to low productivity or high capital output ratio, there will be inflation.

Some types of dynamism are needed. *Investment of today should be greater than the savings of yesterday, then they should be made to match, and then again tomorrow the investment should exceed the savings of today.* This is one way of saying that there should be economic development at the *increasing rate. (atleast from year to year).*

Some excess capacity in old, dying and technologically obsolete industries can be permitted. That is creative destruction. Hence investment has to be even more than just necessary for rising population and rising aspirations. It has to take care of obsolescence also. Domar wanted control on monopolies and strong oligopolies because they keep deliberate excess capacity which militates against full employment. Domar wants such a system in which unsatisfied wants and unsold goods do not go side

(A) Neo-Classical Model of Economic Growth

Prof. J. E. Meade's (of Cambridge University) model of economic growth is the most representative of the neo-classical model of economic growth.[1] His model has all the traits of the classical model. Since it was propounded after several growth theories from Marx to Keynes to Harrod Domar had appeared, his methodology was modern. It was a defense of the classical position in modern jargon.

All models are based upon certain assumptions and this is done to convert the variables into parameters so that the growth equation remains manageable and short. The main assumption of Meade model [indeed of other neo-classical models also] are :

1. Who and how many are the neo-classical economists ? The answer is "innumerable". In fact the last neo-classical is yet to be born ! There is a slight difference between "neo classical" and the 'new classical' economists the former accept some changes in the classical system but the latter do not accept many changes. Solow is another important name amongst the neo-classical economists. Kaldor is partly neo-classical and partly neo-Keyesian. Some essential features of neo-classicism are.

- They do not believe in State intervention like Keynesians.
- They believe in fluid factor substitutability (between K & L) on the basis of the advantage in factor prices. If labour is cheap it will used; if it is dear capital will be used more.

1. There is perfect competition in product and factor markets.
2. There is not government or trade union interference i.e. there is *laissez faire* system.
3. Labour and capital are two factors of production. Labour has homogeneous units. Capital is also homogeneous and "operates as a uniform, malleable, jelly like mass" capable of flexibility responding to any changes in relation between the prices of factors of production.
4. There is unhampered substitution between capital and labour in accordance with the dynamics of their supply and demand conditions and prices.
5. There is full freedom for price setting and for economic contract. Income going to factor of production is determined according to the marginal productivity of the factor of production. The factor prices are equal to contribution to production.
6. There is no problem of demand.
7. All savings are invested via the effect of flexible

- The neo-classical economists believe in the auto-adjustment of the capitalist system. They assert that it is basically a stable system, if not tinkered with.
- The growth rate of the economy depends upon the growth rate of labour and growth rate in capital multiplied by their productivities.
- However, unbridled increase in population without increase in the productivity of labour will require any one or more of following workers will have to

  (A) accept lower wages.

  (B) accept unemployment i.e. displacement by machines.

  (C) limit their population;

  (D) face unsteady growth and lower levels *unless they increase productivity.*
- All (actors of production should receive remuneration equal to their marginal productivities. If they want more, they will have to increase marginal productivity.

interest rate and all workers can be employed fully via flexible wage rate.

8. *Initially* a neutral technological production function is assumed. Ultimately there is diminishing return. The growing scale of production does not influence the growth of efficiency.
9. The elasticity of production factor-substitution is equal to unity. In other words, a change in the relation between profit and wages causes a precisely similar change in the relation between labour and capital, and vice versa. For that reason, the distribution of income does not change.
10. Growth is a function of three principal determinants. *One is capital multiplied by its productivity.*
11. The second is labour *multiplied by its productivity.*
12. The third is the *rise in production due to technology.* Capital is combination of machines with depreciation taken into account. Machines embody technology also.
13. All government policies (fiscal, monetary, wage or income or international trade) are assumed to be neutral. Economy is presumed to be 'closed' initially.

B. The Model

Economic growth is the function of capital, labour, natural resources and technical progress. Since, natural resources are fixed, growth becomes a function of the remaining three factors. If K, L, R are constant then technology will bring growth.

The growth relationship can be shown as under.

$$dY = V \, . \, dK + W. \, dL \times dY$$

(here d denotes change ; V denotes marginal efficiency of

capital; W denotes marginal productivity of labour and Y denotes improvement in income due to technology)

Thus, the increase over the year in the rate of annual net output (dY) is equal to the increase in the stock of machines (dK) multiplied by its marginal product (V) plus the increase in the amount of labour (dL) multiplied by its marginal productivity (W) plus the increase in the rate of annual output due simply to technical progress (dY)

In terms of the rate of growth, this can be put as under :

$$\frac{dY}{Y} = \frac{VK}{Y} \cdot \frac{dK}{K} + \frac{WL}{Y} \cdot \frac{dL}{L} + \frac{dY}{Y}$$

dY/Y: represents proportionate rates of growth in annual terms, in income or in output.

dK/K: represents the proportionate growth rate of capital

1. Factor substitutability will ensure technical progress and it is to be there. Initially for the sake of simplicity a neutral technology function is assumed. In non-neutral technological function, a factor with lower productivity than factor price will be substituted easily. Neo-classical theory is based on Cobb-Douglas production function.

dL /L: represents the proportionate growth rate of labour.

dY/Y: represents the proportionate rate of technical progress during a year.

VK/Y: means marginal productivity of capital as proportion of Y.

WL/Y: means the proportionate marginal productivity of labour, as proportion of Y

If we substitute single letters for these expression, thus:

Y for Yd/Y

K for dK/K

L for dL/L

R for dY/Y

U for VK/Y

Q for WL/Y, then we can write :

Y = U K + QL + R

In simple words, this means that the growth rate of output (Y) is the weighted sum of three rates : *First,* the sum of the growth rate in stock of capital (K) weighted by the proportional marginal productivity of capital (U), plus, *second,* the growth rate of population (L) weighted by the marginal productivity of labour (Q), plus *thirdly,* the growth rate of technology (R)

Economic growth is, thus the marginal product of capital times the proportionate increase in capital, plus the marginal products of labour times the proportionate increase in labour, plus, the proportional increase in output owing to technological change. If technical change is nil and the proportionate marginal products of labour and land add to the increase in income we are back at the Cobb-Douglas production function, i.e., constant growth.

The coefficient can amount to more than 1 *(one),* with economies of scale of less than 1 (one) with diminishing returns to a factor (such as due to land). With diminishing returns, distances between regularly increasing isoquants become further apart, with increasing returns, closer together.

C. Real Growth

The real growth is achieved if the real capital grows (then multiplied by its productivity, it will give real growth). It is depressed by population. The depressant effect of population growth can be included in the equation by deducting from Y that portion of Y which will go towards the maintenance of population.

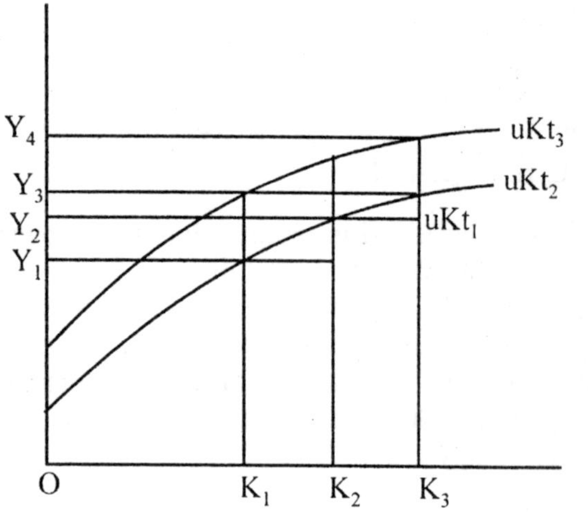

Diagram: 1

The diminishing returns are also depressant. In Meade's model this can be shown by declining marginal productivity of the labour. It will show the depressant effect WL / Y, of which value shall go on declining. Therefore,

1. If population is constant, then real growth becomes a function of increase in capital, or its productivity, or increase in the productivity of labour.
2. If population is rising, then less can be saved. In fact more capital will be necessary. If that is not possible, then only lower wages can increase the relative value of output (i.e. same output at lower wages will give higher share to the capitalist)

D. Conditions for Steady Growth: Critical Growth Rates

Conditions for steady growth require that the rate of change in national income (Y), savings (S), population (I), technical progress (r), wages (Q), profits (U), rents (Z) remain unchanged. It has been seen that the growth relationship is.

$$Y = UK \pm QL + r$$

Taking liberty with the symbols of Meade we can rewrite for easy understanding.

$$Y\text{-}L_c = UK \pm [l_q + l_w] L_r + \phi_r$$

$Y L_c =$ National income net of (minus) demographic consumption of the rising population; c for consumption, L for labour or population.

UK = U productivity of K capital or increase in capital stock multiplied by its productivity

$\phi =$ Increase in real output due to better technology.

$[l_q\text{-}l_w]$ L = productivity of labour (l_q)minus wages paid to labour (l_w) multiplied by total labour

The result will be positive (+) if $L_q > L_w$ [Increasing returns)

The result will be negative (-) if $L_w > L_q$ [Decreasing returns)

There are conditions of stagnation and retrogression. These are when the growth rate in population is higher than the growth rate in capital stock and / or growth rate in labour productivity is lower than the growth rate in its consumption and wages.

Constant population (L) and constant capital (S or K) also mean no progress, if technology is also neutral. It is a condition of stagnation if the growth rate in national income is just equal to demographic consumption of the population plus compensation for depreciation in capital stock. Deceleration will result when conditions of growth become negative. For growth following are necessary :

Lq to increase

Lw to increase relatively less than Lq

L	to increase provided first two conditions are satisfied. K to increase
K	to increase.
U	to increase Same as increase in savings.
Lc	Not to increase
ϕ_r	Output due to improved technology to increase

- We have UK T curve 1 which has an intercept. Some income is generated even in primitive economy without machine capital. Nature provides it.
- On this curve, which is increasing U.K. at decreasing rate OY, income is generated with, ok, capital.
- OY_2, income is generated with, OK_2, i.e. higher capital.
- If, OY_3 income is desired it cannot be generated on UK. T_1 with any capital, unless from inflexion point *x*, UK. T, is lifted upwards with innovations. The OK_3 can generate OY_3 income
- On a high capital-productivity-technology curve UK, T_3 the same OK_3 capital generates OY_4 income

Conditions for Steady Growth : Critical Growth Rate

If population is constant then growth rate in capital should be commensurate with the *desired* growth rate of national income. If population is increasing, then the rate of capital accumulation should be higher to cover the demographic consumption of this additional population. There should be no decreasing returns. A fast rising population will require a high growth rate of capital stock plus increasing returns i.e., contribution of technology. Then technology cannot remain constant. *The dynamic condition (as against the static condition) of growth is that the growth rate in profits should be higher than the growth rate in real wages and this will be possible only with increasing productivities of factors and perfect substitutabilities.*

If factor prices exceed their productivity it is deceleration. If the factor prices equal to the *marginal productivity* it is acceleration. If factor prices equal *average* productivity it is stagnation.

The savings of *all factors* have to rise : of the capitalists, of the workers and of the rentier class. *The rates as well as the total quantities of savings have to rise to secure dynamic growth* i.e., rising growth.

If every determinant is constant then the growth rate will be constant. *This is hardly the 'steady rate' which will be desirable. The determining factors and the determined rate should be in balance at higher levels.* The equality between income (y) and capital (k or s) is equality of steady growth but *rates* have to be constants and not the *levels.*

Actually the constancy conditions in Meade and other neo-classical models are emphasised to highlight that they should not fall and not that their levels be eternally the same. The determining factor be in constant ratios. Growth should come out according to capital accumulation. Capital accumulation should be equal to the requirements of growth (determined by the change in population). The productivities play the role of doing the residue job.

There are three contributors of growth (a) labour and its productivity, (b) capital and its productivity, and (c) their child i.e. the technology and its productivity. All should be in balance (not equal) to the requirements of rising population and its aspiration rate or a natural rate of net increase. The constancy of Y-I,c, means unproductive consumption be constant or be balanced by rising productivity.

Non-stready, growth rates are 'critical'. They lead to inflation or deflation. We actually are always having "a critical growth rate which has a tendency to move towards and away from the steady growth rate". This is the dynamic of development if income increases at higher rate than capital stock savings will have to catch up. If capital increases more than income then savings have to go down but dynamic growth requires that investment or income should rather go up and comes to the conclusion that stability of the national income growth will take place if its rate of growth is equal to the rate of growth of capital stock. Meade calls this the critical level of national income growth rate.

A factor of production gets what marginal productivity is; if it goes down, the income also goes down and vice versa.

In case of the divergences this will happen :

1. As has been seen if the population increases, the productivity of labour goes down and hence the workers (i) either reduce their number, or (ii) accept lower wages, or (iii) accept unemployment.
2. If capital becomes excessive i.e. its rate of accumulation exceeds the rate of growth of income, then rate of interest falls. The savings will be reduced and consumption shall go up.
3. If labour is excessive but demands higher wages, it will be substituted for capital, while contrariwise if capital demands high interests when it is clearly excessive, it will be substituted for labour.
4. Process of adjustment shall continue till the growth rate of population goes hand in hand with the growth rate of accumulation. In a country with increasing population, increasing accumulation can be sustained

only through falling wages and/or increasing productivity, through extra relative labour.

Critical Evaluation

Some Points of Appreciation

Frankly speaking, all those points that can be appreciated in the neo-classical model of Meade are not at all new; they are the classical propositions. One can draw certain inference that (i) population growth should not be excessive, otherwise their productivity will go down and if the labour insists on higher wage (with trade union pressure), workers will be substituted by capital and/or potential unemployment shall ensue; and (ii) the growth rate of accumulation is very important for growth; and (iii) unemployment and excess capacity conditions require downward flexibility of factor prices.

PART-VI

Special Theories of Regional Growth

21

The Cumulative Causation Theory (Backwash Effects Versus Spread Effects)

Gunnar Myrdal's Theories

Noble Prize winner in economics, Late Prof. Gunnar Myrdal has written a lot on the problems of less developed countries. His monumental book "Asian Drama" in three volumes and thousands of pages analyse the development process of Asian countries. Prof. Myrdal is well known for some of his theses, the main of which are (i) the Theory of Backwash Effects of International Trade, (ii) The Cumulative Causation Theory of Economic Development and the (iii) Institutional Reform Theory of Development. In the first two theories the causes of vicious circle of backwardness have been analysed, while in the third we find some explicit suggestions for the development of less developed countries.

PART I

Backwash Effects of International and Inter-regional Economic Relations: Spread-Effects Theory

Myrdal believes that international and inter-regional economic relations in practice involve unequal exchanges in the sense that the weak are always exploited by the strong. Belief in the competitive market benefiting all is misplaced.

Less developed countries face three type of problems

(as analysed in the 'backwash effects theory'). First, the developed countries exploit them in international economic relations. Second the rich regions are also in the semi-colonial position with regard to the backward regions.

Third, the rich people mulct the poor persons of these countries.

International trade resulted in the immiserisation process in less developed countries. When foreigners invested in less developed countries, they usually invested in plantation, mining and a few selected industries These investments created lop sided development in the countries because the nature of development was dualistic. These investments did not trigger off growth impulses in the hinterland.

The precious resources of the nations were drained off. The people by and large remained as backward as ever in the vicinity of big projects. The skilled personnel who worked there developed feudal and colonial approach to the development problems. These were the backwash effects of the development. Capital, skills and people moved out of backward regions to the developed regions, leaving the latter poor and dry.

The spread effects of development were just a few and disjointed or discontinous These spread effects were those which gave expansionary momentum from the centres of economic expansion to other regions, and were centrifugal in nature. The main cause of economic backwardness and regional disparities has been the strong backwash effects and the weak spread effects.

Everything clustered in certain regions from art, literature, education, culture to medical facilities, science, commerce, banking, insurance, power development etc. Big cities developed in port areas. Banking system so developed that the credit-deposit ratios went against the poor regions and while deposits were collected from poor regions, credit facilities for investment were given to developed regions.

Another distressing effect of the past development pattern was that the big industries and urban centres, not only not helped the small industries or cottage industries and rural sectors but positively made them further backward. Handicraft industries died a miserable and lingering death without government support due to unhealthy competition from the developed sector. Even agriculture could not develop in these poor countries and regions.

There were some spread effects from the nodal regions to the hinterland. The hinterland did supply raw materials etc., to the centres of development and in turn received consumer goods. However, these spread effects never helped in the self-expansion process in the rural areas.

The two types of effects were never in equilibrium.* The position was that SPF,> BWE in developed regions while in the less developed countries or regions the BWE > SPE. Spread effects continued to become stronger in developed countries while backwash effects continual to become even more widespread in backward countries and regions. This was the type of "dynamism" in the past, and to a large extent even now between the developed and backward regions.

In developed regions and countries "development becomes automatic process and nothing succeeds like success." In the backward regions and countries "poverty becomes its own cause and nothing fails like failure."

Another aspect of these effects is that while the income

---

* SPE = Spread effects - Forward regions lead boom.

BWE = Back ward effects. Backward sector lead in depression. Backward sectors lag in boom, forward sectors lag in depression. The chasm is always increasing.

elasticity of demand for agricultural products is not high, it is pretty high for industrial products. The terms of trade, therefore, change in favour of the sector which is already developed. When the terms of trade go against the backward sectors, they have to supply more in real terms to get the same amount of real supplies from the other sector/region/countries. This dampens the supply responses further. They cannot increase the prices and they cannot get the advantage of reducing the prices also, because of the low income elasticity of demand.

Money earned in these sectors/regions/countries is not reinvested in these very sectors but is repatriated to the developed sectors, regions and countries. Increased exports from the backward sectors in the past led to inflationary pressure, increasing poverty, balance of payment difficulties, conspicuous consumption and absence of favourable multiplier effects.

There were barriers galore to the spread effects, which included the unhelpful attitude of the rich countries, and regions, sectors and people and also of the governments.

PART II

The Cumulative Causation Theory of Development and Backwardness

The theory of cumulative causation action has been built up on the above two effects vis., the backwash effects and the spread effects. The cumulative causation theory emphasises that *poverty is further perpetuated by poverty* (where backwash effects overwhelm the spread effects), and affluence is further promoted by affluence, (where spread effects overwhelm the backwash effects).

In backward regions problems create more problems; in developed regions auto solutions solve all problems. There is a failure story and there is a success story.

The rebounded effects and circular causation effects are the net result of the backwash effects and the spread effects.

There is inter-locking relation by which in the cumulative process, poverty becomes its own cause whereas development promotes further development. Myrdal wrote :

> "If the spread effects are sustained or accelerated further and backwash effects are resisted or rebounded back to their origin, the pace of economic development of backward regions or classes will be improved in terms of time distances. These two effects originate at the centre of economic expansion i.e., growth centres for lower order support functions and at the growth poles for higher functions. Since the two effects are counter-balanced on tangent areas of the two influence circles, it would be imperative to pressurize a positive force of changes leading to upward movement. The role of "big push" becomes obvious to break through the stagnating situation. Economic incentive to producers, in terms of differential rates of capital subsidy, market subsidy, support price, fiscal support should be granted. These would generate rebound effects on the backwash effects."

Myrdal writes that if the rebound effect are well directed, the spread effects can develop a region. Since the spread effects gradually decline at constant rate with increase in spatial distance from the growth centre, it would be in the fitness of things to locate sub-growth centres, in such future growth potential areas. It would be of much avail to raise intensity of spread effects at point of equilibrium (rather than at existing growth centre), and thereby to extend existing zone of influence to that of other growth centres.

The 'vicious circle' type theory of cumulative causation emphasises that excessive backwash effects keep a less developed country poor. Inequalities do not get reduced on their own but get accentuated. Disequilibrium causes further disequilibrium. He writes :

> "The idea I want to expound in this book is that, in the normal case, there is no tendency towards automatic self-stabilisation in the social system. The system is not by itself moving towards any sort of balance between forces, but is constantly moving away from such a situation. In the normal case a change does not call forth countervailing changes, but instead, supporting changes, which move the system in the same direction as the first change but much further. Because of such circular causation a social process tends to become cumulative and often to gather speed at an accelerating rate."

Thus (as we have seen if the BWE > SPE there will be cumulative causation towards poverty and vice versa), if it is intended that spread effects should overwhelm backwash effects, then state intervention (SI) effect should exceed adverse cumulative causation effects.

There has been an inherent bias in the development of economic theory towards the doctrine of equality because of conservative predilections. Myrdal has been a consistent critic of economic theory based on these conservative predilections. According to him the theory of international trade and indeed economic theory in general was never developed to comprehend the reality of great and growing inequalities and the dynamic process of under-development and development.

Myrdal contention is that "the play of the forces in market normally tends to increase, rather than decrease, the inequality between regions". Once a particular region starts growing faster than the average, the "efficiency wage" in that region tends to fall. (It means that as the efficiency and productivity increase, the per unit wages burden on the cost of production of commodities falls). This region gains comparative advantage over other regions and it becomes cumulative. This has reinforcing effects in terms of industrial development giving rise to widening regional inequality.

Myrdal's theory is centre–periphery model. The favourable effects flow from the centre to the periphery. Periphery supplies raw materials and raw human power to the centre. The centre supplies the technical know-how and finished output for consumption and inputs also. Core activities are at the centre. Subsidiary activities are in the periphery area. After some time the activities in the periphery may give rise to new core regions. This new core region will become the new centre after some time. Then it will be from this place that new peripheral regions will develop.

When periphery becomes the net loser the effects are backwash effects. When the centre becomes the net gainer, the effects are spread effects for the core activity region.

When the spread effects dominate, the core region develops further. In such a case there will be economic integration between the centre and the periphery which will give rise to a more homogeneous spatial system.

When backwash effects dominate, there will be lack of complementarity; and divergences will develop. Periphery will remain weak; only centre will develop and dualism in growth is promoted.

Under such circumstances, the core will continue to experience a circular upward reinforcing trend of favourable effects and the periphery will have a reverse experience.

Cumulative causation theory proves (i) that market mechanism will not bring equality between regions but will increase inequalities, and (ii) nothing short of government intervention will check the backwash effects from getting cumulative.

The process of cumulative causation starts accidently due to "momentum of an early start" and it be just by chance. Once the growth starts, the external and internal economies bring continuous growth at the expense of other localities and regions where relative stagnation or regression becomes the opposite pattern. In backward regions there is outflow of resources, human resources and capital.

Development of infrastructure and directly productive investment brings spread effects, and they induce technical advance and all types of industries grow. "In reality, the expanding, stagnating and regressing localities are arranged in a fairly continuous series on different levels, with all possible gradations between the extremes.

Kaldor's Version of the Cumulative Causation Theory

Kaldor has related his theory to the agglomeration theory of regional economics. According to Kaldor, the principle of cumulative causation is nothing more or less than the existence of increasing returns to scale manufacturing. The rich and big industries can have in capital deepening and can have further access to internal and external economies, and they become even richer. The same is true of regions. Since agriculture market is competitive and industrial market is oligopolistic, the backward regions (where agriculture dominates) lose due to changing terms of trade.

Kaldor has made a good use of the term "efficiency wage", which determines whether the region is gaining prominence or is losing.

He has pointed out that wages in all regions are usually equal and rise and fall in unisom. However, production and productivity patterns in different regions differ. Where productivity rises faster, the efficiency wage becomes lower. Thus the lower the efficiency wage, the higher the growth rate. It can be put in other words: the higher the productivity. The higher the growth rate; or the high productivity-wage ratio is responsible for cumulative causation towards growth while a high efficiency wage or low productivity is responsible for cumulative causation towards backwardness trap. W/P ratio or wage productivity ratio (W money wages and P index of productivity) becomes important. Wages are more or less equal in various regions due to collective bargaining, migration and mobility, and bidding up process. W/P ratios determine fast growing or slow growing or stagnating regions.

Developed countries, regions and sectors may be paying higher money wages, but since productivity is very high, efficiency wage becomes lower than the money wages in backward regions. Circular causation towards development is due to this "efficiency wage effect" only.

PART III

Getting out of the Trap of Cumulative Causation of Backwardness

If the remedial measures are to be conceived, then naturally they will consist of removing the causes. If free international trade has more backwash effects, protection is called for. If market mechanism further accentuates backwardness, the government sponsored and regulated economy becomes desirable. If regional inequalities are promoted through circular causation, then the doctrine of balanced regional growth is to be advocated. In the first instance reverse unbalancing may be done. If the centre and the core are in the semi-colonial relationship with the periphery, then such development -programmes which provide for greater complementarity, integration and linkages are called for, All efforts are to be geared towards ending the socio-economic dualism in development in less developed countries,. Myrdal goes so far as to suggest that the developed countries should now transfer funds and technical knowledge to less developed countries on mass scale so that the latter get the spread effects as compensation for the past backwash effects.

Myrdal has made many other recommendations also. He recommends promotion of capital goods and import substitution industries and also of those industries which permit simultaneous development outside the sphere of modern large scale industry. He wants employment creation to be the main plank for poverty removal.

Myrdal is bitter infact very bitter about the corruption in less developed' economics. Lack' of order, discipline, accuracy and punctuality can be witnessed as national character or atleast as chronic national habit. Widespread superstition, corruption, lack of collective leadership, in-action, lethargy and tranditionalism-abound.

Myrdal is against the model building approach for less developed countries. Models are rigorous but unrealistic. Exercise in model building are fascinating but inappropriate. They ignore social accounting. He wrote :

> "When the models are applied they are selective and therefore, arbitrary nature is usually forgotten. More important, these models frequently pass under false pretenses. In as much as some of the assumption that are essential if the models are to be rigorous are not slated, often the model builders are not even aware of them. This bent is encouraged by ignorance of the history of economic thought and naivete about and contempt for, the sociology of knowledge. The result is that, contrary to the intentions and pretensions of their authors, the models often have only the appearance of logical consistency, rigor, and precision, covering up what in reality is gross looseness in thinking."

Myrdal prefers theory to a model. He rejects the one-sector model or even two-sector model for the multi-structural society and says :

> "In its simplest form the capital-output model contains only one sector. The aggregates in two-sector model are far too broad for these models to lead to a better understanding of South Asian reality. Even if the sectors are well chosen, the fragmentation of the economics is too great and the misplaced aggregation within each sector is excessive."

Myrdal rightly contends that "it is in the agricultural sector that the battle for long-term economic development in South Asia will be won or lost. He is against too much radicalism in agriculture. He wants moderate land reforms because radical land reforms takes the initiative away and reduce the rise of the holdings to less than optimum limit.

A new socio-economic order is to be superimposed, which should be alternative to Marxism. Myrdal's sympathies apparently lie with planning. He does not approve subsidizing the 'big business' by low rates of interest, cheap rates of foreign exchange, protection from foreign competition, and low prices for services and goods from the public sector.

Myrdal laments the collusion among politicians, officials and business people in appropriating the gains of planning to themselves. Myrdal wants far reaching *institutional reforms that* should bring the benefits of planning to the masses that will annihilate the vested interest groups. He writes:

> "The governments ....would be wise to make more and belief use of the price and market mechanism in their planning. Even if under existing conditions, they cannot reach plan fulfilment merely by employing price policies and other automatically functioning operational controls, they should use these controls

> as much as possible, in order to minimise the need for administrative discretionary controls and in order to make such controls, when applied, less inimical to the goals planning, less expensive in learns of administrative personnel and less conducive to corrupt practices (Asian Drama. p. 2033).

PART IV

Critical Evaluation

Critics can criticise anything or even everything of the model. Myrdal's theories have been criticised for the very things for which they stand. It has been argued that the theory of cumulative causation has been blown out of proportion. There are setbacks in the developing regions and there can be development in the vicious circle regions. It can also be argued that even market mechanism can reduce the inequalities and disparities between the two regions. Myrdal model can also be criticized for regarding "accidental factors" as the only factors which start the growth process. Then there are limits upto which a region or sector can go on developing. The same agglomerating factors can bring the laws of decreasing returns when diseconomies overcome the economies.

Appreciation

Myrdal is internationally respected for his views. A western economist, yet he exposed the backwash effects of international trade on the poor countries and regions. Though not a communist, yet he proved that the so called competitive markets instead of solving the problems of backward regions, sectors and people accentuate them.

Myrdal theses have made important contributions to the theories of convergence and divergence, and agglomeration and locational economics and the theory of "vicious circles".

He is for balanced growth and wanted it to be initiated, directed and sustained by the government. He becomes an important supporter of the theory of sponsored growth.

The analysis part of the Myrdal's writings is found to be much more satisfactory than the recommendatory part. He could not develop a complete theory of development, in which he could have written in details about the growth process from the start to the pinnacle.

Myrdal's place in development economics is a little bit shaky but he is on firmer grounds in regional economics where he is studied with respect for his analysis of the cumulative causation of the backwash effects over the spread effects.

22

Theory of Regional Polarisation Growth Poles

This concept was first developed in 1955 by French economists, notably by F. Perroux. In fact the concept was developed on the basis of the borrowal from the growth economics of Schumpter, Hirschman, and Myrdal though theories of these economists were quite different from each other. Perroux first used the term *'pole de croissance'* and by 'growth pole' he meant

> "a centre in abstract economic space from which centrifugal forces emanate and to which centripetal forces are attracted. Each centre being a centre of attraction and revulsion has its own field, which is in the field of other centres"

Growth pole may refer to *industrial or sectorial activities and is functional in nature* and can be defined thus also:

> "Growth pole is a set of industries capable of generating dynamic growth in the economy, and strongly inter-related to each other via input-output linkages around a leading industry or *industries motrice* or propulsive industry/prime-moving industry".

There had been a lot of semantic discussion about the terms 'growth pole' 'growth Centre's growth point' and then 'growth foci'. The first three terms are frequently used inter-changeably.

'Growth pole is functional in nature while the concept

of 'growth centre' is locational in nature. It is an urban concentration where big industries get localised and where professionals of high order provide services not only to the population of the centre but also to the population of the neighbouring sub-systems. These professionals supply what the Americans have started calling (1990) the "intellectual property services'.

"Growth poles (because of their industries and high order services) are such centres as Bombay, Calcutta, Kanpur, Madras* or other metropolitan cities wherefrom the goods, functions and facilities flow. The *industries and the "intellectual property" found here become the 'growth poles'.*

"Growth centres" are big cities and intermediate industrial estates' which are becoming centres of concentrated industrial location. Growth centres are of smaller economic size. "Growth *"points"* are medium service centres. Perroux conceived growth as the process which is essentially unbalanced involving a succession of dynamic poles through time. *Growth poles are key industries which innovate and lead. It* is a leading propulsive industry which has highly advanced level of technology and managerial expertise, high income elasticity of demand for its products, marked local multiplier effects and strong backward and forward inter-industry linkages. Perroux says :

> "Growth does not appear everywhere and all at once, it appears in points or through development poles, with variable intensities; it spreads along diverse channels and with varying terminal effects to the whole country".

Perroux, writing about what promotes economic growth, identified the growth process as "polarisation process and

---

* Now Mumbai, Kolkata and Chennai Kanpur was earlier Cownpore!

then to carry the growth poles (probably smaller) in the backward areas".

Key industries of the key sectors become 'growth poles', and not merely a big city. A key industry has high investment, high output, large reinvestible funds and high density linkages with the activities of the region. It takes as inputs, outputs of the activities around the area and its outputs become goods of final consumption or inputs for further development of other industries. Since it reaps high degree of economies, it provides 'external economies' to other industries. This key industry innovates and it becomes instrumental for the autonomous, supplementary, complementary, imitative and even defensive investment in the region. As the people become materialistically motivated, the original polarisation gets strengthened. Growth process has then different intensities at different places; and, the effects terminate at different times at different growth poles. *These leading industries* (which constitute the growth pole) create, sustain and transmit innovation to other sectors. The dominant firm becomes the 'core' of the growth pole. A dominant firm is supposed to produce a net positive balance of spread effects over the possible backward or backwash effects : thus, providing maximum down stream (forward) and upstream (backward) linkages. As inter-industry linkages develop, a set of industries in spatial juxtaposition that benefit from technological linkages and common agglomeration economics, develop. These industrial complexes and agglomerations give rise to high super-multiplier effects on income, consumption, savings, capital formation and ultimately on the reinvestment.

The main thrust of the growth pole hypothesis is that growth in region tends to be around certain focal points. There will be gravitational pulls towards the polarisation points. Distance reduces the density of flows of development to the interior areas. A growth pole was viewed as a model or an ideal zone of social, economic, institutional and psychological functions/facilities. In an area around the growth pole there is economic activity, at first, of the critical minimum size and then reaching the maximum maximorum in due course of time. The areas of influence of the time get strengthened (in terms of extensive development).

The growth pole of Perroux is 'functional polc' and it is that *Industrie motrice* which, along with interdependent sectors, grows faster than the rest of the economy because of advanced technological practice and high innovation rates.

Perroux had suggested that both economic or sectorial space and geographical space are made up of two contrasting elements. There are active and propulsive elements and at the same time the passive and dependent elements. It was argued that propulsive elements can take along with them the passive elements also. Many observers of the process of economic development aver that this does not happen and leading industries sometimes may not allow small industries to come up.

Perroux's growth pole is 'economic space' rather than geographical space, which he regarded as 'banal'. This was a deliberate attempt to break away from the limiting geographical dimensions' adopted by Christaller and Losch. (Richardson)

In the opinion of Glasson, Perroux gives a typology of economic spaces, the most important being that of economic space as a field of forces, from which he derived the notion of a pole as a vector of economic forces....... as a field of forces, economic space consists of centres or poles or foci from which centrifugal forces emanate and to which centripetal forces arc attracted.

Boudeville's Views

Pottier (1963), Paelinck (1965), Boudeville (1966), Hansen (1969), Darwent (1969) Cameroon (1970), Harmansen (1970), carried forward the view of Perroux and Hirschman (1958). Boudeville gave geographic dimension to the concept of growth pole. He, therefore, wrote about the *regional propulsive industries and agglomerations.* Boudeville formulation became abstract in economic terms. He went on to say that if the growth pole is functional and dynamic *"there can ultimately be only one geographical pole in the country " (!).* Boudeville wrote with reference to the centre and the hinterland and the clustering' was discussed with reference to an urban area. *The concept of inter-related industries was left and only geographical clustering of economic activity in general was taken into account* (!).

Spatial concentration of industries was considered to be more efficient than dispersal *in all cases* (!).

Boudeville erred in asserting that inter-sectorial impacts of key industries did not matter as much as the spatial agglomeration and polarization effects over space. More emphasis was given to the linkages between the centre and the hinterland through the spill over effects of the industries at the centre.

Pottier's 'growth pole' is put forward as *'development axis'.* In his theory of development axes, he integrates the effects of transportation network with urban hierarchies and spatial growth poles. Pottier argues that growth takes places along transport routes and in the centres well connected with transport. Development of transport lines decreases the costs and economies of scale reduce the per unit burden of transport costs. Industry, trade and population tend to be attracted towards the axes of transport network. In such centres the factor and product markets become competitive and efficient and hence they become growth centres and poles. Inter-regional development can be promoted to the extent transport network can be promoted.

In the Pottier's scheme, intermediate towns are not conceived as transmitters of growth impulses.

Hirschman and Myrdal on Growth Pole

Though the names of Hirschman and Myrdal are lumped together in connection with the growth pole analysis, both had recommended different strategies of economic development. *Myrdal very specifically wrote about the development of the backward regions, laggard sectors and depressed ethnic groups and though his strategy may be of 'unbalanced growth type his was clearly 'welfare economics of development'.* Hirschman recommended unbalanced growth through the leading industries. Hirschman recommends concentration of attention on leading and big industries and then their concentration at a certain point of the highest comparative advantage. *Then, growth pole becomes development pole and diffuses development more through social interaction process than merely through inter-industry linkages.*

Hirschman rejects balanced growth doctrine as being "too costly", and wants a group-focused growth. He wants big projects which remain under constant public gaze and are maintained well, thus not involving waste of the scarce capital. He wants such projects which promise the highest possible total linkages. He wanted investment to be made in social overhead capital, as much as is necessary to promote directly productive activities. What Hirschman calls 'trickling down effects' are the same as the 'spread effects' of Myrdal and what are called the 'backwash effects' in the theory of 'cumulative causation' (developed by Myrdal) are 'polarisation effects' in Hirschman's model.

Prof. Gunner Myrdal, the Nobel prize winner in economics, in his earlier theory about "cumulative causation effects" in the development process, gave ideas about 'growth pole'. *It is to be noted that Myrdal did not recommend the strengthening of the growth poles / centres for unbalanced development.* He defines them rather than recommends them. *A growth pole is growth promoting only in so far as the "spread effects' of growth poles are stronger than the "backwash effects' of such poles.* In fact Myrdal warns more about the backwash and exploitative effects of national and international trade which ultimately adversely affect the poor people/countries. *If* (and it is a big if), growth poles (i) ensure more spread effects than backwash effects, (ii) there is no problem of disparities within the periphery of such poles, (iii) if concentration of investment ensures effective use of the resources, then the growth poles are useful. Instead of distributing the resources thinly, concentration can help through total high positive effects of polarisation.

In Myrdal's model growth poles develop because of the market mechanism.

Myrdal says that the main problems associated with economic development are that spread effects are experienced by the developed regions while the backwash effects are experienced by the backward regions and because of this the regional imbalances increase. The growth pole is as good as the favourable effects exceed unfavourable effects by a wide margin and this should percolate in not only the per capita real income but also in the improvement in the quality of life of the people of the hinterland. Spread effects depend upon innovation diffusion and growth attitudes. Diffusion should overcome resistances, and should transmit impulses of development. There will be some phases in the 'logistic curve' of the spread effects. First there will be a slow start, then there will be exponential type *bandwagon* effects, and then as the process reaches saturation point, the curve becomes horizontal to the base line at upper asymptote.

Backwash effects *if they are initially high as resources gravitate towards the pole* and then reach a maximum owing to the lead time in pole projects and gradual build up in agglomeration and urbanisation economies, will form a rising curve first and then a declining curve. A time will come when they will become zero. This is possible only when the spread effects replenish the resources in the hinterland. Backwash effects become zero only when centralisation starts. In case these assertions prove wrong, then the spill over effects of a growth pole will not be positive.

Vertical subtraction of the slopes of SE BE, gives us the TE or spill over effects. There is a point of maximum polarization with negative effects...... A spill comes when the net spill over effects become positive and there is a *cross-over point*. As spill over effects increase rapidly (strong backward effects and backwash effects going towards zero, then the net spill over effects will reach saturation and the upper asymptote is reached.

Propulsive impact of the growth pole was explained with reference to a 'zone of influence', created by 'innovating', 'dominating' 'leading', 'expanding', 'propulsive' and 'linkage maximising' industries. Perroux's growth pole was also based on the 'export-base theory' i.e., if the cluster of industries general large exportable surpluses, it would be an efficient pole.

If such industries can be implanted somewhere then in due course of time more poles can also develop.

Hansen examined the empirical evidence and came to be conclusion that *"it is not polarisation but total industrialisation that is important.'*

Hermansen tried to reconcile the views of economists and geographers. He suggested that growth pole idea be super-imposed on the 'central place models' of Christaller

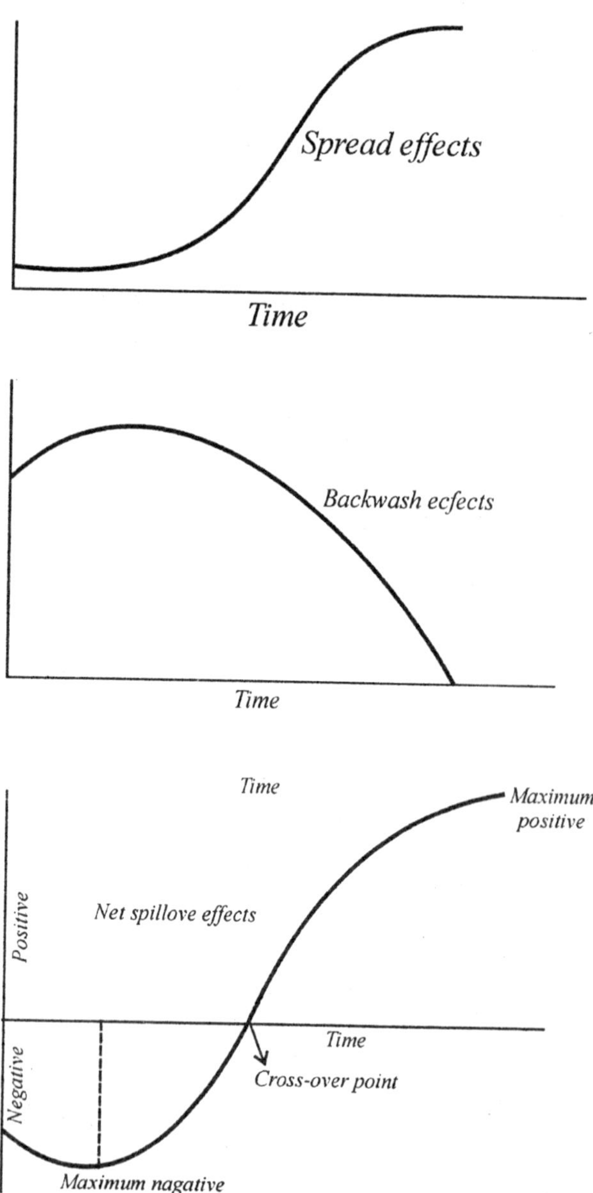
Spread effects
Time
Backwash ecfects
Time
Time
Maximum
positive
Positive
Net spillove effects
Negative
Time
Cross-over point
Maximum nagative

Fig. 1

and Losch. This idea was found even more intractable by writers on regional economics because while the concept of central place is a deductive one, the concept of growth pole is inductive one.

The growth pole hypothesis or theory owes more to the Loschian formulations than to Christaller's theory. As was seen, while Christaller developed the central place theory of spatial development processes, Losch explained the clustering of human activities at given locations and the direction of spatial development processes in order to achieve economies of scale and inter-industry linkages. *Klassen* also emphasised the input-output linkages aspect of the growth pole.

Only when the growth pole theory and the central place theory are integrated with the theory of spatial diffusion of technology, and incorporated, we can have a dynamic general theory of development. A mix of the balanced and unbalanced growth has to be articulated in the explanations.

Summary

Polarisation and Agglomeration: Special Integration

It has been seen that a growth pole requires the following:

(a) a relative large industry or industries;
(b) dynamic nature of industries;
(c) high income elasticity of demand for the product of the pole industries so that demand is not a constraint and whatever is produced is sold also;
(d) high backward and forward linkages and thus maximum total linkages;
(e) spread effects far exceeding the backwash effects to give high net spill-over effects, as early as possible;
(f) there being a lot of continuous innovations in the

industries having the 'bunching or clustering effects'; and

(g) the growth rate to be high in these industries.

There is to be 'flow-line process' instead of just 'batch process' and such a state of affairs gives rise to generation of internal economies in the growth pole industry/industries, agglomeration takes place because of the availability of facilities and functions and these facilities and functions and they further strengthen the agglomeration, resulting in the further generation of net positive external economies.

All these economies result in reduction in the average costs of the products and hence of the price : thereafter enlargement of the national and international markets takes place.

If the diseconomies start exceeding the economies, then there has to be agglomeration elsewhere and new growth centres or even growth poles can develop.

We can have 'pole of development' and / or 'pole or relief. As the first it generates growth in an area where there was no growth. As the second it attempts to reduce the problems of a large industrial complex by establishing itself as a counter magnet. Thus a second growth pole can further the work of the first pole somewhere else. The second pole can help the economy in countermanding the negative effects of the first pole, as they start emerging.

Growth poles can belong to primary, secondary or tertiary sector— —usually of the second.

Critical Evaluation

It is generally seen that in the early phases of development, some polarisation does take place. Ultimately there is dispersion. The problem with the growth pole strategy is that the governments lose nerve even before the positive net spill over effects start emerging. In the early phases there are more backwash effects on the hinterland and there is so much public criticism that growth pole theory cannot be tested. In the words of HW Richardson:

> "This hypothesis has not been tested adequately, partly because of the data limitations, partly because no growth-pole strategy has been in operation long enough, also, it is not universally accepted."
>
> (Regional and Urban Economics p. 171)

Generally it may take 15 to 25 years before a growth pole shows good results and the persons who manage growth may not have patience to wait that long. In the words of Richardson :

> "Given a sound locational choice, aggressive sustained policy measures, perseverance and a strong political will resistant to 'trimming', a growth pole will probably pay off as a regional policy instrument if the planning horizon is sensibly chosen. But this implies too long a planning period for the comfort of most politicians".
>
> (*Ibid.*, p. 171)

Richardson suggests that a 'hierarchy of the growth poles/centres" should be planned to give better result in terms of regional development. It really is a ticklish question to settle the "efficiency equity trade-offs". Unbalanced growth (growth poles) may generate efficiency or economies but dispersal and balanced growth ensure justice, though the problems of shortage of resources remain and growth poles receive greater attention in the early stages of planned growth or in market-machanism dominated growth.

When growth poles/centres are chosen, usually some urban areas become still more developed and when the government tries to relocate some industries, there are more psychological barriers to this than economic barriers. It has also been found that the government tries to develop economic infrastructure (sometimes only 'industrial infrastructure), than social infrastructure and since health, education, housing and welfare facilities (social infrastructure) remain neglected, the hinterland is not happy with the growth poles. These things reinforce the enclave characteristics of the poles. Even if the growth poles are tried to be developed in the backward regions, the core usually exploits the periphery rather than periphery deriving substantial benefits from the core. Enclave characteristic of growth is further strengthened. Eventually in the long run the hinterland may also develop but who has the patience to wait!. Richardson aptly remarks:

> "The result may be accelerated polarization out of the backward regions (including the pole) to the core regions. Policy-makers may for many years find themselves pouring resources into a bucket with a very big hole in it."
>
> (R&U Economics : p. 173)

In many countries the growth pole strategy could not be pursued for long because of the pressures from some groups to do everything everywhere. Poor site selection, lack of resources, and lack of infrastructure support have been responsible for aborting the concept. Economists of many less developed countries became averse to the idea because it came from the West! Communist economists of less developed countries considered the strategy as "an artifact of capitalist society' in which the multi-national companies will dominate the native companies. It was also pointed out that the entire concept is relevant to those countries where there is log-normal city-size distribution, but in less developed countries there are imbalances. Those who were opposed to the congestion, environmental degradation or diseconomies of agglomeration, also opposed the growth pole strategy.

Richardson wrote what everyone feels about the growth poles and he writes with authority :

> "The muddy waters of growth-pole theory might induce the student to turn to an evaluation of policy experience with the technique for more light. .... Unfortunately, the enlightenment anticipated from a survey of operational experience is not to be obtained. On the contrary, if anything, the confusion is increased. Policy makers have interpreted the growth pole concept in very individual ways, have applied it to serve diverse objectives, and have used it to describe quite dissimilar strategies.
>
> Since regional planners are no more immune from fashion and trendiness than the rest of media-bedazzled humanity, the term 'growth pole' has been implanted in their conversations and in their planning documents in contexts that range from the relevant to the widely inappropriate. For example, the designation of industrial estates has been described as growth-pole selection, as has the choice of small rural villages to serve as service centres for rural regions, to take on extreme of the size spectrum, or the promotion of million-plus metropolises as counter-magnets to the primate city, to consider the other."
>
> (R & U Economics p. 174)

If growth pole is selected at a certain urban centre, inequalities are promoted and dispersed poles may mean dissipation of resources. Frequently in the name of developing the backward region, growth pole may be tried to be developed in backward areas and here the efficiency may become the casualty. "Appeasement", in the words of Richardson, may prove to be the enemy of regional planning.

Market mechanism in the past gave rise to the '*natural poles*', while the government planning aims at developing the '*planned poles*'. Planned poles were planned to act as counter-magnets to the natural poles and intermediate growth centres with growth pole functions were tried to be developed. However the big industrialists cornered the advantages of subsidies and infrastructure support without developing the strong linkages with the economy of the hinterland where poor people reside. The inputs of these growth pole-industries did not come from the hinterland, these industries failed to provide employment to the people of the periphery and mostly the outputs of these industries did not become inputs in the small industries or tiny industries in the hinterland. Thus linkages remained tenuous, as in India, and *even planned growth poles* have not so far promoted 'efficiency with justice'.

In India some political parties , therefore, demand that government investment should be concentrated in the development of agricultural and rural economic activities, including the development of rural settlements on modern lines. Rural areas are not to be appendages of urban growth poles/centres. In a country like India *'integrated growth poles' are* difficult to develop because of the vastness of the country and many socio-economic political, and cultural differences. *Indian planners have become too timid and politicians too selfish to risk their posts and position to give importance to compulsory population control programme. India is adding around two crores of persons each year in the population, more of indigents, and the political parties simply want to treat them as 'vote fodder'*

Economists who are against the strategy of the 'unbalanced growth' are naturally opposed to the growth pole strategy. It is, however, perplexing to sometimes find that some economists who oppose unbalanced growth strategy as 'general economists' are quite enamoured with the growth pole strategy as 'regional economists'! Now the social consciousness has so changed that people of all sectors, regions and hues *demand* balanced development. *"Social development poles"* or the active peripheries outside the core regions are desired to be developed. These economists (Friedman is one of them) are unhappy about the over-estimation of the gains of the core regions and under-estimation of the diseconomies transferred by the core to the periphery.

Richardson has rightly written that now the growth pole strategy can work in countries like USA

> ".....growth pole strategies work best when a relatively competitive industrial structure permits large, innovation-conscious manufacturing firms to set up branch plants in intermediate cities."

This view was infact earlier advocated by Lausen.

Growth poles are most likely to result in enclave type of growth. Regional development requires much more. Regions cannot develop without the development of sectors in the region in question and elsewhere; and, regional development will not be perceptible unless sectoral and spatial development strategies are for the development of the folks. Changes in the traditional patterns of development, investment in the skill-building activities, massive investment in the prime-moving activities, changes in the socio-cultural and politico-economic superstructure and probably in the settlement structures will also be necessary. Control of population growth will even be more important in countries like India where the peripheral regions are infested with the progeny of the indigents. Many activities which can act as catalytic agents of development have to be planned for the development of the core and the periphery. Growth pole strategy in countries like India needs modification and co-ordination with the programmes of higher production of basic goods and promotion of social welfare.

Lausen collected evidence to prove that polarisation over economic space distributes itself over the system of cities in such a way that development in advanced countries is becoming less polarised. This is largely due to increasing diversification of business which results in multi-product, multi-plant, multi-city type of organisation in place of one product, one plant, and one city.

"Urban Studies" "On Growth Poles" 1969 pp, 137-161.

Spatial diffusion of technology has also diluted polarisation. Firms now a days do not rise and fall with innovations and they can take new innovations in their stride by adapting themselves. Innovations do not cause earthquake type unheavals in the economic world but merely generate the ripples like changes in investment. Innovations first get embodies in technology used in the production of capital or consumer goods. Though many writers talk about "diffusion of innovations", it should be "diffusion of technology".

The growth pole strategy copes with the problems associated with economic and social immobilities and strengthening of the polarisation depends upon further increase in these immobilities by no means a desirable thing. As the growth pole strategy aggravates inter-regional inequalities, it comes in clash with social goals of economic development. If the spreads effects of the growth poles are to exceed the backwash effects the growth poles, not only the hinterland *space* but also the sectors and people will develop.

It was also seen (as in the erstwhile communist countries) that growth poles promoted by the State were even more anti-people than the growth poles promoted by the market-mechanism.

There was too much emphasis on the spatial diffusion of the innovations, as if innovations can get diffused without the peopie getting involved in it. Innovations are always product-related (sectors). Besides, innovations get diffused only when they are proved to be economically viable. Economic viability depends upon the profitability or the cost benefit relationship and one important aspect of profitability is the demand from the people and the purchasing power with them. Writers like Boudeville took away all the 'organic elements' out of the growth pole strategy. If the persons and sectors are absent in a space, the innovations cannot get diffused over the hinterland.

Economists now a days recommend that agro-based, mineral-based and forest-based industries should be located in intermediate towns and then they can act as 'propulsive' industries. Small and cottage industries *guilds* can have high degree of functional linkages with the rural development. If concentration is the natural outcome of the happenstance economics, this type of dispersal can be secured not only with the grants and subsidies of the government but with active State intervention, infrastructure support and guidance.

It should, however, be conceded that the fault of backward areas remaining backward sometimes lies with the people of the hinterland as well, who may be found to be "lethargic, apathetic to development, non materialistic, and ignorant and may not be keen to participate in the innovating process. (How often do we see that the villagers do not construct a good all weather road with the locally available material or dig a well with their own voluntary labour. They would prefer to remain cut-off from the main centres/roads rather than do this type of *shramdan* or self-help.

There was a time when the growth pole hypothesis got "mystified" and its importance was blown out of proportion by the regional analysts. *The unbalanced growth strategy was presented in a new garb.* Slowly the idea witnessed a burial as the concept got de-mystified. When the 'propulsive' industries were found to be of oligopolies or monopolies or controlled by such interests, the development was found to be "exploitative". Development was found to be asymmetrical and with irreversible domination by the 'vested interest groups'.. Economists who are in favour of 'balanced growth' argued that the ill effects of polarisation are too serious to be ignored. We can study what promotes clustering of industries but not with a purpose to facilitate that. *Sergio Boisier* wrote a chapter with the heading "Growth Poles: Are they Dead? and in that observes;

> "It is difficult to accept the proposition that a polarised developed strategy must be necessarily utilized as a development style which in turn allows the State to assume the role of arbiters in *laissez faire* context. There is no reason at all for an incompatibility between the implementation of a growth pole strategy and other types of State roles." (*)

Diversifed corporate structure now gets preference over the polarised strategy because although the growth pole strategy could induce growth in selected urban areas, its usefulness as catalytic agent of socio-economic change in limited. Growth pole strategy and balanced regional development are as contradictory as *'boiling-icecream.*

Some regional analysis have drawn a distinction between 'climate' and 'space. They criticise that 'space' was neglected by economists. The facts are that 'climate' and 'space' cannot exist without each other. It is not correct to say that economists took into account the 'economic climate' only. Climate is always studies with reference to real space and not ethereal regions. The rural economy has climate as well as space and the same is true about the urban economy. Inter-action takes place both in the space and in the climate. Differences in the real resources and real efforts gave rise to imbalances. Imbalances emerged *despite* economists and *not because* of the economists.

Because of the increasing dissatisfaction with the inequalities of income, the planners find it difficult to continue to support the growth pole strategy, though *the guide-post strategy of the growth poles gives us an idea*

(*) Chapter 4 in "National Development and Regional Policy" Edited by B. Pranlilla. Maruzcn Asia; For and on behalf of the UN Centre for Regional Development, Nagoya, Japan.

about how to weld together the 'location theory', 'the central place theory' and the 'theory of hierarchy of settlements and functions'.

Some regional analysts have asserted that *"effective demand will not be created unless it is created through locational concentration'!* and even go so far as to criticise the entire Keynesian Economics.

This is not correct because lack of effective demand is a problem associated with certain categories of persons (rich persons have declining marginal propensity to consume while the poor persons have lack of purchasing power due to chronic under-employment or unemployment). In the same space there are multi-millionnaires and paupers. Poverty and lack of purchasing power are not space related but person-related and sectoral activities-related.

Conclusion: Growth poles emerged in the past or were developed in the past and may continue to emerge in future or may be promoted in future. Whether growth poles secure development with justice of equitable distribution and the development of hinterland will depend upon circumstances. The greatest hinderance in transmitting development to the hinterland comes from the shortage of real resources and real efforts. The growth pole theory is essentially a theory of the "comparative advantage" and certain frictions have to be overcome if growth poles are also to serve the instruments of economic welfare. The transmission lines for the spread effects have to be strong. If centres of great industries and commerce have a diversified package of propulsive industries, clustering can transmit growth impulses to the hinterland in a satisfactory manner, but probably with active assistance of the government.

23

Growth Centres, Growth Points and Growth Foci

Growth Centres

A growth centre is a locational concept and it does not involve the selection of related industries— as in the 'growth' pole. The growth centre development entails the concentration of investment in the chosen location where economies of urbanisation are promoted to attract more industries. As was seen earlier, the growth pole policy necessitates the development of a selected industrial focus composed of propulsive firms from leading industries; the intention being to foster economies of localisation.

As industry must be localized, a 'growth pole policy' will inevitably result in a growth centre and the generation of the resultant economies of urbanisation. However, this is not necessarily true in the reverse : a growth centre policy may not lead to the development of a growth pole of linked industries. Yet, it is precisely what is needed through planning. Growth centres should have growth poles if not for the development of a very big region, then for as big area around it as possible.

Growth pole explanation is about regional structure while the growth centre policy is about intra-regional imbalance. The basic idea is that growth pole and/or growth centre should promote such economic development that is acceptable from socio-political and ethico-psychological stand points also. Growth poles and growth centres should improve the physical quality of life of the people in the entire space and should reduce inequalities.

There can be growth centres with assortment of industries —a nucleus from which growth could spread into the rest of the region. In addition, development in a limited number of growth centres should also bring rural transformation.

Big industrial estates can become *active* growth centres — the *passive* being those where growth is localised or enclaved and not transmitted. New active growth centres in depressed regions become very necessary for the concentration of infrastructure facilities which facilitate new manufacturing units and agro-based industries.

As a result of the disillusionment with the growth pole model, the growth centre approach was conceived as an alternative strategy. A growth centre can be a district HQ in a multi-level planning. It is not necessary that the industries of the growth centre should be capital intensive involving lumpy investment. A growth centre can have industries based on agricultural raw materials and/or for supplying manufactured goods needed for the agricultural economy. If an urban centre can provide market outlets for the produce of the hinterland and if it supplies vital inputs of development to the rural sector, the centre can be an ideal growth centre. *Growth centres can be much more decentralized than the growth poles.* It is true that decentralisation leads to gradual centralisation at many points and centralisation at different points leads to gradual decentralisation, but it has *now* become imperative that benefits of growth should be available on decentralised basis to the interior areas.

Urban centres already exist and they can be *converted into growth centres* if better linkages are developed with the hinterland. Complementary economic activities can be made to converge at a centre. Growth centres can be developed through planning for the locational convergence of activities in their compatible combination. However, *any geographical agglomeration of activities is not automatically developmental.* There has to be appropriate mix of activities with strong linkages with the economy of the hinterland.

If some large villages and towns can serve the hinterlands with services and become nodal points of transportation network *and have various types of local-resourcess-based industries,* they can become growth centres. A growth centre should provide basic infrastructure, functions, and facilities for the *commercial* agriculture. Growth centres should create such conditions that distress migration from rural areas is arrested.

The growth centre strategy was followed by erstwhile socialist countries as also by many developing countries. Even countries like France, Italy or India had their own versions of growth centres. Under the Community Development Programme, the block head-quarter was intended to be growth centre for rural development Under the new industrial policy of India, the district industrial centre was is to facilitate emergence of the industrial growth centres in each district. We can definitely say that cities like Calcutta, (Kolkata) Bombay (Mumbai) Kanpur or Madras (Chennai) were conforming to the growth poles hypothesis but they failed to develop the hinterland. Infact not only shanty towns emerged in and around these centres but they became examples of unbearable dualism vis-a-vis their hinterland.

A growth centre provides higher order services needed by the people and will have a dominant position in the patterns of interaction. A growth centre is normally an urban centre capable of promoting growth in rural hinterland which can provide finance, marketing, transport, communications, extension, medical, educational, training and other facilities to the people of the hinterland.

Growth centres can have industries of the public, private, joint and cooperative sectors and there can be their ancillaries also. There are principal industries and supplementary and complementary industries. Ancillary industries of the public or private sector industries supply essential components or other materials. Automobile industries buy tyres and tubes, or nuts and bolts (according to their specifications) from ancillary industries. In India many ancillaries of the public sector units were started by politically influential parties who could get permission for the same. They enjoyed monopoly to supply certain things to the public sector units, often at the inflated prices. It was also observed that while the main units were nearly in the red, the ancillaries earned fabulous profits. Now the ancillaries of many public sector units have to compete with others for supplying materials/parts to the main units at competitive prices.

A growth centre must have good-sized industries and/ or many small scale thriving units to become growth centre. In India the structure of industries did not conform to the needs of the rural people. The vertical hierarchy of (a) growth foci/central village, (b) service centres, (c) growth points, (d) growth centres and (e) growth poles did not develop diversified industries needed for the development of the primary sector, the rural areas and the people of the hinterland. Instead of supplementing the traditional occupational skills and crafts, the industries of the growth centres often supplanted them.

In most cases around the growth centres, the prime agricultural land got converted into the residential/industrial land. The villagers were relegated to the interior areas. Many agriculturists became mere landless labourers. Thus many so-called growth centres became 'suction pumps' of the poor people of rural hinterland—but not providing decent employment or incomes. *A growth centre has to act as guide post of development for the hinterland. Housing complex are eating away agricultural land.*

Locations

Conceptually, the growth point and the central places are *not* the same. Central places are numerous and arranged in a hierarchy, whereas there will be very few growth points. *Some economists treat growth points and growth poles as one and the same thing,* but most writers in India treat growth point as a lower order growth centre.

In the words of *Richardson:*

> "Growth point theory implicitly draws upon the export base concept but gives it a spatial dimension, since the key industries are located at the growth point whereas supplying industries, labour, raw materials and dependent services may be dispersed over the zone of influence".

A growth point has its 'zone of influence, while a central place has a 'complementary region'. A growth point sustains the regions, while the central place is sustained by its region. The polarisation flows will be more intense and more varied in character around a growth point than around a central place where the flows consist mainly of commuting for shopping, leisure and other services."

In the opinion of Richardson, growth point is the central labour market where the factors of production move from the surrounding zone which is the factor catchment market. As such, while the income is generated at the growth point, it accrues to other areas.

All growth points should be able to export from their production mix so as to have a high export base multiplier.

There are critical minimum and maximum sizes of the growth point and below and above these limits, diseconomies exceed the economies.

According to Richardson, the 'growth point concept represents a link between the naturally evolved structure of nodal regions and physical and regional planning'.

Propounders of the growth point hypothesis believe that concentrations arranged in a hierarchy and agglomerations resulting from the operation of market forces bring socio-economic benefits. These agglomerations and concentrations are sources of origin of the external economies and are sustained by them. However, if the main centres are over large, then diseconomiess can be generated by them. It will then be necessary that new growth points be developed.

There are 'natural' growth points as well as 'promoted' growth points. The former will have high order central place characteristics. In the latter, they can be created. Socio-economic and technological external economies partly depend upon the natural conditions and partly up on the efforts under the sponsored growth strategy. However, the stress on technical inter-relationships and agglomeration economics suggests a kinship with Isard's 'industrial complex analysis'.

Factors which promote localisation of industries become necessary for developing a growth point/centre. New growth points become necessary to relieve the congestion of the growth points/poles. The government has a big role to play in developing the growth points. In the words of *Richard S. Thoman:*

> "Practically, growth point policy may well involve choices by governments as to which nodes in an existing or potential network can best fulfil selected sectoral objectives. Implementation of these choices

> involves, in large and increasing measures, continuing government policy, and not sporadic, single-incentive actions. Governments therefore are increasingly in a position to change the functions of one or more nodes in an urban network —in other words, to change growth point functions and implications of such nodes. Whether for spatial stimulation, spatial structuring, or other aspects of government policy, growth points can be those places selected from an existing or potential urban network for specified reasons and purposes".

Growth Foci

Shri VLS Prakasa Rao and Shri RP Mishra advanced the concept of 'growth foci'. This concept was derived from the growth pole theory of Perroux and Boudeville. According to *RP Mishra*

> "The growth pole theory has proved to be inapplicable to developing countries marked with dual economies. The growth poles transplanted in such economies have remained poles without a deeply rooted broad base. The propulsive industries located in the poles have failed to diffuse development in the hinterland. To suit the socio-economic conditions of the developing countries, the growth pole theory has been modified and the concept of system of growth foci has been evolved. In a very limited way the concept has been accepted in several developing countries as a tool to develop backward areas and regions while at the same time integrate the traditional and modern sectors of the economy into a single whole".

RP Mishra suggests a *six-tier growth foci.*

At the highest level, there is to be a growth *pole* and at the lowest level a group of villages and hamlets. It seems that in his scheme the first five tier setup transmits growth impulses These six tiers are :

(p. 250 in Regional Planning and National Development. Ed. by RP Mishra, D V Urs and VK Natraj).

1. Growth Poles.
2. Growth Centres.
3. Growth Points.
4. Service Centres.
5. Central Villages.
6. Villages and hamlets.

It should be acknowledged that M/s Rao and Mishra have removed the confused interpretation of the words 'poles', 'centres', and 'points'.

Not only that their six-tier setup is theoretically sound but practical also. This six-tier state of affairs can be found in real life and/or can be planned as well. It is a sound workable Scheme for regional analysis as well as for the national and regional planners.

The growth foci structure can provide/provides necessary complementarities between (a) nodes, (b) linkages, and (c) hinterland, which are three basic, elements which enter into the organisation of space.

Nodes are the central places connected by transport, communication and other linkages. Since nodes differ in sizes and influence, the sizes and nature of the hinterlands also differ. Larger nodes have better linkages and have specialized functions. (For example, though medical colleges may exist at several places, there may be only a few experts who can repair a broken jaw and face bones). Larger nodes have bigger area of influence, also known *as first order hinterlands.* One does not travel from a very distant area to a very big nodal point unless one is in need for a very special commodity or service. The smaller nodes have smaller hinterlands and people from villages may

(p. 175: Regional Planning and National Development: Ed. RP Mishra in a paper on Regional Planning in Iran by RP Mishra himself).

travel to a nearby town to buy just ordinary things of life. *In multi-level planning there are attempts to re-organise the spatial economy by restructuring the nodes, linkages and the hinterlands, so that the processes of centralised concentration gives way to decentralised concentration of human activities.* The restructured organisation can be referred to as spatial framework for multi-level planning.

This hybrid concept (which seeks to incorporate something of Perroux's growth pole theory, Christaller's theory of hierarchy of central places, and Friedman's concept of city as an articulator and mobilizer of the periphery's resources in a process of transition) can serve the needs of socio-economic multi-level planning in less developed countries.

According to Prakasa Rao and RP Mishra, poles lead to agglomeration and dualism. They ignore the rural needs and promote the urban ethos. The growth nodes or poles do not trigger off impulses of development to rural areas nor receive type of support that they should get from the rural areas. The trickle-downism thesis has not proved to be correct and growth poles remain rootless and without moorings with the economy of the hinterland. It has been seen that in a country like India, their backwash effects exceed their spread effects and thus the linkages remain weak.

If in the pre-independence India, the growth poles followed the principle of 'comparative advantage', in the post-Independence period "funds followed flag" — constituencies of important politicians were favoured more in terms of investment. Public sector projects were located not for the best interests of all and 'administration' was considered sufficient in place of 'management'. Rural regions remained neglected. Infact all the seven-sister States of the East remained neglected. The dysfunctional organisation of the secondary sector became exploitative of the rural areas, poor people and the primary sector.

There is to be sectoral integration. Secondary sector should first produce those outputs which are inputs for the development of agriculture and the tertiary sector, *and* the basic goods of mass consumption. If that happens then agriculture will supply more goods of consumption (wage pressure in the secondary sector will remain low), and basic raw materials for several industries. The rural people will have enough purchasing power to increase their liability (i.e, will purchase from them) towards the other two sectors and all the three sectors can develop in juxtaposition. Several centres which supply inputs of development corresponding to the socio-cultural ethos of the people also become necessary. *These centres are generally there; they are to be developed to be functional for providing development inputs to the hinterland's sectors and people.*

Growth foci can provide a network of basic and non-basic industries. *Growth foci is not a centre only but the entire set of conditions of development. It has to provide facilities and functions of development as also the 'extension cultural and social atmosphere' The five-tier upper hierarchy can provide facilities of diffusion of technology, information and infact the culture of materialism.*

The arrangement can be/should be as under :

1.	Cluster of villages	central village
2.	Micro-minor region	service centre
3.	Micro region : sub-regional	growth point
4.	Meso region	growth centre
5.	Macro region	growth pole

The total number of growth foci can depend upon several factors e.g., the size of the country, the dispersal of population in villages, the resource situation and administrative factors. *Growth foci arrangement can have the innovative role of the growth pole and service provisions role of the central places.* Rao and Mishra conceived that central villages, service towns, market towns, growth points, growth centres and growth poles are all part of the system of growth foci. The scheme of hierarchal levels can be put as under, according to Rao and Mishra.

1. *Central village :* This would be one which can serve 6 villages and about 6000 population with marketing, service, recreational, and socio cultural interaction functions..
2. *Service centre :* It can be a small town of population of 5000 or so. It should be able to serve 5 central villages i.e. population of about 30000. Such a centre (in the nature of the administration in India), an extension officer, para medical staff, teachers and village level worker. It will have various types of shops for multifarious primary needs.
3. Growth point : This will again serve 5 service centres, thus a population of 1.5 lakhs or so. This growth point can itself have a population of about 10000 to 50000. They will have good connectivity with the district head quarters. A sub-divisional office or a Tehsil headquarter can fit in with this. The centre will assume agro-industrial character and will have close links with the sister growth points also. Considerable strength can be found in the activities relating to the production, supply of inputs, marketing, processing, service functions etc.
4. *Growth centres :* They can be district head-quarters or other big towns. They can have population ranging from 50000 to 5,00,000. Each growth centre can look after the growth needs of 12 lakh or more population. Growth centres should have somewhat strong industrial base also. This is possible only if

the industrialisation follows a decentralised pattern.

Ideal growth centres are those which can act as counter-magnets to the large urban centres. Already people in these cities are in jitters because of the shortage of housing units, high degree of pollution and a lot of time involved in commuting distances—to speak nothing about the high cost of living and leading a life where personal relations are at a discount. This centre should have facilities of comprehensive banking, higher education (college level), good medical infrastructure, wholesale supplies, storage, collection etc.; ánd comprehensive extension services for the agricultural, rural and agro-industrial development.

5. *Growth poles :* Capital cities and some very important district headquarters can act as growth poles. In Madhya Pradesh, for example, Bhopal, Indore, Satna, Ujjain, Ratlam, Gwalior, Jabalpur etc., can become growth poles. A growth pole in a small state can cover the entire State.

One cannot but agree with M/S Rao and Mishra that such hierachy exists and needs to be strengthened and where it does not, it should be brought into existence.

With government support and with natural course (market mechanism) vertical and horizontal linkages can get strengthened. The role of the government becomes important in that *it can integrate functions over the space in shorter time period.*

Slowly, functions of higher order will gel located in the settlements of lower order and that is how some rural centres become *urban* centres. However, *every growth point cannot become a growth pole.* Rao and Mishra even calculated that Indian needs 30 growth poles and 4000 growth points, with each district becoming the growth centre. These centres are not be *established* but *developed and strengthened.* There is nothing which prevents some higher order functions/ facilities being available in settlements of lower order (For example, a good bone hospital in Madhya Pradesh is located in an interior village in Betul district —at Padar). Time cannot obliterate the functional and spatial hierarchy. *The tasks of regional planning are subservient to the requirements and possibilities in national planning. Ultimately there has to be vertical and horizontal integration of the development of sectors, regions and groups of persons. Vested interest groups will always come in the way of greater equalisation and all the labour and luck are necessary to promote growth, and efficiency and remove inequalities.*

In the growth foci structure, both the centrifugal and centripetal economic linkages can get promoted to increase the economic welfare in the country. Motivation for growth can also become infectious. If the growth foci structure is developed, then the growth pole hypothesis and central place theories get social content and economic practicability.

Decentralised growth will improve the physical quality of life of the people. Connectivity will not be in the narrow sense of transport and communications efficiency but also in terms of social interaction. Not material inputs of development but the psychic inputs of development will also get diffused. In due course of time both real and financial resources will be generated for complementary development.

In this system the growth pole should act as a primate city also of a macro-region. In the growth pole area we can say that the primary activities are not taken up. Even secondary functions are of less importance in comparison to the tertiary sector functions. *Quaternary activities* such as banking, administrative, marketing, cultural facilities dominate.

Growth centres in such a scheme are *essentially industrial centres* producing goods for the national and regional markets. According to the scheme of things suggested by RP Mishra, they may be based on regional or extra-regional resources. The tertiary activities will match the requirements of regional population. In the hinterland of a growth pole where there can be several growth centres, the number would depend upon the resources available and regional development needs. Infact, the growth centres should *relieve the growth poles from the concentration of secondary activities.* The growth centres should diffuse industrial production to the areas lagging in development. *A growth centre can have agro-based industries* in a dynamic agricultural/ plantation area.

A growth point is conceived to be a satellite of a growth centre. There would be several growth points in the meso-region served by a growth centre. A growth point should specialize in processing and tertiary functions.

A service centre has to provide lower order service facilities to the villagers while the central village should have most elementary basic lower order facilities.

24

Central Functions: Centrality Score

APPOGGIATURA

(A Short Note Before a Long One)

Economic development has always to the benefits of all, more so of the poor. This strategy was given various names:

A. Growth with economic welfare.

B. Growth and social justice.

C. Growth with social justice

D. Development with productive efficiency and distributive justice.

E. Growth that percolates down to the poorest.

F. Growth that does not by-pass the poorest.

G. Growth that is inclusive..

> The essence of growth strategy is that it should benefit laggard section or the people, backward regions and under-developed sectors. Centrality score measures the richness or otherwise of the regions about the density of facilities therein the regions in comparison to other regions of we compare the region. We can also know the temporal (between two time periods) positions of the same region or regions. Both relative and absolute positions can be understood.

Growth can be on "top-down" and "bottom-up" principles centrality score measures diffusion and laws of vital function in an area usually a region, or a district or more importantly in the rural economy segments.

Nodes should develop hinterland, if lower order areas have essential functions, we can call growth being right. All space cannot become parallel i.e. of the same type. Inter-spatial and inter-personal differences shall remain higher and lower order centres will have higher and lower order functions. A village cannot have a super-speciality hospital but a medical assistance point should be nearby. Diffusion of technology, innovations, capital- investment and information will improve centrality score. The central theme of centrality score is to reduce the unbearable dichotomy of rural-urban settlements. Rural areas should have many agropolitan centres as urban areas have "metropolitan" centres.

Central functions are infrastructural facilities functional hierachy of high and lower order should percolate, so that lowest settlement has all the basic elementary functions or facilities. Centrality score is a proxy of the application of all the theories of regional economics of development.

> Hermansen, Philbrick, Hagershand, Friedmann, Guttman, and infact our planners wrote about the centrality score/ achievements.

Different functions are selected for different researches and different methods of weight assignments are used. Economist are interested in the quality of functions; geographers in the absence of functions and facility.

CENTRAL FUNCTIONS: CENTRALITY SCORE

Growth in the past revolved around the growth poles and big locational centres. Under the system of planning the main objective of growth is to develop the entire country all sectors, regions and ethnic groups. Growth in the past did not percolate to the lowest level of space and to the poorest of the poor. In 2008 "inclusive growth" was the name given to growth that does not bypass the poor. Spatial sub-systems should also get the essential functions. In the *spatial organisation* both adaptive (passive) and developmental (active) planning become necessary. According to *Hermansen* "spatial organisation is the distribution in geographical space of human activities in a certain order". Spatial organisation will not only include 'space economy' but other aspects also. Orderly 'spatial organisation' promotes economic development and it is in turn promoted by economic development. Realisation of the twin goals of 'spatial organisation' and 'economic development' will require intervention of the State in the form of active planning, However, over the long period the competitive forces of the market do create a spatial organisation which can be conducive to further national economic growth and will also ensure a proper spatial distribution of employment and realisation of the goals of efficiency (higher production) *and* equity. If one is in hurry then important functions are to be located over the sub-systems through active planning.

Most of the development inputs emanate from the cities in the form of quaternary functions and innovations. The rural areas can develop as fast as investment is made to carry these functions/innovations to the interior areas. The real, financial, technological and psychological inputs of development have to be diffused over the entire area. *We should now follow the policy* of *"top down" and also "bottom up"*. The primary, secondary and tertiary sectors and the rural and urban areas are all to be developed in a coordinated way. For this there should be territorial development complexes which can provide convergence of productive activities as well as of functions/services. In this type of spatial organisation there will be combination of the 'bottom up' and 'top down' strategies. We have seen how the growth centres and growth foci type of organisations can help in locating central functions and diffusing them optimally.

If secondary and tertiary activities are located in favoured regions while other regions are neglected, then there will be lop-sided development over the space. Many settlements particularly rural settlements will be deprived of basic necessities. Yet too much dispersal and too many *ad hoc* programmes for the "clientele development" are bound to be less productive unless they are integrated with the development of the sectors. The real goods will be in shortage while purchasing power will be generated and the result will be inflation. *While some regional analysts have emphasised that there should be spatial dimension of the sectoral plans, economists emphasise that there should be sectoral integration of the spatial and clientele development programmes.*

There is theory of area functional organisation also, developed by AK Philbrick. This is the theory of nested hierarchy i.e., of lower order functions and higher order functions existing simultaneously at the higher order centres. *Internal functions* are directed from the higher order centres to the lower order centres in the *area called 'internal area , which is interdependent hinterland.* External functions follow the opposite direction. Thus there is a node, an internal area and an external area. Nodes are circled by the internal area. The *external area of organisation consists of all inter-connections and linkages of the nodes and its region to larger nodes and their regions.*

In between the areas there are *parallel* (of similar nature) relationships as also *hierarchial* relationships. Philbrick presented a seven-fold hierarchy of nodes to show the organisation of nested functions. Nodes of the first to third hierarchial levels were designated by him as the '*focal places*' while the nodes from fourth to seventh were designated as '*central places*'.

1. *First order node:* Lowest level function or common consumption. It is the smallest nodal region comprising of the uniform areas centred around the first, order node.
2. *Second order uniform area* is the grouping of many contiguous farms. The village is a node here and is of second order and here retail trade facilities are available.
3. *When the second order continuous nodal areas are grouped, they form a third order uniform area.* Wholesale trade can be a facility available here.
4. *A spatial uniformed by a group of third order nodal region becomes a fourth order uniform area.* The centre here becomes the fourth order node and the area around it becomes the fourth order nodal region. Here the transhipment facilities are available.
5. *If contiguous fourth order regions are grouped with one fifth order centre,* then the total influence area will be fifth order region. Greater exchange is the characteristic of such a region.

6 & 7. The adding up process goes on to make the sixth and seventh order nodal centres and their regions. Each high order region encompasses the previous order regions. The seventh order centre is the top on the ladder.

Thus each uniform area consists of a cluster of nodal regions of next lower level and in the similar way each nodal region is constituted by a group of contiguous uniform areas connected with a node.

Hagerstrand wanted diffusion of advanced technology embodying innovation over the space for better space organisation. Ideas and innovations should be transmitted from the higher order centres to the lower order centres and that alone can ensure growth percolating to the rural areas. The diffusion model assumes that there its a 'seller' of the innovation and that there is a 'receiver' of the same!, as simple as that. *The diffusion of innovation is treated by geographers as being a function of distance the probability of a message being transmitted; declining with distance between the two individuals.* This is rather simplistic in that it ignores the fact that now innovations travel over the entire world, provided they are of immense consequence and that the diffusion of innovation is a matter of credit and investment, also not only in that line of manufacture but also in the supporting activities.

Market mechanism alone cannot be relied upon for spatial organisation and development. There is need for regional *settlement complexes with high functions,* wherein size, spacing and ordering of settlements are *determined not by the theory of central places, but some other type of centralization and decentralisation.*

Rural and urban development processes are to so intermingle as to bring socio-technological development also. These can be 'urban' centres where (i) services are available to every rural settlement within reasonable distance, and (ii) enough secondary and tertiary activities are created (which will support a large number of primary sector activities) so that employment is generated in the primary sector and also for those who become redundant in that sector as near as possible from their original places of residence and work.

Through appropriate strengthening of functions, *John Friedmann* has advocated the development of *agro-politan centres.* Urban facilities, urban mentality and urbanity are more important to be taken to villages. *City-in-the-fields* can be created in the *rural districts.* If agricultural and non-agricultural activities are dovetailed, the low income of the rural people can be raised. There will be need for linking the agropolitan districts into regional networks by building up and improving physical channels of communication among agropolitan districts and to larger towns and by regionalising certain higher order services and support activities that require a larger population base than is available within a single district. Some requirements of agropolitan centre can be as under:

(a) population between 10000 and 25000;

(b) population density of about 200 per sq, km.

(c) commuting radius between 5 and 10 km. i.e., about 1 hour distance on bi-cycle;

(d) from a town centre, the service population upto 1.5 lakh from minimum of 50000.

For developing a *cluster of villages in* a coordinated manner, it will be necessary to locate some central functions here. *Socio-economic infrastructure facilities are referred to as 'functions' by regional planners.* For a particular function of a particular order, a certain level of threshold population, area and investments are necessary. *Central functions, which are non-ubiquitous* have to be located on dispersal basis. The importance of functions and centres depends upon how sub-functions are distributed to the sub-centres from the centres. Hierarchy of functions should be pain-relieving and efficiency promoting e.g., a primary school should be so located that tiny tots do not have to travel more than 1 to 2 km, also too far to reach it or else even if the threshold population is not sufficient, a primary school should be located in a village to save the children from walking too long. Functional and settlement hierarchies should be optimally inter-related.

Scale of Functional Hierarchy and Centrality

As we know there are different level educational facilities :

primary school

middle school

high school/higher secondary school
intermediate/degree college
post graduate college;
specialized, university teaching departments/special institutional courses.

If lower level function is assigned a weight of 1 the highest order function in a hierarchy of 10 can be assigned a weight of 10.

Thus depending upon the level and extent of functions/ facilities available at a centre, the total number of the weights of the functions can be added up to compare the strength of the centre.

More functions of higher order make a place more important, or atleast there should be larger number or higher quality functions. *Thus, the level of functional hierarchy becomes a decisive part of the whole question of centrality.*

Spatial Organisation

Through spatial organisation, a desirable inter-connectedness interdcpendency is promoted for the desirable interaction over a space. Spatial linkages and interaction are secured between the focal point and the complementary regions. Central places are the focal points; centrifugal and centripetal linkages are interaction; and area of connectivity and dependency is complementary region. There is a hierarchy of the nodes and there is movement of manpower, materials and services in the region. As we have seen, the following theories constitute an integral part of the theory of spatial organisation :

(a) theory of agricultural location;
(b) theory of the location of centres;
(c) theory of industrial location;
(d) theory of the location of functions and tertiary sector.

(e) the central place theories of Christaller and Losch

(f) growth pole theory;

(g) theory of growth centres and foci; [including the variants of these theories]

(h) theory of cumulative causation; and

(i) theory of diffusion of technology innovations over the space,

(j) the gravity models.

The location aspects, the production (growth) aspects, the diffusion and movement aspects and the distributional aspects of the primary, secondary and tertiary sectors are studied with reference to space in the economics of spatial organisation.

There is a spatial structure which is changed through spatial 'planning' to achieve a desired spatial 'reorganisation from hybrid organisation. Spatial planning is decentralised: it is location of secondary and tertiary activities over the space. Allocation of real and financial resources is done accordingly. *It is selecting places for the activities and activities for the places.* A functionally coherent and efficient hierarchical strategy of putting men and activities in developing state, is to be evolved. *However, if spatial integration is without sectoral (functional relationship, there cannot be 'integrated' areal planning.*

GUTTMAN METHOD OF SHOWING FUNCTIONAL HIERACHY

There are several functions and facilities out of which some important ones are selected and they are ranked according to a higher or lower degree of complexity in the dimension.

- Some institutions are present (or absent) in an

area and they provide services at the settlements. They determine the hierarchies of settlement.

- Settlements are listed on the left side of the table of analysis in order of their population.
- At the right side in the rows can be shown the functions.
- The number of each function can be indicated in the appropriate column and separate totals for various types and numbers of functions can be shown against each settlement.
- At the bottom of the table, the number of places having each type of functions is indicated in the appropriate column and the total number of units of each functions is also given in each column.
- In the extreme right hand side of the table all settlements are ranked in order of total number of units of various functions given in the preceding column.
- The place with the highest number of functions gets the first rank. At the bottom of the table are given functions which are available at different places in different quantities i.e., we can find out which function is most available or which function is least available.
- After giving suitable ranks to the settlements and to the functions, *a final table* can be prepared showing the hierarchy of settlements as well as functions in the planning area.

The selection of functions should be done after careful considerations. Sometimes the "central" functions can be too few or too erratic in their distribution. In a highly developed area, this method may not be suitable because of the absence of some crucial functions.

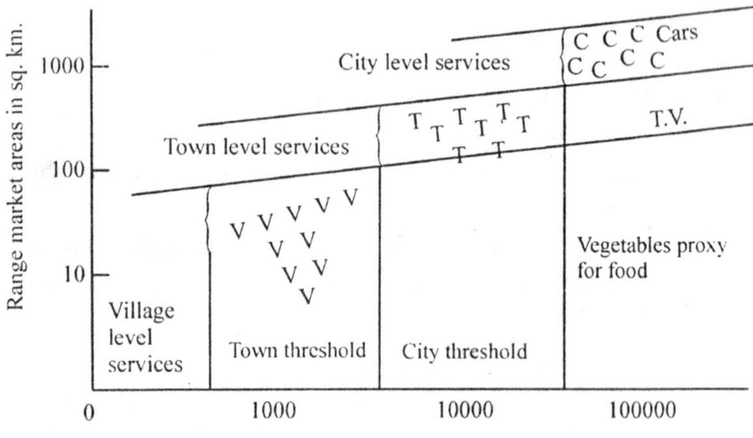

Fig. 1

POPULATION CHARACTERISTICS; FUNCTIONS RANKING AND DETERMINING FUNCTIONAL HIERARCHY

As different, functions differ in importance, they are to be assigned weights. There can be two methods.

First Method

In the first method, the weight of the function is determined by dividing the total number of settlements by the total number of functions existing in the area. If there are 600 settlements and 300 primary schools, then the weight of the primary school is 600 ÷ 300 = 2, Similarly if there are 60 junior schools and 10 higher secondary schools, then their weights are 600 ÷ 60 = 10 and 600 ÷ 10 = 60 respectively Similarly if:

1. Health centre 1 for 500 = 500 ÷ 1 = 500
2. Small post office 50 in 500 settlements = 500 ÷ 50 = 10.

Second Method

All settlements are listed in an ascending order of populations. All functions located per settlement are shown against each of them. The minimum population at which the function appears for the first time is designated *as population threshold or entrypoint.* After a certain level of population is reached, a function may be found in each and every village e.g., now a primary school will most certainly be found in a village of population of 1000. There can be some villages of the same population where the same function may or may not be found. The population at which a particular function is definitely found is designated as *'saturation point'.* The difference between the entry point and the saturation point is designated as 'entry zone'.

From these the median population threshold (MPT) can be calculated. *(Infact mode would have been quite representative).* MPT can also be obtained graphically by plotting the number of settlements below a certain population level which have the function and the number of settlements above this population level where the function is absent. MPT lies in the entry zone, 50% villages above it have the function; and 50% villages below it do not have the function.

'The relative weights can be calculated as under:

$$\frac{\text{MPT of the nth function}}{\text{MPT of the lowest function}}$$

After assigning the weights this way, the functions can be arranged in an ascending order of their values. From this list it is possible to identify some functions of which weights within the group have less variance while among the groups they have far greater variance. These groups indicate different levels at which these functions are being offered and these are designed as lower, middle order or high order functions, as the case may be. The functional hierarchy is determined, on the basis of these levels.

If a function is available at low threshold of population it is a lower order function and the highest order function is one which is available at one or two places of very high population. The rank of an activity can be defined as its order of entry in terms of population. Many a times, only a special type of activity is chosen and the hierarchy of the strength of its functions is taken into account e.g., type of transport facilities ranging from bullock cart facility to supersonics on international routes; or various degrees of medical services available and so on. Different researchers can, therefore, take different set of functions as being relevant for the type of study they want to undertake. For the studies about the basic needs and minimum physical quality of life are concerned, the functions to be taken will belong to one set of activities. If a study is about the growth centres of high order, different sets of functions will be chosen. For the study of the hierarchy of settlements, functions of all the three/four [primary, secondary, tertiary and quaternary sectors] have to be chosen. The minimum population at which a function enters becomes *unsatisfactory* basis when two functions with sufficiently distant entry points are still grouped in one population size class and hence are to be allocated identical central score value, [one function enters at population of 250; another at 750 but the population group is 250-750]. Besides a function is used by the people from settlements other than the one in which it is located. Some writers, therefore, take the MPT and decide about the functional hierarchy. In some cases the importance of the function is too apparent to need devising some method of ranking e.g., primary versus upgraded health centres. Some researchers have tried to assign weights with reference to the entry point population *plus* population served around, which may be subjectively allocated to different function points.

> *Centrality is the collective attractive power of all the central functions present in a centre. The measurement of centrality, therefore, implies a carefully considered list of central functions. From a wide range of functions, some functions are to be selected which should fit in with the topic of the research. The relative importance of the functions will also differ according to the purpose of study e.g., for one purpose education of girls may be important (fertility) but for agricultural yields education of girls is not of the same significance. Someone will always be there to charge that functions have been picked up arbitrarily and subjectively. Thus there is the need for a composite index.*

We can select some essential functions and then the degrees of those functions. In *education* there are (i) primary schools, (ii) middle schools, (iii) higher secondary schools, (iv) degree colleges and (v) universities. To be very precise there will also crop up a question whether well managed "English Medium Public Higher Secondary School" deserves the same weight as the "ordinary one" ? In the field *of medical facilities* there are (i) subsidiary health centres, (ii) primary health centres, (iii) hospitals. Once again the question crops up whether private clinics deserve a higher weight or whether the presence of a trained dai and compounder deserves a weight or what about a setup in which the quality of dispensation is important? In the field of *communications* the ranked activities can relate to one man seller of postal articles, to small post office, to sub-post office to a post office. How do we assign weights to hybrid services a small post office with a single phone connection for all? Similar ranking of services is necessary in *transport services,* (private tempo service, to bus service, to railway station to air link.) Then what about the type and number of facilities? How are we going to assign weights to video-coaches versus rickety buses, which all the same carry as many passengers as there are? Is transport facility in qualitative terms more important than in quality terms? An unserved compartment which carries all with maximum possible discomforts and a compartment which carries passengers in a limited number but in a comfortable way (for which the users may have to wait) may defy relative valuation. The *much ado about the centrality of functions* becomes apparent.

An important task in calculating the centrality of functions, is to rank the functions objectively in relation to each other from the standpoint of their relative contribution to the centrality of the places in which they are located. Because of the considerations of the terrain, distance from the road or being on the roadside, availability of water etc., it is generally observed that *there existed no correlationship between settlement population and centrality.* Many researchers therefore prefer to take MPT rather than population thresholds of villages for studying the centrality of functions. Many 'researchers' have formed a "mutual rejection society" and no one seems to be satisfied with the method of measuring centrality adopted by others.

The enthusiasm of some regional analysts about assigning different weights to sub-functions and functions, and to measure the centrality is not shared by the economists in the same way. It is good to know where functions and facilities are less than necessary and where they are just right. However, the tasks of planners go much beyond that. There is a whole lot of planning to be done to find resources, to train persons to provide functions and facilities, to keep them in working order and to improve them qualitatively. Some regional analysts have gone a long way in illustrating the clustering, the central places, the area of influence etc. In their pursuit of neat cartographic illustrations they have succeeded a lot to *their* satisfaction. Economics will not be at disadvantage if their findings are made use of. However, our tasks are different.

Some regional analysts use the MPT for ranking the (i) settlements, (ii) functions and (iii) complementary areas.

There is a centre, then there are sub-centres and their areas of service. The dependent settlements are so allocated that the total population of the service centres and the dependent settlements is equal to the total population of the Centre MPT.

Many regional analysts agree with the formulations of the economists that there is greater association between population and functions than between centres and functions.

The population sizes of the central places alone are insignificant for measuring the centrality of functions; the centrality is the product of the size of tributary population of the central places. On the basis of 20 functions selected from a very low order function, the centrality can be measured thus:

Function	*Nos.*	*MPT*	*Centrality score*
1. Small shop	420	1000	1
2. Service dispensers (barbers, dhobi etc.)	395	1050	1
3. Stamp selling/dak dak disruption	266	1560	1.6
4. Primary school.	184	2260	2.3
5. Credit coop.	164	2470	2.5
6. Middle school.	143	2900	2.9
7. Bus point.	123	3380	3.4
8. Medicines shop.	111	3740	3.7
9. Revenue/development officials	110	3800	3.8
10. Public health centres	72	5690	5.7
11. Police post.	67	6200	6.2
12. Inputs stocking	60	6500	6.5
13. Higher secondary school	50	8300	8.3
14. Wholesale service	33	12580	12.6
15. Sub-post office	30	13840	13.8
16. Degree college.	18	23000	23.0

17. Telegraph & Telephones	16	24430	24.4
18. Bank	16	26000	26.0
19. Hospital	16	26000	26.0
20. Justice points.	5	30000	30
Total	2299		204.7
Mean score. 2299 ÷ 204.7 = 11.23			1123
Standard deviation.			9.6 app.

$$\frac{\text{Generality Score} \div \text{MPT of a service nation}}{\text{MPT lowest function minimum}}$$

CENTRAL PLACE HIERARCHY

Discontinuous pattern of relationship between population size and functional range, naturally involves the 'stepped' hierarchy of settlements. Different central functions require different population sizes to support and sustain them. Populations live in places and thus central places come into the picture. It is not the population of the place which matters *but the tributary population which assumes importance.* As we have seen this means that the central places will have hierarchy. While the lower order places will not have higher order functions; higher order places *can* have lower order functions also.

The hierarchial grouping of the functions based on the MPT need not correspond to the overall hierarchy of the settlements that may be obtained on the basis of composite centrality scores of settlements. This may be because of several reasons.

(A) There may be no clustering of similar level functions at the central places of the similar/corresponding sizes. The locational pattern of the functions within a area may be irrational having poor location coincidence.

(B) Some higher order settlements may not possess higher order functions and some lower order settlements may possess higher order functions.

(C) Higher order places may not have lower order functions (as expected according to -Christaller's entry requirements). Or, presence of a few higher order functions at places having no corresponding lower order functions can distort the rank order of service centres in a few cases at lower level of hierarchy. Thus centres can have functional gaps existing in them.

The hierarchy of settlements based on their composite centrality index can be more representative of the total attractive power which lies at the core of the idea of centrality. Thus one of way of depicting hierarchy of the settlements is the total attractive power of a settlement, reflected by its centrality scores supported by the number and types of functions present at the centre.

Once the hierarchy of the settlements has been established, we can find out which functions are lacking where and though it may not be possible to provide all functions everywhere, we can find out those spots where certain functions are absolutely necessary. The centres/ settlements can be arranged in various groups e.g., auxiliary central places and service centres of various orders, say, from 2 to 5. (*) Most of the service centres will be found located on road side and almost all the centres on a transport line whether a road or a path. Service centres correspond closely with the distribution and density of the population. The presence, absence and spacing of the service centres is a function of the tributary population. The central region of the district will contain a big part of the population. Slowly the distance between the inter-service centres will decline with the emergence of new centres of distribution.

The nature of distribution of central functions and services is not ubiquitous because of the differences in thresholds. There is a great variation in thresholds of a function itself at different levels of centres. Different weights are assigned to different functions at different levels. Then the functions are to be aggregated. The functions and places can be presented in a tabular form of data matrix. Functions can be shown horizontally and places in the vertically and complete data can be presented.

The weights can be assigned to different sub-functions according to their distribution among all the central places. The principle is simple : greater the scarcity, greater the importance in terms of nodality and, therefore, higher, the weightage. For example, if there are 200 centres and a particular service is found at one place only then the weight is 200. If is found at all the places then the weight is just 200 - 200 i.e., 1. The formula can be :

$$W_i = \frac{N}{F_i}$$

Where W_i is weightage to the ith sub-function;

N is *total* number of central places;

and F_i is number of central places having the function.

The composite value for that function for jth central place will be K

[*] The hierarchical pattern observed by Maithani in Pithoragarh district UP was as 1 : 2 : 8 :10: 125 : 377 : 1628. He wrote : " It *is clear that the observed hierarchy does not conform to any of the theoretical models postulated by Christaller. The K values ranged between 1 ' 1.25 to I : 11.6. To some extent the marketing and traffic principles were found approximating to the formulations of Christaller, but not the way Christaller conceived them.*

See; *Spatial Analysis in Micro Level Planning*, p. 114.

$$C_j = \sum_{1-j}^{K} W_i X_{ij}$$

Where C_j is the compositive value for the function for jth central place.

K is the total number of sub-functions under a given function.

W_i weightage to the ith sub-function.

X_{ij} value of the ith sub function in the jth central place.

In order to arrive at the settlement hierarchy a *composite functional index* is computed by listing the number of each function against the settlements and multiplying it by its weight and then adding up the values thus arrived at. This can be illustrated as under;

CF1 Villages. (Composite Function Index)

Function	*Units*	*Weights*	*CFI*
1. Shops	2	1	2 x 1 = 2
2. Primary school	3	1	3 x 1 = 3
3. Stock centre	1	25	1 x 25 = 25
4. Health centre	1	50	1 x 50 = 50
Total			80

[1] *When the CFIs of all the settlements are computed;*

[2] *The settlements are ranked in a descending order of CFI (can be ranked in ascending order also);*

[3] *From this it can be observed that the CFI may drop suddenly at some points (descending order arrangement) indicating the gaps between the functions in settlements, causing higher deviations;*

[4] *Mean of the CFI and deviations can be calculated from the data;*

[5] *The planners can note where the work is needed to be done in respect of providing essential functions i.e., the settlements and functions requiring each others complementarity can be identified.*

The settlements can be arranged thus;

Between

2000	and	1800
1800	and	1500
1500	and	1000
1000	and	800
800	and	600

and so on. It is quite possible that in a district some CFIs may not have any settlement.

25

Stage Theory of Regions

SECTION-A

Friedman's Analysis

Stage theory of region visualises economic development as process of transformation through successive stages. *The analysis of various regions or their classification is a study of regions at a point of time.*

The stage theory of region is a study of development of regions cover a period of time. Hoover, Fisher, and Friedman have made important contributions to the stage theory of region. A region gets transformed from agricultural to industrial region through successive stages, which can be listed as under;

(i) subsistence agriculture;
(ii) local specialisation based on trade;
(iii) cash crop farming;
(iv) mining and manufacturing;
(v) diversified manufacturing;
(vi) specialisation in tertiary industries for exports.

Friedman developed the stage theory of region to a highly satisfying state. Infact these stages are *based upon the stages of economic development as listed by Rostow* in his famous growth model.

Stage theory suggests that a national economy moves through its spatial organisation from its pre-industrial primitive agricultural position to a *mature industrial stage.*

To explain stages of region we have the stage theory of regional growth like the *sector theory.* Stage theory also considers regional growth as primarily an internal evolutionary process. Both theories explain the process of regional growth.

Flowing stages can be listed :

Stage I. Isolated towns and cities develop which are functionally isolated from the one another.

Stage II. A strong centre emerges surrounded by the periphery. The city gets the colonial and exploitative position. A primate city of large population develops. The ruling classes whether national or foreign usually play a leading role in developing such a city. A city centre 'sucks' more real wealth than gives to the hinterland, though there are both inflows and outflows.

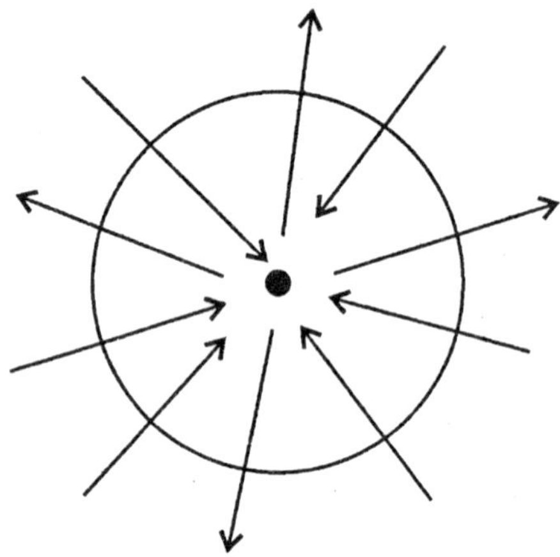

Fig. 1

Stage III. The strong centre remains but small sub-centres also emerge. They have their own peripheries. However, all these sub-centres and their peripheries maintain relationships with the primate centre. At this stage sub-national centres bring resources from their peripheral areas to the national economy. National economy starts growing rapidly.

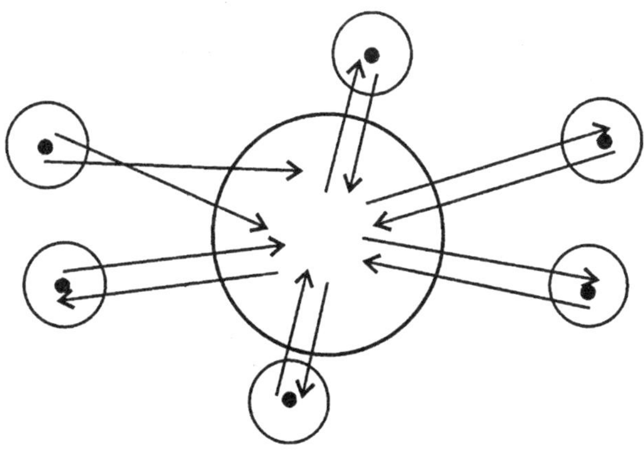

Fig. 2

Stage IV. There *is* greater inter-connection and greater interdependence. Cities get better inter-connected with towns. The national economy is completely integrated into a more homogeneous system, minimising inter-regional economic dualism. In other words, disparities (dualism) are reduced. The growth potential in the nation develops quite a lot because productive 'capacities and capabilities' develop all around. In this stage the spread-effects of growth are available in all the regions.

The stage theory of Friedman is different from the "growth pole" theory of Perroux. Friedman emphasises that national economy integrates and gets stabilized.

Perroux believed that the growth poles can destabilise

the regions. This is because the cities are inventive and keep on influencing the periphery.

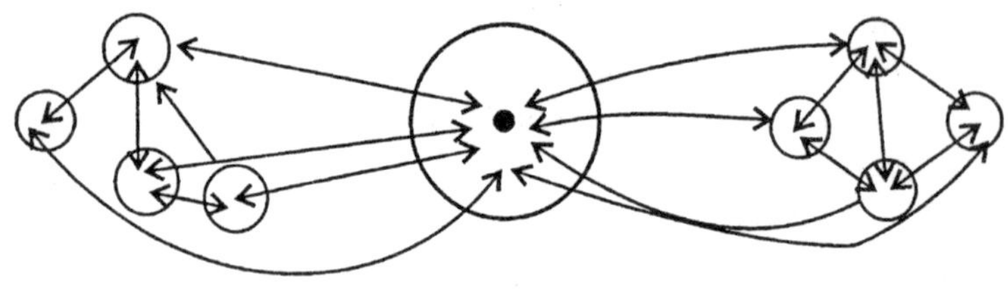

Fig. 3

Friedman emphasized that in the stages II and III, the cities give upward thrust to the periphery through resource mobilisation. In the stage IV there is percolative effect of diffusion of innovations embodied in technology over the space, which is integrative.

Space bound measures are released, horizons of activity change and mobility of people are promoted. Entrepreneurs change their plans, new choices are opened and new techniques are developed. Thus, cities become vital instruments of harnessing resources of the surrounding regions. The regional economy is integrated with the national economy.

Critical Evaluation

It can be said that cities instead of helping the regions often push the hinterland to utter dependence and stagnation and they have not yet approximated to this final stage of spatial structure in spite of the periods of their sustained economic growth. Expanding housing colonies of the city "eat away" many villages and their agriculture.

There are still backward peripheral areas. They may be progressing, but are suffering *relative* decline. In countries like India this is less relevant because non-sponsored industrialisation and urbanisation may take several decades.

There are still penniless families that eke out a precarious living.

Friedman's stage theory of regional growth is not relevant for a country like India because of the structural problems. Friedman's theory assumes that the city shall influence the surrounding hinterland. It will bring into its channel of articulation a significant area. However, if the technological gap and skills-gap were the only problems, then improvements in the transport efficiency (reduction in costs) would have realised the Friedman's effect. In practice, there are poor and backward people in the cities themselves. Hence the cities cannot transform the stagnant agricultural regions because of frictional and structural rigidities. Political leaders from depressed ethnic groups, do nothing for their development.

Appreciation

Friedman's thesis emphasises that an integrated city system is intimately related as a cause as well as an effect, to the process of economic development. It promotes development in the hinterland and in turn gets developed because of the hinterland.

While Perroux emphasized the growth pole theory, Christaller emphasised the 'central place theory', Friedman presented the city as an articulator and mobiliser of the resources of the periphery. All these writers emphasised the role of the central place.

There are, however, doubts whether a centre is also a growth pole or whether the city exercises the centripetal influence on the periphery.

Friedman synthesised the regional economic development process in the following six catch-points.

(i) regional economy is open to external change and there are internal changes also.

(ii) the export sector of the region brings growth of the residentiary sector,

(iii) apart from economic considerations the socio-cultural considerations also determine the regional income and employment pattern;

(iv) regional economic growth may be regarded as a problem in the location of firms;

(v) Economic growth tends to occur in the matrix of urban regions, it is through this matrix that the evolving space economy is organised and;

(vi) there is progressive integration of sectors and activities over a long period.

SECTION-B

Clark Fisher on Stages

In the analysis made by Clark and Fisher, stage theory of region is an extension of the sectors theory of region THEIR WRITINGS WERE ON NATIONAL INCOME GENERATION.

Sector Theory of Regions

This theory emphasizes that the internal factors of growth bring development. Fisher emphasise that as there is development, the relative importance of agriculture will decline.

Agriculture will produce greater output, its productivity will rise and its marketable surpluses will rise, it will provide greater income per hectare to the agriculturists, but the share in the national income will go down. The share of the agricultural sector in the total employment will also go down. As improved technology is applied to agriculture, fewer persons can produce the same outputs and some persons can become redundant. These persons can migrate or can be taken to the capitalist/industrialist sector where they will not and should not demand high wages. It is the secondary sector which provides tools, machines and techniques of new technology, and the service sector which provides the extension facilities (expert know-how). Agriculture develops and only genuinely redundant manpower will go to the urban areas. Those who remain in agriculture shall contribute more because they are using upgraded technology and those who leave for getting works in the secondary and tertiary sectors will also be more productively employed, compared to their employment in the rural sector.

There will be re-allocation of resources. There will be new division of labour and specialisation. *Thus when all sectors get developed in a balanced way ultimately, all regions will also become developed. This is the essence of the inter-action between the stage theory and the sector theory.*

SECTION-C

Hoover-Fisher-Clark's States

Like the sector theory, their stage theory also suggests that *"growth is an internal evolutionary process"*. The stage theory visualises economic development as a process of change or transformation through successive stages. Both the sector and the stage theories of development were developed as complementary to each other.

These writers have conceived five stages of regional development:

Stage I

In this stage the location of natural resources decide the type of agricultural activities. Though agriculture remains in the subsistence stage, there is self-sufficiency because of the low population pressure and low levels of demand. Investment, output and trade remain low. Techniques of production are naturally primitive, but the village 'self-sufficiency' is there for the reasons listed above — there are not many people and not many demands. It is not that all persons produce everything they need, but rudimentary barter serves the purpose. It is the economy of *real production, real exchange, real distribution and real consumption.* In this first stage of evolution, people are rather inert and ignorant and smugly satisfied.

Stage II

Transport systems develop and specialisation also develops as a consequence; or, we can put it the other way round. Simple techniques start being used in the village agriculture and tiny manufacturing sector. People can forge rudimentary tools, which, however, remain simple. Now the people consume not only what they find but what they grow, and grow better, including the commercial crops. Economy becomes monetised as specialisation leads to trade and required transport facilities which are there. All reinforce each other.

Stage III

In this stage, there is greater inter-regional trade which leads to great regional specialisation. Further diversification is the hallmark of this stage. All participants in the economy try to produce outputs which are much more surplus to their requirements so that they can sell them in the market, acquire purchasing power, and purchase goods and services produced by others. Primary sector activities become quite diversified e.g., agriculture, commercial cropping dairying, animal husbandry, pisciculture, sericulture, poultry, mining etc. *A few centres of trade and commerce, social-cultural interaction, industrial development, government etc.,* develop in the space and they provide further diversification facilities to the rural areas. Diversification of activities in rural areas feeds the diversification in the cities.

Stage IV

Increasing population and diminishing returns in agriculture, force the region to industrialise with greater application of the modern technology available. From agro-based industries to heavy industries, there can be several intermediate-goods industries also. Even the real resource application gets diverted to the secondary sector in aggregative as well as relative terms. Industrialisation is accompanied by urbanisation of several centres. The number of size of the firms increases and the *region experiences both the 'economies of scale' and 'economies of scope'.* The agriculturists also start using inputs from the secondary and tertiary sectors on a wider and large scale and they also start using consumer goods of industrial origin in a routine way, presuming that the growth pattern will not give rise to highly skewed income distribution pattern.

Stage V

In this final stage, the tertiary industry also starts exporting services e.g., banks can take up foreign business, insurance companies can insure people and goods in other countries, or firms may extend service facilities in foreign countries. The region comes to a position that capital, manpower (skilled also), and specialist can be 'exported' to foreign countries. There are fundamental changes in the organisation, socio cultural setup, industrialisation, diversification, and standard of living, employment and income of the region.

SECTION-D

Critical Evaluation of the 'Sector Theory and Stages Theory' of Regional Growth

If one wants to find fault with the theories, we can criticise both the approaches viz., the 'stage theory of regional growth' and 'sector theory of regional growth'. Two States of India do not conform to any theory viz. ,

Punjab and Bihar. Punjab has its own number industries but they are no where compared to Bihar where heavy industries dominate the industrial scene of not only the State but also of the country. Punjab has highly commercialised agriculture and with its contribution ranks first in the country in terms of per capita outputs and incomes. Bihar, on the contrary, ranks very low in respect of many socio-economic indicators of growth. Here the sector theory proves itself wrong because despite development of the secondary and tertiary sectors, the rural-side is the quite placid, relatively speaking. If we find lush tracts of high productivity agriculture, we also find that the fields are owned by the big landlords, land reforms notwithstanding. The per capita income and physical quality of life of crores of Biharies are very low. On the contrary, the Punjab villages are getting a look of the small towns and the people of rural areas have become urban and their consumption habits are like that of urban people.

The sector *theory implicitly asserts that the contribution of the secondary sector should be or would be higher than that of the tertiary sector*. In most of the States of India the share of the tertiary sector has grown at a rate higher than that of the secondary sector. There are three possible explanations: (i) industrial outputs are suppressed so that various types of taxes can be avoided; (ii) the backlog of infrastructure development is so high that there is vast scope of investment in that sector, and (iii) various government programmes too ignore the real side of the economy and concentrate more on tertiary sector. (India's official machinery, police and military expenditure (though necessary because of the hostile neighbour), and spending on various *ad hoc* programmes is inflationary and thus the so-called 'contribution' of the tertiary sector goes up.

It will be difficult to believe the hypothesis of the stage theory that "endogenous factors bring the growth of the region". Now a days growth and development in a backward region cannot be promoted unless the growth is "sponsored i.e., exogenous transfers by way of financial and real grants, subsidies, and investment are forthcoming that too backed by extension facilities from the skilled manpower.

Sector and Stage theories both prove that in the end there will be versatile and multifarious development in the region. The region will diversify production and may become self-sufficient at high levels of economic development. This is not necessary. In fact, it is possible that the region may progress along a narrow specialisation and a narrow heat in a region.

There are vested interest groups from the politician, bureaucrats offices, officials, conditions, vigilante groups etc., who misappropriate funds from regional development schemes. Regions stagnate; these persons become multi-millionaires.

26

Divergence Versus Convergence and Balanced Vs. Unbalanced Growth (B.U.G.)

One important question is whether economic growth in regions, left to market mechanism, is convergent or divergent in nature. Will the gaps between the regions narrow down on their own as much as is physically possible or the inequalities will go on increasing, the divergence? If the hypotheses about the growth being convergent' are right, then no State intervention is necessary and regional imbalance becomes self-righting or self-correcting, in the long run. The sector theory of growth suggests convergence: some sectors will become saturated for development while others will become lucrative and that development of one sector leads to the development of the other two sectors in a mutually complementary way. Similarly models of factors flow in the inter-regional trade also suggest convergence of regional per capita income. Diseconomies of space and mobilities promote convergence. On the other hand, such economists as late lamented Gunner Myrdal argued that poor may become poorer and the rich may become richer due to colonial type centre-periphery relationships, and the same holds true for the groups of people. If spread effects exceed the backwash effects of growth, there will be tendency for convergence and the backwash effects exceed the spread effects, growth may become immiserizing for the poor regions and the people. 'Vicious circle theories' emphasize that for some it is a case of 'nothing succeeds like success' while for the others it may become a case of "nothing fails like a failure". Diseconomies, immobilities and drain of human and physical resources make the growth divergent. Theory of 'cumulative causation' emphasizes that growth can be convergent or divergent.............usually the latter in less developed economies. Hirschman and Friedman also emphasized regional growth being 'divergent' in nature.

Some economists argue that though in the initial stages there will be divergence in regional growth, in the long run, mature regional growth will take towards regional convergence reduction in regional income differential. It was argued that in agricultural societies there will be tendency towards divergence, in the industrial societies the tendency will be towards convergence.

Divergence

Divergence in per capita regional income takes place in the early stages of economic development,—— unless the strategy of balanced growth is being implemented through and through, an improbable thing. Complete convergence is scarcely possible and thus socio-politically acceptable divergence in per capita regional income remain even after concerted efforts to promote convergence.

In the colonies of the imperialists the backwash effects exceeded the spread effects and most of the regions and people of those regions experienced the ill effects of divergence and the 'cumulative causation' further accentuated the problems. Wherever the centre is in a semi-feudal and colonial position, it becomes the suction point of the periphery and divergence keeps on getting promoted.

The principle of comparative advantage is quite 'impersonal' and keeps on promoting divergence for quite some time developing nations. Partisan leadership, imbalances in the investment pattern, unequal fiscal transferences in favour of the developed regions and natural advantages in favour of certain regions accentuate divergences. An economy dominated by the primate sector will follow pattern of divergence for considerable period of time. All those industries in which the material index is high, which are based on non-ubiquities, gross raw materials or perishable raw materials will be tied in location and promote further the 'territorial division of labour' leading to further divergence.

Economic development, as we know, is a chain of disequilibria, if giving rise to equilibria at higher and higher points, even if temporarily. Richardson wrote:

> " There is nothing inevitable about the convergence forces. Instead, divergence forces may predominate."

Richardson gives several reasons why divergence may continue and convergence may not take place. *First,* labour may not migrate from the low income regions to high income regions and migration may not be equilibriating. Worse, it may even become disequilibriating by denuding the poor regions of the skilled manpower. *Secondly,* capital too may flow in the wrong direction and high income regions may get all the benefits from agglomeration economics. *Thirdly* innovations and technical progress may not spread evenly and rapidly over space but may cluster in prosperous regions. *Fourthly,* locational shifts in industry may favour high income regions because they have relatively greater access to the inputs of development and industrial activities. *Fifthly,* managers and professionals who provide vital service functions do not move to inferior socio-economic and cultural atmosphere of the backward areas and thus divergence continues. *Sixthly,* the industries of the developed regions have high income elasticity of demand while that of the backward regions a low income elasticity of demand. Changes in national demand also favour the developed regions if they have an industrial composition heavily weighted with high income elasticity of demand and thus divergence continues, seventhly, even if the factor flows are equilibriating and other convergence tendencies were strong, regional per capita incomes would not be fully equalised because (a) factors cannot become homogeneous and (b) differences in occupational distribution cannot be ended. *Eighthly,* there will always be regional differences in the degree of unemployment and underemployment, industrial composition, degree of urbanisation, labour force participation rates, age-sex structure etc. Hence if not all physical, sociological, resource-position, work habits are not equal divergence will continue. *Ninethly,* since properties are immobile, property incomes will be disproportionately concentrated in certain regions. *Tenthly,* empirical evidence of various countries suggests that though the total regional income may have a tendency towards convergence, the per capital income need not have the same tendency. As there are certain tendencies towards convergence, some other tendencies creater further divergence. Had this not been so the 'rank size rule' would not have been there.

Harrod-Domar type models, which discuss the 'knife edge paths' of economic development hold that both labour and capital will move in the developed regions and hence there will be divergence. As against this the neo-classical models emphasis that while the labour may move out from the underdeveloped regions, capital will move in and ultimately there will be convergence.

Concentration and agglomerations lead to divergence in the per capita income. Dispersal and balanced sectoral and regional growth will lead to per capita income becoming more or less equal known as 'convergence'

Convergence Thesis

Through explicit regional policies or compensatory fiscal measures, convergence can be promoted. Those economists who believe that there will be a strong tendency towards convergence of regional growth argue that as the different regions develop at different rates, there will be shortages of factors of production in the developed regions. Infrastructure facilities will get strained in the developed regions and diseconomies will start appearing. Land will become scarce and costly. Developed regions which were attracting factors hithertofore will find that they were paying more than the rates prevalent in other regions. Migration of labour and transfer of capital in due course of time becomes saturated in the developed regions. Many industrial units may seek relocation in backward areas to avoid the degradation in environment and thus may take their units to backward regions. The backward regions may have more resources to be exploited in comparison to the developed regions where resources may start exhausting. There will be slowing down of growth in the developed regions and in comparison the economies of location in backward regions may become higher than the diseconomies of transport costs in reaching there. Marginal returns in the congested regions/sectors may become lower and resource reallocation will be there. In comparison some other activities in the backward regions will be more profitable.

The sector theory advances the arguments that capital and labour will still be cheaper in backward regions and hence there will be greater investment in backward regions/ sectors, leading to convergence. *The factor flow theory* also emphasizes the same but with reference to factors to the sectors.

If the *centre-periphery* relation is such or has been planned in such a manner that centre transmits growth impulses to the hinterland and has 'growth pole' facilities, there will a strong tendency towards convergence. In the *planning economies,* growth centres are established to ensure that there are greater forward and backward linkages with the economic activities of the primary sector and the hinterland in rural areas. If these objectives are realised, regional growth naturally moves towards convergence and the chasm between secondary and primary sectors or between the rural and urban areas narrow down all helping in the process of convergence of the regional growth process.

When a country, to be precise the Central government of the country, follows the policy of planned *balanced development strategy,* convergence can be promoted early unless the divergence was too much and once a reasonable amount of convergence has been seemed, it can continue through and through. However, such instances are rare. If the *unbalanced growth strategy is to undo the past unbalancing,* then also ultimately convergence is promoted. *Market mechanism* can secure convergence by accident and luck and that too in the long run. Private sector investment follows the dictates of the market mechanism while the public sector investment can follow the principle of maximum social returns rather than maximum economic returns only and growth promoted through public sector development *can* help in early convergence.

Now a days, considerable regionalism has entered into politics and leaders of the backward regions naturally want that not only there should be *"bottom up strategy"* but also *"top down"* strategy and thus developed regions may be *'pulled down',* while the backward regions may be 'pulled up' leading to convergence of regional growth. *Frontier spirit* can also promote convergence in regional growth as entrepreneurs realise that there are immense growth potentialities in the backward regions. According to *Perloff and Wing* convergence will depend upon how much the *heartland* can do for the *hinterland;* or *'core'* can do for the *'fringe [Ullman],* or 'centre' can do for the 'periphery' *(Friedman).*

In the course of development, though the central regions may remain dominant but some counter-weight is provided by the emergence of viable peripheral sub-centres. The national economy moves towards integration. Finally, a lot of functional and regional interdependence develops and the integration of all regions into the national economy takes places through *(Friedman hypothesis)* 'the matrix of urban hierarchal regions'. Convergence takes place and only acceptable regional inequalities remain.

Thus a great indicator of convergence is the reduction in the inequalities in the per capita income in various sectors and areas.

The economists of the developed countries had argued that *'low wages in backward regions'* will attract capital there but this was never a factor inducing investment in backward countries where even near starvation level wages could not attract investment.

Conclusion

The debate continues but it can safely be said that complete convergence in per capita income of regions is not possible. Convergence may be achieved in the very long run through market mechanism but if the period of divergence is to be cut short. State intervention may be necessary. The State may pursue the policy of unbalanced growth strategy to undo the past imbalances. However, there will always remain some deterministic tendencies in economic development. The Thar desert of India cannot have the same levels of per capita income as the per capital incomes in the industrial belt of Mumbai. The divergence in the regional per capita income can be brought down to socio-politically acceptable limits.

The *sector theory of regional development as also the factor flow theory of regional development* both emphasise that in the long run there will be convergence. *The cumulative causation* theory makes convergence a function of spread effects exceeding the backwash effects and divergence a function of backwash effects exceeding the spread effects and divergence thus is *ipso facto* not desirable. *The centre periphery* analysis admits the possibilities of both divergence and convergence under the different conditions spelled out in the analysis. *Balanced growth and state* intervention are associated with convergence while market mechanism and development according to the comparative cost principle (unbalanced) growth are associated with divergence. Even if the per capita income gets equalized more or less, the differences in the physical quality of life may remain.

It is a fact of life that factors that cause divergence and convergence will continue to remain operative simultaneously. However, ultimately there has to be convergence and this period can extend till eternity.

The great tasks of economics are to reduce inequalities b not only between regions but also between people and right balancing between sectors. There has to 'equality in affluence' rather than equality in *poverty'*.

During the years 1947-2008, the divergence between regions has been reduced, despite creation of new types of divergences. The population of metros has increased so much that it exceeds the population of the 'seven- sister ' states of the east. Each metro has population exceeding that of Australia. Bhopal for example was a town of about 80,000 population. In 2008, it had population of 14 lakh. Inter-personal incomes have become too divergent. India sometimes claim that Mr., so-and-so is the richest person on earth residing in India. Yet, India has longest number of distitutes in the world, subsisting on the state food thrown by families, hotels and eateries. Growth centre are now bigger and significant, Technology to getting diffused in rural areas. Rural people have consumer durables. They enjoy some comforts. Yet socio-economic continuum and significant convergency are missing in India.

See : Richardson "Elements of Regional Economics" pp. 55-62.

B:

CONVERGENCE AND BALANCE GROWTH: BALANCED VERSUS UNBALANCED GROWTH: [DIFFERENCES: POINTS IN FAVOUR/ AGAINST THE TWO STRATEGIES]

[Summary Points at the Outset]

Yesterday, today and tomorrow it is the balanced growth that should be preferable to unbalanced. However, the growth process, brought highly unbalanced growth between continents, countries, regions, groups of people, sectors, functions and facilities. *Capitalism brought such a state.*

Socialism also followed unbalanced growth strategy. But it was "unbalanced growth to undo the past unbalanced growth". If some regions and sectors got too much of attention, *countervailing* extra attention (unbalanced) was followed to reduce the past imbalances and ultimately to secure balanced growth.

We can say today that *all sectors, sub-sectors, functions, facilities, regions, sub-regions, groups of people, (whether on the basis of rural and urban residence, or on the basis of caste, colour and creed) will never have the same level of growth.* Balanced growth strategy does not insist on the balanced *or equal rates of growth.* That can never be.

Hence at best we can hope that the imbalances will be as less as possible and that will be very near the balanced growth.

These models/theories did not use much of algebra and geometry. They plead and guide in simple words. Unbalanced growth is on the principle of comparative advantage in the market. Balanced growth is "sponsored" growth. In the long run, everyone agrees, there should be balanced growth.

Imbalances, inequalities, imperfections, immobilitises, indivisibilities, inelasticities etc., are to be mastered.

I. Over-View : Points of differences between the two strategies /theories of development.

II. Views of the economists who support balanced growth. Nurkse, Lewis, Meter, Baldwin, Perroux and others.

III. Views of the economists who support unbalanced growth. Rostow, Hirschman, Singer, Kindleberger, Rugina, Bauyer & Yamey, Shehan, Aubrey and others.

IV. Balanced view about the controversy regarding "balanced versus unbalanced growth".

Balanced Growth	Unbalanced Growth
1. It is doing something everywhere.	1. It is doing everything somewhere.
2. It advocates capital widening.	2. It advocates capital deepening.
3. It advocates maximising social welfare and minimising social costs.	3. It advocates maximising profits and minimising monetary costs, based on the principle of comparative advantage.
4. It suggests investment in diversified fields, which increases the 'scope' of economic activities.	4. It suggests investment in 'leading industries' from the standpoints location and functional linkages so that 'growth poles, emerge and the scale of activities improves.
5. It advocates the use of labour intensive techniques, greater employment generation and promoting social productivity.	5. It advocates the use of capital intensive techniques and higher profitability through economic productivity.
6. It envisages that different sectors, regions and activities grow at different rates but in unison in a complementary way.	6. It envisages that different sectors, regions and activities grow at different rates in the competitive way but providing input-output linkages with the help of the dictates of the market.
7. It suggests spatial planning and planning for the depressed, ethnic and economic groups.	7. It suggests 'projects planning'. Macro aspects of development should be left to the market.

8. It recommends that there be social accounting of production consumption and distribution.	8. It recommends that there should be emphasis on higher and higher production. Distribution and consumption pattern will emerge on their own in which distortions, if any, will be auto corrective.
9. It aims at the direct attack on poverty through societal support. Development of agriculture and rural areas to receive top priority. Socio-economic infrastructure facilities be created for balanced development of sectors and regions.	9. It aims at the development through self-financing technique. Only such "industrial" activity be promoted that yields reinvestible funds, liven the development of socio-economic infra-structure facilities be on the principle of 'comparative advantage.
10. The entire development process be sponsored by a planning machinery.	10. Growth should be dictated by the market mechanism. National and international commerce to be free.

Balanced Growth and Summary Points from Some Models

Ragner Nurske believed that if all people participate in the growth process and earn income, then the total savings and capital formation in the country will go up. If all able bodied persons produce goods and services they get income and can demand goods and services produced by others. There will be no glut of goods nor the shortage of goods. All producers will be in complementary position and they will become each others consumers as well. There will be no problem of not being able to sell anything. Forward and backward linkages of production units develop to the utmost extent.

Nurkse brushes aside all objections of the critics of balanced growth and asserts that it is same as no one can say the balanced diet it not necessary. Balanced growth and balanced diet can be managed with less resources also. Balanced growth is the only method of breaking the vicious circle of poverty from both the demand and supply sides. Synchronized application of capital to a wide range of different industries can break the deadlocks of under-development. Productive activities, market, investment and consumption all get enlarged.

The late comers to development (less developed countries) will harm themselves if they imitate the production (technology) and consumption habits of the rich countries.

W.A. Lewis strongly advocated a balanced development between all sectors of the economy. All sectors, sub-sectors, activities and functions need not have a same rate of growth but such growth rates that they are mutually consistent. Labour intensive techniques should be adopted. If the productivity of the people engaged in agriculture rural activities is raised, the same works can be performed by fewer persons. The 'genuinely redundant' persons should be transferred to the cities/industry, The transfer will be

---

Many authors have defined balanced growth without subscribing to it and many authors have defined the strategy of unbalanced growth without giving approval to the same. In this chapter we have kept the views of various economists and definitions part separate. *Kindleberger* for example is for unbalanced growth but defines balanced growth, similarly Lewis is all in favour of balanced growth but comments on unbalanced growth as well.

The entire discussion should be oriented towards the problems of 'development' (not merely of growth) of the less developed economies. The views of the authors advocating either strategy have been presented in a succinct manner and not presented two times in full once as the discussion of the theory/model and then as part of the discussion of the BG versus UBG.

Balanced growth has also been defined as a condition when capital stock grows at the same rate as human capital (but for LDCs we cannot call all additions to population as increase in human capital). Balanced growth has been quoted in some books with reference to UN as the condition of "full employment equilibrium" which in *not* correct because balanced growth for LDCs is a strategy *to reach* full employment. The present author, therefore, has serious reservations about the so called a 'steady growth path' as 'balanced growth strategy' for the developing economy'.

'orderly' and not distress migration. The urban wages be such that they are equal to rural wages *plus* "30 percent extra" to compensate for the high cost of living in the urban areas. If these aspects are taken care of, then production will increase in a hitchless way *without inflation.* Lewisian scheme was better than the Nurkse's scheme who wanted that the rural people be taxed equivalent to savings in consumption of the migrated persons. With this the wages of the urban labour be paid. The second scheme is unjust and difficult to put to operation.

Meier and Baldwin deserve mention because their early electic work had been of great importance to the students of the early economies of development. Their arguments are of Lewisian variety. Several growth points are to be chosen; investment has to be on broad fronts and in various parts/sectors of the economy. Balanced growth ensures that the participants of all the three sectors increase their liabilities (purchases) from other sectors and mutually support all activities. It is a doctrine of increasing the "external economies".

The doctrine of balanced growth is pro-poor but if the rich are (sort of) penalised, capital formation and investment shall suffer. The poor are to be helped to develop themselves.'

It will be futile to believe that balanced growth can be achieved with foreign assistance: self-help is the best promise. Balanced growth, however, is not forced self-sufficiency or autarky. If in the name of balanced growth, the economy gets too much regimented, controlled and over-regulated it will inhibit growth. The market cannot be abolished; it may be required to subserve the needs of planned development. In such a paradigm, the public cooperation will be forthcoming if the people see that this strategy is meant to provide benefits to all. Balanced growth aims at optimum interface and the use of natural resources, human resources and the 'produced means of production (capital and technology).

The Central and the State governments have to strengthen the infrastructure support and should run them efficiently. The experience of the decades of fifties to eighties of the twentieth century of direct participation in the manufacturing by the estate proved capital consuming by the 1980s. Now the state should better concentrate on public utilities rather than put its nose in productive ventures. Indicative planning may be necessary. Regimented planning of socialism or of mixed economy type will not deliver goods. Balanced growth objective can still be pursued even if regimented planning stands discredited. It will be impossible to achieve the same unless the high birth rates and high death rates amongst the poor and in the rural areas are brought down sharply and early.

Balanced growth should mean sticking to intermediate technologies. The labour force has to be converted into 'human capital'. Then only it can create capital. The factor

---

1. In this connection it may be mentioned that the policy of reservation in India has moved from one extreme to another. The States are providing reservations over 50 p.c (even 80 p.c, in complete defiance of the Supreme Court verdict and the centre can do nothing.) A compromise can he had with only four provisions.

   (A) By whatever number there is additional entry of the person belonging to scheduled castes, scheduled tribes and other backward classes' the seats in professional and other educational institutions should be increased. The central and the state governments of this big nation can find resources for the same.

   (B) The second generation reservation benefits be not given, except to janitor class and the cobbler class, who can get them in perpetuity till their complete socio-economic salvations.

   (C) The creamy layer concept should be seriously implemented, i.e., they should not get the benefits.

   (D) Reservations in government jobs will not be as much a problem as the denial of getting education to meritorious students of the so-called upper classes. That is to be avoided at all cost.

disproportions have to be overcome. There will be ineffectiveness of the diffused investment if leakages of funds are not checked. A corrupt political-administrative setup and balanced growth do not go together. Lumpy investment can be made under balanced growth also provided the government functions well. This doctrine was very popular and was considered to be the answer to poverty but the emergence of mafia in all countries made people realize that the public sector became a sector which was looted by both by the insiders and outsiders. It is true that the private sector leaves no opportunity to indulge in massive profiteering but the mutual competition becomes a safety valve. If there are difficulties in the path of implementing this strategy, the objectives of the same cannot *completely* be jettisoned.

Francois Perroux, a great name in regional economics, also argued for balanced growth and averred that it is the best way to avoid cyclical fluctuations. In unbalanced growth there is "haphazard piling up of projects" and "incoherent juxtaposition of measures." Balanced growth, in the opinion of Perroux, increases social productivity and real outputs of the economy. There are three distinct advantages;

(A) Maximum real output per capita and minimum fluctuations in employment and aggregate output are secured.

(B) There will be diminution in the disproportions between sectors; and

(C) There will be diminution of tensions between regions and groups.

Despite difficulties the doctrine of balanced growth is worthy of putting into practice.

C:

UNBALANCED GROWTH AND SUMMARY POINTS FROM SOME MODELS

The classical economists advocated unbalanced growth, to be left to the forces of the market and even socialists advocated the unbalanced growth to be achieved through planning. Both believed that there will ultimately be balanced growth in the country. The classical economists believed that market mechanism itself will do it. The Marxist planners believed that 'deliberate unbalancing to undo the past unbalancing' will secure this.

There are two strong bases for advocating unbalanced growth. First it is based on the principle of comparative advantage and secondly, it will be within means (real and monetary resources will always be insufficient for balanced growth). Investment in leading and profit earning activities located at the points of greatest advantage will secure low costs of production. This will promote sales inside and outside the countries. Growth process will be self-financing. *Here the nation has to look after the 'production' and the 'employment' will look after itself.* Those who advocated balanced growth believed if employment is provided in diversified and well spread-over activities , then production will look after itself. Leading sectors will have real and not artificial linkages sustained by government intervention, which will be necessary for balanced growth.

W.W. Rostow is a very strong advocate of the doctrine of unbalanced growth. He wants growth through 'leading sectors', big projects and big industries. These are 'growth poles' which are of course locational in nature but more than *that functional* in nature. When these growth poles develop there will be supplementary, complementary, imitative and supportive investments. They will develop urban centres and functions. There will be upstream (backward) and downstream (forward) linkage activities.

Growth will spread from these centres. Such projects and great industries will earn profits and from the reserve funds they can invest further. Growth need not be financed with the help of deficit financing. Growth will follow certain stages and the economy will reach maturity.

First, the heavy industries, then intermediate industries and then consumer goods industries of all sorts will develop. Too much labour will not be pitched against too little capital. There will be vertical and horizontal transmission of economies. Technological upgradation will take place with rising profit and capital formation.

A.O. Hirschman is the most leading economist advocating unbalanced growth on the ground of serious shortages of capital, capital goods, skilled persons and shortages of even essential raw materials and infrastructure facilities. Advocates of balanced growth are regarded by Hirschman as being engaged in 'children's parallel play' and in finding an 'escapist solution. If a country was ready to apply the doctrine of balanced growth then it would *not be* underdeveloped in the first place i.e., only developed countries can pursue this policy. There are no managerial talents to look after all the planned activities.

Growth decisions should better not be political *only;* price signals should be respected and even the State action should obey them. Hirschman regards balanced growth 'unattainable' and 'undesirable.' All leading countries progressed on the basis of unbalanced growth only. Growth process is a series of the chain of disequilibrium and the disturbances in equilibrium brought by market mechanism. They will ultimately lead to higher growth point. The tensions and disproportions are growth inducing.

"The nightmare of equilibrium economics, the endless spinning cobweb is the kind of the mechanism we must assiduously look for as an invaluable help in development process."

H.W. Singer: He is also is favour of unbalanced growth and says that though it is correct that balanced growth can solve many market difficulties, it will be premature. *"Think big"* is okay but *"act big"* will be unsound. The unbalanced growth strategy respects market mechanism more and makes the entire system elastic. Singer regards balanced growth doctrine as incomplete, implausible and even potentially dangerous and not suitable for early stages of economic development. However, there should be no, "white elephant projects' in unbalanced growth. One point which balanced growth strategy emphasises is investment in socio-economic infrastructure and that is valid for unbalanced growth also. Balanced growth cannot create *both demand and finance;* this can be done by unbalanced growth. If we pursue balanced growth, we will become victim of 'double counting trick.'

Singer extols the principle of comparative costs and recommends that LDCs should import capital goods and start profit earning industrial units. Exportable goods should be produced. External loans and capital intensive technology will help. Unbalanced growth does not mean that agriculture is to be neglected. In fact agriculture itself can develop better if there are industrial goods to help its development. Deficit financing could be resorted to but the main aim should to be to secure profits for reinvestment.

Singer wanted that a nation should save at least 12 p.c, of its GDP to start growth . Productivity should be increased to reduce capital-output ratio. Some austerity be also practised. There are several costs to be met for developing agriculture industries, tertiary sector, paying the external loans, managing migration and other development works. Mobilisation of savings, some additional taxation, external loans, credit creation, import of capital etc. can take care of the other side.

In the Singer model the growth rate of the country is the function of net savings ratio multiplied by the productivity of investment (inverse of COR) from the sum of which the rate of annual increase in population should be deducted.

$$G = s.p - r$$

Where G stands for growth rate of national income *(economy):* s stands for net savings rate and p stands for productivity of new investment per unit of capital (inverse of capital -output ratio) r stands for rate of increase in population.

Suppose $\frac{S}{Y} = \frac{25}{100}$

COR inverse = $\frac{25}{100}$

then $\frac{25}{100} \times \frac{25}{100}$

$$= \frac{1}{4} \times \frac{1}{4} = \frac{1}{16}$$

$$= \frac{1}{4} \times 100 = 6.25$$

is growth rate. If population growth rate is .2%, it should be deduced = 6.25 - 2 = 4.25 p.c.

Evaluation

Singer uses Harrod-Domar type equation in which one additional element i.e., the negative role played by the increase in population is also incorporated.

Singer has very correctly emphasised the dualism in development as also the importance of increasing savings, capital productivity, labour productivity as well as labour intensity and the need for controlling population.

Kindleberger considered balanced growth as an 'empty slogan'. He feels it is better to start somewhere than everywhere. If balanced growth is pursued then capital will fall short of the requirements, machinery will be overloaded and grave mistakes are likely to be committed.

Prof. Rugina was against the balanced growth doctrine because it was allowing "a backdoor entry to socialism". In the name of promoting balanced growth, the government would assume over-riding powers and would curtail freedom of enterprise. There will be eventual failure, to hide the failure the government would turn to an over-regulated economy again. The government would not stop short of regimented socialism.

Marcus Fleming wanted unbalanced growth because he believed that 'complementarity between sectors/activities is a myth' and 'competitiveness is real and efficiency-promoting'. It will be the shortage of capital which will be felt first in implementing balanced growth. He wanted that Government should help those industries come up which are having increasing returns and this will be highly useful to the entire economy. Balanced growth doctrine will give immense powers to trade unions which would seek higher wages and will not try to increase their productivity.

Bayer and Yamey, J. Sheahan and H. Aubrey, amongst others, also prefer unbalanced growth because though lower amount of capital is used per activity, the total amount of capital investment will be very high. Not only the present supply of capital will be short but the future capital formation potential will also go down. Too much labour will not be pitched against too little capital. Growth through leading sectors will mean economic growth on a solid foundation.

There will first be vertical transmission of external economies and then horizontal transmission of external

D:

BALANCED VIEW ABOUT THE BALANCED AND UNBALANCED GROWTH CONTROVERSY

Complete balancing is not possible but there should be an optimum degree of unbalancing. The case for balanced growth rests on autarky and of the unbalanced growth on specialisation. Complete international specialisations is not desirable from the point of view of national defence. Hence there have to be some efforts towards balanced growth also, particularly from the point of view of employment generation. But the controversy should not be carried on to the extreme. Paul Streeten wrote:

"Both doctrines have certain faults. The trouble with advocating unbalanced growth is that, for countries embarking on development unbalanced growth is inevitable, whether they want it or not and governments and planners do not need the admonition of the theoretician. All investments create unbalanced growth because of rigidities, indivisibilities, sluggishness of response both of supply and of demand in these low elasticity economies and because of mis-calculations."

The real point is that it is to be kept in mind that unbalancing should aim at ultimate balancing.

In case of the unbalanced growth also we will take the

See Hans W. Singer : *The Economics of Underdevelopment*
J. H. Boeke : *Economics and Economics Policy of Dual Societies*
J. H. Boeke : *Three forms of Disintegration in Dual Societies.*
J. H. Boeke : "Western influence on the growth of Eastern Population'. *Economic: International.* May 1954
Benjamin Higgins : Op. cit.

view that unsteady growth is not unbalanced growth. It is not something to be explained in terms of equation but a strategy of which rationale is to be explained.

In unbalanced growth there is concentration of industries at certain places and that leads to divergence between regions and sectors. Ultimately, when balancing poles emerge, then several points of concentration become 'dispersal' points and that leads to convergence of incomes.

Unbalanced growth thus starts from concentration and divergence and ends up (or should) in dispersal of activities and convergence of income. There is no balancing between SOC and DPA through and through that is simply not possible. Sometimes SOC becomes more than DPA requires and vice versa. The trials and errors and the adjustment processes start from the position of imbalance and end up or should end in a position of balancing.

Unbalanced growth strategy is a strategy of 'growth through profits' and efficiency from the short period to the long period. It is pragmatic and practical and *it lays emphasis on "internal" as well as "external" economies.* Horizontal transmission of external economies comes later; first the emphasis is on vertical transmission of internal economies. In this system the 'surplus' comes out of 'plus' i.e., from the profits of the important ventures with maximum linkages. It is development via industrialisation. The other two sectors play the supplementary role. In the balanced growth it is hierarchal development. First agricultural and rural sectors are developed and *the secondary and tertiary sectors are so developed that they subserve the needs of the development of the primary sector first.* Then the secondary sector is developed and the supplementary roles are played by the primary and tertiary sectors. The tertiary sector (SOC) is always in the limelight.

Unbalanced growth doctrine is of 'specialisation' of

techno-economic efficiency rather than of socio-economic efficiency and is a doctrine which keeps a country abreast with development paradigm of the world.

The points against the unbalanced growth are the same as were the points in favour of balanced growth.

The doctrine of unbalanced growth neglects all issues of the anti-poverty, programmes and of reducing the regional disparities. With its greater emphasis on *capital goods industries (resulting in long gestation period)* and low priority to consumer goods industries *(resulting in goods lag),* it can become inflationary. It is disliked by workers and the masses. The linkages effects do not come out as conceived and growth becomes 'enclave' growth.

Prof. Gerald Meier (Leading Issues) has summed up well about both:

> "Each approach has been overdrawn.....has become highly qualified...and the controversy is essentially barren... It may be concluded that while a newly developing country should aim at balance as an investment criterion, this objective will be attained only by initially following in most cases a policy of unbalanced investment.

Thus there is no dispute about the long term balanced growth. The only practical solution seems that there should be an admixture of both with the blend differing from country to country according to socio-economic conditions.

See: Respective Growth Models of the authors mentioned (hereinafter). There is a good chapter on BG & UBG in Gautam Mathur's book on Planning. Paul Streeten (Economic Weekly) April 20, 1963. International Economic Association's Special 'Economics Stability and Progress in the World Economy." *The Economic Journal, June 1955 and Quarterly Journal of Economics. Feb. 1958.*

PART-VII

Regional Planning

27

Regional Planning: Multi-Level Planning

A. Regional planning : Nature and scope

B. Tools and techniques of Regional/Micro level planning. Constraints in micro level planning.

C. Multi level planning : Meaning, Nature and scope.

D. Integrating Regional Development in Multi-Level planning.

A : Regional Planning: Nature and Scope

Regional planning is "bottom up" planning and is an antidote to the ill effects of "top down" planning. The *pro-to-type* socialist planning was centralised and highly regimented. That planning was concerned with the body ignoring the parts and limbs. It was not realised that the whole body can be dead with a big slash in hand! Regional and local problems were not appreciated or taken into account. The assumption was that if gross input-output relations are optimised, the benefits shall percolate to the lowest level. This was the thesis of 'trickledownism'. It also assumed that if we look after the 'growth and a high rate of growth at that' then poverty will take care of itself. It was also believed that all sectors, sub-sectors, activities and functions shall develop ultimately. Growth will secure better distribution through production relations. There will be growth and social justice in opulence. If better redistribution is desired it will be still better if it is not equality in poverty but equality in prosperity.

Backward regions remained neglected and what was worse the depressed ethnic groups could not get the benefits of development in non-socialist countries as much as they should have. The growth process bypassed them. Regional planning is concerned with the problems of backward areas, though not of the depressed ethnic groups. The revenue block becomes the lowest unit of micro level planning. Then comes the district. A government or a system (like the *panchayats* in India) can have problem redressal at the cluster of village level or even village by village. There is emphasis on the use, development and conservation of natural resources and on the fuller development and employment of manpower. Regional planning will further the territorial specialization for employment generation and income propagation for the benefit of the people of the region primarily. The "exports" of the region to other regions are to be increased and the "basic" (exporting) industries/ activities are to be developed. Of course there are the objectives of increasing production in various lines for basic needs.

Autonomous planning, financing and implementation and monitoring are neither possible nor desirable. Higher level benevolence is also necessary to finance development of backward regions. Technical and real inputs are also to be infused. *In regional planning the society institutionalises the planning of supra-urban spaces; it is particular type of structural solution to the problems of societal self articulation to economic problems. Regional planning is aprioristic to specific regional ends.* Location of functions, facilities and projects in region become important.

Even if *pro-to-type* planning was defunct in 1991 in the world, the need for finding solutions to regional planning through *programmes and projects* which can become planning, cannot be left.

Regional planning includes urban, town and country

planning also and gives greater importance to agro-climatic zonal planning of agriculture. Regional planning gives greater importance to pockets of poverty and activities of the poor persons. *However, regional planning ipso facto is not planning for a balanced growth. It also pursues the policy of starting big projects in a region. Regional planning has to be made pro-poor and pro-neglected activities to be of some consequence for balanced development.* Then only it can stop areas of vitality becoming suction pumps of the static regions. Regional planning seeks to undo the relegation of the backward areas to semi-colonial position. Backward areas need not lose their high order manpower and resources in the raw form to advanced areas. The work of value-adding can be done in the region itself rather than in any other region. In the centralised planning, as we have seen everything or most of the things happen in a few regions; in regional planning most of the regions have most of the things or, if that is not possible, something/many things. A region is extricated from the vicious circle of stagnation.

Regional planning is not uniform in the matter of programmes and projects but the objective is the same-to develop the region according to the endowments of the area. It is essentially a corrective planning also. Since the institutional and structural levels of regions differ, the types and degrees of planning of various activities and functions differ. *Regional planning has to achieve the national goals also as they are perceived in a regional planning; the national obligation are not discarded.* Cohesiveness in planning requires centralised planning/programming but vitality in achievement requires decentralisation and regionalisation. *Regional planning is problem solving for the region as also bringing its development at par with other regions.* Regional planning is a partial dimension related to physical plans at the local level but the region remains an organic part of the plan for the country.

Regional planning conceives development *of* some,

growth poles. These *growth poles are not merely cities;* they are leading industries. The industries become 'leading' if they have maximum linkages with the hinterland and with the activities in the region. The linkages are forward (downstream) and backward (upstream). (A textile mill will have backward linkages in the form that persons will grow cotton and then all activities which provide inputs for growing cotton will develop. These backward activities can be industrial in nature e.g., providing tools and implements, fertilizers and pesticides, fencing equipment etc. Some mining activity is also stimulated. The chain is long. The forward activities relating to packaging, running shops and establishments etc. There are still some other forward and backward linkages e.g., in forging sewing machines. Here again the chain can be long). *Growth poles are locational in nature alright; but they are important because they are functional in nature.* They trigger off subsequent activity linkages for employment generation and income propagation. That is what should be.

If the industries located in a backward region are such that they do not take their raw material or manpower from the adjoining areas they remain show-piece guide posts for the region. When a region gets benefits, the nation also gets benefits.

There have to be growth centres/nodes of growth. A network of growth *foci* (wherefrom people can avail facilities) helps in the development of regions. *However, such growth foci always exist even without conscious planning.* The small towns are centres wherefrom the villagers avail services or buy things or where they sell their outputs.

The networks of growth centres have to be so developed with functions and facilities that they trigger off further growth impulses to the hinterland for other activities. *A region can plan two markedly separate polarized nodes in order to fulfill their potential. Planning a homogeneous region is easier but two or more heterogeneous regions can also be combined.* All depends upon the calibre of the planners and availability of resources of all types. A region can be defined in prescriptive as well as descriptive terms. Planning can be on the basis of homogeneity as well as on the basis of functional interaction between polarized regions.

If regional planning solves the problems of the region without aggravating the problems of other regions (hence of the nation), then it is superior to other forms of planning.

The national goals can be realised through regional planning in the matter of increasing maximum production and generating maximum employment. The mining activities of different regions will be different; the soils and water positions for agriculture will be different; the motivations and skills of persons of different regions are different; the socio-cultural ethos are different; and the leads and lags of the regions are different. As such *not one uniform ready-made policy but tailor-made policy* becomes necessary for formulating-implementing plans.

National planning aims at allocating resources over the regions while regional planning aims at allocating resources *within* the region. Regional planning is *local physical planning primarily.* Traffic densities differ in different regions; hence the network of roads and railway have to be different. Deposits and loans positions of different regions differ and hence banking should have to be different. Deposits and loans positions of different regions differ and hence banks should have differing institutional structure. *Regional planning is differential institutionalisation as well.*

Procedural regional planning seeks to chalk out the methodologies of planning while substantive regional planning seeks to first have the data base and feasibilities studies. Now-a-days some regions become 'autonomous' regions within the country. In unitary form of government the states/regions do not acqu re autonomous status. Regional planning is not merely physical planning; it also seeks to achieve socio economic objectives. Regional planning is not merely urban planning and is thus supra urban.

However, we would reject the charge of some regional analysts that economics had been non-spatial discipline or that the classical economists used to be in the wonderland of no space. Economists are realists and had always been so; they never were dwellers of ethereal regions. Even Adam Smith discussed the problems of a backward/depressed region-and the region which was discussed by him was India's Bengal! Malthus discussed the problems of over-populated regions in a different vein than of the under populated regions. In the former, control of population was considered necessary by him, in the latter, more capital formation. Ricardo discussed the problems of those regions where diminishing returns in agriculture applied in a special with context. His rent theory was based on differential fertility of different regions. Some economists discussed the problems of total demand and total supply as well as of sectional/sectoral demand and supplies. The sectors were many a times based on territorial division of labour. *Economists always discussed the problems of inter-sectoral activities and interpersonal incomes.* Those who propounded the balanced and unbalanced growth theories always had regions in mind, apart from groups of people or sectors. If economic development of the tribals was discussed, tribal space came into focus *ipso-facto;* so was the case of mining, forestry etc., *the regional analysts should not have condemned economists of the past to show the importance of their views. Their criticism was based on their ignorance, if not on prejudice.* If price theory was discussed with reference to time, it was also discussed with reference to space (price discrimination; or polypolistic competition in concentric circles). Factor mobilities and factor price differentials were always discussed with reference to space and activities therein. Even the founding father of economics, Adam Smith, discussed the problems of "the journeymen" i.e., of migrant labourers over different regions.

Regional planning is best promoted when rural activities are developed and when urban areas provide industrial and infrastructure linkages and get the same from rural sectors. The external economies are to be made available. Industrialisation and urbanisation are part of regional development process. Regional planning involves that greatest benefits be derived from the process of polarisation. Regional planning will secure 'sustainable regional development' without harming the regional environment and bio-diversity. If resources are used there are efforts to develop and conserve them also.

Regional planning objectives in India were pursued with (i) metropolitan regional planning, (ii) urban centres planning, (iii) sectoral programmes and their spatial integration, (iv) rural development, (v) development of industrial estates and growth centres, (vi) tribal development programmes, (vii) river valley projects, and scores of adhoc relief, rehabilitation and employment generation/poverty alleviation programmes, (there are more that three dozen of them). The Finance Commissions had been making special devolutions to end regional imbalances. The planning commission had been provided hundred per cent finance for certain programmes. The hill areas, desert areas, arid areas, semi-arid areas, tribal areas, forest areas, wasteland areas, mining areas etc., all were given special programmes.

Decentralised planning, district level planning, block level planning and now *panchyat* level planning are all cited as regional planning. *The most comprehensive plan of regional planning drawn for the development of agriculture and allied activities in India had been "agro-climatic zonal planning" in India.* There are sub-plans for some special regions. In each state special provisions are being made for development: Jharkhand and Bihar, hill areas in West Bengal tribal areas in Orissa and Madhya Pradesh etc., have been promised special allocations of funds for special programmes. *Regional planning is being promoted in India as a part of national plan.* This is an aspect which is regarded as the 'beauty' or 'bane' of planning by those who appreciate or deprecate the same.

Regional planning is implemented in a hierarchy of regions but all types of regions are covered. *Regional planning is relevant only when regional differentiations exist. If all regions of the country are virtually in the same state, then regional planning becomes unnecessary.* It is because of territorial differentiation of resources, that there arises the need for regional planning. The nation is territorial 'system' and the regions are sub-systems. Some regions are so different that they become a system in themselves. All these systems or sub-systems are to be instilled with a dynamism that all develop in an integrated way. A planning region has got to have operational facility. Socio-political cohesiveness is also necessary. Environmental and economic planning have to be integrated. Regional planning is regional problem solving technique without accentuating problems of other regions. *All planning is inter-disciplinary and not merely regional.* It is perplexing why only regional analysts claim that regional planning is inter-disciplinary. Planning exercises are made by economists and econometricians but they have to take assistance from the persons of all disciplines about the techno-economic aspects. If leading regions are chosen for planning, it becomes unbalanced growth strategy. Regional planning is something which is not peculiar to developing countries or socialist countries only; it is relevant for developed capitalist countries or socialist countries only; it is relevant for developed capitalist countries as well. *However, it is to be remembered that if there was planning there was always a spatial dimension to it, though the term 'regional planning' might not have been used for the same. Now the sectoral development will have to have spatial dimensions also, as spatial development will be based on different sectors, sub-sectors, activities and functions.*

Single level sectoral planning followed the principle of 'comparative advantage in location' to secure minimum per unit cost of production. Cities and urban areas got more attention and the vast rural side was neglected. This strategy gave rise to areas of life and vitality on one hand and the areas of utter poverty and stagnation on the other hand. Developed areas in the past acted as suction pumps (they still do) pulling the more dynamic elements from the more static regions. The remainder of the country is relegated to second class peripheral and 'semi-colonial' position. In the quasi-colonial position with the centre, backward areas lost their trained manpower, reinvestible funds and resources. Cumulative causation made these backward areas because they were backward.

This cause effect-trap drains the region because the vicious circle of backwardness takes the people of these regions in it:, firm grip.

It has now been recognised that since regions differ in endowments and level of growth and living, corrective micro levels planning will be necessary. Since the institutional and structural levels of regions differ, there is need for different types of planning with different degrees of intensities in different regions.

Micro level planning generally considers the levels at which national development goals, targets and policies can best be given their spatial dimension and related to physical plans at local level. A regional plan is an integrated comprehensive plan for a micro region, forumulated so as to best serve the country. A micro level plan is not just a set of schemes to be executed within a region.

Micro level planning discards the philosophy of 'trickledownism' or percolation doctrine'. A national plan is not discarded planning cohesiveness requires centralization planning, while vitality in planning requires decentralization. A comprehensive spatial or zonal distribution of activities, projects and programmes is inherent in regional or micro level planning.

In most of the less developed countries, the institutional structures in all sectors of the economy differ. Economic functions are not provided at the same pace in different regions. To end the regional disparities, the development programmes of the most developed regions cannot be stopped, but the pace of the most laggard sectors, regions and ethnic groups can be increased.

Regional planning is a partial dimension related to physical plans at the local level. A regional plan is an integrated comprehensive plan for a region, formulated so as to best serve the needs for that particular region as an organic part of the plan for the country. Regional planning is to be harmonised to further the national interests and regional interests. The regional plans can be made complementary even in a mixed economic setup where competitive market mechanism prevails.

B. Tools and Techniques of Regional/Micro Level Planning

Many techniques are used for micro level planning. (1) Regional accounts have to be prepared, (2) Leontief type inter-industry input-output analysis can be made, (3) Comparative cost studies have to be simulated, (4) Cost-benefit analysis of the project (preferably social cost benefit analysis) has to be projected, (5) System and its sub-systems have to be identified, (6) Mix and share analysis has to be made, (7) Linear programming exercises may be undertaken and (8) Regional multiplier may be estimated.

Data Base. Adoption of the sophisticated techniques will first require that the data base be strengthened. Data base at micro level (even at district level) is usually very poor. In many less developed countries data are cooked up (by changing the of data this way or that way). Sometimes to show the 'progress' in the district the data are constantly adjusted upwards in a 'systematic' manner, while actually there may be no progress in the district. A secular trend is presented while fluctuations might have been occurring. The district administration should have data about age-specific birth rates internal migration, marketed and marketable surplus, input output relations, output capital and labour-capital coefficients in the past investment projects, expected profitability of the future projects, agriculturists' responses to price stimuli, utilisation pattern of credit and its impact on productivity etc.

Detailed statistics of national income and related aggregates, important demographic particulars (as for example knowledge, attitude and practices about family planning, mean ages at marriages, morbidity and mortality pattern), sectorwise investment production and transport cost prices, consumption, saving and their pattern are all necessary.

Inter regional flow data will be necessary. Horizontal and vertical compilation of such data will be very necessary and then other regions can make use of the data prepared in other regions. The main problems in this connection are the existence of (i) insufficient staff in this branch, (ii) lack of expertise (they can collect raw data but cannot interpret it), and (iii) sometimes the 'cooking of the data' to show progress. In less developed countries the quality of persons engaged in offices is much lower even for general administrative purposes and very unsatisfactory to tackle the dynamic problems of development. Poor pay structures are also responsible for this lack of talent and good work.

Inventory Preparation

Each district must have a good inventory of resources. The quantum of known resources must be estimated. An optimum rate of utilisation can be worked out. A manpower balance sheet is to be taken. The degrees of employment and under-employment have to be understood. Estimates for training the manpower to suit the development needs must be worked out. It should also be seen what should be the critical minimum size of the investment programmes both in the financial real terms to utilise the manpower effectively.

A district planner must have knowledge about the potential rate of use of water soil and other resources. For example, it should be known how quantum of sub-soil water and flow of water can be utilised. It should also be known that if alternative schemes of development are to be implemented what will be their cost-(financial and real)-and benefit ratios. These things will enable to fix productivity and employment targets. They will also enable in chalking out programmes of employment creation, income propagation and generation of the reinvestible funds.

Identification and Development of "Growth Poles"

Centres which act as growth poles or which can act as growth poles should be developed. Then impulses from them will permeate down to the lower level as also radiate outward extensively into the surrounding areas. The prime-moving activities and stimulants will have to be identified and seen that they can be developed in required quantum. Growth poles-as clusters of human activities functionally linked with other larger and smaller clusters, sending socio-economic impulses to clusters lower in the hierarchy and receiving similar impulses from the centres in higher hierarchy can become catalytic agents of development.

A growth pole will have to be a centre having localized mix of economic, social, institutional and psychological facilities inter related with each other to create internal and external economies and extending their influences to surrounding areas in proportion to the size of the localized facilities. The concept is not the same as industrial concentration. Growth poles will be necessary for corrective or micro planning between 'concentration zones' and 'dispersal zones' i.e., will have to act like transition zones. Growth poles will have to be essentially an ideal or model regional centre of activities creating conditions under which regional growth can be accelerated. Growth poles ensure largest spill over effects' of the total linkages.

Infrastructure Development

Though power, transport, communications and credit infrastructure will come from the national system, some minimum infrastructure facilities should be available in the district. Micro region will have legitimate expectations about 'enlarging the distribution network' of these facilities. Their availability only can enable starting of the directly productive activities which will help the micro region planning authorities to develop the region and to lift, as many families, as possible above the poverty line.

Preparation of the Regional Accounts

There are sophisticated exercises but at least rudimentary formulations must be done. Input-output tables are necessary for meaningful planning but at present level of data base and district level personnel expertise only heuristic substitutes are possible to the sophisticated planning. The district planning machinery should so organise itself that in due course of time it should know the inter-district and inter-regional flows of commodities. It should know how much is imported and exported, in and out of the district, how much is consumed and used as inputs. The monetary values of these commodity and service flows give us monetary flows. Then the balance of payment can be calculated and the planning machinery can know the direction and extent of the corrections necessary to improve or mend the position. Inter-regional linkages can be improved.

Social accounting will involve a study of who produces what, who owns how much, or who consumes what. In case of backward classes, some special efforts will be necessary to improve their lot.

Ranking and Allotment in Micro-Regions

An index of economic development is to be prepared to determine what should be the rate of growth of income in different regions to reduce the regional disparities of economic development and what would be the proportionate regional allocation of a given total investment compatible with the pre-assigned rate of growth of income. Production lines have got to be selected and production and productivity pattern worked out. Consumption savings and export-import ratios have to be planned. Funds should be available on the basis of economic and not political considerations.

Ranking of the regions will be necessary. Various weighted indicators like per capita income, expenditure, percentage of persons engaged in the primary, secondary and teritary sectors, roads per sq. kilometre, electricity consumption. Percentage of land irrigated houses of a certain type per 10,000 population, number of schools, number of medical facilities per 1,000 persons and so on should be used to prepare a list of the regions in the ranking order. Present low ranking should entitle districts to get more allotment.

Full employment should receive greater priority than merely full production; people should receive more priority than things. A micro level plan must also have a time horizon to even out bunching of projects under different programmes. Floating of district development bonds will not be a bad idea if enough funds are not available from the institution and the government.

Location of Projects: Implementation

Micro level planners should do their best to attract foot-loose industries. Unless the district administration has performance budgets, micro level planning may fail. It is seen that the efforts that go in formulating a plan (and more important than that writing its preamble) do not get the same support in implementation.

Each district must have development squads. They should be composed of experts, public men, administrators and economists. These squads should include experts on agriculture, rural housing, sanitation, small scale industries, demography etc. A vigilance squad should see that corruption leakages are not there.

Constraints in Micro Level Planning

A region is not a nation within a nation. It has to accept the central hegemony. The monetary system and policy, the price structure and policy, the industrial structure and policy and the entire juridical political superstructure have to be taken as given. A district planning machinery will have no legal right to check the people of city areas and other districts sharing the gains of development.

In the beginning district planning is likely to be somewhat undecided and heuristic, moving towards more rigorous planning as experience is gained and data base improves. It will be a big task on the part of the planners to take co-operation from all types of political groups for the effective utilisation of manpower. District planners may have to compete for the import of capital with other districts.

Narrow sectionalism and parochialism have no place in regional planning. Sectionalism breeds separatist tendencies whereas regionalism should mean unity and integration. Micro level planning de-emphasises centralisation in economic growth but it also tries to strike a balance in political authority by striking an effective and natural medium between uncontrolled individualism among the states and a complete centralisation of administration at the federal level.

Optimal regional development may be inconsistent with national development. There are at least three major reasons why this may be so. First, there are multi-dimensional economic goals, the preference patterns of region may be such that there will not be a consistent ordering of these goals at the national level. Secondly, even if maximum outputs were the only goal, each region's share in relocation costs needed to achieve it may not be equal to their share in the resultant gains. Thirdly, in either case, external economies or diseconomies in production extending across regional boundaries have not been taken into account.

Micro level regional planning will have to utilize many instruments e.g., location instruments, capital instruments, technical instruments (infrastructure), welfare instruments (special schemes), direct control instruments (licensing) and carrot and sticks instrument (subsidies versus levies) to undo the past unbalancing. Without the co-operation of the central authorities all these things may not be possible.

C. Multi-Level Planning

Discussion on planning no longer revolves round the need, and importance and conditions for successful planning. In recent years it has been realised that sectors received all the importance in planning while the backward areas and classes were neglected in the sense that lop-sidedness in development could not be reduced, much less ended.

It is only recently that multi-level planning has started

receiving attention in economics. In multi-level planning, the essential thrust is that all districts or even blocks should merit equal attention. A sub-region whose boundaries are co-terminus with the administrative boundaries is to be the hub of planning activity. This sub-region should be contiguous geographical area, should have nodal points of development and should have a homogeneous administrative machinery capable of formulating and implementing integrated area plans. A resource inventory and a reliable and adequate data base are necessary before planning can start.

In this connection it is being considered that at present only district level planning may be practical because homogeneous administrative machinery capable of formulating and implementing integrated area plans may not be below that. Similarly it may be difficult to find nodal points of development. As such district planning is regarded by many as the lowest level of planning that may be possible even in countries like India. Village or even taluk level planning may remain a distant goal.

Multi-level planning is a sort of system approach. Lower sub-systems cannot be made self-sufficient. Autarky is unthinkable in smaller sub-systems. If at all it is to be conceived, it can be done for a few activities or productions of the lower order. Lower sub-system of a hierarchy of sub-systems can be self-sufficient in some agricultural and primary sector outputs. For inputs of even these activities, they may have to look towards other sub-systems. Only at the highest level, planning objectives are to be for achieving viability, self-reliance, and instituting multifarious activities and healthy linkages with the sub-systems. At sub-system levels, the pressing problems of the 'life and death' importance can be solved.

Multi-level planning, some economists are of the opinion, should start from the village itself. Foci of development should be the village. If not one village, then atleast a cluster of them be treated as one unit. Development of a region is a process which can trigger off from within. That is the reason why a single outpost type big project located in a backward region fails to provide the necessary linkages and incentives for the development of a region, internal chain of development reactions is more important than the external.

Meaning

Multi-level planning means, planning is done at several territorial levels atleast at the central, state and district levels and in some cases in special regions level (multi-purpose river valley projects). Where the sub-divisions of the country are many and they enjoy a high degree of autonomy, the levels of planning may increase.

Before multi-level planning can be attempted it will be necessary to (i) identify different levels of planning with territorial, spatial and administrative jurisdiction, (ii) discover a hierarchy of the level functions, (iii) be certain about the degrees of the inter-government technical, financial and administrative decentralisation, (iv) to estimate the viability and constraints, and (v) to estimate how far the growth stimuli will be exogenous to the region.

Multi-level planning and regional planning are not the same. In multi-level planning, a national plan is not just disaggregated into various regional plans. Multi-level planning gives greater attention to spatial problems than merely to sectoral planning. Integration is the essential hall-mark of multi-level planning.

Then, there should be 'consistency' in the multi-level planning. (1) There should be internal consistency in the

See: O.S. Srivastava, "Regional Economics", Anmol Publications, New Delhi. For all about regions and regional economies and references.

planning of consumption and savings; then of savings, deficit financing (including external loans) and investment. In the light of these parameters the multi-level flow of resources and investment pattern will have to be devised. (2) Secondly, there should be consistency between the rate of growth of various sectors of the economy in the light of various determinates of GNP and then the regional sectoral rates should be such that national growth rates are achieved. (3) The regional input-output relationship should accord in their totality with the notional input-output ratios.

D. Integrating Regional Development in Multi-level Planning

Integration is far more important than just co-operation or co-ordination. Before attempts are made for integration, the commodity, services and monetary flows should also be understood so that efficient linkages can be established between them. There is a hierarchy of levels with appropriate decision making authorities at each level. In multi-level planning it is necessary that the sectoral and spatial plans at micro, meso, macro and national level should be integrated in a consistency framework to achieve optimisation.

The supply and demand imbalances of input and output should not emerge at a later date. Various projects should be complementary and supplementary to other projects.

One example of integration development activities will be establishment of the linkages in a multi-purpose irrigation development project. Once a project is implemented in all its technical perfection (we are not taking into account here the hitchless completion of the project), then further activities must be well planned. Schemes for the rehabilitation of the displaced persons in the new command (reclaimed) areas. Construction of the displaced persons in the new command (reclaimed) areas. Construction of canals, provision of loans to agriculturists to use better inputs, development of transport linkages, development of marketing facilities, storage facilities, soil management and land shaping, dairy development, and finally the development of the agro-based industries should be planned simultaneously.

Integration will have to be vertical and horizontal. There is a hierarchy of vertical regions and there should be integration between these levels. The vertical hierarchy is well known as (1) national level, (2) macro level, (3) state level, (4) meso level, (5) district level and finally (6) block level.

If there is vertical integration, then, according to the needs there can be disaggregation downwards or aggregation upwards. If there is no integration, the national planners will not know whether down to the lowest level the same amount of efficiency, time-bound implementation and implementation within the resources can be achieved. Nor will they be able to know whether targets or output can be achieved.

The sub-system planners on the other hand will not know whether the inputs for their development more physical than mere financial-will be available from the nation, which in fact means from other levels of planning.

The potentials and constraints of all levels should be known to the planner of all levels. Therefore whatever be the process-disaggregation or aggregation the regional levels must show consistency. If national input-output tables are prepared, the exercises with regard to levels of lower hierarchy should also be done.

Evidence of multi-level planning being done on the right lines will be visible if the national plan is disaggregated not merely on the sectoral basis but also on spatial basis. This will be *vertical* integration. *Horizontal* integration involves cross-sectional and sectoral integration. While horizontal integration had not been lacking so much in the past, it was vertical integration that was rather tenuous. Then the time pattern of development should be such that there is *temporal* integration also. It means deciding the things that are to be done in the short, medium and long periods. There should be integration between plans for settlements, sectors, people, function and levels of planning over a time period.

If there is a single type of integration, the chances are that the growth pattern will continue to follow the unbalanced growth pattern. If horizontal and vertical, temporal and functional, all types of integrations are taken care of, there will be balanced growth. Non-co-ordination and lack of integration at various levels will leave some areas backwards and the targets at lower levels will not be realised and the needs at the lower levels will not be taken care of. Lack of horizontal integration will mean disturbances in the input-output relations, (output of one sector , say coal, becomes input of other sector, say steel, which in turn is the input for construction and so on.) These linkages and relationships are to be studied in a time pattern i.e., how much and what should be available at what time. (When Bhilai steel plant was constructed the Russian planners even planned how the goods train moving on such and such date and carrying such and such material will reach the site even if it meant over-taking the express trains!)

Integration also involves anticipating constraints and taking measures to ensure that they are removed in time. If dairying is to develop, facilities for veterinary services and chilling must be planned; if higher agricultural outputs are planned, facilities for storage, marketing and transportation should be planned. Some such activities should be planned that the output does not remain unsold. A time pattern of starting production lines that will provide forward linkages must be envisaged and implemented. Similarly no project can come up. Backward linkages should also be assured infrastructure and several activities and functions should be planned in a co-ordinated way.

Multi-level planning can succeed when these consistencies are present not at certain sector levels or in certain areas but for all economic activities and territories, of course, the integration process will not always be smooth. Integration equilibrium will be of ephemeral nature to be superseded by disequilibrium. Efforts are to be made to achieve the new equilibrium as soon as possible. Human ingenuity alone will secure this. What is physically possible should not be made difficult through financial constraints. Monitoring by experts will secure this integration.

Putting together of the existing sectoral or development plans, does not automatically make an integrated plan. Planning may be comprehensive and multi- sectoral without being integrated. A plan becomes integrated when forward and back ward linkages are thoroughly analysed and their implications in terms of organisation and investment are incorporated in the plan. Integration exercises are to be anticipated *ex ante* and then compared with the *ex post* positions to introduce the correctives. Integration is not a mechanical exercise but an organic one.

The Issues Relating to Organisation and Regionalisation

1. The organizational set-up can be (and usually is) something of this nature. As a new plan is to be formulated, proposals are invited from the departments of a government which in turn gets them from the units of the department.
2. The broad objectives of the schemes/projects/ programmes can be given by the central leadership. For example, various levels of planning agencies in the country can be briefed that this time "more importance will be given to the minimum needs

programme" or "there will be direct attack on poverty", "at least one member in each family will be assured of employment for a fair minimum income", or "family below the poverty line will have to be identified and brought up above the same", or "such and such quantum of progress will be,desired in such and such sectors."

3. Proposals will be invited from the units of various departments and then they can be summarized blockwise, districtwise, meso regionwise and finally statewise. The state will also then break up the proposals sectorwise and may also disaggregate them ethnic group wise (e.g., in case of scheduled tribes and scheduled castes in India). While the district and/or sectoral plans are prepared *janpads, panchayats* or local (urban or city) authorities may also he consulted.

4. The state level exercises are done by the state planning division. The sector and space contents of the plan are to be spelled out. While formulating the state level plan. It will be necessary to take into account the national priorities and directives yet at the same time give the spatial contents of the plan in such a manner that local potentialities and priorities are also identified.

5. There should be functional integration in the sense that one thing should lead to another. Agriculture development plan is related to irrigation development, power development and provision of basic inputs. They have also to be planned. Presuming that agriculture will develop at a certain rate, the marketable surpluses are to be estimated and plans formulated for their utilisation. The entire gamut of changes in infrastructure and superstructure will form the strategy of the plan.

6. There will be 'indicative directions' to the private sector as to how much is expected of them to achieve some goals and priorities. They have to be assured of the basic socio-economic infrastructure and administrative support (institutional credit, reduction in the red-tape, incentives, technical advice, facilities, and social services), besides the package to concessions.
7. Before the finalization of the plan, the draft should be circulated to a group of experts (economists, public men, leading journalists, private entrepreneurs and lower level authorities) to elicit their response. Feed back can help in revising it suitably.
8. The state plan may be discussed in a meeting of the zonal planning 'bodies', if any. If no such 'bodies' exist it will be very desirable that there are such 'bodies'. This will help in formulating a good plan of development for a natural/ geographical region than merely for a functional region. If necessary, some revisions in the state plan can be made as a result of the feed-back of comments.
9. Finally, the plans of the states will be summarized, pruned and reframed in a national plan. This plan will aim at horizontal and vertical integration of the highest order. The central authorities (Planning Commission, Central Ministries and the Cabinet and the National Development Council) will be in a better position to know the quantum and type of foreign resources and aid, which is a thing entirely foreign to the State planners. They can know the nature of input-output relationships; decide about the capital-output and labour output ratios and fix the targets and growth rates in the light of the stability it can assure and assume. It is always incorrect to enforce cuts across the counter without

any consistency. Regional discrimination on the basis of political differences should not come in the way of formulating a plan of national consensus and development perspectives.

10. Ultimately, the states can adjust and disaggregate the sanctioned plan to give it better sectoral and spatial contents. Now the function and activities can be so located as to achieve the goals of growth as well as removing the past imbalances so far as they are not guided by physical considerations. (A hydroelectric generation unit can be located only at the waterfall or dam site.)

Regionalisation

It is rather difficult to by-pass the administrative regions either in the matter of formulation of the plans or their execution. However, nothing should prevent wider co-operation amongst the states of a homogeneous functional region. This can be done if as discussed in the point (9) above there is co-operation amongst the states of a zone in formulation some schemes/projects of inter-state importance. These projects can be implemented through joint monitoring or through special authorities created for them.

When the central planning authorities can feel the pulse of nodal regions through remote control, we can say multi-level planning is on right lines.

Lower Level Administration

While experts of international fame may be available for drafting of the plans at the national level, the manpower at the state level cannot enjoy the same level of prestige in the matter of economic expertise. Persons in charge of manpower planning may know next to nothing about the subject and may think that the work simply involves keeping an inventory of technical personnel. There may be no co-ordination in the programmes of employment generation and making the people employable in long term perspective.

Planning is Entirely Missing

There exist independent evaluation agencies in the states or any other lower levels. The same persons who execute the plans give a certificate of excellent performance to themselves! There is no agency or authority which can monitor the implementation and order the corrective actions. The publicity division of the state does keep a time bound programme of publication the 'achievements' sometimes ahead of the actual implementation! No efforts are made to plug the leakages. These leakages are leakages of corruption, inefficiency, waste and demographic increase.

Various ministers and secretaries are too busy to devote serious attention to the principles and practices of planning. Short period meetings are wasted in issuing of cliche-ridden statements, ritualistic sermons and other inanities.

The machinery at the state level should consist of the representatives of all the ministries and representatives of various spatial divisions. Unless there are experts of sectoral and spatial planning, no meaningful exercise in planning can be undertaken. Specialists in various fields should not be "administration spokesmen" but should have independent individuality and expertise of their own.

For special functions, special working groups can be appointed which will report to the higher co-ordinating bodies, e.g. working groups on population control and medicare and working groups on education and skill building. There should be working groups on transport, irrigation, agriculture, dairying, forestry, communications, finance, power, mineral development, prospecting Industrial developing and so on.

Since economic planning cannot be done in a social

vacuum, the social fabric also gets changed. In non-planned economies the dichotomy and dualism are always present between the rural and urban areas; between the rich and the poor; between the developed and backward sectors and regions. Only under a planned system the material natural, human, real and financial resources can be marshalled in a coordinated manner, planning is a short-cut to win the war on poverty.

The vicious circle can best be broken under a planned system whereby necessary savings, capital and investment allocations can be managed. The latent talents become active forces of progress.

In a planned economy, if the market mechanism is also to be retained, then it can be so modified and improved upon that the national needs are subserved. Market imperfections can be removed and a co-ordination can be obtained in the factor and product markets, as between the markets of various goods and services over different regions. Similarly there can be effective co-ordination between the commodities market and the financial market. The banking system and other financial agencies can be made to lend credit to the priority sectors. In non-planned economics, the small savings of the common people are handed over to certain capitalists who use the money for increasing their profits rather than promoting social good.

Briefly, planning is necessary for

(i) the optimum use of the natural resources;

(ii) increasing production and productivity per person per unit of capital and per unit of time;

(iii) maximisation of employment and ending under-employment;

(iv) increasing the socio-economic productivity;

(v) increasing the economic infrastructure like power,

transport facilities, developing ports and harbours, improving communication network;

(vi) increasing educational, training and medical infrastructure facilities;

(vii) checking erosion of productive capacities i.e., securing afforestation, flood control, insurance against droughts;

(viii) optimising consumption and saving; increasing nominal as well as real capital formation and investment;

(ix) canalising investment between various lines of production according to a national priority plan;

Various Regions:

- *Homogeneous or Formal;* there is geographical, economic or any other type of homogeneity. In Harrod-Domar type models, entire country is taken as homogeneous. It is fit for a single or two sectoral modeling.
- *Heterogenous, functional or nodal region or polarized region:* It is full of non-homogeneity in which there is a hierarchy of settlements and functions. Some nodes or centres renege to which and from which linkages develop. Growth poles emerge.
- *Depressed, Backward and Vestigial regions:* vestigial regions are poor in resources, inhabited by poor tribal and are declining or are static.
- *Macro-Major Region:* As zone of seven-sister states of the East or the four southern states of India.
- *Macro Region:* A state of India, generally.
- *Micro and Micro-minor Region:* A district and a block.
- *Meso Region:* Like Bundelkhand or Chhattisgarh or a commissioner's division.
- *Administrative Region and planning Region :* usually the same but a river valley planning region will cut-across the former.
- *Manufacturing, metropolitan, urban and neutral* (intermediate) Regions. They are what their names suggest. Other types of regions are; mineral region, tribal region, forest region, river valley region.

(x) increasing the per capita availability of basic goods, raising standard of living in real terms and increasing the physical quality of life;

(xi) bringing equality between demand and supply;

(xii) reducing the inequalities of income and asset-holding;

(xiii) prompting industrialisation after increasing productivity in agriculture (thereby reducing the relative share of agriculture in GNP and total employment);

(xiv) to reduce the balance of payment deficits and if they cannot be reduced in the short period of plan for the similar effect in the long period; meanwhile to secure better management of the foreign exchange resources; and

(xv) for promoting a state of autarky, in as many lines of production as possible.

28

Applied Economics of Regional Planning

Developed countries of Europe and North America have rural-urban continuum. So is the position in Australia and New Zealand. However, in *a* country like India even after 60 years of planning, the unacceptable regional disparities remain.

The tasks of regional planning have become even more difficult because now only indicative planning remains.

Now the location of economic activities will be on the principle of comparative advantage. Private investment is now of much greater importance. The impact of the planning process is becoming less and less visible. Budgets are more discussed than the five year plans. Public investment, ever more massive, is not yielding matching results. Productivities are low and leakages are high. They are higher than ever. The theme of corruption leakages cannot be avoided when discussing public sector investment. We examine following combinations:

Sector	*Sector*	*Exploitation.*
Public	Public	No exploitation.
Private	Private	No exploitation
Public	Private	Public sector does not exploit private sector.
Private	Public	Great exploitation

Politicians, their kith and kins acting as contractors,

bureaucrats, officers, mafia groups, industrialists and traders (avoidance of full compliance of tax is one factor), etc., now siphon off a lot of funds.

> As soon as vehicles are purchased road tax for 10 years is collected by State and Local Governments but the city roads are full of pot holes. Anti-incumbency factor votes out governments on the issues of drinking water, good roads, electricity and minor mercies from the governments. The Governments prefer to go out and come next time rather than not take their conventional cuts from the allocations. Regional disparities and poverty persist, not despite planning but because of planning. The best thing that the Planning Commission of India can do is to disappear. It is faceless now.

Though the above observations are not wrong we can say Planning Commission should be mended rather than ended. It should have statutory powers of booking erring persons who misappropriate funds. A wing of the CBI or any other agency should be attached to it !

District Planning is on paper only. The data base is almost totally fake. Figures are changed on the tables. Collectors and other officers of the district are not allowed a five year term to complete a plan. No one is answerable.

> The panchayat system has not changed much the face of the rural side and the regions. Much work could have been done had the house not been divided on political lines. It is quite common to kill the elected representatives. Many lives are lost during the elections also. The father of the nation, Mahatma Gandhi wanted partyless village panchayat system. As is well known he was for achieving self-sufficiency *in* food, clothing and shelter first for each family and each village. He was not against industrialisation.
>
> GANDHIJI DID NOT WANT "RURAL, INDUSTRIALISATION" HE ACTUALLY WANTED

> "RURALISATION OF INDUSTRIES". Each district, block or cluster of villagers can have a hierarchy of occupations/livelihoods that can ensure employment to all. Employment is both goods producing and income generating. He wanted production near the rural masses for the masses and by the masses.

If these principles are kept in view then regional planning can deliver results.

> Regional planning should make best use of the resources and should enable the region to cope with the shortages of other resources. Geographers conceived many regions and not all of the energy that was used in doing the work had been fruitful. Geographers criticised economists for ignoring space but in their schemes of things monetary economics, investment-interest economics, fiscal economics and even techno-economic model building was not there. They unnecessarily created scepticism about regional *economic* planning.

Both the homogeneity and hetrogeneity of space are to be taken into account. In the actual field planning we cannot always get homogeneous regions. Uncommon plans are needed for uncommon regions. There should first be strong ordering of the problems and then strong ordering in the allocating of efforts (not merely investment). Physical, financial, human and technical inputs will be different for different regions.

> Regional planning takes stock of the (i) resources of the region, (ii) manpower inventory, (iii) present and potential levels of development and (iv) provides necessary investments for use of production methods of appropriate technology.

Regional planning is always sub-national planning. We do not take a continent and then include a few countries in the "region". We take a country and can take a few States as a region. We can delineate a region within a

State. Unless the country is very small, regional planning is sub-national planning

Mostly regional planning is in the administrative region. Same spread of forests may cover say Karnataka, Tamil Nadu and Kerala in India yet the planning will not be for the entire forest region but of the forest ranges within the States. The States may coordinate the planning but the jurisdictions may remain separate.

> Regional planning is regional-problem solving planning. A region in danger of Tsunami, a desert region, a snowy region, a forest region, a mining region....will have different action plans for solving the problems. The solutions/schemes of flood prone areas will be opposite of the schemes in the drought prone areas. If there are possibilities then cooperation/coordination can ensure that the flood waters of one region solve the drought problems of the other region.

Different regions have different types of hubs. They can have different transport systems. The habitats may differ. Land uses can be (will have to be) different. The cropping pattern and the pattern of industrialisation will differ.

There can be separate regional planning for urban regions, as the urban regions differ. The regional planning for rural areas will be very different from the urban regional planning. There can be minor differences in rural regional planning, if we leave aside totally different cropping pattern.

Many a times there can be parochial tendencies in regional planning. These are to be avoided. Therefore, a central authority is needed. There is freedom for regional planning but only so long as that is not adversely affecting other regions and the nation. Everyone has the right to walk on the road; but not in the middle of the road .

Regional planning has got to be problem solving and

yet income generating. An arid region can be planted with appropriate trees and the seeding may be done by aeroplane. These trees should provide wood, fodder-leaves and preferably some type of fruits. Then cattle, sheep, camels, goats or other animals that can withstand the climatic conditions can be introduced and propagated. Down-stream activities can then be promoted. Regional planning now a days is best implemented in an administrative division comprising of a few districts. It can be trans-divisions also. Bastar forest area extends to Andhra Pradesh and both can be taken for planning. Coastal Andhra and Coastal Orissa can have one plan. Uttaranchal and Himachal can have one plan. A regional plan for developing a vast can also have States-component. The same is forest-based activities in a few districts can be replicated else where. Instances can be multiplied.

National planning at best is sectoral e.g., for agricultural development, for rural development, for industrial development (by types) for infrastructure development etc. Regional planning is disaggregation of this sectoral planning State-wise and then region and sub-regionwise. All sectoral development plans should have regional dimensions incorporated in them. All regional plans when aggregated should give totals that are equal to the totals of the regional plans.

> Funds can be allocated for programmes within the plans, like providing permanent drinking water facilities to the problem villages. This expenditure can be under water-resource management. It can be booked under any other items also, depending upon the national accounting system should.

Ending destitution, ending poverty, ending illiteracy, ending poor health facilities, improving transport and communication linkages, improving roads, providing drinking water, increasing agricultural productivities, increasing value productivities of farming activities, improving sanitation and habitats, promoting silviculture and fruit-forestry, controlling situations of floods/droughts, having multiple forestry in all vacant spaces etc., are prime tasks that can vary in quality in different regions. Each region should have primes-moving activities that provide full or fuller employment that ensures a permanent income. These things will take time but it should not be a case of "from here to eternity".

Same institutional and administrative setup will work. There can be specialist consultants and people's representative as also some neutral knowledgeable persons. They should not have their own axes to grind. Key district administrative officers should not be transferred till a five year plan is completed.

Allocation of resources both public and private has to be rational i.e., according to the strong ordering of the problems of the region. There has got to be optimum resource use in the public sector investment because it is presumed that this will be there in the private investment. Private investment, however, is for profits and not philanthropy. There should be simultaneous efforts for regeneration of the resources which can be regenerated and also for resource discovery.

> The first step for regional planning should be to end poverty. Growth process should address this issue first. There is no objection to others becoming much better off but not at the cost of coming in the way of poverty alleviation and poverty eradication. Destitution should be ended as early as possible, within five years of starting regional planning.
>
> This is rather simple on paper but difficult in implementation yet is possible in application. Destitute and ultra-poor families can be identified. Their skills of whatever nature can be listed. Members who can be put to work can be identified. They can be given such productive employment that *n* number of persons

> at n size of recompense can get the targeted income that lifts them over the poverty line on enduring basis. There should be self-employment multiplier at work.

Project planning can be essential part of the regional planning. Activities that are already there need to be made efficient. All efforts have to be made to increase the physical productivities of land per acre, per package of inputs and per person employed. For increasing the value productivity, cropping pattern can be modified. Empty lands should be used for water harvesting and/or planting of fruit-bearing trees. Commercial and small industries hubs can be established. Regional planning will have to be supra urban. There are always evil designs on good goals and they emanate from the vested interest groups of the region. They have to be extinguished. In rural areas of India as with the people inhabiting the slums, the informal lending system is in vogue. The money-lenders-cum-traders charge 3 p.c., 4 p.c. 5 p.c., interest per month, sometimes charging as much as 100 p.c. per year or per any term of less than one year even. The interest is deducted from the lending amount in advance. Even in 2008 this practice is there even as the banks are going rural. The money lenders borrow from banks to lend to the people ! The poor persons are in the trap because of their consumption of liquor and habit of gambling, and of course their large progeny.

> There is a impossibility condition in villages. Landless workers get employment; @ 40 per day but in total hardly for 4 months in a year. Two persons of a family thus can Rs. 9600 per year or Rs. 800 per, month for a family of six or even seven.

Illiteracy is to be removed. Family planning is to be promoted and social attitudes are to be made progressive. A State Government, irrespective of the party in power, should practise these.

> Madhya Pradesh Government forbade private practice

of the doctors, including of the teaching staff of medical colleges. The result was that most teaching staff resigned. The medical colleges of the State face threat of the All India Medical Council that the degrees of the colleges will not be recognized. The doctors/ teachers are appointed on a contract salary of Rs. 12000 per month with the condition attached that the contract shall expire automatically after one year with no promise of renewal. No other fringe benefits are given no dearness allowance, no medicines are provided and there are no facilities for even a minor of operation theatre with aseptic conditions. Most, if not all, the doctors who opt of such "package" are either the poor record holders or those who are waiting for opportunity to establish their own clinics, where Rs. 12000 can be earned in a day or two. In a state (name not being given), teachers (named "Guruji", and Shiksha karmies get Rs. 500 to Rs. 1000 per month for primary school, Rs. 1500 or Rs. 1800 for middle school and Rs. 2.500 to Rs. 4000 for higher secondary school. Bribes are taken before appointment for salaries are not paid for months Promise is given that they will be made Permanent. They agitate for the payment of the salaries once or twice a year. In return they are beaten by the police each year without fail as they try to march towards the residence of the Chief Minister or the "Governor.

It is insisted upon that if the students fail, the salary will not be paid. Therefore, the examinations are conducted in such a way that everyone is given a V pass certificate, even as they cannot read the numbers on a car plate. "Board Examinations" for Vth and VIIIth are abolished so that the villagers remain happy with the pass results and the MLAs are not voted out. Many unteachable students take admissions in the college courses where they protest for "strict marking", if they fail. Many Non-English knowing students are admitted in M.B.A. and B.E courses.

In backward regions, sorcery is practised. Each year dozens of women are killed because they were "witches" bringing diseases in villages or were declared as causing deaths of someone or were respcnsible for the droughts ! Unsafe deliveries are common. Superstitions abound. Planning proper as well as regional or district level planning could not end social backwardness nor could ensure the unity of purpose for developmental activities. Worse, the rural-side was totally divided on caste and party (political) lines in the State, as elsewhere in India. Social development vacuum cannot permit regional planning.

Corporate involvement in the development of the interior areas of the country brings recursive effects on the development of the people of the hinterland. The big project may completely bypass the people of the rural areas. Infact they may obliterate some villages and uproot the villagers, while at the same time converting the agricultural land into urban land. This is a disastrous thing that is happening in a country like India.

Advocacy planning is now prominent in India. There are groups which legitimately plead for the development of the scheduled castes and scheduled tribes. Then now there are the groups that advocate the development of the "other backward classes". Caste considerations have become supreme. In the advocacy planning two unfortunate things have entered.

> Fifty p.c. reservations are now accepted in India. First is that howsoever developed a persons belonging to SC/ST/OBC class may be the person is entitled for all types of reservations. Means test is left; only class test remains. There is no expiry date for reservations.
>
> Secondly, howsoever a poor may be in the so-called upper classes, there is no consideration of any type for the person. Means test is not applied.

Narrow parochial politics dominates the pluralistic planning. We should advocate innovative allocative planning for the development of regions. A prime moving activity can be found for the region. There can be a few prime-moving activities. They are new activities. Then resources are to be allocated for optimisation. Neither sectors nor groups of people are neglected.

Regional planning theory should combine the (i) general principles of planning, (ii) urban planning, (iii) rural areas planning, (iv) sectoral planning and (v) special planning for the depressed ethnic groups. The tasks are formidable indeed. The system planning is to be combined for the environmental planning. Economic implications of the social change and social consequences of economic transformation are to be taken care of. It should be hitchless planning rather than combative.

Techniques and Methodologies of Regional Planning

1. Resource inventory *be* prepared.
2. Human resources inventory be prepared.

   Various resources will be quantified by quality and potential use. There should be a time plan when all those who should be in employment, who seek employment and who can be in employment should be employed. Children are to be kept out *of* the work force, unless the work is of taking training in certain skills. Sweating of the aged is al*so to* be avoided.
3. A time profile of the works/programmes/ projects to undertaken in a plan should be prepared. If the planning is right there is no reason why within 10 years all able-bodied persons seeking employment cannot be èmployed for providing basic necessities of living.
4. Finances necessary are to be evaluated and this is

See "Regional Planning" by Alden and Morgan, Leonand Hill Book.

to be done with reference to the appropriate technologies that are to be chosen.

5. Rural areas provided many livelihood patterns, like agriculture, animal husbandry, floriculture, pisciculture, floriculture, epiculture, food forestry, food processing, processing dairy products, handicrafts, ...

   Guild production can be encouraged for a cluster of villages. All persons can work in sheds where electricity can be provided. Other inputs of development can also be delivered easily.

6. Raw Model building can be there. There can be input-output exercises. If very refined type exercises cannot be done, there can always be as to where from the inputs will come at what costs and where the outputs can be used, sold and consumed. Market mechanism can work. If orders are placed the producers arrange the inputs. If they cannot be arranged then the planners will be informed about the same.

7. Location aspects are to be sorted out so that the production is at the least costs for the masses, near the masses and by the masses. Private entrepreneurs will certainly step into or they should be encouraged.

8. "Exports" to other regions can be estimated. Regional multiplier can be worked out. Instead of indulging in region-wise exercises, it will be sufficient to calculate how much can be sold at various prices and income generation should be worked-out. Profit ratios can be worked out. There can be some activities which are not providing much employment and/or not bringing sufficient income. They can be down-sized and other activities can be started.

9. There can be social accounting also to find out whether

the depressed ethnic groups, destitutes, and people below the poverty line were sufficiently benefitted.

10. Forecasting can be done for future plans of action.

There should be monitoring of the activities. This monitoring is to be about the physical productivities and efficient storage, transport and marketing. There should be profitable activities. This monitoring is not to be of socialist type of planning whereby everything is known to the planners. This monitoring should be of the "extension service type".

29

Economics of Project Planning–I

Feasibility studies
Formulation of project profiles
Implementation of project
Rural projects
Utility Transforms
GANTT, PERT AND CPM

Meaning

A project is a scheme for investment of resources. A project is a building block of an investment plan. Every project has a sub-project, but somewhere a line may have to be drawn. A sub-project can be treated as a separate project. For example, the construction of a dam and the construction of canal net-work can be treated as separate projects also, though both the activities are quite inter-related. One sub-project can be rejected in favour of another sub-project. (For example, there can be different types of residential quarters for a mining project). Many considerations enter into accepting one sub-project in favour of another .

PART-A

Formulation of the Project

Identification

First the project is to be identified. This project should be a prime-mover i.e., a project with maximum of linkages.

If good projects are taken to the rural side, it will mean taking jobs to the people cutting the distance of migration from rural areas to the urban areas. Such projects can utilise the raw materials and manpower of the adjoining areas and generate employment, output and income. Projects which can be expected to give maximum catalytic effect in promoting further development should be selected. On one side the monetary, opportunity and real costs of the selected project should be low and on the other the project should promise high rates of output, employment and income. Project should be such that they can be executed within the inputs available.

Those projects be identified which should receive high priority in the country, region or the people of the area. The projects which generate externalities should receive priority. The project should provide long term productive capacity and income. It should generate very high amount of spread-effects, and demonstration effect.

There can be several projects such us irrigation system, land reclamation, flood control, power plants, construction works relating to railways, roads development, afforestation, dairy development, health project or even developing education system.

The project can cost millions of money units and can be a localised unit or spread over project, (e.g., a big dairy scheme spread over hundreds of villages). A project can be an 'enclave project" designed and supervised by foreign consultants, executed by contractors and suppliers and managed with the help of expatriates. Most projects should be executed with local talent and resources. Economists, financial analysts, engineers, agronomists, demographers, architects, rural sociologists, energy specialists, public health experts, environmentalists, educators, physical planners etc., have all an important role to play in project planning.

Formulation of the Project

Project formulation covers all the steps necessary to bring a project to the point where its technical, economic, and financial feasibilities have been established and it is ready for appraisal. The funding agency cannot straightway give loans for the project immediately after its identification. The project formulation and feasibility studies have to be completed before funding is provided.

Starting of a project involves decisions, based on technical judgments, about the site and location of the facility, and more broadly, on the appropriate technical features of the project itself. This is the stage in which soil, hydrographic and hydrological investigations have to be undertaken, and the suitability and adequacy of the natural and other resources required for the project determined. It is also the stage where alternatives are systematically explored. The alternatives should be cheaper and equally efficient or equally costly but more efficient. This is done through feasibility studies, which provide the preliminary design and engineering of alternative technical solutions and make a preliminary assessment of the economic benefits of each.

The project can be prepared by an expert national or international agency (IBRD does that work for less developed countries). It is not the bigness of the project that should matter but the effectiveness.

In case of the rural projects, the labour intensity should be high and the project should improve agricultural operations and productivity. The differences in income, skill and quality of life between the rural and urban areas should be reduced by such projects. Rural project should be desired by the local people and should provide great linkages and feedback effects. It should have lower indivisibilities and gestation period.

Intermediate technology can be used in the rural projects. As far as possible the project should use local resources, have local manpower for work and local market for the output.

Before formulation of the project, the resource inventory and input inventories are to be prepared. Feasibility and viability studies are to be undertaken and technical details about the erection of the project are to be worked out. Project planning cannot be independent of the national planning, it is a part of the national planning. Project planning determines the success of the national planning.

Project formulation will involve simulation of the analysis of resource use capital availability, productivity expectations from workers, profitability expectations etc., If low profits are expected from 'A' strategy, 'B' strategy may be evolved for a project. Project formulation should subserve the national goals and should be within the resources. A balance between the ideal and the workable formulation is to be struck.

Decisions are to be taken about allocation of resources and technology mix. Output streams are to be worked out. Ideal cost-benefit relations are to be targeted. Project formulation is the preparation of the pre-investment report. It is an investigation process which precedes investment decision.

First there is PIR (pro-investment report) work, and then there will DPR (detailed project report) work. Project formulation requires preparation of detailed specifications and designs, engineering drawings, site investigations and foundation design for the project premises, detailed design of the process or other equipment and time schedules for the implementation of the project.

The concept of capital-output ratio which is so popular with the planners for planning exercises is in fact more related to the projects. The capital output ratios of various projects are average as national capital-output ratios for various sectors. Right from the blue-print and drawing stage to tender-calling and construction stage, these capital-output ratios are to be calculated. The fifth five year plan of India mentions:

"It is necessary that in order to ensure the growth output envisaged in the plan, the efforts at project formulation need to be intensified. It is only on the basis of actual projects that feasibility of the output targets contained in the plan can be tested".

The fifth plan also recorded:

> "One of the reasons of the poor performance of several key sectors in the fourth plan is that preparation and evaluation of projects and issue of sanction were undertaken much after the plan had been finalised and the project concerned had been included in it".

Project formulation provides a scientific basis both for the development and installation of an information system as also for the determination of the target information against which the information obtained can be evaluated. In the words of Gunnar Myrdal:

> "Planning in effect is a learning process in which intuition is transferred into hunches and hunches into knowledge, political pressure into technical consideration, wholly independent into partly instrumental valuation, and in which the obstacles presented by social inertia and vested interests, the inhibitions of the planners and the area of genuine ignorance and uncertainty are gradually reduced. Project formulation is one of the basic techniques through which planning can change from one institutional base to an institutional and rational base".

Project planning assumes great importance in those

countries where physical planning (rather than mere financial planning) is considered more important. Planning is as successful as the success of the project and the project evaluation is based upon whether the project fulfils the planning objectives.

In any plan formulation work, the government, the financial institutions, the entrepreneurs and the planners (including the personnel of the entire administrative set-up) are involved.

The role of the government is important in project formulation. Frequently, the state governments feed the Central Government with wrong data so that the project is not rejected. Project reports are merely proforma-proposals in which even wrong details may be fed. At the State level the machinery for project formulation is rather weak. At the Central level the expert machinery may not have enough powers to reject a project if a very important politician at the Centre or the State is backing the project. It is necessary that the expert bodies and the politicians should have a balanced say in the project formulation and acceptance.

Financial institutions approve a project only when the capacity for the repayment of loan is established. A project may be socially good but if it cannot generate enough surplus for repayment, financial institutions would not, like to fund the same. Some agencies can fund a project even if self-generated resources may not be forthcoming, if the government guarantees the repayment. The government can always repay the loans from the tax revenues. However, this negates the very principle of project planning. In the long run every project should yield the revenue directly or indirectly for self liquidating repayment.

If the project belongs to the private sector the *entrepreneur* does the work of formulation of the project. The private enterprise makes the profitability analysis of the project as against the social cost-benefit analysis that may be done by the government agency for its projects. International lending agencies prefer private projects of the established industrial houses. If the financial agencies are captive (i.e. nationalized banks or insurance companies), then the government projects can get finance merely by asking.

A private entrepreneur has to understand the licensing procedures, import and export policies of the government, price control, limits on expansion, and incentive packages. Their time dimensions have to be understood. Those who formulate the project must ensure first that there are no losses and then to see that gains and profits are as high as possible. It will be of no use to formulate a project, the line of production of which has been banned by the government, howsoever profitable it may be. A *formal* project for the manufacture of banned drugs cannot be formulated.

When there is a project idea, there will be an *inventory taking* team which will go into the details of investment. The locational aspects will be decided and detailed propositions will be drafted. *A sponsoring body* will have to be searched. Then the project formulation team of experts will start the detailed work. *Outside agencies and consulting agencies* may be consulted for financial and technical guidance and aid. *The feasibility report* that will be prepared by the agencies will not only tell whether or not the project will be viable but also how and to what extent it will be so. There will be detailed instructions in the report about the *allocation of resources* and investment in a time pattern. The special task force of implementing the project will have its own *performance-budget.*

There are non-quantifiable projects also *(like adult education, family planning drive, or rural health projects)* of which only social-cost benefit analysis can be made but not the direct profitability analysis. There can be several quantifiable projects in (i) agricultural sector, (ii) mining and quarrying sector, (iii) manufacturing sector, (iv) construction sector, *(v)* electricity, gas, water sectors, *(vi)* transport, communication, storage sector, (vii) irrigation and flood control sector and (viii) social services.

Feasibility Studies

Feasibility studies are an important part of project formulation and deserve full analysis. There are certain choices which must be exercised. In the first instance, it is to be judged whether a particular type of project can be undertaken at all. There must be domestic and foreign competitors. There may be resource constraints or demand constraints. If they can be overcome, then the project can be chosen.

Next question arises whether the project will be viable here or somewhere else. Its best location is to be found out. It should be located in such a manner that transport and others diseconomies do not overwhelm the location economies.

After locating the project, it is to be decided as to how much is to be produced, what quality is to be produced, how is it to be produced (technology mix and factor mix) and at what price the output is to be sold. Presuming that there are certain indicators for all these things, the profitability can be simulated. Externalities can also be taken into account e.g., expected tax burdens or administrative obligations and help. In the end it can be found out whether the project will work successfully and successful working will include whether it can finance its own expansion or repay the capital borrowed.

Data regarding all these aspects are to be collected and projected. Additive (self-generated), complementary (from interaction) and break-through (through extra efforts and chances) opportunities are to be imagined, or anticipated. So also the possible opposite conditions are to be taken into account. A project planner should hope for the best but provide for the worst.

Opposite conditions involve risks which should be foreseen and efforts have to be made to avoid them. In other cases, it should be planned how non-insurable risks can be borne. One who is well aware of the trends in the business, industrial and capital (shares) market can be a good project planner. A project formulator should be aware of economic rules, regulations and tax structure and these things are to be taken note of in project formulation.

Project formulation is not something independent of or in addition to plan targets. There are projects to implement the plans. Therefore what types of projects are to be established or implemented will be decided by the plan proper. The plan formulation and implementation will require how best to do it and realize the targets and objectives of planning.

It is in case of the private project that risks of a wrong project are high. In a planned system the project has a certain place in the schemes and plan. In the private enterprise system the project may face uncertainties due to competition. In a planned system a position of monopoly or semi-monopoly in a region is assured. A public project faces death-like condition because of malfunctioning while private project faces difficulties because of the cut-throat competition but very rarely of inefficient working.

Mistakes about estimates of input supplies, availability of raw material, manpower, infrastructure facilities, capital etc., can pose serious problems. If output-capital ratios are not realized, there will be further problems. These problems will get compounded if there are marketing (demand) problems. In project formulations all these cost benefit analyses are to be made in advance.

Profitability analysis will be made for economic projects

while social costs and social benefits analysis will be made for socio-economic projects (education, health development). In this case the feasibility studies will be of different type.

Not all projects which do not satisfy the feasibility criterion are rejected! Sometimes some projects are formulated and implemented at the behest of the planners. In this case it will be the duty of the project executives to make the best out of the very bad conditions. After all, the decisions of the publicmen or the elected representatives of the people become supreme.

Not much relevance of socio-cost-benefit can be traced in many defence projects. Of course, whatever is to be done should be done efficiently but sometimes the problems of military expediency may not allow such studies to be made because some different considerations far outweigh.

While formulating a project the endogamous and exogenous forces of constraints and spurs can be anticipated. The social environment has also to be studied.

It is also to be judged whether the project is within the competence of the persons. If the requisite manpower is not available then the manpower is to be trained. Competence analysis is to be made and the conditions are to be created in advance. Condition creation is to be taken note of in the feasibility report. Several questions are to be raised and listed. Answers to them are to be recorded. The score will tell the project makers where they stand and what sort of correctives have to be introduced. They can also know with what sort of 'liabilities' they have to live.

Techno-economic Analysis

Techno-economic analysis is a part of the feasibility report. The same aspects e.g., demand forecasting, costs of the project erection, costs of running the project and producing various levels of output, physical and time inputs needed, financial and physical return expected etc., are studied in the techno-economic analysis.

In sequential terms, project formulation shall include the works relating to evaluation of a project in terms of feasibility prospects, techno-economic prospects, time profile, input prospects, financial prospects, social cost-benefit prospects and re-investment prospects.

Without all such studies (simulated or otherwise), a project may have to be shelved midway through and it may involve colossal losses. Such analyses help in not taking up the project at all if insurmountable difficulties are revealed later on.

When a project is to be implemented the forward and backward linkages are to be examined. If there is a project of readymade garments, so many things of backward linkages have to be taken into account—to name just a few: whether sewing machines and materials will be available, whether cloth of the types required will be available, whether yarn and cotton will be available, or whether necessary inputs (fertilizers, pesticides and farm machinery) etc., will be available for the cotton growing. In case of the forward linkages it has to be examined whether the trained manpower for running the project will be available (if not what type of training programme will be necessary), and whether selling outlets will be managed. Such projects can be several: some fail miserably while others experience roaring success. The type of things that are sold should cater to the tastes and fashion; publicity shall also count. These things are to be planned in techno-economic research for the preparation of the feasibility report.

PART-B

Implementation of the Project

Literature on 'formulation', 'identification', and 'appraisal' of the project is now legion but not so much on 'implementation'. Certain policy guidelines about implementation can be identified.

1. During the project formulation stage, the stage of implementation must have been simulated after careful considerations. It is believed that the simulation work must have been as possible. During the implementation stage, it will be necessary that all these stages of implementation should be completed within the time schedule allotted. There should be minimum overlapping of the stages, unless the overlapping was planned *ex ante.*
2. The second point to be kept in mind in the implementation stage will be the realization of the physical targets during the time period contemplated. The output stream should be the same as contemplated.
3. The third point of importance will be to complete the works within the funds allotted. The physical targets are to be realized within the financial allocations. In case of inflationary pressures, some adjustment will be necessary for which the project planners cannot be blamed. However, inflation results when all project planners fail to realize the physical targets of output within the financial allocation and within the time period allotted. Long gestation period and lower output and /or higher financial outlays are what bring inflation. This is the fault of the central monitoring authority and the wings of government which look after the financial (monetary and fiscal) management during the formulation stage.

4. The implementation machinery will have to realise the targets of capital-output ratios, capital-labour ratios and labour-output ratios as were contemplated during the formulation stage.
5. The management of the sinking fund (for the repayment of the loan that must have been taken for running the project) will be yet another important task of project implementation.
6. Those who implement the project must keep an eye over changes in technology, taste, cost-price structure, profitability etc. The labour-management relations should be such that work is not hindered. Constraints must be anticipated and overcoming planned for. A close watch is to be kept on input procurement. Productivity targets, over-fulfilment targets (if any), transport and marketing aspects. The cash flow is to be managed so that the liquidity does not suffer.
7. Ultimately the profitability is to be so ensured that reinvestment funds are generated from within.

A Note on Rural Projects

It has been seen that rural projects can be of various types e.g., development of minor irrigation works, making a cluster of villages approachable during all seasons byroads, improving sanitation and rural health, propagating adult education and family planning, launching 'social forestry scheme', plant protection drive, drive for warehousing and grains safety, drive for making agriculturists use HYV seeds, drive for developing *fertigation* techniques in an area, dairy development and dung-gas plants development, a project for land reclamation, checking soil erosion and land improvement, or developing agro-based industries.

The fundamental aims of rural project will be to (i) increase the development consciousness through changes in socio-cultural-economic atmosphere, (ii) make the basic goods available, (iii) utilise the rural manpower more gainfully, (iv) make a direct attack on poverty, (v) have low capital-output ratios and high labour-output ratios, and (iv) should have a short gestation period. The pattern and volume of production will have to be planned, input-output relation have to be worked out, value-adding streams have to be estimated, and incremental capital-output ratios have to be worked out. Surpluses and marketing procedures are to be planned.

It will not be prudent to make rural projects import-replacing or exports promoting in the early stages of development, unless the project relates to food self sufficiency. If such projects are started in rural areas which make available output for exports, the projects will have the same backwash effects for which the old colonial system was notorious. Local self-sufficiency of wage goods and promotion of the inputs for development should merit greater attention.

The development of rural projects also depends on some urban projects e.g., fertilizer project, tractor manufacturing projects, project for manufacturing insecticides, projects for supplying irrigation pumps, project for supply bins for storage etc., however, such projects as cattle-feed supplying projects or small tools-supplying projects can be established in rural areas themselves.

Power cannot be generated in rural areas nor can transport equipment be manufactured here. The technical personnel will also come from urban areas e.g., doctors, trained teachers, engineers, etc. Para-medical or similar lower rank cadres can be trained from the rural stock in due course of time. Considerable scope exists in rural areas to utilize the services of under-employed persons (women in particular) and seasonally unemployed persons.

Even for rural projects such exercises as about (a) risk

and uncertainties, (b) innovations, (c) demand forecasting, (d) cost-sensitivity trends, (e) price trends, (f) competition possibilities, (g) tax possibilities, (h) finance and infrastructure availabilities etc., have to be undertaken.

Rural development is to a very large extent a function of the availability of water and water availability depends upon monsoon. 'The only certain thing about the monsoons is its uncertainty" and insulation against the erratic availability of water should be ensured through various projects. This can ensure flow of agricultural surpluses. Nothing probably matters more.

Rural projects can be great sources of money for the urban planners. For example, trees planted under "vana-mahotsava" (afforestation) programme in India whither away even before the bills of expenditure are cleared. A rural political-economic watch dog must oversee that rural projects do not become means of siphoning off the funds for the benefit of a vested interest group. This aspect is very important.

For the rest, the rural projects formulation procedures are more or less the same as of urban projects. A rural project bureau can also be set up for different regions. Non-viable rural projects will set disheartening precedents. Projects can be in any sector-private, co-operative, or public. Tax laws, if they are pragmatic, can keep away the administrators from showing 'losses' and the true picture of the working can emerge.

There can be several rural projects particularly for handloom cloth, dress (uniform) making, doll making, furniture making, paper and cardboard making, tool forging, match box making, solvent extraction, making of brooms and brushes, carpet weaving, bone digesters, utensil making, bricks from paddy husk, oil from paddy husk or even corn, fruit growing orchards, mini-cement plants, footwear and leather goods, soap making etc.

PART-C

Special Notes

Project Planning and Production Management

Management has to give sufficient attention if the time dimension of the project is long and project is being started from scratch. The management has to keep in mind that all projects are unique in themselves. Even when one project is similar in nature, its geographical location is unique to itself. Non-repetitive project decisions, therefore, become necessary.

A permanent team of expert managers has to be concerned with all stages of project from identifying the project, to location, deciding the size, maintaining the required capital-output, labour output and capital-labour relationships, realizing a certain benefit cost ratio, doing everything in a time strait-jacket, and monitoring the implementation and evaluation.

There are irreversibilities involved. The bigger the project, the greater will be the nature of indivisibilities. In big projects, mistakes prove very costly. Wrong decisions and wrong timings of activities will even cripple or render a project bankrupt. There exist ruin threshold in long-term planning situations where a single decision can push the company across a threshold from which there is no return.

Decisions which have short cycle effects can also bring grave losses. However, there may be very great scope of correction if attended to early. Non-reversibility characterizes long-term planning and distinguishes it from short-term cases. Some short-term wrong decisions can bring strikes and loss of machine time and labour time, higher overhead burden or cancellation of orders from customers or return of defective goods.

If the project has large degree of repetition in its operations then the system can be regarded as stable. In such cases past experience can be used for forecasting future. There are many long period projects where there may be no precedence. In such cases judgment assumes great importance. Problems tend to be unique and special methodology will have to be evolved.

In case of such long period projects for which new decisions become very necessary it will be very important for the project managers to record their experiences as the project goes by. All project details should be so recorded that they are not forgotten over the long period. Activity sequence can be maintained. Project control must be so observed that the resources are optimally allocated over the time. If need be, strategy will have to be changed or modified. Experience should be recorded so that predictions become possible.

When long term projects are being planned project decisions are frequently founded upon opinions; and opinions differ. It will be an important function of the administration to record the reasons of disagreement of opinions among the top management cadre. Time will vindicate one or a few other opinions. These have to be taken note of. That strategy should be adopted that gives scope for flexibility. Then, corrective actions can be taken easily if they become necessary. That strategy that promises very high profits but at the same time may end in catastrophe, is not to be preferred.

Sensitivity analysis becomes important for long period project planning. There can be projects where only one strategy is to be chosen. It is clearly the best of all. Then there will be no question of sensitivity analysis. It will not be a problem at all. When different strategies are available, then sensitivity analysis becomes important. The optimal combination of variables, the value of slack variables, and the optimum value of the objective function can be found out. While the optimum solution states what to do now, given the objective function and the constraints, the sensitivity analysis raises questions about opportunities and what possibly could or should be done to improve the solution to the managerial problem.

In sensitivity analysis, the marginal gain and marginal losses of increasing and/ or decreasing production with alternative strategies is to be found out. Then choice is made. Some decisions are of great importance. Others may be of only marginal importançe. If small changes bring large effects, the system is said to be "sensitive". Sensitivity analysis supplies narrow probability ranges. Sensitivity estimates can be applied not only to forecasts, but to outcomes as well. Sensitivity analysis thus represents an important planning technique. A manager needs assessment of the critical areas for sensitivity analysis with clear guidance.

Sensitivity analysis becomes necessary whenever it is necessary to know the reliability of various economic alternatives. The believability of the sensitivity analysis is a manager's option and responsibility.

Utility-Transforms Study

They refer to the study of the alternative projects. One project may have high expected rewards yet at the same time high penalty rates (high possibilities of losses also). The other project may have less expected reward as well as minimum penalty. A balancing is to be done. Low penalty rates are to be preferred. Considerations about the penalty side of the pay-off scale are very important.

If a project has high probability of loss, it means that the project will not be flexible in operation options. The possibility of ruin threshold is high. Losses will curtail other profitable activities. Reserves may be destroyed and further expansion may become limited. The project becomes vulnerable.

A project manager has to evaluate pay-offs in the unique different way relevant for the project. The pay-off is to be considered with reference to the capital. A profit from Rs 50 lakhs to Rs 51 lakhs is only 2 per cent increase. As against this, an increase of Rs 1 lakhs from Rs. 1 lakh (i.e., to Rs 2 lakhs) is 100 per cent increase. Thus the transformation of outcomes to utilities is a critical management function. What may be good for a large project might spell ruin for a small one. Risks and utilities are to be carefully weighed.

Once projects could be managed (and used to be managed) on "trial and error basis" (also known as GANTT METHOD, after Henrey L. Gantt). However, in the modern world where stakes are high, this will not help. A modern manager is confronted with several and serious sub-optimal situations. He wants to achieve optimization everywhere. Thus project planning becomes a critical function. Errors with wider ramifications can lead to the destruction of the enterprise. Potential ruin situations are to be identified and avoided. Great deal of both theoretical and practical efforts will be necessary.

Now-a-days, the 'time' is also an important cost factor. Project managers have little time to take decisions. They do not have great computational time to handle problems. Hence the aid of computers is taken.

In a simple way a project planning chart can be prepared. On the left side of the chart, stages can be written (planning stages; materials procurement stage; fabrication stage or stage Nos. I to n. sub-assembly stages from 1 to n and the final assembly inspection and testing and certification). On the right side the dates can be plotted. Many dates will overlap i.e., next stage may start even before the previous stage is complete. Material procurement and fabrication may continue side by side. Shifting the dates may be necessary and can be receded.

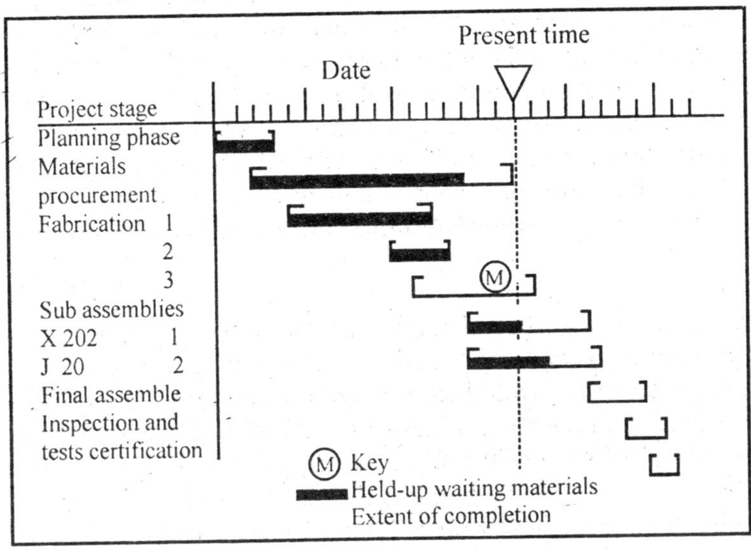

Fig. 1

All projects have technological sequences and constraints. It is very rare that there are no constraints. These constraints are to be anticipated and overcome. That sequence is to be selected that assures the best allocation of resources with minimum constraints. Optimizing project activity requires good judgment and even intuition. Co-ordination and dovetailing are very much necessary.

A project planner has to beat so many odds. In times of inflation, early and bulk purchase of necessary things can save a lot of money which will be spent more when the price rises.

The above chart is a simple chart that keeps track of what has happened in terms of what was thought should have happened. It is a suitable device for control and accounting. This chart, however, does not tell us how the resources could have been allocated better.

The pendulum like line can be kept moving to show where the project people stand. As the project progresses, it will move to the right.

A Note on Some Procedures regarding Project Planning

There are some terms and procedures regarding project planning. *Systems Analysis*

All problems are first anticipated and simulated. Their optimum solutions are also evolved. A scientific system is perfected which analyses the data of the problems and judges the efficacy of various solutions in a simulated way. It can also solve the on-going problems. The main feature is that for every problem there can be alternative solutions. The solutions are judged in all their ramifications. That solution is to be chosen which is not only consistent, but also cheap, quick and effective. It is better to think about the possible solutions; They should not remain intuitive. A good decision comes out of experience; but experience comes out of a bad decision.

Now-a-days the help of the computers can also be taken. The problems may be identified and solutions programmed. The computer can give a solution which will be error-free and speedy. Machines and men can co-operate in a systematic manner to know the problems and solutions.

Operational Research

In any system as a whole there are parts. In each factory, there are various sections which produce a part or process a part of the whole. There are purchase, production, and sales divisions. Then there are sub-divisions. A part must function well so that the other part can also function well. It is quite possible that while 95 per cent of the system is working well, 5 per cent may not be and this can, in due course of time, make the working of the rest 95 per cent difficult and even impossible.

In the *operational system approach,* the individual components of the system should function in consonance with each other and the smooth functioning of each component is essential for the overall well-being of the system.

First, the problem is understood: *secondly,* the comparative importance of parameters and variables is understood in a system; *thirdly* a solution is conceived deductively (logically or intuitively) and based on empirical studies (numerical methods); *fourthly,* solutions are conceived and tested (field experiments or simulation) *and fifthly,* solutions are finally implemented.

In any project planning, certain tactical problems are to be tackled. These are:

(1) *Allocation problem* under which how much to invest and how to allocate the resources are analysed.

(2) *Inventory problem:* Unnecessary inventory accumulation puts a dead weight on the organization; and absence of inventories may mean that for the want of a nut, the whole project may go dead.

(3) *Replacement problem:* The project planners must make maximum use of the machines before they become obsolete and for that sinking fund provisions should be adequate.

(4) Solving the *queuing problem* i.e., a situation should not arise when due to under-production, customers cannot get the required goods; this means not utilizing the market potential fully.

(5) Finally, the *routing and competitive problems* are

to be solved so that cross transportation charges are not incurred and adverse effects of competitive losses are avoided.

PERT and CPM

PERT refers to Programme Evaluation and Review Technique while CPM refers to Critical Path Method.

In any project there are some critical choices. If a project has a long gestation period, it means high investments, high overheads for that period, and lack of goods supply for the period. It may, however, mean that in the long run the goods supply may be abundant. Opposite effects will be there for projects with short gestation period.

The above two methods were developed independently but are almost synonymous in meaning and content. The methods are used from Army, Navy and Air programmes to the programmes of various firms producing commercial goods.

The aim is to reduce the time and costs of (i) project formulation and finalization, (ii) construction, (iii) working, (iv) maintenance and (v) over-hauling. It is simulated that if the working of the project follows various paths, what will be the trade-off between costs and benefits in terms of time. Past experience can also be a guide for future action. Interrelationships and the time paths of development can be studied with the help of charts and diagrams.

Different components of work can be accomplished in different ways, in different time periods, and at different costs. The completed event becomes a "milestone". These "milestones" can be identified and shown on a graph in a circle. Code number may be given for these accomplishment-landmarks. An arrow can trace the way which is least time consuming yet most efficient: This will be the critical path. One path which enables to reach the goal earliest at minimum costs (wastes) and maximum outputs is to be chosen.

30

Project Economics and Planning—II

A. Project Appraisal and UNIDO method.

B. Profitability and cash flows.

C. Socio-cost benefit analysis. Shadow prices.

PART-A

1. Project Appraisal

This is to be done during the implementations as well as after the completion of the project. However, the appraisal should better start mid-way through the completion. Some aspects like whether the work is being done according to the blue-print and within the time costs, as on-going process If that is not done, then there will be cost over-runs and time over-runs. Six important aspects are to be kept in view;

Technical aspects: These relate to the right use of the inputs and right flows of outputs. The engineering aspects regarding quantities and qualities involved have got to be looked into. If, for example, it is a rail-road construction project, it has to be checked whether the best alignments were obtained and whether the project can handle load density. All allied aspects e.g., right quality of the culverts, bridges, signaling system, communication system, safety outlets etc., are to be planned.

Economic appraisal: Examines the inter-sectoral

relations as also the benefits costs relationships. If benefits have not started accruing, the time pattern of costs is to be evaluated.

Commercial appraisal: It relates to whether the prices paid are right and if the production stream has started whether the prices received are the optimum. *Financial appraisal* relates to evaluating the inflows and outflows of cash. Viability of the project can be re-evaluated. *Managerial evaluation* is about the productivities or work effectiveness of all the persons involved. Right persons have got to be at right places at right time for right payments and for right productivities and/or significance. *Organisational appraisal* is a little bit different from managerial appraisal. Here we are concerned about timely and right decision making.

Intra-project works, inter-project positions and relations with the government and outside agencies are also to be evaluated.

2. Project Appraisal in Developing Economies

First of all, all costs should be as low as possible. These are physical costs (real inputs used), monetary costs (real quantities multiplied by prices), capital and labour costs (their values) and opportunity costs (income from the next best alternative). The question of opportunity costs actually arises before the start of the project. The best project should be chosen.

Benefits should accrue to maximum number of the persons and for the benefit of the people in general. On any day, an irrigation and flood control project is far superior to a private sector brewery. (In Ratlam, Madhya Pradesh, the government ran an alcohol plant). Public projects should generate employment and should help in eradication of poverty through increasing the income streams.

The norms of evaluating a private sector project are internalized. The norms of evaluating a public sector project are different. The points may be the same but the view points differ. In the public sector projects, public good is the prime consideration. A private brewery can discharge the effluents in the river system. The tanneries of Kanpur (earlier Cawnpore) have destroyed the Ganga and the governments could do nothing.

The planned benefits-costs should come out more or less the same, *ex post.*

Shadow rates of interests used to be used in earlier evaluations. "Shadow prices" are those prices, which if established will equate demand and supply". The importance of shadow prices was at a time when prices used to be controlled. There used to be official rates of exchange between US $ and Indian rupee. The market rates used to be higher for dollars and lower for the rupee. For example if the official rate was $ 1 Rs. 26, in the market, it used to be $ = Rs. 36 (more or less). Hence the shadow exchange rate could be Rs. 36 or between Rs. 26 and Rs. 36. Shadow rates of wages, interest or whatever are used when market mechanism is not allowed to have its full sway Now there is liberalization, privatization and globalization. The real prices are market prices. *The concept of shadow prices has lost its relevance.*

Discounting of benefits has also undergone a change. The basis of "discounting of benefits" is that "present gains" are more important than "future gains". Costs of the projects are incurred now. Benefits come in future. Hence future benefits should be discounted. Benefit of Rs. 100 today is more important than one year afterwards. If the rate of interest is 10 p.c., then after one year, the benefits should be 110. Then 10 p.c, on Rs. 110, which be Rs. 11 and hence the benefits of second year should be Rs. 121.

We say the discounted benefits of one year of Rs. 110 at 10 p.c, rate of interest are equal to Rs. 100 and of Rs. 121 two years hence at the same rate of discounting are Rs. 100. Hence the future benefits should keep on increasing at the rate of discounting.

UNO does not consider this right. *All projects which provide immense social benefits for the general masses should be evaluated without discounting of benefits, If discounting is done then we can "prove" that all public sector projects will be costlier in comparison to their benefits. There will be adding of interests also in the costs. This will be double drag on the evaluation of benefits.*

The use of shadow prices and the practice of discounting of future benefits may be theoretically correct. But western economists used them more for the public projects than for the private projects. There intention was to prove the suitability of private projects and unsuitability of the public sector projects. Their views were sinister. UNO ruled that if at all a discount rate is to be used it should be 3 p.c, or less. There are immense benefits of planting such trees in desert region that can withstand and climate and that can check the march of desert. Benefits of such projects should not be discounted at all.

[See IMF's Finance and Development. March 1979 Vol. 16. Number 1 p. 30 for views about the rate of discounting). Once upon a time the western economists used to discount the benefits of the projects in developing economies @ 18 p.c.!

3. UNIDO (United Nations Industrial Development Organisation) Their Guidelines for Project Evaluation

There are very longish guidelines couched in language that readers would find tough. In simple way, the points can be listed as under:

First, it should be evaluated whether the projects completed the goods gap (brought more supplies to match the demand), the way it was planned. *Secondly* some projects do not close the goods gap directly but indirectly e.g., power plants that make production possible. All infrastructure development projects help the production units indirectly. Good roads, good railway services, development of ports and harbours etc., are all such projects that help the production indirectly. Their efficacy should be evaluated — the outcomes has got to be the same as was conceived. *Thirdly,* the physical and monetary costs should come out as were planned. Monetary costs can differ by as much as the inflation rates are. However, if most of the projects have "inflation-escalation clause", the outcome should match this position. *Fourthly,* the project should not have inflicted social costs on the society as of having created pollution or having left pollution uncontrolled. *Fifthly,* projects relate to the traded goods and to non-traded goods and services. They all had certain objectives about profits or utilities. Non-traded projects can be about the expansion of medical and educational facilities. They can be about provision of safe drinking water or provision of all-the-year-round connectivity. It is to be evaluated whether the quality "utilities" (services) were provided the same way as were planned or conceived. *Sixthly* for productive projects 'productivity' is to be measured and for public utility projects 'efficiency' is to be measured. Both should come up as were planned. *Seventhly, shadow prices or border prices should be used for evaluation if necessary.*

B. Profitability Analysis: Cash Flow Analysis

Benefits-costs analysis is a wider concept. Profitability is a narrow concept. Most, but not all projects, run for profit. Profit should be commercial profits. What percentage of profits is to be regarded as 'commercial profits'. If the long term rate of interest in any country on the deposits is

10 p.c, then atleast 20 p.c, profits on the total capital can be regarded as commercial profits The floor of 10 p.c, will be known as "wages of superintendence" or "proxy of interest earnings". Profits to be profits should be supernormal.

Cash flow is the net inflow of cash over the outflow but of future years. The future profits are to be discounted on the same principle as was discussed earlier about the benefits.

While discounting of benefits may be misplaced, discounting of cash flow is not Rs. 100 today are better than Rs. 100 one year hence. One year hence, they should be minimum 10 p.c, extra. The discounted future flow should be equal to a figure of the present e.g., Rs. 100.

Financial Analysis

This analysis relates to 'book-keeping and accountancy" and is of great concern to commerce students. Sale and purchase accounts, profit and loss accounts and the position as is transferred to the balance sheet are all to be studies. To an economist, it is of great concern that the fund raising through equity bonds, debentures and/or bank loans should provide the cheapest combination. In any profitability analysis, it is very necessary for the planners to find out the break-even point. It is that point where total costs become equal to total revenue. There are two points for the same.

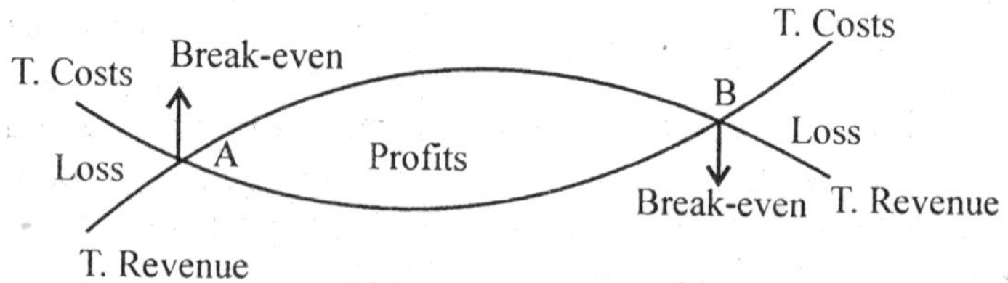

Fig. 1

These is logic in reaching point A, Profits are there thereafter. There is no point in crossing B. There are only losses thereafter. If "C" is costs and "R" revenue and *R* is *equal to px i.e., price multiplied by x quantity of goods, we can have breakup of "C" also.* C = vx + F. Here v represents the unit variable costs; x represents the volume of goods and *F represents the per unit total fixed costs. Price setting will include proportionate part of the fixed costs per unit + variable costs per unit.*

Operational leverage should be high and this means capital-output ratio should be low or output-capital ratio should be high. The position with regard to the following should be as under:

Net worth should be high. Net worth is equal to equity capital plus reserves and surpluses and net profits. Net profits, as is well known are equal to the gross profits depreciation-taxes.

$$\frac{\text{Rate of return}}{\text{(to be high)}} = \frac{\text{Net profits}}{\text{Net worth}}$$

$$\frac{\text{Turnover ratio}}{\text{(to be height)}} = \frac{\text{Net sales}}{\text{Total capital}}$$

$$\frac{\text{Operating ratio}}{\text{(to be low)}} = \frac{\text{Operating expenses}}{\text{Net sales}}$$

$$\frac{\text{Deby-equity ratio}}{\text{(to be low)}} = \frac{\text{Debt}}{\text{Net worth}}$$

IRR or Internal rate of return should be high.

It is the average discounted rate of cash flows of a project.

PART-C

Socio-Economic Cost Benefit Analysis or Benefit-Cost Analysis

As is known there are economic benefits which can be calculated in measurable production, income, employment, profits and some other variables that may be chosen. The social benefits are not sometimes measurable. Spread of education is social benefit but the quality of the type of students that emerge cannot be measured. Degrees of skills cannot be measured. Medical and sanitation projects improve the health and efficiency/productivity of people. They can do better work but these qualities remain immeasurable.

Thereafter there are direct and indirect benefits. The indirect benefits are in the form of upstream and downstream total linkage benefits. These benefits cannot be measured to several stages. [One cannot say that because of the production of sugar, people started taking tremendously high amounts of sugar and with certain other causes, they became diabetic. Hence sugar industry brings harms instead of benefits. Such calculations are not done. Nor can we say the production of sugar gave so much of energy that India won the world cup).

Direct benefits one or two stage costs benefits can be measured.

In the cost benefit analysis, (i) physical costs or real costs, (ii) opportunity costs, (iii) time costs, (iv) costs calculated at shadow prices or/and border prices, (v) psychic costs and above all (vi) monetary costs are calculated.

Psychic costs are immeasurable but they are there. If projects create pollution or if forced labour is taken or if there is under-payment to the workers, the psychic costs of the projects will be high. They are to be kept near zero. All other costs are ultimately translated into monetary costs. *Shadow prices/costs/benefits have now become less relevant because controlled prices and exchange control are not there. It is the market mechanism that rules.*

Hence the actual prices can be taken for the calculations of benefits and costs. *[We have shown in an appendix page, the calculation of shadow rate of interest].*

If there is mass unemployment in the country, the wages in the organised sector will be higher than the shadow wage rate. If workers are invited to work on "tender basis', the actual rate will be lower. This lower rate at which the demand and supply will be equal will be shadow rate. *It is to be remembered that there are several categories of workers and hence several shadow wage rates.* The shadow wage rates will not be starvation wage rate. It should be the critical minimum wage rate in conditions where labour abounds.

For the private projects the internal rate of return (duly discounted) will be enough.

The simple rule is that while net profits rate as a ratio to the total capital is the main criterion of judging the benefits, for the public sector projects the indirect benefits — as many as can be easily measured and are visible and apparent— can also be included. Public projects enable private projects to come up. Those are also the benefits. So far as the costs are concerned, all costs (listed above) should be low.

Appendix

We can illustrate calculation of shadow rate of interest. A notional and representative rate of interest in India can be taken. For example, the notional rate of in India can be taken as 12 per cent. However, anyone can question this figure. The actual rates of interest can vary from 4 per cent (subsidised rate of interest for scheduled caste and tribe people) In rural areas of interest was (2006) 3, 4 or 5 p.a., per *month* i.e., 36, 48 or 60%! Of course short-term distress borrowing and usurious rates of interest in rural side could be even 200 peer cent!

A formula for shadow rate of interest can be devised:

$$R = \frac{G}{S_p + \frac{I - P_y}{P_y} \cdot S_w}$$

R = shadow rate of interest

G = growth rate.

S_p = rate of savings from profits.

P_y = rate of profit.

S_w = savings from wages.

If, for example, the G is 5%, S is 25 cent, P is 50 per cent and S_w is 5 per cent, then the shadow rate of interest will be 16.6% worked out as under:

$$\frac{5}{1 - \frac{50}{100}} = \frac{5}{0.3} : 16.6$$

$$\frac{25}{100} + \frac{50}{100} \; \frac{5}{100}$$

Now:

(A) IF the growth rate were to be 10, then the shadow rate will be 33.3 per cent. In other words. The shadow rate of interest will go up to higher capital requirements.

(B) If the rate of profit goes down to 40 per cent, and other variables remain the same as in the above solution, then the shadow rate of interest will become 15.38 per cent i.e., will go down with the fall in the rate of profit.

(C) If the rate of savings goes up form 25 per cent to say 33 per cent, then (when all other variables of the equation remaining the same), the shadow rate of interest will be 13.15 per cent i.e., shall go down with the increase in the supply of savings.

(D) If the savings rate of interest wage earners goes up form 5 per cent to 15 per cent, then (all other variables remaining the same) will go down to 14.28 per cent i.e., go down.

Thus shadow rate of interest will go up in the society if (a) higher growth rate is required, (b) savings go down, (c) profit go up. Opposite will happen in opposite conditions. The equation simply emphasises that (i) if demand goes up and supply goes down, the shadow rate of interest will go up. If the demand goes down and the supply goes up, the rate of interest will go down.

SELECT REFERENCES

1 E.F.M. Durbin : "Problem of Economic Planning."

2 Maurice Dobb : "An Essay on Economic Growth and Planning."

3 Herman Finer : "Road to Reaction."

4 Ranger Frisch : "Planning for India: Selected Exploration in Methodology."

5 S.E. Harris : 'Economic Planning."

6 P. van Hayek : "The collective Economic Planning."

7 Indian Planning Commission : "Five year Plans", "Mid-Trm Appraisals."

8 Oskar Lange : "Essays on Economic Planning."

9 W.A. Lewis : "The principles of Economic planning."

10 Lionel Robbins : "Economic Planning and International Order."

11 Ludwig von Mises : "Planning for Freedom."

12 Ferdynand Zweig : "Planning of Free Societies."

13 W. Birmingham and A.G. Ford : "Planning and Growth in Rich and poor Countries."

14 Charles Bettelheim : "Studied in the theory of planning."

15 S.S. Wadia : "Techniques of Planning."

16 Zinkin : "Growth, Change and Planning."

17 Maurice Dobb : "Economic Growth and Planning."

18 U.N.O. : "Measures for Economic Development in Underdeveloped Countries."

19 U.N.O. : "Report: Seminar on Formulation and Execution of Development Programmers," Puerto Rico, 1950.

20 Hollis B. Chenery (Ed.) : "Studies in Development Planning."

21 Gregory Grossman (Ed.) : "Essays in Socialism and Planning."

22 I.M.D. Little and J.A. Mirrlees : "A Manual of Industrial Project Analysis it Developing Countries."

23 Gerald Meier : "Leading Issues Development."

24 Ignacy Sach (Ed.) : "Planning and Economic Development."

25 y. Shvyrkov (Ed.) : "Soviet Planning: Principles and Techniques."

26 Jan Tinbergen : "Development Planning."

27 P.K. Mattoo : "Project Formulation in Developing